Safety in Numbers

Safety in Numbers

From 56 to 221 Pounds,
My Battle with Eating Disorders

A Memoir

Brittany Burgunder

Safety in Numbers:
From 56 to 221 Pounds, My Battle with Eating Disorders—A Memoir

Published by Wheatmark®
1760 East River Road, Suite 145
Tucson, Arizona 85718 USA
www.wheatmark.com

ISBN: 978-1-62787-322-2 (paperback)
ISBN: 978-1-62787-323-9 (ebook)
LCCN: 2015948245

Cover design by Nicole Pollack

SAFETY IN NUMBERS IS lovingly dedicated to Dr. Habib Sadeghi, Dr. Linda Schack, Dr. Barbie Lucas, Lisa Palm Alkadis, Dr. Pedro Guimaraes, Paige Esparza, Tracy Quinn McLennan, Jane and Jon Anderson, my grandparents, and Mike and Pat Gorby, and Los Osos Valley Equine Farm.

I want to especially thank my sister, Kasey, and my parents. Without their unconditional love, support, and belief in me when everyone else had given up, I wouldn't be here today.

And to everyone who's ever felt alone, lost, hopeless, or broken...this book is for you.

Table of Contents

Foreword		xi
Letter to My Niece		xv
Preface		xvii
1	The Wonder Years	1
2	A New Friend	5
3	Boost Up Your Life	19
4	Gym Hopper	23
5	Third Time's the Charm	29
6	When You Bite the Hand that Feeds	35
7	Future Tripping	43
8	Good Intentions	52
9	Merry Misery	62
10	Possessed	73
11	How to Save a Life	81
12	Not My Time	98
13	Survival of the Sickest	113
14	TrappED	132
15	Tricks of the Trade	147
16	Singled Out, Shut In	159
17	Home and Horrible	174
18	Night of My Life	188
19	False Freedom	202
20	Hi! Welcome to Fat Camp!	207
21	PFC, Please Save Me!	214
22	Panic in Park City	223
23	Back to LIFE	228
24	Confusion and Delusion	238

25	Psychological Paralysis	255
26	The Truth Will Set You Free	262
27	Hooked on Colonics	276
28	Chronic Chaos	285
29	The Reality of Recovery	294
30	Sleepless in San Luis	301
31	Fighting the Feelings	305
32	Psych Wards Are for Crazy People	313
33	You Have No Rights	322
34	Rules and Regimens	330
35	Making the Choice	341
36	Welcome to the New Age	352
37	Beauty and the Feast	366
38	An Apocalypse of My Own	374
39	Repeat Offender	384
40	Tell Me You'll Open Your Eyes	395
41	Letters of Love...or Not	400
42	A Weigh Through	408
43	Perfect in Every Weigh	417
Epilogue		427

Foreword

REGARDLESS OF THE DISEASE a person may be dealing with, I tell all my patients that in order to heal they must change their relationship with their illness. This can be difficult especially when we've been taught to see disease as a threat that must be eradicated with maximum force and as quickly as possible. This creates an adversarial relationship with illness, and what we resist will persist until we change our concept of it and ourselves as we go through it.

The two biggest misperceptions that keep us from making this important change in perspective are that disease is purely physical and has nothing positive to add to our lives, and because our bodies are sick, we are somehow broken; there is something *wrong* with us. I firmly believe that we live in a mind-body and that every physical manifestation in the body has a mental-emotional component. Socrates himself said, "There is no illness of the body apart from the mind." Health, along with the other circumstances of our lives, is the physical printout of what's occurring for us on the subconscious emotional plane just beyond our awareness. As such, illness is the body's external way of trying to get our attention that something needs healing on a deeper emotional level. In this way, illness is actually our ally. When we identify and address the deeper issues within us that need healing, the body responds in kind. If we see illness as our adversary, its vital message is lost to us. Even if we are successful in defeating it through surgery, drugs, or other interventions, our victory is only temporary until it reappears in a similar or different form to try and get our attention once again to look within.

I've seen this dynamic play out countless times in the lives of my patients and even my own.

This doesn't mean that we don't take the necessary steps to heal our bodies. It just means that we don't assume an adversarial or fear-based attitude while we're doing it. It requires that we see illness as our partner on the journey toward healing important deeper issues of the heart that we would never have realized had it not acted as our signpost. In this way, we don't have to love our illnesses, but we can appreciate and learn to work with them as we explore our inner emotional terrain. This is the beginning of true healing.

Once we change our concept of illness, we must change our concept of ourselves as we go through it. This consciousness shift can be even more challenging because disease often brings feelings of inadequacy. Our bodies are broken, therefore we must be broken in some essential way, too. Fortunately, nothing could be further from the truth. Everything necessary for healing is already inside of us, which makes us complete. We're not missing anything. Illness is simply the catalyst to take the journey within and find the healing answers we need to create better lives for ourselves. When we're sick, it can seem like our lives are falling to pieces, but if we take the proper approach to illness, it can put the pieces back together in ways that make us and our lives even more beautiful than before simply because they were "broken."

There is a Japanese pottery technique called kintsukuroi. I was introduced to this art form after I was invited to Japan by the Ministry of Health to speak at a conference of alternative medical physicians. The legend of kintsukuroi perfectly explains how brokenness is really an illusion with the purpose of creating great beauty. In the 15th century, shogun Ashikaga Yoshimasa sent a precious but damaged Chinese tea bowl back to China for repairs. He was quite disappointed when it returned with crude metal binding holding the pieces together. He quickly employed craftsmen of his own to find a more aesthetic repair. After the metal clasps were removed, the pottery shards were set in place with a lacquer resin. To hide the adhesive and add elegance to its appearance, the craftsmen sprinkled powdered gold over the seams of the repair. In the end, the result of the broken pottery was a piece that was more beautiful than it was before. In fact, what started as a repair method for broken pottery quickly became an artisan technique to beautify ceramics in Japan. Kintsukuroi actually translates to "golden repair" or "to repair with gold."

Imagine how our concept of illness and ourselves would change if we reframed the experience in the understanding that we're going through a transformation process from which we'll emerge even more beautiful than before. Imagine how differently our bodies would respond. This is a profound and positive consciousness shift that resonates at the cellular level.

Things of great beauty rarely just appear. More often, they're the result of a fashioning process where pieces are removed or rearranged in a way that gives rise to the perfection out of something that we mistakenly saw as imperfect in the first place. A great sculptor doesn't see a blunt block of marble. He sees the angel inside it and removes the pieces around her so that she may be freed. A diamond that begins as a crude, dull crystal must face four weeks at the grinding wheel before its brilliant scintillation can dazzle us. Old glass soda bottles must face the hammer first before their colorful pieces can be reassembled into a stunning mosaic.

When I think of Brittany and all she's been through, I think of kintsukuroi. At the lowest point in her struggle, she was able to surrender, make illness her ally, and summon the courage to take the inner emotional journey that every healing experience requires. Her reward has been the creation of a life more beautiful than she could have imagined only a few short years ago and all out of the remnants of her previous life where not a single piece was wasted. She chose to see the wholeness in her experience with illness and, by working with it rather than against it, wholeness was reflected in her outer world.

Life fashions us into spiritual works of art based on what we've been through, and it has been my privilege to be Brittany's partner for part of that journey. Now, it brings me great joy to see her empowering others in the same way to recognize that their biggest opportunity to make their lives a masterpiece is their biggest obstacle.

Dr. Habib Sadeghi
Los Angeles, 2015

Letter to My Niece

To my lovely niece, Brittany,

"Time Time Time heals real life

And the scars that descend upon you

And how we true forget the making of the perfect life, That That is…That That is…"

These are words from a song I wrote last year, and watching from afar the world of Brittany unfold, I find myself wanting for an answer to her life Healing Path, for she is a bright, strong, and adventurous young lady who we all love so much.

And yet in this state of mayhem she writes extraordinary heartfelt words of encouragement to whomever reads her work, work that comes from a very deep level. She has a good heart and a loving family to help and support her.

There is always hope, and God bless her…Brittany fought through some of her darkest battles, yet is releasing such love and hope for others going through this world with scars of fear and doubt …

With love,

From Uncle Jon…singer/songwriter

Preface

I FIGURE IF I must have a damn tube up my nose against my will, then I should be able to benefit from it. I try to bargain with Dr. Schack, such as having lights out at 12:30 a.m., 8 pieces of gum, and more ice cups. I don't think she is buying it, and I am too chicken to pull the tube out myself. My throat is so incredibly sore. I can't sneeze or cough because I am too weak. My skin is so dry that I have to put coconut oil on it every few hours, and it still doesn't help—not to mention I am always worried the calories are saturating into my skin. I am having a really hard time seeing. I can see, but everything seems a little too dark.

How did I get here? What happened to me?

1

The Wonder Years

"If only you knew how beautiful you are unconditionally. Don't you know it's enough if all you do is
breathe?" ~Britt

I GREW UP A healthy, strong girl in San Luis Obispo, California. I was
smart, athletic, and your average hormonal teen. I had loving parents,
a passion for horses, and a talent for tennis. Everything in my life
pointed to success and happiness, but that was never the case. No one
would have suspected that my life would spiral down in the future,
but I wasn't surprised. Perhaps I wasn't as "average" as I portrayed. I
was shy in school. In fact, I never had any close friends and was bullied
and teased on a constant basis about everything, including my love
for horses, my height, acne, and even the way I dressed. I was always
a good student and got top grades, but I was hiding behind an inner
drive that told me I was never good enough. At home my parents
never suspected I struggled socially in school or was ever bullied. Why?
It was simply because I didn't really talk to my parents. I was very shut
off, and after a day at school trying silently to deal with my utterly
low self-esteem, I would often find myself explosively yelling at my
parents and unleashing my built-up insecurity on them. My parents
were always loving and supportive and never very controlling. In fact,
sometimes I wish my parents put a little more pressure on me than
they did, such as they had with tennis or horses. But why would they?
   I put so much pressure on myself that I was a mental wreck.
Nothing was ever good enough for me. I couldn't just be a nationally

ranked tennis player; I had to be the number-one professional player in the world. I couldn't just be a talented rider; I had to compete at the Olympic level. At least that was what my mind made me believe. After all, it was my understanding that to be liked, popular, and noticed, you had to be the best. I had no idea where this idea came from. I believe my self-esteem and shame about myself was so incredibly profound that I thought being the very best at something would mask the real me. If others noticed me for my external abilities, then maybe they wouldn't see the terrified little girl balled up inside. Unfortunately, this idea of using external qualities to mask who I really was later manifested into something more, something that I could control to a greater extent. I couldn't necessarily control whether I would win a tennis match or a horse show. But I soon learned that I could take charge of my food and weight . . . or maybe I should say that they took charge of me.

When I was younger I was healthy. Now, what does *healthy* even really mean? Well, for me it meant that I was 5 feet 5 inches, 125 pounds, and extremely fit. I participated in high-level athletics and never got sick. The problem wasn't apparent on the outside—yet. What was going on inside was stirring up a monster. I looked in the mirror every day at someone I hated—someone who was too short and had bad skin, curly wild hair, and fat legs. I had no concept of what body image was at the time, but mine was so terribly wretched that I would play make-believe fantasy games in my head where I was the "perfect" girl. I would have blonde hair and blue eyes. I would be skinny, popular, beautiful, tall, and famous. It was the only way to escape my reality. I prayed daily that I would turn into my fantasy girl, but each day I woke up to the same ugly face.

I didn't have friends. As I said, I spent my elementary and middle school days quiet and alone, with the occasional insult from a peer. Inside, all I ever felt was loneliness. I didn't feel I deserved friends or that I was pretty enough or cool enough to fit in. I would watch with jealousy as all the popular girls would get the guys' attention. Those girls were always hanging out in groups, going to parties, dressing up, and seeming to have perfect lives. That was how I saw it, at least. I looked in the mirror and knew I wasn't one of those girls. I was athletic and strong, not skinny and petite. Something clearly was wrong with me, I believed, but one thing I knew for sure was that I hated myself.

As depression and disgust began to enter my life, I found myself caught in new habits that were manifesting. I started making lists and hoarding food in my room, never to be touched. I had an overly loving relationship with gum. I spent hours on the computer comparing myself to people I wished I looked like. It was obsessive compulsive disorder (OCD), but at that point, I didn't know why I had to perform these new rituals each day. All I knew was that I couldn't stop, and completing the tasks made me feel safer and calmer in my head full of racing thoughts. I even stumbled upon some eating disorder chat rooms and pro-anorexia sites, which actually promoted eating disorders and described ways to hide them from the rest of the world. However, I still had no idea what an eating disorder really was. I didn't read magazines or watch much TV. It just wasn't something ever brought up or mentioned in my life.

My parents always told me I was beautiful and so lucky and talented, but instead of making me feel better, it only made me feel guilty for being good at certain things. It only made me place that much more pressure on myself to use the "talents" I had to their full potential. My parents believed supporting my horseback riding and tennis would boost my self-esteem, but slowly I was crumbling under the pressure I placed on myself.

Everyone told me to relax and have fun and that I shouldn't take everything so seriously. But this was serious. This was my future. This was a matter of fame and popularity or being a nobody and an utter failure. My parents couldn't have known what was coming, but they knew I was changing. My mom had OCD of her own, and although she ate a very normal, balanced diet, she did mention to me that I should start eating healthier. Throughout elementary school and my first year of middle school, I found love and comfort in food. In fact, you could easily call me an overeater, but my athletics kept me in a normal weight range. Well, soon that love for food became something else I could hate and blame for making me the way I was.

Genetically, perhaps, it was the perfect storm. My dad attended Dartmouth and graduate school at Stanford, becoming a successful lawyer before deciding to take a job as a business and law professor at California Polytechnic State University (Cal Poly). He was a perfectionist, all right. He always went above and beyond and never took a sick day. I wanted to make him proud. I grew up closer to my dad and characteristically had his tendencies. He and my mom were almost complete opposites, in fact. My mom was very outgoing, a free spirit, and more holistic. She graduated from UC Berkeley as an art major. She was expressive, showed emotions, and didn't place many, if any, boundaries or rules on me.

But I was a good girl, so there was no need, right? Well, I craved those boundaries. I was a kid, but I felt the responsibility of an adult. I wanted someone to step in when I threw a tantrum and take away that power. I wanted someone to step in and say, "I'm in control, not you." But that didn't happen. I learned that if I screamed loud enough, my parents always gave in. I felt unsafe, out of control, and ripped from childhood. My dad and mom fought on occasion over me. Both had such different parenting styles, which made sense given that they were so different. Either way, I was unknowingly being primed for disaster—a disaster that was out of everyone's control and unfortunately so misunderstood.

The pressure and expectations I put on myself were so unrealistic that they were guaranteed to result in failure, but maybe that was what I wanted. I needed something else to focus on. Something else to take the pressure off. Some excuse. Some measurable progress.

I needed something that would help me control a life I was seemingly resigned to not being able to control. All I wanted was a close friend, someone I could rely on and trust. All I wanted was some structure in my life and for someone to tell me "no." All I wanted was to feel loved and that I was good enough. All I wanted was to be an accepted person. All I wanted was to be happy in my own skin. Sometimes wants can blindly lead you into giving up all your rights as a human being.

2

A New Friend

THE SUMMER OF 2003 was one I will never forget. I was 14 years old and going to be a freshman in high school. I was going to attend 3 summer tennis camps and was very excited. Never would I have thought it would be the summer I started to slowly kill myself. The first camp I went to was an amazing experience and opportunity. I worked hard and for the most part ate healthy. I was very excited for my second summer camp and to show the new coaches what I was made of. Unfortunately, I didn't really click with any of the other girls, and I felt completely left out. We ate all our meals in the cafeteria, and the buffet style setup of food overwhelmed me. Before I could even really process what I was doing, I was eating plain salads for lunch and dinner. For breakfast I ate 2 or 3 baby muffins, which

I would eat as slow as a mouse, crumb by crumb. No one really paid attention. Occasionally I got a few stares, but nothing major.

After 2 weeks at this particular camp, I was transported along with a few others to the next camp, my last of the summer. I called my parents the minute I arrived and cried, begging them to take me home, but with no luck. That night the group went out for ice cream, but I was the only one who stood there with nothing. It was a long walk down a big hill to get to the tennis courts from the dorms we were staying in. Just a few days into the camp, I was so weak I could hardly climb up the hill.

I occupied my mind with counting calories. I wrote down everything I ate on a small piece of paper. With my activity level, I should have been eating at least 2,500 calories a day, but I decided that I had to stay between 900 and 1,100 calories. Calories? How on Earth did I even know what such a thing was? I enjoyed this game I was playing with myself, though. I liked calculating values of food to get an end result of about 1,000 calories, and I enjoyed the art of eating the same thing every day. I found safety and comfort in knowing that in a world of never-ending change, I could count on my calories being the same each day. I could tell people were starting to notice, and I often got weird stares from other campers. But I felt utterly alone, and this was my control.

Eventually the misery ended, and my parents brought me home. They were shocked when they saw me. I had lost about 15 pounds since they had last seen me. I remember my mom commenting on how much weight I had lost and how much it alarmed her—and I loved it.

High school began that fall—or should I say *hell* school? I was just one freshman among the 1,200 students. I hated high school with a mad passion. It had nothing to do with the teachers or the school itself, just the overall atmosphere of the students and the annoying cliques that were formed. I had completely changed my appearance. I went from an athletic, healthy-looking girl to a scrawny, stick-thin frame. So, why wasn't I happy? On the outside, I felt I was perfect. I wore cute clothes and got straight A's. I was a varsity tennis star and always had a huge smile on my face. My skin had even cleared up, and I blossomed into a beautiful young girl. But the seed of self-hate had been planted long ago.

So, yes, at a distant glance, one might think I had my life packaged up neatly and successfully, but looks could be so deceiving. I needed everyone to believe I was perfect. At least that is what I thought I had to portray. On the inside, I was more miserable than anyone could ever imagine. What I didn't realize was that when my eating disorder and I started our long-term relationship, I would have to make sacrifices. I was always tired, cold, and paranoid about people talking about me. I no longer got any attention from boys and quickly lost the wow factor in my tennis game. My eating disorder (ED) belittled me constantly, screaming negative messages and demanding unrealistic standards. What was worse was that I was no happier with my appearance. I still stared into the mirror with the same criticism no matter what. The small amount of confidence I had going into the school year had now vanished. I looked different physically, but inside I was still the same.

I became more and more consumed with food. I was still counting calories and shrinking away. I weighed around 110 pounds at this time, perhaps less, but I was all muscle and bone. I became obsessive compulsive about school. I stayed up past midnight working on homework to go above and beyond to get that A. I didn't enjoy anything anymore; I was just going through the motions. My life was nothing more than school, tennis practice, horse training, homework, and bed. I became obsessed with my one and only friend: ED. I didn't really understand what an eating disorder was. I knew I was weird about food, but I didn't see it as a problem.

But I was wrong. I think my parents were just as confused and unaware of what was developing as I was. They made me see a few therapists and a nutritionist on occasion, but everything was spiraling so quickly, and I didn't listen to anyone anyway. My desire for eating healthier or having perhaps a so-called innocent diet had taken a deadly turn. My mom and dad were terrified and startled, but they were very supportive and tried their best to understand what was

7

happening and how to help. But I wouldn't let them in. I wouldn't let anyone in. It was just ED and me, and I took care of my misery with the distraction of my eating disorder's tormenting comments and slave-driving demands. My mind was no longer consumed with being a loner or even wanting to be a professional tennis player. I was quickly losing myself and turning into a person I never wanted to know.

The obsessions only escalated, but I still had no concept of what having an eating disorder meant. I didn't know treatment centers existed. I didn't know many others in the world suffered in the same way I did. I had no idea that what was happening to me was a problem on some level.

Things continued to flow in a very wrong direction. I would freeze yogurts, have every drink with a bunch of crushed ice, and eat with a baby or plastic spoon. I had to eat the same thing every day at the exact same time. I made lists compulsively, chewed gum to pass the time and control hunger, cut my apples up into microscopic pieces, tore up the turkey in-between my diet bread, and ate as slowly as I could. My habits were taking over my life, yet I accepted this. At least I had something to focus on other than my unhappiness.

I felt safe with my eating disorder. It was a best friend and an authority figure to me, a parent—someone I could always depend on to accept me and be there for me. It was also something I knew I could control. I couldn't control my future, but I could control ED. It also became my excuse for not performing my best in tennis. Using my eating disorder was a way to avoid any responsibility for myself. It was a built-in defense. I was so terrified to give 100 percent and fail that I figured it was better just to never know.

The biggest problem was I couldn't place the blame on anyone but myself. Sure, my lack of social support and jealousy of my younger sister—who seemed to have friends and happiness—played a role, but ultimately the cause of my eating disorder was driven by a deep-rooted insecurity, a perfectionistic attitude, and genetic factors. It wasn't anyone's fault, not even mine, but it became a survival coping skill for me. I thought ED was holding me together, but it was doing the opposite. My desire for more and more control led me to become that much more out of control. But it was out of my hands at this point.

Perhaps a small level of revenge and rebellion existed on my part. My mom didn't necessarily set boundaries, yet she often over-mothered me and would treat me like a little kid, which was part of her own OCD and control issues. But ED was something she couldn't take from me, and I liked that. If only I had known that she nagged me constantly out of pure love. If only I had known that my little sister wasn't born to replace me. If only I had known that I was accepted just as I was....

Everything was falling apart for me. I was now 15 years old. I started to give up all hope in life and couldn't see things getting any better. Five hours of sleep became a luxury for me. I was irritated, stressed, anxious, and extremely unhappy. I became too weak to play tennis; I had lost my desire to play anyway. I had trouble walking up the stairs. I weighed close to 100 pounds and ate 1,000 calories a day. I would make promises to myself every day that it would be my last day of living with this monster and that starting tomorrow, I would end my dependence on ED. That tomorrow never came, but deep down I don't think I believed ED was all that much of a monster anyway. I didn't want to live with ED, but I sure as heck couldn't imagine my life without it.

A month later I found myself on a plane headed for Wickenburg, Arizona, to go to a residential eating disorder treatment program called Remuda Ranch. My mom told me a week before I left. I had no idea what I was about to enter. My parents were only doing what they believed to be the best next step. They saw their daughter slipping away, slowly killing herself. They believed residential treatment would be the cure and that I would come home a new person. I wanted to hug and disown my parents at the same time. I was furious with this idea of treatment, although there was a sense of relief that someone else would take control of the reins.

When I arrived at the ranch a mental health technician, or MHT, as we called them, showed me my room and then took my suitcase. She told me we could search through my belongings later. Search?

What kind of place was this? The MHT told me all the other girls were at lunch but that they would be back soon. She took me back downstairs into a big room with a couch and TV. I sat on the couch shivering. It was February 4, 2004, and quite cold in Arizona. A few minutes later, a girl walked into the room with some sort of tube hanging out of her nose. I was absolutely horrified! Why was that in her nose? She looked a few years older than I was and was so terribly skinny. She introduced herself and welcomed me. She said she was 17 and an overexerciser. She told me she would run 30 miles a day and that her heart rate got down to the low 30's. "Thirty miles?" I thought to myself. I felt weak and like such a failure all of a sudden. I never did anything close to that.

A few minutes later, about 30 girls swarmed me.

"Are you an A, B, or C?" was the first question out of their mouths—no hello, no nothing. I looked at them wide-eyed as if I had missed something.

"What?" I managed to whisper.

"Are you anorexic, bulimic, or a compulsive overeater?" one asked.

"Oh, I'm anorexic," I replied, but all of a sudden I didn't feel very anorexic or sick compared to a bunch of toothpicks with tubes hanging out of their noses. The girls were really sweet and so open about what they were going through. It caught me by surprise.

For once I didn't feel so odd talking about my weird habits, fears, and struggles. It was such a surreal moment. Maybe I wasn't as alone as I thought.

Later that day, one of the MHTs sat me down and explained the rules:

- No shaking your leg.
- Must stay seated at all times.
- 30 minutes to complete meals and 15 minutes to complete snacks.
- Hands must be above the table when eating at all times.
- No napkins.
- Must eat 100 percent of meal or else get supplement (which was a high-calorie drink called Boost Plus).

- No flushing your own toilet.
- No sharp objects.
- No food talk or talk about weight or numbers.
- Must wear shirts with no pockets while eating and absolutely no jackets.
- Everyone starts as a level 1, and the highest level is 4.
- Church is every day except Sundays.

The list went on and on and covered what I felt were completely ridiculous and pointless topics. I didn't understand what all these rules were for because I was too new to the disease. Later, I realized you weren't to shake your leg because you might be trying to burn calories. You must stay seated and not stand was also to prevent the possibility of trying to burn calories. The time limit was imposed because people would take forever to finish one meal if they could. Hands had to be above the table so that you couldn't try to hide food. Napkins were not allowed for the same reason. Flushing your toilet was not allowed because people who were bulimic might try to throw up. Sharp objects were not allowed because people might try to cut themselves. There was to be no talk of food or weight because it could trigger people and make them want to act out on their disorder. Pockets and jackets were not allowed to prevent hiding food. Shoes were not allowed because some patients attempted to run away.

Remuda worked on a level system to give patients an incentive to comply with the program. The higher the level, the more privileges they awarded you. All of these rules seemed ridiculous to me, but only a few years later I would be a master at finding ways around them. I was horrified when I realized that I would be at this circus for 60 days. I was only 101 pounds, but by the end of 2 months, I would be obese! Were they out of their minds? I wasn't even sick! I spent my three 15-minute phone calls each week crying and begging my parents to take me home. Eventually I became more accustomed to the routine and felt a sense of belonging.

I had a fantastic therapist. It felt as if for first time in my life someone understood me and listened to me when I spoke. He tried to help me get to the root of my problems, but I put up a smile as my defense every time I became uncomfortable. In fact, my whole stay there became a game to me. As others competed to become the sickest patient, I competed to become the best recovering anorexic. My happy face was a disguise to hide so much shame, but I convinced myself I truly was happy. I never wanted to reveal my pain to anyone because it would mean I did have problems and that I wasn't perfect after all. I did everything in my power to be a leader and centered my choices on what the staff would want to see, not what I truly felt.

I made some very close friends at Remuda. I found myself being the popular one. I was the one everyone wanted to know and be around. It felt great, but at the same time it was a hard act to keep up. I watched girls cry, scream, hide food, break rules, exercise in their room, and act out in any way possible. I was so mad that they were able to get away with it. I told myself I wasn't struggling when really I was. I was on a 3,000-plus-calorie a day meal plan and not enjoying it. The doctor recommended a feeding tube because it would make it easier for me to consume all my calories. The girls who had tubes had smaller meal plans and at night had Boost Plus dripped into their tubes while they slept. I said no because I was too afraid of losing control. At least I could choose not to eat if I wanted to. If I had a tube, I feared they would add more calories in my tube at night.

I didn't understand why everyone else so badly wanted a tube. It was a competition of who was the sickest, and clearly you needed a tube to compete. I went on smiling and being the caretaker of all the other girls who were having a hard time. Who was going to take care of me? I remember the only time I cried was when my dietitian told me that my goal weight had changed from 110 pounds to 120 pounds. *What?* I thought I was done with the weight gain, and now I had to put on 10 more pounds! I loved my dietitian but didn't trust her at this point. As soon as I went back into the big room we spent our days in, I started crying. It was only for a few minutes, though, and afterward I apologized for my silly behavior.

Toward the end of treatment, all the girls experienced family week. Parents came for a week of one-on-one sessions as well as group therapy with other patients and their parents. It was an amazing experience, and I finally felt as though my parents understood me and that everything would be OK. My dad told me he was glad I wasn't like the other girls at the ranch; they were so sick and stuck. That certainly made me feel proud, but what if I was more like them than he realized? I didn't want to let him down. My parents left, but I was expecting to be going home with them soon enough.

Then my therapist told me that he wanted me to go to their step-down program called Remuda Life. I looked at him as though he was crazy. I had just spent 55 days in this jail, and now he wanted me to spend another 60 days at this transition program? I told him no way it would happen and that I was going home no matter what. Despite my protests, I eventually gave in to their recommendation, knowing it would look good toward my quest as the perfect recovery patient. A week later I was unpacking my things at Remuda Life, which was located an hour or so from the main ranch.

Remuda Life was in many ways the same as Remuda Ranch, but it did have more freedom. The facility took up an entire cul-de-sac. There was housing for the adolescents, housing for the adults, offices for the therapist and dietitians, an MHT office, and an office for church. At least it looked more like the real world. I already knew most of the girls there because they had left the ranch before me.

Remuda Life was much better than the ranch. I almost came to enjoy it. About 15 adolescents were split up into 2 houses. Meals were still stressful and supervised by an MHT, but they were much more relaxed and with a much smaller group, which was nice. One girl there was a big trigger for me. It was not because I didn't like her—I did—but it was because our eating disorder rituals were very similar. We were both very controlling. We always had to be the last one done eating, the one taking the smallest bites, and the one who got the plate with a seemingly smaller portion. She also had this obsession with water. She would sneak glassful after glassful of water and drink it very quickly all at once. It never made any sense to me at the time, even though only a few months later I, too, would be gulping water in an effort to make myself feel full artificially.

The highlight of the week was the cardio walks at night. We were allowed to power walk around the cul-de-sac as fast as we wanted for 30 minutes 3 times a week. I found it hilarious because some of the girls were so serious about it and walked faster than most people running. True dedication, I assumed. The other highlight was youth group every Wednesday night. We got to leave our little world and drive about 15 minutes away to the building where it was held.

I enrolled in the local high school while at Remuda Life. I had been doing home study while I was at the ranch and wanted to finish out the school year attending regular classes. My classes were easy, I made friends, and as an added bonus, I was able to throw away my afternoon snack. I found myself becoming increasingly anxious and on edge. I had about a month left, and I was still hooked on my anorexic behavior and mind-set.

Remuda was a nice little vacation. Having to gain weight wasn't fun, but I had no other responsibilities besides eating. I was now 118 pounds and no longer sick. I had no excuse not to be great, successful, and happy. Going home meant all the expectations and pressures would return.

My parents picked me up in early June to bring me home. I couldn't believe the day had actually arrived. At the same time, I was panicking. I was about to leave a special world where I was popular, felt pretty, and had lots of friends who would listen to me and, most importantly, who understood me. I lost a big part of myself that day, but I had no choice. My discharge plan consisted of seeing a therapist and nutritionist, a meal plan of 2,500 calories a day, and no athletics for a few months— yeah, right. Within only a week or 2, I was back on the tennis court playing tennis with my dad. My dad knew he wasn't supposed to be playing tennis with me so soon after returning home, but I assured him that I wasn't like those other sick people and that it would only help me forget about anorexia. He took me at my word, hoping that the tennis would help give me a reason to stay healthy and strong.

The problem was that I had a surplus of new tricks up my sleeve that I never would have been exposed to had I not gone to Remuda. It was a blessing and a curse.

Shortly after restarting tennis, I also got back into riding horses. I immediately fell in love with a young gray mare at the barn. Her name was Scandalous. She was 5 years old and well on her way to becoming a dressage champion. I was in heaven when her owner offered me the chance to start taking lessons on her and showing her. We were chemistry in motion. Our bond was evident from afar, and I loved her more than anything—even more than my eating disorder.

I picked up my very first journal early on in my eating disorder. It was the one safe outlet I had to share my daily struggles and triumphs. It was as if it was a witness to the chaos. I journaled religiously. I had to find some way to relieve some of my obsessive and mind-torturing thoughts. So, I now share with you my journey firsthand and in its authentic form. It started with my mom and me journaling back and forth to each other, but after just a few entries of our journal exchanges, I realized I wasn't ready to be so open and honest. I wanted ED back to myself. I wanted to be sick again. In fact, I wanted to be so sick that I would have to go back to treatment where things were safe, I had friends, and I was understood.

July 18, 2004

Hey, Britt! Some say that things get tough before they get better. I do know that to feel joy, we have to experience sadness or pain or else we wouldn't know what joy felt like! Maybe it's not that difficult. We humans like to make everything more difficult and harder than it has to be. Past hurts—if we don't work through them—become present hurts. Put them in God's hands. Forgive them, bless them, and let them go. If we hang on to them, then we can't move forward. We become stuck. Everything will and always does work out. What are you afraid of if you let go of your eating disorder? We'll still love you and give you loads of attention. You get to be you, Brittany, a great 15-year-old kid. Don't try so hard; that's not the point. By letting go, the gifts come in. See? Just the opposite happens. The harder we try the more resistance comes back. You don't need to be "somebody." You get to and need to be Brittany Leigh Burgunder because she is good enough and we love her. XOXO, Mom.

August 13, 2004

Yeah, forget journaling with Mom. She can't know what I'm really thinking. I know she wants to help and get closer to me, but I don't trust anyone, not even myself. It's easiest to let ED call the shots. I know I'm slipping back, but part of me can't help but get a high off it. I like being underweight because I know I can always eat as much or anything I want and it would be good for me. I like knowing I have that option, even though I am not healthy at my weight. I want to be 112 pounds, but I am scared once I get there, I will have to gain more. So, if I stay below 112 pounds, then I know if I gain weight, the worst I will be is 112 pounds, and that's what I want anyway. I am doing so great, and I am going to beat ED! Ugh—I just completely contradicted myself.

2005

The year 2005 came and so did another year full of ups and downs. My lessons with Scandalous kept improving; each day our bond grew stronger. I played tennis more seriously and switched coaches again. I was now training with Paige, the assistant women's coach for the Cal Poly tennis team. She was the most special person in my life. She was my sister, mom, best friend, role model, coach, and support. She was positive and motivating and a hard worker. She and I got along great and formed a strong relationship. She knew me very well and didn't let me get away with anything. She accepted nothing less than 100 percent and expected commitment and hard work. She knew all about my eating disorder and struggles and made it clear to me that I could not have both an eating disorder and a successful tennis career. I practiced daily for upcoming tennis tournaments and horse shows. In my third show with Scandalous we received all blue ribbons and high-point champion.

I was homeschooling for my sophomore and junior years of high school but was taking a majority of my classes at the community college. I loved this. It gave me a lot more time to pursue tennis and horses, and the boys were much cuter. I felt like my life was being put back together. I was happy with myself. ED was there but didn't really have a say.

2006

The year 2006 started out better than ever and ended in disaster. I started working out more at the gym and, although not addicted, made it a necessity in my life. I finally gathered enough confidence to face my old high school again. It was my senior year, and I felt the need to return and make it better than ever. I returned feeling full of confidence, but it was quickly crushed. I played the number-one position once again for the tennis team with good results. Still, it was a tough year for me. I was no longer the freshman phenom who had no expectations. I was now the senior who was carrying loads of pressure to perform. Academics kicked my butt, too. I was academically successful, receiving good grades in all my honors classes, but it required a lot of work. Along with tennis practice and riding Scandalous, I was starting to break down again.

February 6, 2007

After an emotional but correct choice, I am now finishing the school year on home study again. The good: I'm much happier, am still considered a student at San Luis Obispo High in all my classes, and will get my diploma. The bad: I sleep too much during the day and stay up and eat much too late at night. I have unfortunately become obsessive with exercise and am now requiring myself to burn at least 1,250 calories at the gym. One thing that has been tough is Facebook. I have now reconnected with all of my Remuda friends and a few extra. Although I absolutely love having contact with them, it is also very triggering because many are still struggling and have lost a lot of weight, which I can see by their pictures. It makes me get back into that competitive anorexia mode again. I know I'm losing too much weight, but I love the feeling and am so addicted right now. I haven't been playing tennis almost at all for the past 2 months because I am too weak.

March–May 2007

The next couple of months were all downhill for me. I was obsessed with exercise and had a gym membership at 2 different places so that I could exercise more without people noticing my repeat visits. I kept forcing myself to burn more and more calories and never missed a day. I started seeing a psychiatrist. I was not on any medication, and he was very much like a therapist instead. I continued to have decent tennis lessons with Paige but knew I was holding myself back physically from my full potential. Having ED as my excuse seemed the best way to go, though it saddened me, always wondering, "What if? What if I gave 100 percent effort and was physically strong and healthy?" ED was such a perfect built-in defense to rely on. My fear of the unknown was far too great not to have ED as my safety net. I was now requiring myself to burn 2,300 calories at the gym. It was taking over my life!

I noticed my heart rate getting really low, and my weight was staying around 100 pounds. Everyone was so worried and nervous. I had to wear a 24-hour Holter heart monitor, which pissed me off because I had to find the right outfit to wear so no one would notice while I was working out at the gym. I did reduce my exercise from burning 3,000 calories to 2,000 calories, but 2,000 was still a lot. My blood work came back poor in addition to my other struggles.

3

Boost Up Your Life

"Dare to let go. Dare to trust. I promise you won't fall. I promise the fear is worth it. And I promise moving forward will reward you in ways you thought impossible." ~Britt

June 30, 2007

I'm at Stanford Hospital in the Lucile Packard Children's Eating Disorder Program. An ambulance transferred me here after spending 2 nights at our local hospital for stomachache, headache, and very low blood pressure and heart rate. I was shocked yet relieved. I don't want to be in the hospital, but I certainly wouldn't be able to maintain my crazy life much longer. I got a really nice doctor at my local hospital, and I begged him to let me stay until I was better, but he shook his head and said they didn't treat eating disorders. I had the choice of being transferred to Stanford or an eating disorder program at UCLA. I ended up choosing Stanford because I had a friend who had gone to both Stanford and UCLA and she said you gain less weight at Stanford.

I hate it here! I have to have Boost 5 times a day and have to use a commode (a chair enclosing a chamber pot) to go to the bathroom. I am on bed rest and can't even take a shower until my vitals improve! The only good thing is that it is regular Boost (240 calories) not Boost Plus (360 calories), which I was surprised about. The girls here are really sweet, but one is so thin and triggering! The staff is really nice, too. I refused my Boost and caused a lot of commotion with the nurses today, but eventually I drank it because of the threat of an NG (nasogastric) feeding tube. The program kind of works like Remuda except it is purely a medical stabilization program versus a therapy model. I have to wear stupid electrodes on my chest all day and night so they can keep an eye on my heart rate, and I have to have my blood pressure taken every 2 hours! I don't want to gain any weight though and plan to lose it later on. I don't know how long I will be here but hopefully not too long because I am having a hard time.

July 1, 2007

Today was a little bit better. I had a nice talk with my roommate in the morning, however, my stomach and head are continuing to kill me. I didn't get the best news from the doctor. My weight has dropped to 99 pounds, my heart rate at night is really low, and my sodium levels are dropping from where they were at the San Luis Obispo hospital. The doctor did say, though, that I could probably get off bed rest in less than a week. After bed rest comes the wheel-chair phase. They allow you to eat in the dining room with the other patients but don't allow you to walk. You also get to start eating food instead of the Boost. On the last level you are able to walk and only need your vitals taken every 4 hours and do not need to wear a heart rate monitor anymore. For now I am not allowed to leave my bed and dull little room and must drink my Boost alone with a nurse. I am so bored and frustrated! All the nurses and doctors are really nice and cool, though.

July 3, 2007

Last night was really hard and triggering for me. During dinner, I started comparing myself to others and watching all their stupid food rituals, such as eating bites so small there was nothing there and eating super slowly. I couldn't believe the nurses let them get away with it! I guess it's much different than Remuda here. At Remuda, you could not get away with one food ritual without being caught and corrected. Here it seems they just want you to finish your food and don't care how it gets done. Anyway, it really bothered me. It made me feel like a failing anorexic and fueled my competitive side.

July 5, 2007

This has been a difficult day. It started with a huge 800-calorie breakfast. No, I'm not exaggerating, and it made me feel like a fat ass. Then I talked to the doctor. He said if my vitals and night heart rate were good for the next 48 hours I could go home Saturday. Unfortunately, right before lunch I had bad vitals. When I stood up I started blacking out again, and my blood pressure dropped to 71/39. Well, hopefully I can go home Sunday.

July 6, 2007

Ugh! I am so pissed because at lunch we got ranch dressing with our carrots, which was 220 calories, but I didn't realize that it only equaled 6 ounces of Boost as a replacement, which was only 180 calories! I had already started eating the ranch before I realized, so I ended up having an extra 40 calories. I am so mad! We are allowed to replace any food item we want with Boost if we don't like it. Usually the Boost comes out equivalent in calories to the food item, but sometimes the Boost option is a little bit less or a little bit more. In the case of the dressing it would have been a little bit less and clearly the better option. I am so scared to go home because my dad says I have to be gaining weight and progressing, but I know I'm going to struggle and want to lose weight. I almost don't want to go home. The only good thing is my heart rate is 46 at the lowest at night now. I have also decided to take a year off before going to UC Davis, the college I chose, and they accepted my deferment, which is great!

July 30, 2007

Life isn't the greatest right now. I have been home for about a week, but I went to the ER last night. I wasn't feeling well, and they admitted me for very low blood pressure and heart rate. Oh, great! I spoke with the same doctor I had last time. He once again told me I would have to be transferred to Stanford or UCLA. I was shocked. I mean, I didn't feel well so I went to the ER just to make sure I wasn't dying! The last thing I thought was that I would be admitted, but now I have no choice but to go through this whole ordeal again! The doctor wouldn't even let my dad drive me; he said I had to go by ambulance. I, of course, chose Stanford since I knew the program and staff. Paige, my coach, called me to play tennis but, gosh, I don't know how I can tell her I am here—again.

4

Gym Hopper

"It's amazing how much power a smile holds. It's contagious and brightens people's day. It's also the most powerful camouflage. For that person who seems to have it all together is merely masking the pain of drowning tears. Don't be so quick to assume." ~Britt

August 20, 2007

I got home from Stanford on Wednesday and have totally changed myself for the better! I have been consistently eating breakfast by 10:30, lunch by 2:30, snack by 6:00, dinner by 9:00, and snack and bed by 10:30! I went to the doctor today, and my blood pressure was OK, but my weight was 112 pounds! Yikes! I have been so upset. I hate how my legs now touch and how everyone is commenting on how great I look. Don't get me wrong, I like the compliments, but at the same time it freaks me out because then I feel the need to keep it up and fear of failure sets in. At least I will hopefully be able to ride, play tennis, get a job, and drive soon!

September–October 2007

Things continued on without too much drama. I slowly started getting back into going to the gym again and was getting obsessive. I went from burning 400 calories to 1,200 calories. I was extremely upset because I saw my weight on my dietitian's scale, and it was 118 pounds! I didn't get it. I had been working out like crazy, I was not getting my period, and I was eating under 2,100 calories! What was going on? I had my 19th birthday and had a really nice time with my dad. I was kind of upset, though, because my mom got into a huge fight with me and left to go to my grandma's house. My sister, Kasey, ended up going to one of her friend's birthday parties, so no one spent my birthday with me, which made me incredibly sad, although I tried not to show it.

October 28, 2007

Today was one of the worst days of my life! I got on our scale at home, and I weighed 111.2 pounds with no water. Thankfully, only I saw that. Then I quickly drank 2 glasses of water and weighed 113.6 pounds when my dad wanted to see it. Because of my weight, Dad took away my gas money, car keys, and upcoming tennis tournament unless I weigh 115 pounds Friday morning with no water. What! I got so unbelievably upset and screamed, cussed, cried, and even broke a plate. I feel like my life is controlled by a number, and I hate that my dad does morning weights because I can't water load. I just got so upset because deep down I desperately don't want to gain weight. I played tennis today and then went straight to the gym to burn another 800 calories. I just want to stay at the weight I am and don't think I can gain the weight, even if it is only a few pounds.

November 22, 2007

Happy Thanksgiving! Today, however, has not been so happy for me. In fact, it has been a terrible day. I stayed in bed until 6:15 in the evening, and then while my family and relatives were eating Thanksgiving dinner, I was out driving to the gas station to get my Diet Sunkist soda. I hate this disease so much, but at the moment I feel no strength to even challenge it and its pull on me to lose weight. My exercise has become out of control again, too. I'm praying for a miracle—a big one—because I feel desperate!

December 14, 2007

I am very worried about myself. I am absolutely out of control with my behaviors. Today I did the most exercise in months, burning 2,000 calories! I had way too much artificial sweetener too: I had 4 flavored waters sweetened with Splenda, 1 diet soda, 1 pack of gum, and a ton of sugar-free syrup in my drink from Starbucks. I'm also eating later than ever and am now having my dinner at 1:00 a.m. I really need an intervention or something. I can't stop myself! Clearly I'm depressed, too, and have a bad case of OCD and anxiety, but frankly I'd never agree to seeing a psychiatrist, let alone allow a medication to pass through my lips. I was on a very low dose of Prozac while at Remuda, but I soon stopped it. I mean, I don't want to take a medication that might interfere with my weight loss. Even worse, it might make me gain weight! No, the fewer variables in my life, the better.

December 24, 2007

Today was kind of a big day for me! I went to the gym and burned 900 calories. Then I went to another gym to work out before it closed. Yet, while sitting in the car in the parking lot, I decided my exercise needed to be put to an end, so I drove off! I am now going to limit myself to 1 hour a day at the gym and get back into tennis. I am also lowering my calories by at least 300. I can't be exercise dependent to control my weight. It's better to do it with food the anorexic way. Merry Christmas to me!

January 3, 2008

I had a revelation today—not only do I *not* want to recover or get better but also that I can't recover. I have never felt this way before. I think I have been in denial, believing, "Oh, I can change if I want" or "I still have time to change." Now I think I am facing reality for once and am realizing the scary hold my disorder has on me despite having an amazing support group right now. I feel as though nothing can help me, not even going inpatient. I know I'm giving up my life, dreams, tennis, and opportunities, but I feel as if I'm doomed and plagued with this disease forever. I just pray that after a few weeks of being out of denial, I will be able to change. I burned only 950 calories at the gym today. It is just getting so difficult.

January 10, 2008

I went to Starbucks with Dad. He told me to turn this disease around or else Scandalous is gone. He also told me how hard my eating disorder is on him and how depressed he is. I can't stand seeing how much of a negative impact this has on my dad, yet I suppose it's not enough for me to let go. I get worried that without ED I will have no reason to struggle, be unhappy, or fail. I fear that if I am fine, people will expect me always to be happy and successful and keep it up even if I am unhappy or don't always come out on top. There is too much pressure and disappointment involved with giving up ED. It's better to create a miserable life where things can't get any worse opposed to living a happy life where things can only get worse. I suppose I like controlling the uncertainty of life, but how's that working for me?

January 23, 2008

After I finished my workout at the gym, this cute guy came up to me and said, "I never hit on girls at gyms and I think that it's really stupid, but I just wanted to tell you that you are so gorgeous and so sexy. I used to come in here and just do my routine, but now I also look for you and look forward to seeing you." Anyway, as nice as his compliment was, it made me feel like I'm not skinny enough if he thinks I look "good." Oh, I hate this battle!

January 24, 2008

I had an excellent appointment with my therapist. I made the statement that "I want to destroy my body enough so that it becomes undesirable." I am scared of failure, yet scared of success and the attention. I don't want to die, but I don't want to truly live in the world either. My parents and my therapist both agree that I am doing great emotional work and that I need to sit with my depression and find out who I am and what my purpose is. But what if I never find out?

February 12, 2008

Well, 2 days ago I woke up late and dragged myself to the gym and could barely make it through burning my routine calories. I then got some groceries and came home to my grandma's feeling extremely weak. I've been living with my grandma the past few days to get a breath of fresh air away from my parents. Anyway, I knew there was no way I was going to make it through my evening workout. After talking to my grandma for 30 minutes, I finally got up enough courage to call my dad and tell him I was taking myself to the ER. He wasn't happy, but I knew I had to go just to make sure I was OK. So, I got there and weighed 104 pounds. Surprisingly, my blood pressure was fine, but my heart rate was averaging 36 beats per minute, so I was admitted.

Today is Tuesday, and I have been in our local hospital since Sunday night. For the moment I think my doctor is OK with letting me stay here until my vitals stabilize, even though he was thinking of sending me back to Stanford. My therapist, on the other hand, is strongly pushing for me to be transferred to Stanford or another program like it for 2 weeks to help show that I am "working the program." It would be a waste of money, though; I have no intention of gaining weight. I am living off Cheerios, apples, coffee, and gum while I am here. I am trying to stay under 1,000 calories because I'm not exercising. My blood pressure has amazingly continued to be fine since I was admitted, yet my heart rate stays around 35 and 36 beats per minute during the day. I'm getting occasional back and chest pain.

Things have been tough with my parents, and I am extremely bitter, resistant, and mad. I now get no car, no gym, no food I like to buy, no freedom, blah, blah, blah! I'm pissed! On top of that, I asked my mom nicely if she would bring me a few things from home. Not only did it take her 2 days to bring them, but she didn't even bring everything I asked for! Mom thinks it's my fault I am in the hospital, and therefore I deserve to suffer. Well, if only she knew this was the last place I ever wanted to end up and am miserable. I just feel so neglected, lost, confused, unloved, and hopeless. I want to scream and never stop!

5

Third Time's the Charm

"Setbacks allow us to take a step back and look at the view from a whole." ~Britt

February 15, 2008

Today has been eventful. I woke up with leg cramps and not feeling the best. Then, out of nowhere, my dad comes rushing into my room saying I am being taken to the adolescent unit at Stanford again that afternoon because my heart is in so much danger. The whole morning the doctors and case manager were trying to get me transferred to a different hospital but without luck. Nobody would take me because I am too medically unstable. My therapist was shocked at my vitals and heart rate and said I was in immediate danger and had to be transferred as soon as possible. My personal doctor outside of the hospital told me he would no longer be able to work with me. I guess I am scaring all the doctors and nurses here.

Of course, despite my protest, the ambulance came at 1:00 in the afternoon. After watching my heart rate average around 30 to 38 beats per minute, I was back at Stanford for the third time. Thankfully, one of my favorite doctors was working this week and knew my history. She said my heart rate at the previous hospital was dropping into the 20's at night and that it is very serious. My therapist is mad at me because, despite being so close to death, I still don't realize the danger I'm in or want recovery. I did decide to drink my Boosts tonight because I haven't had anything else. I am so very miserable and confused right now. I don't want to get better, but I don't want to die. Please help me to see that this is all part of the plan—I'm desperate!

February 16, 2008

I had a decent talk with my therapist from home. He is most concerned with how my mind is thinking and working as opposed to my weight. So, my plan is to keep my weight low but keep a positive, healthy mind-set—even if it is only an act.

February 18, 2008

I came up with a discharge plan today that I'm planning to present to my parents. It includes seeing my therapist, checking in with a doctor, limiting gym to 30 minutes, continuing to work at Abercrombie where I recently got hired, continuing to improve my mind-set even though I don't want recovery, figuring out my living situation, getting a second job, and having no weight requirements. I am so much happier now that I feel I have a good discharge plan. I'm pretty mad at the moment, though. I almost got away with having just one Boost at snack instead of 1 ½, but my stupid conscience and I had to question it until the staff realized their mistake. Well, that's the last time that will ever happen. At least I have learned from my mistake!

February 20, 2008

I am getting some special privileges. I get to start my meals and snacks 30 minutes later than the scheduled start time, and I get to chew ice with my Boosts, although it does count as water. I also get to know my weight 2 times a week versus 1. Me and my stupid bargaining. However, everyone who gets food receives 40 minutes for lunch and dinner, and the staff members say since I am on Boost, I should only get 30 minutes. I have been protesting and saying I'm going to take 40 minutes no matter what. I might lose some privileges, but, oh well, at least I am not refusing. I am really enjoying being able to start 30 minutes later than the scheduled time. I get to be the last one done and feel as though I have won as the slowest eater even though it's different.

February 24, 2008

Ah! I'm having a terrible morning again! I'm trying to refuse breakfast, but it probably won't work. There is the prettiest rainbow outside my window that I have ever seen with all the colors, even pink! I talked to the doctors. They again emphasized how sick I am and how I definitely need to be here—although I completely disagree. My heart rate did increase to 39, which is progress but still not enough to move to wheelchair. I'm so confused. Part of me wants my vitals to improve so I can get out of here with minimal weight gain, yet part of me is scared to go home and tackle life.

I am refusing lunch. I will probably be brought to court because of my continued noncompliance, but I don't really care. The nurse brought me Boost around 2:00 in the afternoon, which is too early for snack. I told her I refused lunch, so I don't know why she's thinking I would have snack. I threw the Boost on the ground and made a huge mess. I finally calmed down and had one Boost for a late lunch and am now having 1 ½ for snack. I'm planning to have 7 total Boosts today. I'm scared of what my consequences from the program will be tomorrow—but it's worth it.

February 25, 2008

Ugh! I have to have real food today. Breakfast was brought with a huge, ugly banana! I freaked out, but it was either a banana or Ensure Plus, so I chose the banana along with oatmeal, cottage cheese, raisin toast, and butter, which calculated to about 500 calories. I spent a long time in my room thinking of what my 3 hate foods would be. We get to choose 3 food items that we will never be served here. Obviously, you're supposed to pick 3 foods you truly despise, such as onions or cilantro, but clearly I'm going to pick foods that are the most threatening caloric-wise. I talked to the dietitian later and decided that my 3 hate foods would be pasta, cheese, and syrup because those items are served a lot. I also mentioned a lot of other foods I never wanted, but she couldn't promise I wouldn't get them. I just have to worry about things like peanut butter, cookies, pudding, etc.

February 27, 2008

We could be getting another admission today or tomorrow, which makes me anxious to see the new competition. I can hear almost everything since my room is across from the nurses' station. I like that, but it can also be noisy and stressful.

I am struggling so much with food. I mean, yes, I am eating fear foods and foods I haven't touched in years, but it still feels as if I am only getting worse and more consumed by my disorder being here. I am eating the same, if not more, calories than I was at home, but at home I was also burning 1,800 calories at the gym. Here I sit on my ass 24-7!

I always scrape and hide as much butter and leave as much excess food on my plate as I can. It's like a game to see how much I can get away with. I have also been trying to drink a cup of water before weigh-ins by pretending I'm brushing my teeth, and I am holding in a little pee to make my weight seem higher so they will slow down my weight gain. The nurses don't seem to care though and have been letting me do it. However, one nurse told me they are documenting every little thing I do against the program and are gathering more information to use against me in court. Then a judge could rule that I can't take care of myself and set up a conservatorship with a doctor or a parent making decisions for me.

March 5, 2008

My heart rate fell to 34 beats per minute once last night—scary. I was so tempted this morning to just go for it and eat all of my breakfast, but I couldn't. The doctors came in right after breakfast with some news. They now have to involve the social workers, legal workers, insurance, and other people in deciding my case. They say I am getting worse. They say they can't keep me here because I won't increase my calories fast enough to improve. They say they will watch my next 5 meals to see how well I do and if I complete 100 percent (of my calories), otherwise they could be discharging me tomorrow! They told me I need triple the amount of food I am getting on my meal tray but that they have been giving me less because they knew I wouldn't complete it and didn't want to waste food. What? I can hardly finish half of what is on my tray now!

I had a good talk with my nurse tonight. She made me think things over a little harder. She told me how dangerous it is to do what I am doing, how I am killing myself, how my heart is shrinking, my bones are deteriorating, my brain is shriveling, and my life is fading. Do I want to spend my life in hospitals? Sure I'm skinny and want to be skinny, but who am I trying to impress? I'm ruining my life, and each time I do this to my body the longer it takes for it to recover and the more permanent damage I do. There will be no second chance. If I die, that's it! Who cares how skinny I was or how good at anorexia I was if I'm dead?

March 6, 2008

My parents eventually arrived for a team meeting today. It only lasted about 10 to 20 minutes, though it felt as if time stood still. I was called into the meeting halfway through. Dad told me that I must eat everything or he will get a conservatorship over me and have me tubed. I reluctantly agreed for fear of getting my rights taken away, and everyone is very happy. I am being forced, though. It's not my choice, therefore, I don't feel like such a failure and bad anorexic.

I completed 100 percent of my 700-calorie lunch! Ugh! I had to sign a contract saying that I will complete 100 percent and eat on time and within the time limits or else I get tubed. This sucks, but I have no choice. My parents left, so I am now alone again faced with my biggest fear. Ah!

March 7, 2008

I met with my therapist here. She had me write down my ED rules: I must always be the thinnest in the room, eat less than others, be the last one finished eating, take the smallest bites, eat balanced meals, eat as slowly as possible, water load and stay full to create an artificially higher weight, be satisfied with my weight during my heaviest time of day, freeze foods so they take longer to consume, eat at the same times every day, eat the same number of calories each day, eat alone and have something relaxing to do while I eat, eat in the car if I'm on my way somewhere, save something to eat while I work out, and save my calories for as late as possible in case I slip up. My legs must not touch when my feet are pressed together. My collarbones and chest bones must show immensely. My hip bones, back bones, and ribs must protrude. My skinny jeans need to fit loosely. My weight must be below 100 pounds. I can never eat without some sort of distraction. I can't eat until everything is taken care of and in order. I have to work out longer and harder and be more perfect than any other girl. Ugh—tough, pathetic life.

Well, I completed all my lunch. I took an extra 5 minutes, but at least I did it. I must say, I feel so happy! It's as though a dark cloud has lifted. I feel good about finally complying with the program and doing what I am supposed to. Maybe it's just a relief knowing I have boundaries now and can surrender the fight. I know when I go home I will struggle with restricting, but at least I feel happy now. My blood pressure has been better all day today, which is good! For snack I got a chocolate milk, banana, and peanut butter, but the supervisor was a little clueless so I hid the peanut butter. I know that wasn't a good thing, but there was no way I was going to eat it.

March 10, 2008

Erg! I hate how my bones don't protrude as much anymore. The doctor even told me I look better today. It was intended to be a compliment, but I took it as an insult. Don't these people know anything? I talked to my therapist here and vented for a while. I told her it's so hard because I spent so many hours slaving away at the gym unhappily to achieve this body, and now I'm being forced to give it up after all that grueling work. I had a nice talk with my dad later. He is proud of me for my progress and how I have turned things around here. I have decided that I will follow the rules for my dad here, get out, and then control my eating again at home in a less dangerous way—if there is such a thing.

6

When You Bite the Hand that Feeds

"Perfectionism is searching for faults to justify low self-esteem. It is a guaranteed failure and fantasy."
~Britt

March 19, 2008

I slept OK last night. I arrived home yesterday afternoon. Dad was anxious this morning about making sure I got up and had breakfast with him. I understand his worry, but I wish he had given me a chance. I had a lovely breakfast with him around 10:15. Dad says he has faith in me but that the Stanford team thinks I need to have a conservatorship. Mom and I have been fighting on and off all day about food and calories. I went to take a nap, and she woke me up shortly after I fell asleep by asking me how much turkey I was going to put on my sandwich for lunch. I hadn't even made it yet! I was still in bed, and she just went on and on about how many slices I would eat and asking what else I would have! She is just so stressed and having a hard time staying calm.

Another explosion took place around 7:00 in the evening. I was arguing with my dad about something that had to do with the computer, and all of a sudden my mom butts in and starts going off about calories, food choices, etc. The subjects weren't even related! I got hysterical! I reacted that way mostly because I feel as though

I haven't even been given a chance today. I had it all planned out to spend a lot of nice time with my family, and instead it was all fighting, worrying, and lecturing. Eventually things calmed down a bit, and we all had a nice dinner together. My total calories for today are 2,050. I can tell I am already slipping a bit in weight, and Dad can tell, too. I'm so scared about how things are going to work out. I really hope tomorrow is a much better day!

March 30, 2008

This morning sucked! I slept in again, and my parents were trying to get me to wake up. I told them I wanted to sleep a little more even though I knew I should get up. My dad is also having a nervous breakdown right now. I took our dog for a long walk. I am now walking for 45 minutes to 1 hour. I can't let it increase more than that, though! I took my blood pressure at Rite Aid today, and it was 85/53—not too bad, right? I was able to eat lunch by 6:00 in the evening, have a snack by 8:30, and have dinner with the family at 8:45. We had salmon tonight, which I knew would be hard for me, so I threw away the yolk of my egg at snack. I'm so mad at myself for not eating the yolk but will try to eat a few extra calories before bed.

I had a nice time with my mom at Starbucks after dinner. I explained to her that ED has become somewhat of an authority figure for me and serves as a boundary. Growing up my parents always eventually gave in to what I wanted if I persisted long enough or whined long enough, and it made me feel as though I never had any boundaries and I had too much control. Well, ED became my authority figure and set boundaries for me, and *he* never gives in to me no matter how much I protest.

Ah! Dad is absolutely losing it tonight!

March 31, 2008

Dad was a complete mess last night, crying, moaning, cussing, and barfing. He went upstairs to the guest bedroom, and my room is right underneath. I could hear everything. Finally he was quiet, and I had a good night's sleep. Dad and Mom both pointed out my apparent weight loss. I admit I can tell, too, but it is none of their business! Please help me fight. I will win!

Dinner was chaotic. My parents freaked out about the small frozen dinner I was going to eat even though it was a challenge for me. Here I am about to eat something difficult and different, and all I hear from my parents is how I'm restricting and taking the easy way out. I somehow made it through dinner, and then Dad and I went to get coffee. He explained that he's so scared of losing me. It's scary for me, too. One minute I feel as though I haven't exercised enough and that I ate too much, and the next minute I'm panicking because I fear I ate too little and that I'm going to die or my health will fail. I can never find a middle ground. I just can't win!

April 1, 2008

Dad came into my room this morning to hug me and tell me his horrible dream about him burying me! Please, no! Don't ever let that dream be even close to the truth. His dream really scared me, but we had a nice moment hugging.

Scandalous is being put up for sale. My parents agreed there is no way they will continue to pay for a horse when I don't even have the strength to ride. How has ED taken over the number-one position in my life? I can't believe I'm going to be losing my best friend. I'm almost numb thinking about not riding her again and can't really contemplate it. What has ED done to my mind? Scandalous could always overpower ED, but now?

April 6, 2008

Mom got upset about me going to bed so late last night. I do it because it's comfortable, it's something to control, and I am afraid to let go and lose control to sleep because I am afraid I won't wake up. I posted pictures later today on Facebook that were taken of me yesterday. Everyone is saying how pretty I look, but part of me wants them to say I look too skinny. I am still eating only about 1,700 calories and walking for about an hour. My mom asked me about going to another treatment program. I just gave her a look and walked away.

Will this never end? I can't wait for college so I can make my own decisions!

April 10, 2008

I was thinking today about why I even have ED. I mean, it seemed so pointless until I thought about it and realized ED has given me more than I imagined. ED provides me with boundaries. It is an authority figure, a focus, an excuse for not being the best, a friend, something I can rely on, control and certainty, a stress reliever, an identity, a way to bully myself first and to distance myself from getting too close to people, a way to avoid and at the same time receive attention from others and my family. ED is a punishment for my flaws, an attempt not to grow up, and something "special." ED keeps me protected from disappointment and hidden so I don't have to make choices or try new things. In a word, ED keeps me "safe" in my own little world. Of course, those are the positives. The negatives would ultimately lead to death.

I talked to Dad tonight, and he shared his concern about me again. I told him one thing that is really helping me—and not ED—is not being involved with people associated with eating disorders. You see, every time I would go to the doctor, ED would be praying my vitals were scary bad or at least worse and that my weight was lower. Then there would be shock and attention around me, even if it was negative. It was like a game to me to try to have worse vitals and scare doctors even more each time. Also, seeing doctors or therapists made me feel I had to keep myself "sick" and be doing bad. If I were doing OK, then why would I need them? In the 3 ½ weeks I have been home, I haven't been to a doctor or therapist once. By keeping myself disassociated with doctors and ED-related things, I believe I will be able to let go of ED easier because one of the purposes it fulfills would no longer exist. At least that's what I want to believe for now.

April 16, 2008

Tonight was rough at home. I looked at the 3 chickens my dad had put in the fridge for me for the next few nights. They were quite large, so I took them out and cut off a piece from each. Of course, Mom overheard Dad saying, "Don't do that," and she came in and started blabbing about how I wasn't doing well. I started screaming and yelling. Why can't my mom just butt out? Why can't my mom stay calm and rational? Why can't my mom let me live my own life and make my own decisions? We started arguing. Half-crying, I said, "I just want to like myself." She replied, "Yeah, that would be nice because you're killing yourself and this family in the process." My jaw completely dropped. Does she not realize that I criticize myself by the second every day for how crazy my lifestyle is? I say negative things to myself all day long, so it's hard when my family points out my flaws, too. I really need to hear compliments and praise from my family because I don't receive it anywhere else. If they can't compliment me I know ED will, which is more reason to not get better!

April 18, 2008

I feel like my parents base how much they will support me only on my looks. I am caught between wanting to be dependent and independent. I don't trust one person on the face of the Earth, not even myself. I feel abandoned by God; I don't feel good enough for him. I allowed ED to become my best friend instead of trusting that there is a greater plan for my life. Sadly, I don't trust anything good will be waiting to catch me and take ED's place.

April 30, 2008

I went to an AA meeting tonight even though I've never had a drink or tried a drug in my life. I really enjoy the meetings. Alcohol and drugs are a different form of self-destruction but have the same characteristics of addiction that can accompany an eating disorder. A common theme people kept sharing was how they could give up alcohol as long as they had drugs or they could give up drugs as long as they had alcohol; it wasn't until they could have neither one that the real work began because they had nothing to fill the hole inside of them or numb their pain. I could so relate! "OK, I will eat more as long as I exercise way too much" or "OK, I won't exercise, but I'm going to restrict my calories." That's what I need to work on: keeping the exercise in line and not restricting to make up for it.

May 2008

Things continued to go downhill for me. I slowly started increasing my exercise and decreasing my calories. I started playing tennis again but only to burn calories. I was too weak to be competitive. Soon, on the days I didn't play tennis, I was walking up the mountain for 30 minutes instead of just walking around the neighborhood. I also stopped eating any food containing gluten. I felt so much better not eating it, but then it became another obsession and rule to follow.

June 17, 2008

My exercise is now up to 2 hours and 10 minutes, which is as much as I was doing before Stanford but at the gym! At least it is probably with less intensity, right? Every time I stare in the mirror now, I see a skeletal face with soulless eyes. It is so scary! I want to be able to let my weight fluctuate and not care. I want to be spontaneous and go out with friends. I don't want to be held prisoner to having to eat at certain times and the same foods every day. I don't want to worry I'm going to die every day and not be able to sleep. I want to play tennis again for real. I want to take back everything so that I could still have Scandalous. I want my family to be happy. I want to be able to have energy and know I am safe. I want to be able to skip exercising and eat normally. I want to be able to eat cake on my own damn birthday. I want to be free from my insanity. I want to be Brittany!

June 30, 2008

I didn't feel great today. I could feel how low my heart rate was. I also was having slight chest and back pain. I didn't feel dizzy but felt almost as though I were floating and could drop to the ground at any moment. I did decide to do a 30-minute walk over a 40-minute hike, which I guess is something to be proud of? I hate that it always takes me severely flirting with death before I make any sort of change. Then, of course, when I do make the change, it only lasts until I feel a bit better and then it's back to destroying myself slowly again. It's not as though I want to destroy myself. I know I am a great person, friend, student, and athlete. I also know that I am OK looking, but for some reason I just feel so undeserving. ED is my addiction, not my choice.

I went to a few markets tonight and paced around but did much less walking because I felt weird. After I came home, I went for a 30-minute evening walk and had a little more energy. But again, I was getting that odd sensation as though my heart was hardly beating and I could drop to the ground. I am starting to get low back pain, too, which makes me worry about my kidneys. My voice is getting weaker lately, and it's getting harder to breathe. I'm always almost hyperventilating when I see myself in the mirror. I can't live like this! I now know for a fact that I am dying and will die soon if I don't take some action.

Dad came into the office where I was, sat down, and said, "Look, Brittany, here are the facts and truth. You are not going to make it, and you are going to die soon. You will not make it." I started hyperventilating because he was right. I felt odd. I then walked into the kitchen and drank an Ensure Plus that was in the fridge. Ah! I feel as though I've never been so stuck and so ready to give up ED at the same time. Mom always says that things are the hardest and worst right before a change is made. I decided I would reduce my walking by 1 hour starting tomorrow. I was petrified of going to sleep with my heart rate being so low, but eventually I just couldn't keep my eyes open any longer and sleep took hold of me.

July 3, 2008

Today was very scary! I woke up to my parents' extreme worry about me and how I should not exercise at all and probably should be taken to the hospital because of my appearance. I was upset because today was supposed to be my first day of less activity. I left to go to the market and was feeling ill. I had no energy, was very hot, and felt as though I would collapse.

I came home and told my parents I would do no walking today. Mom came home a mess about me and cried, saying how she now saves all the notes and phone messages I leave wondering if it will be my last! She is so afraid she is going to have to bury me and so is Dad. The neighborhood all knows about me and calls me the "crazy walker" because I am walking all the time. Stupidly, I went back to the markets tonight and did a little walking until shoulder pain stopped me in my tracks.

7

Future Tripping

"Everyone holds his or her own key to success and happiness. It's just that sometimes you have to test out a lot of wrong keys first to find the one that fits." ~Britt

July 15, 2008

I only got a few hours of sleep last night so I could wake up early and pack for the 2-day visit to UC Davis with my dad. I slept for a bit on the drive up and didn't eat anything until 6:30 in the evening. I am so weak, groggy, and mentally stupid right now. I just can't think! Dad and I walked around downtown Davis until 8:00 at night. The weather was perfect! I absolutely love the town. It is very similar to my hometown but smaller with fewer stores and things going on. It feels much safer and sheltered, though, which is nice. I could not have picked a better school!

We finally decided to eat at Bakers Square, which was right across from our hotel and is basically identical to Denny's. There were so many delicious and fun-looking restaurants that I know Dad would have loved to have taken me to, but they looked too threatening to me. I ended up eating way fewer calories than I expected, but it was so nice eating with Dad in a new place and at a normal time. Gosh, I want to change so badly, create a new routine, eat at normal times, and eat with people. I feel like if I spent a week at Davis or anywhere else, I could do that and adjust my schedule. Knowing that tomorrow

I'm going home to my familiar house, people, and food is what makes it so hard to change. I am so excited to meet new people and reinvent my life at Davis, but like Dad said, if I can't start to make some changes now, then people will easily be able to see I have a problem, and it will be very hard to change with the pressure of school.

Dad said I very well might die before I can even get to Davis if I don't take a few steps forward. I would really like to hope he is exaggerating, but I don't know.

My greatest fear is that I will bring this demon—or shall I say, ED—with me and again create an image I dislike. I really don't want to ruin this opportunity. It will be my life for the next 4 years! This is where I will meet great friends, perhaps my husband, get amazing academic opportunities, and do fun things with athletics and horses. I can't blow this! I at least need to go into college strong so that I attract people. I can always lose more weight again. It would be much worse to start school so laughably anorexic that I scare everyone away. Because then, even if I tried to gain weight and get healthy, I would still carry around the anorexic label and might even die before I could get well. It seems like a no-brainer decision, right?

July 16, 2008

I absolutely love Davis, yet I know I won't survive a week if I don't improve my health. I have only eaten 1,350 calories today, including vitamins and gum, which probably shouldn't even count! What happened to me? I almost feel hypnotized. I don't want this eating disorder, but I feel as though I'm consumed with it now and that there is no turning back. I tell myself that as soon as I get to Davis I will change, start over, and be happy. Yet, subconsciously, I hear that voice inside my head saying it will be no different.

July 17, 2008

What a day! I walked around markets for hours and didn't eat anything until 5:30 in the evening. I went back out to run more errands, and I was really late coming home. Dad called me furious! He said I was never to be out even close to that late again and that changes will be made. I finally made it home around midnight, and I fought and cried with and hugged Dad. I am killing him. My parents sat me down and said this was an intervention: no more walking, must gain weight, going to supervise food, and no more late nights or else I would be put under a conservatorship and tubed.

I was panicked, yet in a way this was the moment I've been waiting for—someone to force me to change since I can't seem to do it myself. My parents say I'm days from death and should be hospitalized now. After much bargaining, we settled on a few significant changes: one 20-minute walk, eat earlier, go to bed earlier, markets and errands must be done during the day, and I must eat 100 percent of my food. Mom is still saying I must increase my calories a ton. I hate how my parents want to watch me eat as well as demanding I gain weight. I suppose it is better than being on bed rest and eating 2,500 to 3,500 calories with no freedom at Stanford, but it still makes me just want to rebel and fight.

I have been acting on a more rebellious side of myself than I had when I was younger. It is mainly with my parents—and doctors, I suppose. Maybe I am just protective of ED. I am the type of person who likes to prove people wrong. When they say something is impossible, I give it my all to make it possible. Too bad I'm using my willpower and determination toward something negative. If only I could channel it toward something positive.

I am excited not to restrict and to eat and go to bed earlier. I'm just not sure it will last. I am terrified of changing my familiar routine, but I do need this boost before Davis. Once I get to college, I can do whatever I want and can finally make decisions without my parents' interference.

I am now having tons of trouble thinking clearly. I can't even speak or form sentences correctly sometimes. It's as though I try to think about something and say something, and my mind feels empty and blank. I feel I have no more depth right now than being the "walker" my neighborhood has labeled me. I wish so badly I could go back to 14 years old and make different decisions. I wish I had taken the tennis academy scholarship I was offered before ED took hold. I wish I had gone out with friends the few times they invited me. I wish I had taken the compliments I received to heart rather than thinking I was worthless. I wish I had said yes when guys asked me out. I wish I had gone to another treatment center after Stanford. I wish I still had Scandalous. I wish my mind could think about something other than calories and weight. I wish I still had a happy family. I wish I didn't hate myself. I wish I still had a life.

July 20, 2008

I did lots of market walking and errands today. When I came home my parents asked for my written calorie list of what I would eat for the day. I gave it to Dad, who was fine with it until Mom searched all my foods to get the exact calories. I was so mad because she was extremely rude about it. She found my string cheese, which I was trying to pass as 80 calories even though it is only 50; thankfully, I hid the wrapper so she believed me when I said they were 70 calories. She also found my sugar-free pudding, which was 45 calories, but again there was no box, so I said it was 70 calories. It was a very unpleasant, 30-minute ordeal. Eventually it passed, and when Dad recalculated the calories, I was 100 short. Dang! I added 1 tablespoon of peanut butter with Dad, but when he left the room, I spit out a good amount that I hadn't swallowed yet. I also restricted ¾ of my egg yolk; I was worried that my parents would be watching my later meals, so I took advantage of restricting the egg while I had the chance. After all that my parents did not watch me eat or make me show them my food—yes! I hate ED and myself for restricting, though. I flush more food down the toilet each day than I eat!

July 21, 2008

Today was honestly one of the worst days of my life! I did great with going to bed by 1:00 last night, and I got up early this morning for work at Abercrombie at 8:00. After my shift, I began my "errand walking" for 2 hours and 30 minutes and then came home to grab my snack. I took the string cheese my parents believed was 70 calories and 1 tablespoon of peanut butter, but again I spit out 75 percent of it after they saw me put it in my mouth.

I then left to do my next hour of errand walking. I parked on a hill above the bank and then walked to the bank and to the drugstore and the market. I walked back up the hill to get my string cheese out of my car and then I walked back to the market. I got home late, and that is when the hell began. Dad opened the house door furious! Apparently the whole town is worried about me and has been calling my parents. I guess someone called today to say they saw me walking all around town and in markets—shit! Dad was also pissed about the string cheese because he looked it up and found out it was really only 50 calories. Anyway, to sum it up, I have never seen my parents so upset in my life. They completely cut me off from absolutely everything. My life is crap now, and my mom is a bitch! The damn rules: food eaten by 11:00 at night, computer off by 11:00 p.m., no keys, no activity, must eat right when I wake up, must eat 2,000 calories, parents must measure and count each of my foods as I prepare them, parents must sit with me and watch me eat every bite so I don't restrict, can't have any privileges until I gain weight or look better. I hate them! This is war!

July 22, 2008

Today I was able to get away with throwing away my whole egg and a whole bunch of other things, but my mom decided not anymore! She has been the meanest person ever! She just randomly states throughout the day, "Oh, computer off by 11:00. I want to check your Facebook. Food eaten by 11:00. I'm going to count your crackers and watch you go to the bathroom." Dad wasn't going to do any of that except now he is backing Mom up! I hate her! Dinner sucked! I ate 100 percent of a huge piece of chicken. I must find a way to restrict and exercise, but I have no escape! I literally had to stuff my face with almost all my food back-to-back to make it by 11:00 at night or else be kicked out of the house or tubed and put under a conservatorship. Dad says I can only get my freedom back when he can trust me and sees me trying and gaining weight. I guess I will have to comply, but I don't think I will ever want to get rid of ED fully.

I got a call from my guy friend I met in the hospital today telling me he is back at Stanford. He said he has been doing OK weight-wise but that his heart rate got too low and they admitted him. How ironic. I should be there, too. Ugh! Just the other day I had my mom hugging me and telling me how proud she was of me, then bang! Craziness! I am seriously going insane and would almost rather be dead. I can't take eating so much with no activity. I can't, I can't, and *I can't*!

July 23, 2008

Just when I thought things couldn't get worse, they got much worse! Dad came storming into my room at 7:00 this morning saying he found food and my string cheese coming up from the toilet. Shit! He was fuming! He said I now have to be supervised in the kitchen with all of my food and that every bite would be watched. He then went upstairs only to storm back down a minute later with the scale and said if I didn't get weighed I was kicked out. He was completely serious. I had just peed and had only a nightshirt on. I told him I wanted to get on it first without him looking and it read 91.5 pounds! I was shocked and confused because on other scales I was around 98 to 100 pounds when I was clothed and had a lot of water in me. The difference couldn't be that much. I am convinced our scale must be wrong, right? Well, then I had to step on with Dad looking, and it read 90.5 pounds! Even worse! He was furious and ordered I drink 2 Ensure Pluses and eat 2,700 calories a day and be weighed weekly to make certain I was gaining a lot of weight.

Shit! If I had only just eaten 100 percent of everything yesterday, it would have still sucked, but at least I would be able to eat in the office, be more trusted, eat 2,000 calories versus 2,700, and not have to go by numbers on the scale. I blew it! I have completely destroyed my dad's faith in me. I had to recalculate a whole new meal plan to equal 2,700 while Dad watched me eat all my food. Surprisingly, even with everything that happened today, I have acted polite and cooperative. Tonight Dad said today is the first day he has been genuinely proud of me in a long time. I think I am just in shock and too embarrassed to put up a fight this time. I know that if I gain more weight than I'm comfortable with, then at Davis I will want to lose just a little, which always leads to a downward spiral. I hope my parents allow me to gain enough weight to get stronger but not so much that it scares me so that I can maintain a good balance.

August 6, 2008

Today was the first day of my 2-day orientation at UC Davis. It was pretty warm out already, which is always a conflict for me. I love warm weather because I am always cold, but it also means wearing shorts, tank tops, or short sleeves, which in turn means I can't easily hide my obvious problem. I checked in, put my belongings in my temporary dorm room, and then gathered with about 400 other students to go into a lecture hall. I met 3 really sweet girls, and we had fun talking and sat together.

I had dinner with my roommate in the cafeteria that night. The cafeteria was extremely nice and was just like a food court with many different style foods all around. It was buffet style, which was cool. I am so worried about my health and calories! I can tell I've lost a lot of weight and am not eating enough. Despite my worry, I still ate dinner like a freak. It was just so overwhelming with all the choices and unknown calories. Oh well, tomorrow is a new day. I can always eat a little extra here for a few days and then restrict at home. This school is just incredible! I have had 1,000 calories today at the most. Eek!

August 8, 2008

I got home today from Davis. I shared with my mom how scared I was, which triggered her into a panic and caused me to feel attacked and ignored at the same time. I just wanted her to listen and tell me I would be OK. Moms are supposed to be there for you and hug you while you go through your teenage problems, right? I didn't want her to explode and start lecturing me. Doesn't she know that I am fully aware of the poor decisions I am making? Doesn't she know how guilty I feel? Doesn't she know I want to change? Doesn't she know I hate myself? Doesn't she know I feel like such a burden already?

August 20, 2008

Last night I heard my dad go upstairs into the guest room right above my room, and I could hear him crying about me again. I went upstairs around 3:40 a.m. and asked him what was wrong. He said he was worried I couldn't break my habits and calorie level. He was afraid I would die. We had a nice talk. I assured him I had complete control over my actions. I mean, I do, right? I did 2 hours of compulsive walking today. I did do better with not restricting, though I'm sure that's a result of exercising more. I did 2 extra fast walks alone tonight because my parents went out to dinner. I feel so guilty, but it's as reflexive as breathing now.

August 23, 2008

I was able to get away with restricting pretty much everything today. Only when I started making my sandwich did my parents get suspicious, but I still got away with restricting it, too. My younger sister, Kasey, called me from a friend's house to say hi and that she loves me and she's sorry she hasn't been there for me. She also said she is scared I will die in college and will never see me again. Ugh! That certainly made me feel guilty and scared. I hate how I affect others so much. I know I am destroying myself and I don't really want to, but I definitely don't want to destroy my family in the process.

I was looking around on YouTube tonight, and I listened to the song "Deadly Beauty" by Faces Without Names about a girl who dies from an eating disorder. It terrified me and made me cry hysterically. I called Mom to come talk to me. She said I was OK because my vitals are good, yet I know I'm not OK and that my body has already been through many years of abuse. I'm scared. I don't want to die!

August 24, 2008

I had a really great talk with my dad late tonight. We talked about how I must go for it. No more chances. ED will never make me happy or let me live. College is my last shot, and it can be amazing. I told him it's hard because I have so many years invested in ED. Dad said it was the worst choice. I can now pick a new one and leave ED behind.

Doesn't he know how hard I have slaved away at perfection? I can't just drop the past 7 years of my life like they never happened. All that work for nothing!

I told Dad we should have a binge day and go out to breakfast, lunch, and dinner without counting calories. He said that would be a dream come true. I think I said it just to make him happy, just to make him believe I had the right mind-set. The honest truth is that I would love to have a binge day or at least a day where I could eat off-limit foods. I have been with ED for so long now that I really don't ever crave foods besides what I already eat. I could pass up every single kind of dessert or unhealthy food easily. I'm rarely hungry either. I mean, I enjoy eating when I allow myself, but it is a very controlled and sacred thing. I don't ever see myself eating normally. I wouldn't even allow myself 1 bite of mashed potatoes! I don't really know if it's because I'm afraid I won't stop. No, I know I could stop. That isn't it. I think it just comes down to "losing." If I give in, even to just 1 bite, then I am no longer the best and no longer competitive in the "game" of anorexia. I'm so scared, though! I'm obviously stuck in this disease, yet I'm not intentionally trying to lose weight—at least not consciously. I really think I want to gain some weight, especially going into college. I even wince when I look at myself in the mirror, so what will others think? I'm so tired, too. I'm going to bed around 4 in the morning now!

8

Good Intentions

September 20, 2008

Today was the day we drove up to Davis so that I can move into my dorm tomorrow! I got up early after only 3 hours of sleep again to get my hair done. Mom and I pretty much fought and yelled at each other all day. She's incredibly scared. So am I. I've been extra "babyish" and "obsessive" today because I feel as though it's my last day to be taken care of, not have to grow up, and stay stuck in the old Brittany.

I'm really, really scared. I have no energy and look as though I should be dead. So, why am I still struggling so much to eat more? I hate how I look and think I'm too thin and sick, but I'm paralyzed to change it. I'm addicted to the disease! Now I am sitting here up at night feeling guilty and starving. I was reading all about the UC Davis equestrian team and am so excited, yet I need to make dramatic changes to try out for the team in about 2 weeks. I pray with all my might that starting tomorrow I can live ED-free and let go and be the true Brittany, as well as gain some weight. I really need to eat and take risks and be different. I am ready to start my new life in my heart, but I'm just so worried my mind doesn't understand.

September 21, 2008

Well, I got moved in today! I met a lot of people and ended up hanging out with a few. I really struggled with food though. I hardly ate during the day and then ate a ton at night but still only about 1,700 calories.

September 22, 2008

I went to the dining hall around 5:00 this evening and ate a few strawberries (it was the first food I ate all day). A bunch of the girls on my floor and I hung out in one of the dorm rooms. Everyone was getting ready to go out to the frat parties downtown. It was around 11:00 at night! Aren't they worried about getting a good night's sleep before classes? I met a lot of really cool and "popular" girls, but they were all into drinking and getting wasted. They snuck in a bunch of alcohol and were dancing in the room. I eventually left and said I would go out tomorrow but felt left out because I wasn't into drinking.

September 28, 2008

I talked to my mom today and vented to her. I told her how lonely I felt because all the girls were hanging out laughing in their room with music blasting and I didn't feel included. They all know each other from high school, and although I like them and think most like me individually, they still never seek me out to include me.

I'm mostly worried because although ED is gone and I want to gain weight, I still eat all my food alone in my dorm room. I have some nasty old habits to break. Wait...did I just say ED was gone? I hate to admit it, but that's false. Why do I keep lying to myself? I might want *him* to be gone, but ED is stronger than ever right now. Besides, I know ED will always be my friend, invite me, and be there for me, unlike the people here.

October 23, 2008

The past 2 weeks or so have been OK and nothing more. Lately I have been almost binging at night on almonds because I get so scared about my health and being alone in my room. I have one of the few single dorm rooms, which ED clearly thought would be the best choice for me. Yeah, well, it's not so great. Then again, if I had a roommate, she would think I'm absolutely nuts considering all the odd food I have stored in my room and how late I stay up. Maybe that would force me to change, though? Yeah, well, forget that. I can change all by myself! I had my first anxiety attack on the 16th of this month, and it was the scariest thing ever! I thought I would have to go to the ER! Dad eventually calmed me down, but it really unraveled me. My parents came up to see me for my 20th birthday. That was nice but also kind of awkward. I felt bad that I didn't have a lot of friends to introduce them to.

My room is packed with food I brought from home. I have a huge plastic bin full of nutrition bars and 2 shelves full of sugar-free Jell-O, broth, and a bucket of really tiny fruit. My whole dresser is full of diet soda, Powerade Zero, and an obsessive amount of SmartWater. It looks as if I'm hibernating for a year! I'm creating the same life I had at home, and I am blowing it socially. I have so many people here that I could reach out to, hang out with and eat with, but I am just overly rigid. I am so lonely and have no friends. I just have people I say hi to. I never eat in the cafeteria and eat way too late as well.

I am also doing way too much activity and am starting to get addicted to the gym again. I walk on an inclined treadmill for 45 minutes now. It isn't very strenuous, but on top of everything else I do, it adds up. Not to mention just the act of entering the gym is bad news. The gym scale says I weigh 102 pounds. I really thought I would weigh less. I know I'm clothed and have a lot of fluid in me, but is it really correct? I'm still getting very anxious at night and am afraid I will die. I need to—no, I *have* to—change!

November 8, 2008

I was out of control with exercise again today. I rode my bike downtown; biked to the horse barn; rode Casanova, the wonderful pony I'm leasing; biked back to my dorm; walked to University Mall; walked back; went to the gym 3 times; walked to Rite Aid and back; walked to Rite Aid again and back; and then walked to Starbucks and back. My gosh! I did a total of 2 hours and 23 minutes at the gym. I am getting so compulsive. I really shouldn't forget to mention that I pace around the dorm hallways late at night when everyone is asleep. We are talking 1 hour a night of walking circles around the dorm hallways with my headphones in! Am I really that ridiculous?

November 13, 2008

I am so tired! I went to class, did some laundry, finished my essay, had a class review session, took a 1-hour nap, and had an equestrian team meeting. I did a total of 9 miles today on the treadmill for a total of 2 hours and 41 minutes.

A girl who was walking out of the gym at the same time stopped me and said, "You work out a lot. My friend and I noticed you come every night. You look like you are in great shape." I responded with, "I'm an athlete..." She then said, "Oh, OK, so I'm sure you know what to eat." She mentioned all the programs and classes through the university, such as nutrition drop-ins, and how things can get stressful. She said she was a senior. She was really nice, yet I'm sure that she was trying to help me and knew I had an eating disorder. I felt kind of embarrassed and didn't really know how to respond. Part of me wanted to put my hands up and shout, "OK, you're right, I have a problem!" But the other part wanted to look at her as if she were nuts. I think I settled for something in-between. I guess it is pretty obvious that I come to the gym back-to-back 4 times every day. I need to start spreading out my gym sessions. I am getting scary skinny. My legs are still not where I want them, but they are getting better. I am waiting till 10:00 at night to eat anything. I had been going to bed around 4:00 in the morning, but now I am going to bed around 5:00

a.m.! Everything keeps getting later and later for me! My legs are so sore and heavy right now. I know I am losing weight and not eating enough. Not to mention I walked around outside for a while and then paced the halls like a madwoman. Ugh! Seriously, Brittany?

November 22, 2008

I slept in and then went to the farmers market. I bought 4 full bags of miniature-sized fruit! The gym closes early tonight, so I went a little overboard with my exercise. I did a total of 2 hours and 25 minutes! I then walked to Rite Aid and Starbucks and then walked outside for 30 minutes in the freezing air. I then paced the halls for 1 hour. I've decided I really need help. I am still going to bed at 5:00 in the morning. I am severely sleep-deprived. I am really scared, but don't feel in danger... at least yet. I am lonely, stuck, addicted, happy, confused, stressed, free, and lost all in one. I really don't want to die!

November 30, 2008

I slept in and then went to the gym in the early afternoon. At least I am spreading out when I go more now. I went to the horse barn to ride Casanova. He was awesome, but my position is horrible over the jumps once he gets going because I'm too weak. I then did some homework and listened to the dorms slowly fill back up with students returning from Thanksgiving break. I decided to stay in Davis for Thanksgiving. Too much hassle to go all the way home, especially when it would interfere with my food and exercise schedule. I have the worst stomachache tonight I think I have ever had in my life! It is probably the combination of way too much liquid and artificial sweetener: 44 ounces of diet soda, 14 pieces of gum, and 2 packets of Splenda. Please make it stop! I am going to bed at 5:00 a.m. and will get only 4 hours of sleep before class. I just don't understand! Am I really this addicted to eating and staying up late, or am I really that scared I will die in my sleep? Only 13 days before Christmas break, thank goodness! My total gym time was 2 hours and 32 minutes today. Not to mention the 1 hour of hall pacing. Oh, what I would do to turn back time.

December 5, 2008

I got up before class and went to the gym for a bit. I went to class and then to the health center for my appointment with the doctor my parents are forcing me to see. Dr. Freeman is a physician but apparently works with a lot of people with eating disorders. I love her! We talked for about an hour. I was completely honest, and she said everything was completely confidential. She was so nice. It was a relief to admit to someone the hell in my life. She set me up with a counselor for eating disorders next week and said there are some great ED support groups, too. She said they could create a little treatment team for me, which sounded OK. She was really worried about my vitals, though. I was 95.6 pounds with UGG boots and tons of layers on, my temperature was 94 degrees, my blood pressure was 92/39, and my heart rate was 43. Ugh! I have to get blood work and an EKG. She made a special appointment to see me on Wednesday as well as Friday. Still, I went to the gym for the second time and then went to Starbucks and then, hey, what do you know, I went to the gym a third time! I didn't do quite as much "other" walking, but still did 3 hours and 33 minutes at the gym!

Oh my gosh! I am so cold right now! Five layers are not keeping me warm even with the heat turned all the way up in my little room. I am going to bed at 6:00 in the morning now. I am going to die!

December 9, 2008

I could hardly wake up today and slept until 2:00 in the after-noon. I keep telling everyone on my dorm floor that I have stomach issues to hint as to why I am so skinny, but I wonder what they are really thinking. I had such terrible stomach pain! I couldn't even drink water! I decided to skip the gym time today and still eat around 1,200 calories. I wobbled over to class and took a hard final exam while I winced in pain. I had another final right after the first, and I was 15 minutes late because I was not feeling well. My teacher asked me if I was OK, and I surprisingly answered truthfully and said, "No, I am really sick." I took the final anyway and then debated going to the health center. I eventually decided to go.

I made it to the health center around 8:00 tonight. They called an ambulance within 10 minutes of my arrival to get me on IV fluids. The doctor at the health center seemed to already know quite a bit about me from my meeting with Dr. Freeman. He was very worried about my vitals and anorexia. He said he used to be an ER doctor for 10 years and wanted to hospitalize me ASAP! My heart rate was 43, temperature was 93 degrees, and my blood pressure was OK.

When I got to the ER my weight was 85.2 pounds! Oh my gosh! I hadn't had anything to drink or eat all day, but I must say that weight does better match my appearance. I can't even sit in a chair anymore without excruciating pain because all my bones stick out.

They gave me an IV and took some blood work. The nurses at the ER told me the doctor at UC Davis was very worried about me. Everyone was really nice, but I was eager to leave, so I promised them I was OK. I finally got myself discharged about 2 hours later and had a taxi take me back to the dorms. No more gym and more food! I went to bed tonight, or morning, around 6:00. Erg! At least I am done with all my finals so I can sleep.

December 11, 2008

What a day! I was able to get up this morning and get blood work and an EKG done by 11:45. Dr. Freeman had left me a message on my cell phone and an e-mail saying it was urgent I get this done because of my lab results from the hospital...but I thought the ER doctor said they were OK? Well, I got my EKG done. Then my doctor came in to have a serious talk with me. She told me I needed to be hospitalized today! She said I was at severe risk for "refeeding syndrome," a possibly fatal complication of nutritional restoration, and that I needed to be hospitalized for quite a while to stabilize. My labs came back decent enough except my phosphorus was way too low and my white blood cells were dangerously low. She ordered a phosphate supplement for me. Then she and 2 other doctors came in one by one and literally begged me to agree to hospitalization. I refused and said I would be careful and do it at home because I didn't want to be away for more than 3 weeks. They begged and begged, but

I still said no. I wouldn't even let my doctor talk to my dad to explain how sick I was and what to expect. They were all intensely frightened and honestly told me they thought I would die on my own. They worried about me sleeping in the dorms tonight and didn't even think I could wait until Saturday for my dad to pick me up! Ugh!

I was so tired and weak I could hardly walk, and they made me sign a form with a witness basically saying I was refusing their serious recommendations. Dr. Freeman said I could possibly go to the local hospital here for intravenous food and monitoring for a few days, but I said no to that also. I weighed 87 pounds, but I think I look even worse than that. I have an appointment tomorrow with her again. I love her, but she is just so worried...too worried? She told me that if I was going to do this on my own at home that I must be very careful increasing calories because of the risk of refeeding syndrome. She said not to increase my calories over 1,200 to 1,300 and that maybe after 1 week I could increase a little if I were doing OK.

December 12, 2008

I was exhausted this morning. I had my doctor appointment at 1:00 this afternoon. I eventually made it down to the health center, but the ½-mile walk felt more like an eternity. Dr. Freeman was very upset and worried about me last night and talked to a trusted colleague of hers who said to do a "mental status" exam on me to make sure I could make decisions for myself. It was just a bunch of random questions such as what day of the week it was and so on.

My doctor said I am 70 percent of my ideal body weight and that I meet hospitalization requirements up until 85 percent body weight. She said she wouldn't be so terrified of my weight if I could get my heart rate, temperature, and electrolytes more stable. She told me to check in over break and to see my doctor at home to check my electrolytes.

My energy level was nonexistent all day. I just wanted to collapse and sleep. I walked around for a bit, though, and then walked to meet with the counselor my doctor had suggested for me. I really liked her. I spent most of the time filling her in on my history and what has been going on recently. I could hardly stand up out of the chair after my appointment with her and honestly didn't think I could make it back to the dorm! I did finally make it back, thank goodness. I called my dad, who is picking me up tomorrow, and filled him in on some things, including that I was eating only 1,200 calories and wasn't advised to increase, which really upset him. I hope being at home goes well. I still did way too much activity today and went to bed at 5:45 this morning.

December 14, 2008

Well, I'm now back in San Luis Obispo. I slept until 5:00 in the afternoon today! It was disturbingly hard to wake up. It poured rain today, which was a nice change. I went a little crazy because of sleeping in so late and not doing as much activity as at Davis, so I decided to take a walk at 5:40 p.m. in the pouring dark rain and 46-degree temperature. I had planned on just walking around the neighborhood, but I ended up walking all the way to the Rite Aid about 2 miles from home! It was not smart.

After I got home I took the car and went to 4 more markets to pace around. I'm crazy! I have no strength. I am going to bed at 6:00 in the morning tonight. I am so scared to die, yet so scared to live. I am not having my first bite of food until after midnight now. I am in such a terrible spiral and hate-love my addiction to weight loss. Then again...I couldn't stop myself if I wanted to. It's as if I'm possessed. It's not me inside telling me what to do...it's ED, but ED is real...I have no other way to explain it.

December 17, 2008

My heart rate was only 34 last night when I took it! After much arguing in my head, I decided to give my suffering body a rest. I plan to reduce my calories and rest all day. I went to see my old therapist at 1:00 this afternoon. I was so tired I could hardly speak, drive home, or keep my eyes open. It was freaky, though, because I literally could not think or process words. I then slept until 9:45 in the evening and afterward got Starbucks. My parents are sort of staying out of my way, but I can't imagine what they are going through. Now when I stand with my heels together there is at least a 3 1/2-inch gap between my thighs. I can feel my heart barely beating! I need and want to gain weight but really don't know how. My muscles are cramping up, and my body hurts like crazy even if I just barely bump into something. I really hope my doctor's appointment goes well tomorrow.

December 19, 2008

I was awoken to an urgent call from my doctor I saw yesterday saying my blood work came back and was not good. My sodium and chloride as well as my blood sugar were dangerously low. She said I am at risk for a seizure, which explains why I have been so weak, sleepy, and having cramps. She told me to go to the ER right away for an IV and monitoring. About 3 hours later, I finally decided I would go.

I arrived at the ER, and the nurse started an IV. I was ridiculously lethargic. My sodium levels came up a little eventually, and the doctor asked me about going back to Stanford. I gathered what little strength I had to project a firm *no*. He dropped the subject. He wanted to keep me overnight at least to monitor me and get my sodium back up to normal, but I again said *no*. He was disappointed but said OK, however, I had to sign something saying I was leaving AMA, against medical advice. He told me not to drink a lot of water today, to have lots of salt and calories, and to return immediately if I feel worse at all. He told me to get my blood work rechecked immediately. He really wanted to make sure that I was confident in my treatment team at Davis and in my support at home. My weight was taken after about an hour with IV fluids in me, but I still weighed 85.6 pounds. I guess I was hoping for less. How can I hope to lose weight while simultaneously hope not to die? I am just disturbingly *hopeless*!

I left and put my head down for a bit when I returned home, and then later I went to 5 markets! I did way too much activity today. I am so scared! I drank too much water tonight as well. My back and hand keep cramping. I just want a hug. I just want to feel safe. Doesn't anyone know how to protect me?

9

Merry Misery

December 21, 2008

Today is my sister Kasey's 17th birthday. I went to bed last night (morning) at 8:00! I am becoming nocturnal. I wasn't too tired, so I decided to not really go to sleep and just kind of get up and push through the day to help readjust my internal clock. I was feeling so weird that I actually chose to take myself back to the ER. The doctor wanted to admit me overnight because he was very concerned with my weight and electrolytes and wanted me to be monitored. I finally gave in and agreed. I am so tired. I talked to my new doctor upstairs even though I was so out of it. He suggested something like Stanford or hospitalization again. I clearly stated no and said that things were just beginning to turn around and improve. He told me there was no way I could leave early and that I had to stay overnight. I only ate about 600 calories. I am so sorry, Kasey!

December 22, 2008

My heart rate has been as low as 38 at times. I talked to the doctor this morning, and it was not great news. I forgot most of what he said. I do remember him saying I was in serious condition and that he can't release me home. He said I will die and that my weight is too low. He said I couldn't even sign out AMA! He also told me that I can't make decisions for myself and that he talked to my UC Davis doctor and my local doctor and that they all agreed I needed to be an inpatient. He said that my UC Davis doctor wouldn't accept me back to her care in my current state. He also said I would be staying another night for monitoring.

I am praying I can be released home after a few days here. I need to do some serious begging and convincing tomorrow. I decided I will have to take winter quarter off from horses and probably do the IOP, intensive outpatient program, in Sacramento by bus for my UC Davis doctor to accept me back. Dad threatened to conserve me again! I am walking on eggshells right now despite all my recent actions, such as quitting the gym. Dad says I must come home and eat 3,000-plus calories—shit! I never should have come in to the hospital to get my sodium checked. Everything happens for a reason, right?

I called Mom to ask her to bring me a few things. Of course we got into a huge fight, or at least she got into her crazy mode when I starting listing some foods I wanted her to bring. She told me I'm in a hospital, not a resort, and that I have to eat the hospital food. I finally gave up and asked Dad, but when he came he brought no gum, no mints, and no sugar-free flavored water as I had asked! He told me he chose not to bring those items because I don't need them and that maybe when he sees me actually take some "real" action, such as downing a Boost Plus, he will bring them. Anyway, I freaked but knew I had some emergency backup gum and mints at least for tonight.

December 23, 2008

I still went to bed around 4:30 this morning despite being in the hospital. I woke up early, though. They drew my blood and did vitals at 5:00 a.m.! I was so anxious for the day and to talk to the doctors. The doctor eventually came in. It was a different one than yesterday, thank goodness! He was really jolly and outgoing. I definitely liked him much better. He came up to me and asked me why I was here. We ended up having an awesome and productive talk! His name is Dr. Dale. Apparently, the previous doctor was going to involve the court and have me conserved to the hospital, force-feed me, and hold me until I was better! Thankfully, Dr. Dale and I both greatly disagreed with that approach. He said he was going to overwrite him and release me tomorrow or Thursday morning at the latest. He even called my dad and told him I was almost good to go! My sodium did drop a little, so he wanted to monitor me another night, but that's really the only thing keeping me here.

I had a nice talk with my dad. He said I could go back to UC Davis after I told him I would see a treatment team. Paige, my tennis coach, and a friend both visited me today. It was so incredibly nice! They are hands down the most important people in my life other than my family. I feel I can be honest with them, though I do worry I am freaking them out. My friend told me I still look beautiful and gave me a CD he burned. I have been in the best mood after seeing them! I truly feel as though I am giving up ED and am going to get my life under control. I also don't have any cramping or weakness today!

Dad came by later, and we had a great time together. I told him how I was going to get my life back. He told me that would be the best Christmas present ever. On another note, I have been quite sick tonight. I have been having intense diarrhea all day. I haven't been getting terrible cramps but just an awful stomachache. I mean, I must have gone to the bathroom over 40 times by 10:00 tonight! I finally told the nurse, who called the doctor, and he ordered a stool test and something to calm down my stomach. A little later my temperature, which had been consistently in the 97-degree range all day, became undetectably low for the next 3 times the nurse took my vital signs. I had also been complaining all night of being unusually and chillingly cold. When she couldn't get my temperature the 4th time she took my vitals, and she had to take my temperature rectally. It was 93.1 degrees!

She called Dr. Dale right away, and he was very worried and sent me straight to the ICU. They gave me some sort of warming blanket and were able to monitor my vitals more closely. I finally started to warm up after hours under the blanket. Everyone was really nice and helpful. I am still having terrible diarrhea and stomach pain, though. The doctor called many times throughout the night. I haven't really been able to sleep at all either. My potassium dropped, so I am now getting potassium through my IV.

December 24, 2008

Today was one of the scariest and worst days ever! What a contrast from yesterday being so great. I didn't sleep at all last night, and the nurses ended up having to put in a new IV because the potassium was stopping up and burning my arm. It still hurt just as bad through the new IV, and they could barely run it. They gave me something to help with my stomach pain. As it was some sort of narcotic, it completely knocked me out even though they only gave me half of the normal dose.

I awoke to a burning IV and eventually groggily noticed Dr. Dale had showed up in the ICU to see me. He came over with me half-asleep, touched my shoulder, and said I was wasting away and not eating and that he was going to have me 5150'd, which meant put me on an involuntary psychiatric hold! I was in utter shock. "*What! Why?*" He said, "Because you are going to die." He was quite firm and a bit frantic in a way. I almost passed out in disbelief and confusion. What had changed from yesterday to today? He went back over to the computer while I shouted at him to explain to me what the heck was going on. "I thought I was going home today." He replied, "I changed my mind." Then he started questioning me about refusing my food and vitamins. I think he got confused with the fact that I skipped one of my Neutra-Phos doses and equated that to refusing food, too. That is completely false; I ate all my food! It was all a huge whirlwind. Eventually he came back and said I would have to talk to "crisis" today. If they said I could go, I would be discharged. He said then he would not medically be able to keep me longer because I was stable.

He told me he had to call my dad to inform him of my possible discharge. He wanted to talk to him about my health, but I protested. He finally said OK because he legally can't share medical information because I am an adult. Dad later told me the doctor scared the shit out of him by saying, "She is a sweet girl but absolutely hopeless." He said that Dad should be ready at a moment's notice to have me be sent by helicopter to Stanford and that there were other things he wished he could tell him. I talked to the crisis lady for like 1 minute, signed something, and she said I was good to leave!

Dad came about 30 minutes later, and I was out before noon! He was quite frazzled. I was still out of it from the meds. He had to help me walk out because I could hardly stand. I grabbed a hard-boiled egg and protein shake right when I got home, I was so scared, but I ended up throwing out ½ of the shake and all of the egg yolk. I then slept until 11:00 at night.

Dad brought my meds down to my room even though I still couldn't really wake up. My diarrhea is thankfully better but not completely gone. I feel and look as though I weigh 60 pounds—this is ridiculous! I don't feel as if I even have a body! Why do I struggle so much just to add a tiny egg then? I finally woke up and felt slightly more energetic. Dad and I sat down and had a good 30-minute talk about everything going on. I explained to him in detail what happened in the hospital. I think I made him feel a little better about me, I hope. Ugh, I have to go back to school in a week!

December 25, 2008

Merry Christmas! I wore jeans and 3 layers of shirts, but my appearance still upset Dad. I had a great time opening presents and giving my presents to everyone. I later went to Starbucks and then the drugstore. It is so draining to have to keep finding words to convince Dad I truly am making progress, want recovery, can do it, and can go back to school. I really can! I did increase my calories from 800 to 1,300! It is quite scary to eat more yet my body is also scary. I must take a deep breath and do it! I worked on organizing my room all day and then went upstairs around 5:00 in the evening to pretend to eat peanut butter and 1 egg when I only ate 1 egg white.

Later I told Dad I was really tired as I sat right in front of the space heater even though it was warm inside. Dad said, "That is the one thing you always need to tell me...if you feel tired...because that is when Dr. Dale said your body is crashing and you need to be taken by helicopter to Stanford." I got scared and added a protein shake, which made me feel a little better, but I still threw out ¼ of it. It was only 150 calories!

December 26, 2008

I went to bed extremely late last night, which I suppose is nothing new. Dad woke me with that firm, interruptive voice I hate and said I needed to eat more today and prove to him I can go to college. I was pissed because I had just talked to him a few hours earlier; I thought we had an understanding. He was really nervous, I guess, because he has to pay my winter-quarter tuition soon. I got up, and Dad came into my bedroom as I was getting dressed and had another mini-freak-out because of my appearance. Even I admit I look skinnier today, if that is even possible? I can feel my metabolism starting to speed up a bit, though.

I was planning to go downtown for an hour or so, but Mom started getting all frazzled with me. As I was leaving, she started saying I shouldn't go out, needed to be conserved, needed to eat more, blah, blah, blah! Then Dad got involved, and we all went off to war. Thankfully, Mom was about to leave with her friend, but Dad and I had a heated argument. He was raging and saying to go drink a Boost Plus now and that he wanted to read all of my doctor's e-mails or read all my journal entries. He just went on and on, but after almost an hour, we somewhat resolved our argument. I pretended to add 3 tablespoons of peanut butter to my normal caloric intake even though I really had none. It kind of satisfied him enough at least to let me out of the house.

I went to a ton of stores and did a lot of walking. I also left a message for my UC Davis doctor and the IOP near school. I came home, and my family was actually in a decent mood. I lied to my dad and said I ate a string cheese while I was out. Dad pulled me aside a little later very worried because apparently I was talking very drunkenly and slurring my speech. He was quite scared. Mom also mentioned something. I felt OK but even I noticed! Oh, please get my family and me through this!

I got this weird notice today from the post office saying they tried to deliver a confidential letter today but that it couldn't be left without being signed for so they will return with it tomorrow morning at 9:00. It was from the student health center at UC Davis. Uh-oh! Dad said when things have to be signed for, it means they are very important. He prepared me to be told perhaps that I couldn't go back to school for a quarter. I pray the letter turns out to be no big deal, please!

December 27, 2008

I got up around 11:15 this morning and went to the post office to get the scary UC Davis health letter. It turned out just to be a personal letter from my doctor stating she couldn't currently treat me and that I needed to go to a refeeding program, then IOP, etc. At least it said nothing about not being able to return! I then went to 5 markets and walked obsessively. I felt kind of weak and had another huge fight with my parents about calories, that I have to be in bed by 4:00 in the morning, and that I must gain weight. They are scared shitless and said I'm failing every second. I really need to binge tonight. I can't look at myself in the mirror! Boost Plus tomorrow? A binge is much better than just increasing my calories. It doesn't feel as much as if I am choosing to eat more. It's just kind of an out-of-the-blue loss of control, and if I gain weight it would be because I ate way too much and that makes me feel better. Again, it is creating an excuse. Why do I always do that to myself? Why can't I just accept what life brings to me, good or bad?

I pray some sort of plan will work out and that the IOP will accept me. I don't know what to do, though. I really need to go to Stanford, but I would have to take this quarter off. Or I could go to the IOP but would have to deal with my deteriorating health and do part-time status at UC Davis, so I wouldn't be completing as many units. Dad won't stop hassling me with talks. He does make tuition payments tomorrow, so I guess he can be uptight. I hate that he keeps saying he's so mad at me, especially when I am really trying now.

December 28, 2008

Last night before bed I showed Dad the letter from my doctor. It basically said I must do a refeeding program or go to the hospital and take winter quarter off if I wanted her care.

I spent the whole night crying, in shock, yelling, negotiating with Dad and then with Mom. Both said nope, I basically blew it, and it wasn't their choice. I didn't go to sleep until 8:00 in the morning! I ended up sleeping all the way until 3:30 in the afternoon. I then somehow pulled myself out of bed but felt severely lethargic. I am just not well. I was planning to pretend to see one of my friends and then walk around downtown a bit to get in some activity, but I ended up deciding to sleep all day. I had some diarrhea last night, and I have awful cramps today. I am still pretending to have 3 tablespoons of peanut butter and cheese, but thankfully I am able to get away with having it without my parents watching. I did drink a Boost Plus in front of my dad; however, I had poured it all out, added 3 ounces of almond milk (30 calories), and filled the rest with water the previous night. No one ever knew the difference! I only had 1/3 of my protein shake. I also only ate 2/3 of my egg white. I am having the worst stomach cramps.

My UC Davis doctor finally sent me back an e-mail late tonight. It was really encouraging. I think I may honestly have a chance of going to school Monday, taking minimum units, and doing the IOP! I sent her a long e-mail back with a lot of updates. Dad was really happy. I will let him read her e-mail in the morning. My appointment with my hometown doctor has to go well, though, as far as vitals and blood work. Please, please, please! I am scared because I am still losing weight and I look dead now. It is extremely difficult for me to walk up the stairs. Even bending down takes tremendous effort! I really can't even sit on a chair without my butt killing me! It is like I have this physical block to letting go completely and improving despite how much I hate my body. I really hope things work out!

December 29, 2008

I woke up with a decent amount of energy and had my doctor's appointment. It actually went well! My blood pressure was 100/62, my heart rate was 56, and I weighed 90 pounds with UGG boots, tons of layers, and a lot of water in my system from water loading. We talked briefly about my hospital stay and my plan for UC Davis. She declared me medically stable and said I was safe to go to school on Monday. I also got a referral from her for the IOP.

Dad paid for my tuition today—yes! I really hope my blood work comes back OK. I am only going to be taking 13 to 14 units, and I will be a minimum-progress student this quarter. But I plan to take summer classes. I then went to some stores and did an excessive amount of walking. I didn't have my Boost Plus or my almond milk version. I am so hungry, and I don't look like a person anymore! I do want to gain weight, but I am scared to overdo it. I still have terrible cramps and diarrhea today. My family is really happy but equally worried. I am still going to bed insanely late, but I will definitely change that when I go back to school.

December 30, 2008

I awoke from another phone call saying my potassium is too low. Ugh! I had to pick up my potassium supplements from the pharmacy. It is probably just from the diarrhea. It is such bad timing though. My UC Davis doctor called to say how worrisome my recent blood work I had to send her was, that the IOP wouldn't currently take me, and that I needed a hospital program for refeeding. She said she is terrified for my life and health. She did say if my potassium was higher, she and the IOP would probably treat me. I told her it was only because of my diarrhea, but she is worried it might not go away or get better as fast as I hope. I have another appointment with my hometown doctor tomorrow. I will call her after.

This sucks! What awful timing! Dad was very encouraged because he said I look and sound way better today. He said he could give me until Monday to see that my potassium level is increasing, would take me to Davis, and would stay with me during the weekend. If my health declines, he will pull me out and take me straight to Stanford. No! I am so excited for Davis and to change and recover. I don't want anything to stand in my way. I need my UC Davis doctor to monitor my blood work frequently while I'm on potassium supplements. I need my levels to increase so she will take me! I still went to about 9 markets today and walked a lot. Why do I always have to fool myself into thinking my lifestyle is OK?

December 31, 2008

I am so drained and hardly got any sleep last night. I had my doctor's appointment today. It didn't go so well. My blood pressure was 80/60, my heart rate was 48, and my EKG was decent. She told me it would probably be a good idea to go to the ER for the day at least to get a potassium IV. I decided against that, obviously. I had a good talk on the phone with the intake lady from the IOP, so I am really hoping it is going to work out! The only problem is how far away it is from campus and the fact that freshmen aren't allowed to have cars. I am happy, though, because Dad is probably not going to stay at all this weekend. I feel awful, though, and am so tired. I need to start sleeping, geez! I did so much activity today. I can barely function right now. I feel as if I am here but not even living anymore. It is so terrifying I almost can't acknowledge it.

January 2, 2009

I slept for a total of 30 minutes last night; I never really went to bed. I got up and packed, but I was so weak, tired, and ill that it was taking forever. I was so exhausted and sleep-deprived that by noon I told Dad we should just leave Saturday morning instead, which was a good choice. I finally finished packing and then took a nap until 9:30 in the evening. I then got up, and it ended up being another insanely late night. I look dead, and I have class on Monday! I am so frail it hurts to bend down. I look as though I weigh 60 pounds. How much better would I be feeling if I got a good amount of sleep? Dad is really worried but is going to let me go. I don't want to die! Is it really OK for me to go?

10

Possessed

"The further you fall into the hole, the higher you have to climb to get out." ~Britt

January 4, 2009

I slept all day today. I could hardly get out of bed to pee. It was almost not even worth it. I had an insane amount of diet drinks today. Everyone is back in the dorms now. I eventually got up around 6:30 this evening and explained to a few people how terribly sick I was over break in case they wondered why I looked so awful. I mean, I guess they were concerned, but they almost didn't seem to care. No one was stoked to see me. I then went to the bank, Starbucks, and Rite Aid. I really tried to go to bed earlier, but it is still going to end up being 4:00 in the morning. I have a 9:00 a.m. class! Oh well, I just need to get through tomorrow—hopefully on adrenaline—and pray I can get out of bed. I am having some slight chest pain. Please let me live—please!

January 5, 2009

I ended up going to bed between 5:00 and 6:00 in the morning despite really trying to go to bed earlier. I thankfully did have a lot of adrenaline today. My mind won't stop racing. I did somehow manage to get up and ride my bike to my 9:00 a.m. class. Afterward, I had another class. I love both of my teachers so far. I just want to scream and scream, though. I look like a skeleton, have chest pain, and can't walk up the stairs for the life of me! I now have to take the elevator up to my dorm. I am an absolute wreck! I have my appointment with the IOP tomorrow and am going to have to find a cab to take me. I see my UC Davis doctor today. I'm scared she might call 911 despite my rights. I am so hungry and tired! I am telling all my dorm mates I have a serious stomach problem, which is at least partly true. Why can't I eat? I am so scary tired tonight!

January 6, 2009

I am scared I am going to die! I am so skinny now in ways not possible, I think I might barf! Terrible day! The IOP doctor was scared I would die right there and begged me to allow him to call for an ambulance, but I refused. OK, I am so tired now. I have to go to bed. Good night!

January 7, 2009

Today was a living nightmare. I could hardly walk again and got no sleep. I keep getting hungry in the morning, so I usually binge on diet drinks. I have an 8:00 a.m. class today and am having chest pains. I almost fell over when I first got on my bike! I did miraculously make it through my 3 classes, but I just can't walk anymore. Each step feels like I am carrying 10,000 pounds. Walking feels foreign to me now. I don't have the stamina or strength to balance or keep myself upright for that matter. After all my classes today I started feeling very ill. The dorm leader came to talk to me and ask how I was doing. I told her about being sick a couple days ago. I feel a little better now. I did have a good talk with my parents. I briefly talked to my UC Davis doctor and told her that I would get a therapist and do groups and stuff since the IOP wouldn't take me. She kind of said OK, but who knows what is going to happen.

January 8, 2009

I slept through my first class because I got no sleep again last night. I slept until 12:15 in the afternoon and then had to get up for my next class. I could hardly move and got anxious and worried. I forced myself to class though. I love my classes and learning, but I just don't feel alive anymore. Both of my ears popped again today during class, and it is the worst feeling ever! It just started happening a few days ago, but it keeps coming back! It feels like when your ears pop in an airplane when changing altitude, yet it is painful, too. It makes it hard for me to hear myself talk and to think, which scares the crap out of me! The only way I can relieve the pressure is to lay down flat or sit down with my head between my knees. I just don't understand and am completely helpless.

I am freezing today! My ear pressure is still terrible. I took a short nap and only went out once to Starbucks and Rite Aid, but still I am going to bed at 4:30 in the morning. I really hope I will be able to get up tomorrow. I keep tripping over stuff, and I can't walk anymore. The worst is when I sit down on the ground; it actually takes me 10 to 20 minutes just to push myself up again. I mean, really now, picture me on the ground for 15 minutes literally trying to figure out how simply to stand up. I almost want to go inpatient. My ears finally unplugged, but I am afraid they will stop up again. I don't want to know what other awful things my health has in store for me.

January 9, 2009

OK, so today was one of the worst days! I didn't really sleep again but did make it through my 9:00 class this morning. My UC Davis doctor called to check in and said she might be able to arrange it so I could leave for treatment this quarter and still get to keep my dorm room for spring quarter. I said no even though I know I probably need it. There is just no way I could leave my perfect classes, teachers, and dorm. I did feel really weird this morning, to the point where I agreed internally to eat anything, but after waiting it out for a bit I felt better and decided I didn't need to. I later went to the library and started feeling unusually tired and not well again, along with my ears popping and getting all stopped up.

I made it back to my dorm and drank an extra 3 ounces of unsweetened almond milk, which is only about 15 calories, but I still feel guilty about it.

So get this...I spilled water all over my computer, and it broke. A bit earlier, I accidentally dropped my phone in a cup of water and broke it! I can't see the screen at all! Luckily, I can dial out and receive calls, but I don't know who is calling and I can't see the screen, so I think I lost all my numbers! How ironic is that?

I fell asleep and awoke to the worst phone call of my life! It was a nice man calling from student judicial affairs. The university, crisis center, housing, and SJA have unanimously made the decision to make me leave this quarter to get treatment. I only have 2 choices at this point. I can leave voluntarily and return in the spring to get my dorm room back, be a part-time student, and work with my UC Davis doctor. Or I can leave involuntarily, but I do have the right to present my side at an SJA hearing. Dad highly warns against this, although I'm not sure why.

Maybe I have to trust this is the plan? I had so many freaky things happen back to back, such as my disaster meeting with the IOP, spilling water and breaking my laptop, dropping my phone in water and breaking it, and once again spilling a huge cup of water on my lap! What is the significance of spilling water? Geez. Not to mention I have been practically cut off from all communication without a properly working computer and phone. I am restricting my calories tonight since I will probably be going to IP—inpatient hospital treatment—anyway. I am devastatingly pale. Everyone on my floor has been so nice and supportive, though. Time to gain back my life and health! I am going to bed around 5:30 in the morning, but who cares now? Please guide me, someone!

January 10, 2009

Well, today was actually a good day! I was up all night worried and anxious about my health along with thinking about being forced to leave and all the ways I could possibly change the university's decision to allow me to stay. Anyway, I finally came to a decision that I would call my parents and discuss with my dad what my home life/plan could be if I choose to leave voluntarily and get refeeding monitoring at the hospital. I told him I would choose to get help voluntarily because I know I need it. I also told him I could not live at home or in San Luis Obispo afterward, and he agreed. I had him look up some hospital phone numbers for me, and I said I would call him later. I have been doing some research on different treatment centers. I have added back a lot of eating disorder friends on Facebook, so I have been asking them about programs and which one I could get away with gaining the least amount of weight at. Hmm . . . we will see.

January 12, 2009

I am so tired! I had a great intake with Del Amo, which is a hospital/residential eating disorder program in Torrance, California. After talking to one of my friends who had been there, I decided it would be the easiest program and the one I could complete without gaining too much weight. They were very nice on the phone. I got all my questions answered and an idea of how it works. I ended up going to the ER for labs to send to them, but they were disturbing. My sodium and potassium were very low, and everything else was off. The ER doctor said I needed to be admitted because I could die if I went home, but I signed out AMA. I had too much to get done. He even classified my AMA at crisis level 5, which is apparently the highest. Yikes! My weight was 84.9 pounds. I had water loaded like crazy and was clothed in a minimum of 5 layers because I have to be at least 67 percent of my ideal body weight for Del Amo to take me.

I slept the rest of the day and didn't go out once. I am still not eating enough though . . . maybe about 1,000 calories? Everyone on my dorm floor has been amazing and is doing anything to help me and run errands for me, which is so nice! Then again, this has to be the worst way to interact with people. Tomorrow I have to meet with the nice guy who left the voicemail telling me I had to leave UC Davis. I hope I feel OK.

January 14, 2009

I hardly slept last night. I am outrageously weak and lethargic to the point where I thought about calling 911. Instead, I kind of dozed off again until 3:00 in the afternoon. Then I debated whether to spend the rest of the day in bed or go out. It was a really nice day and I had stuff to get done, so I chose to get up. I looked at my legs in bed and was in shock. It was as if I was staring at someone else, or something else, because I certainly don't look human. I have to eat way more, but I just can't. I don't even know how to explain it! ED just won't let me. It's my body, but ED controls it. I am going home on Sunday. Everything is 90 percent set at Del Amo. I should arrive there on Thursday.

I walked pathetically slow to Rite Aid to buy diet soda. Then, despite feeling extremely tired and weak, I called a cab to take me to Safeway to buy some sugar-free Jell-O and the Powerade Zero I like. I can't begin to say how awful and faint I felt! I walked every single aisle of the market like a 90-year-old woman. I got back to my room and tried to take a nap without success, so I walked to Starbucks and then all the way across campus to the library to use the computers to check my e-mail. On the way I tripped in my slip-on shoes and fell, but the scary thing was that I did not catch myself! Yes, I was carrying my purse and a water bottle, but I didn't have reflexes even to attempt to stick out my hands to catch myself. I swear I am going to take care of myself for real tomorrow, eat lots of food, and stay in bed. Why am I struggling so much? I know I am going IP in a week, but I am only going to prolong my stay the way I'm going. I'm not even sure I will live until then. No, I will! I am still getting that terrible ear pressure. It usually happens once I start walking or moving around a lot. I am having terrible pain in my upper middle back right now. Please don't let me be having a heart attack!

January 15, 2009

I woke up feeling even worse. I am having a hard time getting dressed now. I have no strength to even pull a shirt over my head and can hardly bend over to put on my socks and shoes. I often have to sit with my shirt or sweatshirt halfway over my head and rest for a while before I can find enough willpower to get it over my head completely. Then I have to rest again before I can get my arms through the sleeves. When did getting dressed and undressed become something I couldn't take for granted anymore?

I returned all my textbooks for this quarter. I then got blood work done at the health center for Del Amo, hoping it would be better than the results I got from the ER. I could hardly walk to the health center, though. My water bottle with only a little water left felt like a brick to carry. I started falling asleep as they drew my blood. My weight was 80 pounds with tennis shoes, a million layers, and a ton of water. I talked to Dr. Freeman briefly. She is so happy I am going for treatment. I wanted to slap her and hug her at the same time. I know she is saving my life, but I feel as if she is stealing it. My results thankfully came back a lot better! There are still a lot of things off, but I think it is decent enough for Del Amo. I had to have the escort service give me a ride back to my dorm because I got so weak. Please let me make it until Thursday!

January 17, 2009

I didn't leave my dorm today until 4:00 p.m. I kind of panicked about leaving so late because I wouldn't be able to do as much activity even though I should be doing none. Well, I certainly made up for leaving late. I must have walked a total of 20 miles throughout the afternoon and night. I went wild! I did have an unsettlingly true horoscope today: "Investigate what is going on around you. You understand much less than you think you do. Stay open. A profound change is in the offing, be it at home or within yourself."

January 18, 2009

I am home now. I ate about 1,100 calories today, which is way too much for doing less activity. Then again, today is the worst I have looked physically and the worst I have felt mentally. I am really not feeling well tonight. It is late right now. My stomach hurts, and I can hardly walk!

January 20, 2009

Mom helped me organize my room and clothes a bit as well as all the stuff I brought back from my dorm. My parents are being so amazing! I don't get it. They are treating me as though I am the best thing in the world. Do they think I am going to die or something? They are nuts! I am having terrible back, ear, head pressure, and pain again today. Who is this monster I've become?

11

How to Save a Life

"You can do anything, but not everything. You don't have to save the world, just yourself." ~Britt

January 21, 2009

Well, today is really the 25th of January. I just haven't had the time to journal the past few days, so I am now journaling for the past days right now. Let's see... the 21st was Wednesday. I don't remember many details from Wednesday except of course for the fact that I felt the sickest yet. I think I slept in really late after going to bed around 7:00 in the morning and could barely walk. Still, I had to go to some markets and stores so that I could at least burn some calories. I also needed to finish all my packing because I was to leave for Del Amo EDU (eating disorder unit) tomorrow morning, and Mom and her friend wanted to leave by 9:00 a.m. All I remember is pulling another all-nighter packing. It was scary because it took me literally hours just to pack! It was as if I couldn't think straight and was paralyzed and couldn't move. Everything was moving in slow motion. I still feel like that, by the way. I begged Mom to leave an hour later so that I could finish packing and get a quick 1-hour nap. She said no and that I should stay up and keep going. So, I kept deliriously packing and still was hardly ready by 9:30, which was already way later than my traffic-nervous mom wanted to wait.

January 22, 2009

The car ride down to Del Amo EDU was much too quick and all a blur because I was so tired. Not only that, but guess what sucks big time about Del Amo? No gum, hair straightener (so people don't burn themselves purposely), cell phone, tweezers, laptop, mouthwash unless alcohol-free, blankets, iPod, scarves, necklaces, nail polish, camera, mints, perfume, razors, journals with a spiral back, plastic bags, head bands, dangling earrings, pens, pencils, and all types of makeup in a glass bottle—to only name a few. Apparently all these items can somehow be used to self-harm. This place is crazy! I'm so confused.

Anyway, backing up a bit now: we made it to Del Amo and went inside to wait. It is actually not in the main Torrance hospital but in a single-story building kind of adjacent to it. I waited for a few minutes and then signed some papers with one of the intake ladies. I was told to say goodbye at this point. I hugged Mom weakly and went back.

Many adults first greeted me. I guess some were eating disorder patients and some were trauma patients. They were all really kind from my first impression at least. It was a nice enough and clean building but looked just like a hospital wing. There was a big hallway with a bunch of rooms on both ends and a nursing station. It was cold and not very welcoming or comfortable-looking, though. To my right was another narrow hallway, a bathroom, and a dining room.

I was asked to sit down on a chair, and then some lady sat down with me and tried to help me come up with a meal plan for the rest of the evening and morning because the dietitian had already left for the day. It was an enormous struggle. I declared that I am gluten-free and as much sugar-free as possible in addition to pleading with them that I had not been taking in more than 200 calories (lie) and that I was not ready to eat more. It was extremely hard, but eventually I ended up having a small bowl of plain shredded lettuce and 3 tiny slices of an apple—and that was it for dinner. The one nice thing is we can have tea with a packet of Splenda at meals and are allowed 2 diet sodas a day. I very slowly dissected my food and deliriously met all the girls there. Most were pretty nice. There were 8 of us including me. I just don't get it. They have like 10 to 16 smoke breaks all day, and yet they won't let me have 1 piece of gum, which is nowhere near as bad for you!

After dinner I waited to get my luggage searched. They took all my tea, gum, phone, etc. One awful thing is that we can't have any strings, so I had to cut the drawstring off my favorite sweats and pull out all the drawstrings from my other pants. Now they won't stay up over my waist! I must say I was not in good shape there. I mean, I had worked my body and health so far down to the point where I could not bend down or pull off a sock. It took me 10 minutes straight just to pull off my sweatshirt, and I was seriously debating asking for help. When I sat down, it was a monumental struggle to get up again. I was shivering uncontrollably at night and could hardly walk straight. Not good. I met the main nurses, and they are awesome, though!

For evening snack I had 1/3 of an apple and that was it. Again, it took me forever just to finish that apple, but I eventually did while everyone else finished and either went on smoke break or back to get ready for bed. I guess I could eventually get used to these strict rules.

January 23, 2009

Well, now this was certainly an interesting day, to say the least. I didn't sleep very well, so I was up early and not feeling well. I got my vital signs taken, which were decent enough, I think. Then I battled to get dressed and put on a bit of mascara. But I got interrupted to get my blood drawn, which took forever because the nurse could hardly get any of my blood out. Next I went to breakfast and had 1 egg white and a few small cubes of cantaloupe. It wasn't terrible calorie-wise, however, it was much too early for me to be eating.

I then got called back to see the doctor to examine me for the first time. I guess that didn't go the best. I was still so tired I forget the details of our encounter, but I do know he was concerned with my appearance and me. I also remember that about an hour later or so I was told that I was being sent to the ER to get my lab results processed quicker than they could get themselves and to make sure I was medically stable. So, I unhappily got in the ambulance they had called for all of the 30 seconds of walking distance ride to the main hospital, Torrance Memorial Hospital.

The hospital was very busy, but after about 6 hours in the ER, the doctor told me that they were admitting me. I guess my sodium was a little low, I think? I don't even think it was that bad. I don't really know what the main reason was. I think Del Amo was just scared because they aren't exactly a medical facility and wanted to make sure I got a bit more stabilized for their program. One shocking piece of news I did hear—which must be wrong—was that I had weighed 50 pounds that morning at Del Amo, which is 1 million percent not correct. Yes, at the doctors' offices at home, I was weighed after water loading and with tons of clothes and shoes, but still there is no way I am this low! I made them weigh me again at the hospital, and my weight really was in the low 60's after a bunch of fluid . . . though not 50 pounds. My admit weight in the ER, though, was 56 pounds! This is ridiculous. I am living in a dream right now! Or is it a nightmare?

Well, what I didn't realize is that the main hospital I am in now has its own eating disorder type-refeeding medical stabilization program. It's even worse for me than Del Amo EDU! So, there was no getting away with eating a small amount of calories. Apparently, the nurses and doctors get many ED patients throughout the year who come to this hospital program. They have a whole team of doctors, therapists, psychiatrists, and dietitians who know all the anorexic tricks. I mean, people actually check into this hospital just for ED treatment, refeeding, therapy, recovery, and weight gain. Ah! OK, I am getting ahead of myself right now. I am still journaling for Friday, and I found out all this stuff later on.

Back to Friday: I was taken up to a room and hooked back up to my IV. The only thing I remember is wanting to sleep. I am pretty sure they did at least force me to have some evening snack, even though I did get away with refusing dinner. I had 1 huge apple and was only going to eat 1/2. But I had hardly eaten the rest of the day, so I just ate the whole damn thing. It took me well over 30 minutes to finish. I cut it up into microscopic pieces and stared at it as if it would attack me. I guess I do look pretty anorexic in the mirror even though I want to be skinnier. At least the nurses told me I look anorexic. Anyway, no diet sodas, no Splenda, no gum, no brushing teeth right after meals (I do anyway), no eating in bed, only 30 minutes for meals, no thin straws, and no TV, magazines, or writing during meals. OK, I am getting ahead of myself again.

Back to Friday: I finished the apple and explained to everyone how hard that was for me because I am used to eating only 200 calories at most throughout the whole day and only after midnight. Their reply was that was good, but it was time to change. I think I went to bed then. I could still hardly get myself out of bed at night just to pee because I was so weak. I had to have the nurse help pull me out a few times, and that only hurt my body even more. I also slept with about 7 heavy blankets because I was still freezing at night. But all the blankets did was add weight, not warmth, because they are made of that awful rough material and are not soft or fuzzy at all. My temperature and blood sugar have also been low the whole time, but that's enough writing for Friday!

January 24, 2009

OK, well, today is really the 26th, but I am still trying to catch up on my journaling. Hmm...let's see...what happened Saturday? I really can't remember many details about this day except for I refused all my food until I talked to the dietitian. Finally we came up with a challenging meal plan for me. But I did choose it, so obviously it wasn't too bad. This is what I came up with:

Breakfast: 1 egg white, small bowl of cantaloupe, and tea with 2 packets of Splenda; *Snack:* nothing, I am not ready; *Lunch:* 1 egg white, small bowl of cantaloupe, 1 can of Diet Coke, 1 can of Sprite Zero, and a thin straw to drink with; *Snack:* nothing, I am not ready; *Dinner:* 1 egg white, small bowl of cantaloupe, 1 can of Diet Coke, 1 can of Sprite Zero, and a thin straw to drink with; *Snack:* ½ apple and black coffee with 2 packets of Splenda; *Other:* 5 packs of sugar-free Orbit Bubblemint gum, 8 chewable sugar-free Pepto-Bismol, and 10 sugar-free chewable Lactaid.

I gave the dietitian a copy of this for my challenging meal plan. I am pretty sure she said it was fine! Although I should mention this was the hospital dietician, not the eating disorder–specific dietician I would soon face.

Saturday ended up being OK because I was able to get away with eating just cantaloupe and 1 egg white for dinner and 1 whole apple again at night, and that was it for the whole day. I have a sitter with me all the time, which means a nurse is always in the room with me. Thankfully they don't watch me very closely when I eat so I am able to get away with hiding and throwing away stuff. I really just don't remember this day very well.

I was extremely weak still and on a banana bag IV drip, which is bright yellow. The nurses assured me it was just a bunch of vitamins, so hopefully no calories, thank goodness! It is taking me forever to eat. I mean, I figured I would be able to eat quicker if I chose to, but I can't even do that. My finger has been getting pricked every couple hours because I've been having low blood sugar. My temperature has been really low as well, around 92 to 93 degrees with normal averaging 98.6 degrees. Unfortunately, I had to stay another night even though I wanted to be discharged back to Del Amo. The only other thing I can really remember is begging everyone for a piece of gum, but no one would give me any. I froze shivering again that night under 7 blankets, but at least I got more sleep than usual.

January 25, 2009

Today, from what I can still remember, was pretty awful! I was expecting Del Amo to pick me up that morning, but apparently they were still deciding whether I was stable enough for their program. So I had to stay at least another day, be taken off the IV fluids for the evening and night, then get labs and vitals retested in the morning and then get evaluated by a psychiatrist. I was really disappointed, yet figured I could wait one more day. I had an endoscopy early that morning to check out my stomach pain and make sure I didn't have any weird inflammation. The good part about that was I got to skip breakfast. I then had to have lunch. I had 2 egg whites, but I threw one away when no one was looking. I also had 10 carrot sticks and a bowl of cantaloupe. It wasn't a ton of calories, yet I knew that was only the first of many other meals and snacks to come, and it was only 12:30 in the afternoon, not the morning! Also, if I didn't comply, I could be tubed!

Later I had snack, and that was dreadful. I loved my nurse, Lisa, but she knew all the eating disorder tricks and was obviously well informed on eating disorders in general. I was brought 3 celery sticks and one of those peanut butter tubs. There was no way I was going to touch the peanut butter, so I begged for something else. I eventually chose the dry tuna option; however, Lisa ended up bringing me a ton! There was nothing I could do but eat it or supplement, so I choked it down. I then had really low blood sugar and was practically forced either to have juice, Gatorade, or pudding. I reluctantly drank about 3 ounces of Gatorade, and it didn't even help! For dinner I had an egg white, gross chicken, peas, and rice, and so I chose to supplement all of my meal but the egg. I only made this choice because nurse Lisa repeatedly told me the supplement used was the no-sugar-added vanilla Carnation Instant Breakfast and that I needed about 12 ounces of it to replace my dinner. I have had the no-sugar-added version before. It is only about 150 calories, but I know the regular kind is 240 calories. I believed her, but as soon as I tried it, I knew it tasted like the regular version, and 2 days later she even admitted she was wrong. I am so pissed and am never supplementing again, but at least it's over with. So much for trusting people. I had a huge apple for evening snack and went to bed. I think I had about 800 calories for the day, but my calculations could be off. I look ridiculously inhuman. Not a good day!

January 26, 2009

I wish I could say Monday was a much better day, but if you can believe it, it was way worse! I woke up and decided it was all right to eat breakfast because I had planned to go back to Del Amo. The doctor even said I am good to be discharged and my vitals and blood work were stable. I even had a psychiatric evaluation, and the psychiatrist said he would give me the OK. However, one of the ladies from Del Amo came over to talk to me and told me that despite everything, there was no way they would or could accept me because my weight was far too low—below 67 percent of my ideal body weight. I still can't for the life of me figure out how I lost so much weight! If I weren't able to see the scale myself, I would say they were all lying! Then again, I guess I do look pretty bad.

I begged and pleaded to convince her to let me go to Del Amo and gain the weight there. She just kept saying no because of the type of facility they are. She did say I could go to some other refeeding-type place and return to Del Amo once I had gained a lot of weight, but that it would probably take me at least 3 weeks doing so before I would be ready to go to Del Amo. With spring quarter at Davis approaching soon, that was not an option. She left with me devastated. The only good thing was that she brought over all of my luggage. I've been able to sneak all the gum I've wanted for the past 2 days.

I had a really harsh talk with Dad. He told me my one and only choice was to go to UCLA ED center and that he was going to conserve me if I didn't go. Let's just say it was a very emotional and hard phone call. But we eventually came to some agreement, and a social worker gave me UCLA's number and helped me call them. I eventually got through only to find out it was at least a week wait because they were full and had no available therapists. They said there was a possibility that it could be earlier but not likely. I did fax over all my insurance information and filled out and faxed back an 8-page survey everyone must complete, but I am still stuck at Torrance-stupid-strict-ED program-hospital until a bed opens up. I am so pissed!

I called my parents back to update them quickly and said I would call them the next day. They said fine. I still couldn't believe what had happened with Del Amo! UCLA would be my absolute last choice, I think, yet I really pray I get in soon, don't have to stay past 3 weeks, hardly gain weight but gain some strength, do great therapy, get out of there, and return to UC Davis . . . yes, that could work. I am trying to trust in your plan, God, but I can't see it right now.

I am so incredibly weak! I can't get out of bed or walk without help. I can't bend over at all! I also can't stand that long without intense back, head, and ear pain. I actually look worse than a few days ago. I am scared! It was a really hard day, so I skipped a lot of meals and food. I ended up having 2 egg whites and a small bowl of cantaloupe for breakfast and then nothing the rest of the day until evening snack. I chose not to eat my suspiciously large apple until 1:00 in the morning, but no one seemed to mind. I also had 9 Pepto-Bismol, 8 Lactaid, 21 pieces of gum, and 3 sugar-free powdered teas. I think my total calories were about 450 at the most.

In late 2009, I got a copy of my medical records during my stay at Torrance Memorial Hospital and have added one of the doctor's notes. This provides some perspective as to how professionals perceived my condition compared to my own view.

> Since coming to this hospital, she has been stubbornly defiant and quite passive-aggressive. She is refusing feeding tubes, refusing to eat in any substantial manner, refusing IVs, refusing medication, refusing to let anyone talk to her family. She is insisting that she be transferred to UCLA... apparently, at least, as of this moment, there is no bed. Del Amo Hospital refuses to take her back because of her medical status. She is clearly quite bright and she is now playing a classic power game, demanding that her sitter be removed, demanding that she be moved to a regular medical floor, and demanding that she should be allowed to pick her food. She states that she will not eat unless she gets her way. She claims that she can't go home, can't go back to school at this point, needs to be in a program, but at the same time she demands that she be taken away from the unit because, "I do not want to be treated like a child." She is currently on the pediatric floor. She denies depression. She is not currently in any way suicidal nor has

she ever been suicidal in the past. She denies hallucinations. She is not delusional in a classic sense, but she states that "I do not trust people" and she believes that her weight currently is "just fine but I need to be stronger." She claims that her energy is good, but I doubt that is true. Allergies: "sugar and gluten," although I doubt that she is truly allergic to these. Strengths and assets: she is clearly quite intelligent and she is enrolled in college. General: the patient is awake and alert. Mood and affect are cheerful. She is quasi-delusional regarding her body weight status and her general inability to grasp the seriousness of her illness although at some level she does realize that she needs some care. She is quite incapable of following any reasonable medical directions at this point. Insight and judgment are poor. Concentration and attention span are within normal range. Fund of knowledge is adequate. Intelligence is high-average. Abstraction ability is good. Discussion: . . . I hope that the social worker is looking into this situation and trying to get this patient moved as quickly as possible. In the interim, Dr. Allen needs to determine whether the patient's medical condition represents an acute medical emergency. If it does, I would recommend she [Dr. Allen] consult with the hospital risk management team and consider an emergency court order to force-feed this patient via NG tube should this be required to keep the patient alive. In the interim, under the law, if the patient's medical condition becomes life-threatening, a doctor can treat prior to the court order if it is an absolute life or death situation. In the event that Dr. Allen does not judge either of the above to be relevant, then Dr. Allen will have to go through a tedious negotiation process with this patient to try to find a way to coax her to eat as she is quite skilled in manipulating and fighting unwinnable power struggles with authority figures, which is a classic anorexia situation.

January 27, 2009

I can hardly keep my eyes open right now. I had no energy the whole day! I did make it through a nice shower, yet it took all of the little energy I did have. I had terrible back, ear, and head pain as well even though I was only sitting in the shower. My pee has never had such a foul and strong odor as well as it being a dark yellow color. The doctor said it was dehydration and something to do with my kidneys. I am getting freaky-looking. I mean, after actually looking at my body, I can almost fully believe I really do weigh in the 60's or whatever. I think my labs are still OK though. I absolutely hate Dr. Allen, the doctor I have right now. She said she would call the court to get me conserved and tube me if I don't comply! I don't like her. She told me that I have to follow the whole plan, which is 1,000 calories per day until UCLA can take me next week. She said if I don't follow her plan I have to leave AMA, go home, or transfer. I had no choice but to say OK, yet for some reason I ate almost nothing this day. I didn't have breakfast or it seems anything until lunch for some reason. For lunch I guess I had a small bowl of lettuce, a tomato slice, a small Italian dressing cup (that I threw away), 1 orange, and a bit of dry rice pilaf. But again, I hid about ½ of the rice in my napkin and threw it away in the little trash bag I have attached to my desk. I also had some diarrhea. I am just not doing well.

I still can't grasp the fact that I can't get out of bed, change my clothes, or sit down on the ground for a second without help. I was sitting on the floor going through my suitcase. I had to ask the nurse to help pull me up, and I couldn't even help her. I had no strength! It took literally 3 minutes straight of her just trying to lift me from the ground; it was ridiculous. Ha! And I was once an elite athlete. I hate how I can't have diet soda now because the nurses I am getting now know the eating disorder protocol. I am 20 years old, not 10! Thankfully, everyone knows I can't eat gluten and sugar for the most part, yet I don't know how well that's going because my blood sugar has been really low, like around 38, whatever that means.

I have now decided to declare myself a vegetarian and say I can't have liquid calories or supplement. Oh well, if only I knew that today would end up being one of the better days, I probably wouldn't have complained as much. Again, I threw away a lot of my dinner and had about 450 calories for the day. I am going to go to bed now. I don't feel well. Just bad diarrhea, tired, and scared. Please, let tomorrow be a great day and for me to love my new eating disorder doctor, Dr. Schack.

January 31, 2009

It's been a few days since I have journaled now. Yesterday, from what I remember, was horrible! Today I have been getting no sleep and have a terrible stomachache. I had an X-ray this morning, but I think it was normal. I still have awful, brownish-colored pee that smells terrible, and I feel really dehydrated. Today was a lot better than yesterday, and I still love my nurse, Lisa, even though she is strict with the rules. I am getting a little bit stronger now; I just have trouble getting out of bed at night. My stomach hurts so much, though! I keep choking on everything I eat, even an egg white the size of a pea! Dr. Schack says it's because my stomach has no fat. She is worried my intestines are rubbing against each other. What the heck? I really think everyone is overreacting.

Dr. Schack, who is in charge of the eating disorder program at Torrance, explained all the rules to me in detail today, so it was nice to have some clarification even though I agree with none of them. I am still having a social worker look into other ED places that could take me medically, however, maybe this could work. It is an eating disorder program; I just happen to be the only one here and am not allowed to leave my room. I am thinking I could spend 2 weeks here and then return to Davis. I am not allowed to have any diet soda or Splenda, but I do get to have 4 pieces of gum a day.

My bathroom has to be locked, and all the rules here are strict. I'm hoping this means I will get to leave sooner as opposed to finding a more lenient program. Maybe I should just stay?

I had amazing talks with my parents and Kasey today! I got a visit from the "echo" lady who did my echocardiogram exam last night.

I prayed with her pastor on her cell phone. She sang to me, and we talked. She also brought me a few gifts. She gave me the most gorgeous necklace that she was wearing, which was obviously worn but clearly incredibly special to her! I never take it off. Her name is Sheryl, and she is a tall, beautiful, black lady. I swear she is an angel. I just get such a weird feeling when I am with her but only weird because it is the most incredibly magical feeling. Mom even said she had dreamt of a black lady taking care of me! My EKG today looked good, but the doctor who did the one yesterday said I do have some fluid buildup and that if I don't give my body continued nutrition I will eventually get heart failure or would be at risk at least. Again, I really don't think it is that big of a deal.

I took a really nice shower today. Afterward, I felt incredibly light-headed but thought I could stand up real quick to do my blood pressure. That was a mistake. Everything went black for a couple of minutes, and I got really hot and couldn't see anything! Lisa told me my blood pressure dropped to 40/28! I started feeling better after 15 minutes, but it was scary...too much heat? All my labs have been OK, I think, except for having very low phosphorus, so I am now going to take phosphorus powder that I have to mix in water. I just hope it's sugar-free! I have to eat 900 calories tomorrow—dang! I get to know my weight every other day, and today it is 62.3 pounds. I have a huge rash on my butt. It hurts like heck! I think it's from sitting so much and my bones rubbing my skin, but I don't remember. My aunt and uncle are visiting me while passing through L.A. on Monday, which I'm excited about. I am so tired, though. I will write more tomorrow.

February 1, 2009

I talked to Dr. Schack this morning. She said I am incredibly sick and that I almost went to the ICU last night. She said my sodium is OK and that my potassium is fine because I take supplements. She said I have a bladder infection and gastritis and could die anytime! Huh? She also told me my liver enzymes were high. My AST is 664, my ALT is 712, and my ALKPHOS is 268. Apparently the normal range is supposed to be around 40 at the highest. Hmm. She told me I would need 1,600 calories just to maintain my weight, but I know that is a lie. She also told me I am the sickest patient she has ever had, but I don't know what she is talking about. She must have always treated eating disorder patients that were pretty much OK. She kept telling me I could die at any moment and that my stomach could explode just from sitting and eating because it is so fragile. Oh, please!

She agreed to increase my calories by only 50 each day because she thinks it's the safest. She said with refeeding, once you start you can't really go back and that I need to keep slowly eating more. She really wanted to have a meeting with my dad to put his face to his voice because I am so critical and just in case something bad were to happen. Bullshit! Well, I did agree, but I only allowed her to share certain information.

So anyway, this means I get to see Dad tomorrow—hooray! Mom is being incredible. I figured she would be so mad at me that she wouldn't even speak to me, but she is being the complete opposite. They can't honestly believe the doctor that something bad might happen. I really am not that skinny. I am so tired, though, and can't write anymore.

February 3, 2009

Dr. Schack said I have to have my IV still. I am allowed to have my mouthwash now but only if the nurse pours it for me because I have been consuming too much. Dr. Schack doesn't know what is causing my ears to clog up. My AST is 597, and my ALT is 744 today. She told me I have to be in bed and have lights out at midnight. She said cold water is better for hydration. She said we could discuss the room search policies later. Yeah, I am so mad because my room got searched, and all my hidden gum was found! She kept saying I could still just drop dead. I was able to see my weight today because I had a lovely but clueless nurse. I even got away with having my whole iPod in my gown pocket for my weight. I think I weighed 64.1 pounds—with a full bladder, of course. Still much too much, but we will see about that.

February 4, 2009

I met with Dr. Schack again this morning. I am not really journaling that much right now because I am so tired. I do make sure always to take notes during my meetings with the doctors so that I know what orders I can and can't have and, of course, how to get them anyway. Dr. Schack said I am allowed to eat in bed even though the rule is to eat in a chair with a table. I am just not strong enough to sit in a chair, which really is kind of laughable. It's nice to stay in bed, sure, but the fact that I can't sit in a chair without terrible ear pressure and whatnot is certainly a failure in my mind. In fact, when I asked, Dr. Schack said I couldn't eat anywhere else other than my bed—what the heck? I'm sure I could prove her wrong, but I feel too awful to try right now. She said my AST is 708 and my ALT is 859 today. My creatine, which has something to do with my kidneys, is only 153. I guess it is supposed to be greater than 600. Still, I really don't know what all this means, and I don't really care. She recommended my mom bring me petroleum jelly because my lips are so dry and cracked. In fact, my whole entire body is really dry. To give some kind of a visual, my skin is like that of a lizard. Dr. Schack said I still have to be observed during meals and 15 minutes afterward but really I think I would be fine on my own. She said my liver issue is really serious and scary and that if they get any higher, I will be in big trouble. Come on; I don't feel that bad.

The rest of the day was actually quite stressful, I guess you could say, but I'm so tired, I cannot go into it in detail. I will mention that I fell in my room today, and no one was with me. It was such an unreal feeling. I could not for the life of me stand up even with holding on to the dresser. I was eventually able to get someone's attention to help me, but I couldn't help but sit there in disbelief, remembering a time not too long ago when I dominated in conditioning drills and enjoyed running lines on the tennis court.

I've re-hidden some gum I still have, so I hope no one finds it this time! I have been able to hide a lot of my food during meals. I am having a hard time, though, because I am not really getting the help

I need. Sometimes I have to wait 30 minutes just to go pee because I need a nurse to help pull me out of bed, help me walk, pull me up off the toilet when I'm done, help me walk back to bed, and then help me get comfortable in bed. The simplest task takes forever. It's crazy and something I have always taken for granted. My aunt and uncle visited today, though, and that was amazing! I love them so incredibly much! I have so many bruises all over my body and everything hurts. OK, well, that's enough for today.

February 5, 2009

Today has been uncomfortable, to say the least. I am having terrible stomach pain and diarrhea, but that's not even the worst part. I can't control my bowels at all right now! I just keep shitting my pants—literally—while in bed every 30 minutes or so. I have to wear diapers, for goodness' sake! It also smells so odd and is just so gross. Dr. Schack told me my AST is 884 and my ALT is 937 today... I don't think that's good. She said I could go outside in a wheelchair when my temperature is over 95.5 degrees for 24 hours without the Bair Hugger, which is a warming blanket. Yeah, right, like that will happen! I am still cold even with the Bair Hugger. I have the blanket on me all the time, which is nice but annoying. It's actually more like a mattress with boiling air in it and is so light I have to put a heavy blanket on top of it so it won't fly away.

My weight today is 63.3 pounds. I only get to see it Mondays and Thursdays now. Dr. Schack told me my liver issue was due to refeeding syndrome, but I am really not eating that many more calories than I was at home, so I don't know what the big deal is. She told me it's OK to have a full cup of ice with each meal and have ice cups whenever I want as long as I don't go over my fluid maximum. Thank goodness, because I am as addicted to chewing ice as much as gum now. Mom and Dad came today. But I was so mad because only Dad was supposed to come, but Mom showed up without even telling me! I have been so tired today. My eyelids feel as though they weigh a pound each. Everyone has assured me I will still look anorexic if I gain 10 pounds, which made me feel much better. I'm sure they are getting annoyed with me asking them every 2 seconds, but too bad. My stomach hurts unbelievably badly.

I do not have any entries for the next week, only a few notes. I remember I was deathly ill, literally, and that I ended up in the ICU with an NG tube. I was told I might need a liver transplant and was asked repeatedly if I wanted to be resuscitated if I were to go into cardiac arrest. I remember telling them to get the fuck away from me and quit asking such foolish questions.

12

Not My Time

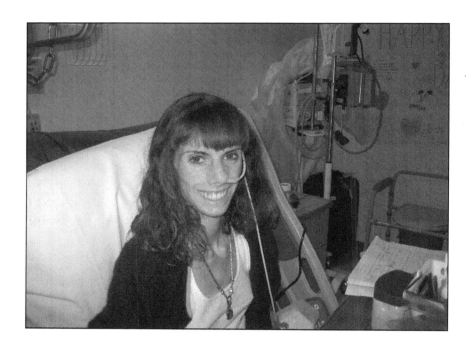

February 8, 2009

My AST is 2,808, and my ALT is 2,262. Why can't I think? I don't feel well. What's going on? Please help!

February 9, 2009

AST is 2,555, and ALT is 2,161. Staph infection in my left hand from the IV, and I can't move my thumb now. I have a lip fungus.

My weight is 59.6 pounds. I have an air mattress now, which doesn't hurt my body as much. I have Duoderms (special padding) all over my body because I have been getting bedsores. I also have red dots all over my body where I think blood vessels burst. I haven't been able to walk either. I mean, really... I can't walk. I can't even lift my arm above my head in bed. I can't even wipe myself. I have to go to the bathroom in a bedpan and have the nurses wipe my butt for me... definitely not my proudest moment.

February 12, 2009

I have to have 1,000 calories through my tube today. It's been weird not eating anything but ice for the past couple days. After only 2 days, though, my liver enzymes are back in the 1,000 range. Dr. Schack said I almost died and that I am the sickest and skinniest person ever documented who is surviving. Whoa! She said that even once my liver is back in the normal range, it is still at risk of jumping extremely high again very quickly now. She still isn't so sure about me being discharged in 2 to 3 weeks, but I have planned otherwise. I weigh 62 pounds today, but she assured me I would gain slower while having a tube, though I think that was just a lie.

I still have to have a sitter 24-7, though, which sucks especially because a lot of them don't really understand that I still need help moving around and stuff. A lot of the times when I tell them I have to go to the bathroom, they just stare at me like, "OK, so go." They don't realize I can't sit up or even walk, for that matter. I guess it is nice sometimes, though, to have someone help me grab a tissue, grab my cell phone, or bring me my journal, but then again these are all things that should be easy to do even for a toddler!

Dr. Schack told me she is leaving and won't be back until the 23rd, which sucks because what if the new doctor is stricter? Sheryl brought me a gigantic teddy bear, which is half my size—literally! I always love it when I get to see her. Mom spent the night with me last night, which was so nice, but I had a really hard time sleeping and getting comfortable, and so I don't think she slept much.

February 13, 2009

I figure if I have to have a damn tube up my nose against my will, then I should be able to benefit from it. I try to bargain with Dr. Schack, such as having lights out at 12:30 a.m., 8 pieces of gum, and more ice cups. I don't think she is buying it, and I am too chicken to pull the tube out myself. My throat is so incredibly sore. I can't even sneeze or cough because I am too weak. I try to cough and nothing comes out. My skin is so dry that I have to put coconut oil on it every few hours, and it still doesn't help—not to mention I am always worried the calories are saturating into my skin. I am having a really hard time seeing. I can see, but everything just seems a little too dark.

I have to have 1,080 calories today by tube. I am getting some new formula today with more protein and fiber called Isosource. Dr. Schack said that I could gain weight slower but that it is unlikely an additional 6 pounds would be enough for UC Davis to take me. Clearly she doesn't understand what she is talking about. Guess what happened later today? I stood up and walked! I was so happy that I started crying hysterically in Lisa's arms. I can't believe it. No one thought I would even be able to stand for at least 2 more weeks! I am so proud. I even stood on the scale. Hooray! I weighed 61.2 pounds. No more getting weighed on a bed scale, which was the most uncomfortable thing and made me feel just like Free Willy in one of those slings raised up over the surface. OK, so I didn't really walk that far, only a few steps, but it is still progress!

I met with a hand doctor today about my stuck-thumb issue and infected hand. He said I would likely need surgery to remove my vein. I don't want to think about that right now. He also told me that my liver enzymes are back down around 400 now all the way from 2,900 and that I am making one of the fastest recoveries they have ever witnessed. I really wanted to walk to the windowsill because I was feeling daring, but I took about 4 steps and blacked out. Hey, I still took 4 steps! Dr. Schack told me I might not even have permanent damage—wow! Then again, the seriousness they keep referring to isn't real to me. I hear their words, but it just doesn't apply to me personally. My throat is so sore. I can't have that much water or ice because I am already getting so much liquid through my tube. OK, I am really tired now!

February 14, 2009

I met with my new doctor today, who is taking over for Dr. Schack while she is away. Her name is Dr. Lucas. I really like her! She said I have to have 1,100 calories today and that I am only gaining ounces. My ALT is 378, my AST is 439, and my ALKPHOS is 687. Hooray! Normal is still less than 40, but it is still an improvement. She said she is going to talk to my GI (gastrointestinal) doctor about when the tube could come out. Unfortunately, she later told me it would be when my liver enzymes get below 100.

I was able to stand for a second and walk up on the scale even though I blacked out on my first attempt. I feel stronger today physically, but I still don't feel well. I was able to move around more in bed and was even able to turn and lie on my stomach for a second! It was so awesome and felt so weird to be in that position and stare at the opposite wall. It has been so long since I could really move around. It still seems as though I am going to be here forever. I am continuing to have trouble seeing, especially at night. I really hope my liver is better tomorrow so I can get my tube out. I hate not having control!

February 15, 2008

I had a really good sleep and am able to move my body enough now to avoid getting completely cramped up. I am so much stronger today! I was able to stand on the scale a little longer before things went black. It feels so amazing to stretch. Everyone keeps saying that I look so much better, but it is still kind of triggering, because if I look fine, then I should either a) start losing more weight or b) at least be able to go home. I don't have to use the Bair Hugger as much anymore, which I think is kind of cool. I feel much better except for the fact that I weigh 64.9 pounds! How did I gain so quickly?

Everyone told me it is just fluid imbalances, but how the heck am I supposed to trust that? I have the worst cramps right now! I am so sleepy, which I think might be from the antibiotics for my hand and C. diff, which is a colon infection causing my excessive diarrhea. It still bothers me that I can't keep my eyes open very well. I really hope I lose weight tomorrow!

February 16, 2008

I don't feel well at all! I had an average sleep, but last night I had the worst sore throat, left earache, stomachache, and diarrhea. To make matters worse, my nose was stopped up, and my anxiety was skyrocketing. I really thought I was dying! I even went to bed by 11:00 p.m. instead of 12:30 a.m., I was so scared and ill. Apparently, it's pouring rain outside, but I can't get up to see out my window. I am nervous because my muscles feel very tingly and heavy this morning as well as my left ear being all clogged up, which makes me feel as though I can't take a deep breath. I am really light-headed, dizzy, and sick to my stomach, and the tube is only making me feel more anxious and claustrophobic. There is just so much pressure in my left ear, and it's making me feel crazy! I tried stretching my muscles in bed while lying down. Everything feels so heavy and weird.

I attempted to stand for my weight but blacked out just sitting on the side of the bed. I tried a second time and barely made it. I was 65.1 pounds, but I guess all my fluid is messed up. I just don't feel right. I really need this tube out! I had a stressful talk with Mom later. She was going off on me about how she is concerned I don't want recovery, lecturing that I will not be going back to Davis anytime soon, that I have to gain a ton of weight, how she doesn't believe I even feel bad about everything I've done to the family, and on and on and on. The fact is that I really do want recovery, but I need my parents to quit forcing me to voice it to them. I want to get better deep down inside but don't always know how or if I want them to know I want to get better sometimes.

After our stressful talk, I had a bed bath and had a ton of energy! I was even able to wash my face and get up enough energy to cough slightly and blow my nose! I then had a great meeting with my GI doctor. She said that my tube could possibly come out tomorrow if my liver levels went down enough. She said I would transition to food and keep increasing my calories but that I wouldn't gain over 2 pounds a week. She explained that if the tube came out too soon, my liver could get even worse than before and that I would need the tube back in twice as long. I suppose I can wait a few more days.

After the GI doctor left, I called Dad to tell him the exciting news about my tube coming out soon. He half laughed and half yelled at me when I told him. He was like, "What are *you* talking about? That tube isn't coming out for a very long time." I said, "Huh? What are you talking about?" And he replied, "You have to keep that tube in for a long time to make sure you get all your calories and don't hide food." Anyway, it was a big argument because I obviously knew I was right and that the tube would be out in a few days because I had just talked to the doctor! Thankfully, the doctor was still outside my room and came back in overhearing our conversation. She explained to my dad on the phone that the tube would come out soon and that I would eat food and that this was good news.

Dad then apologized and said that was good, but then we had a heated 30-minute talk about basically the same thing Mom addressed. He started stating how I would not go home or to Davis after being here, that I would have to be at least 95 pounds and would have to gain weight and recover now! He said I have no choice and that it would be many, many months before I could do anything and lots of other absurd stuff. Anyway, I guess I chose very good words because we actually finished our talk pretty happy. Dad said we could take it day by day.

Next, I met with Dr. Lucas and had a very good meeting. She told me all my lab values were OK and better. She said I am being bumped up to 1,380 calories, which seems really scary. I guess it's not too much, right? She told me a few interesting things, though. One was that she feels I am manipulating her! She said she feels I don't want recovery and that I don't want to give up ED because I keep pushing her for more ice, gum, and sugar-free stuff. She said she is only making guidelines to save my life and keep me safe. She said she spent hours on the phone today with doctors about me and loses sleep over me because she doesn't want anything bad to happen to me under her care. Anyway, we ended up having a great talk. I cleared up all the confusion to make sure she knew I was not manipulating her. OK…maybe a lot of things I said were bullshit, but she seemed satisfied at least. She pretty much told me that there was no way I would be ready for UC Davis in the spring, though, which really bummed me out.

One thing she said that caught my attention was that my red blood cell count is 2.1; normal is around 3.8 to 4.0. She is so worried a specialist is now working with her. She thought I might even need a blood transfusion! She is going to draw labs again and decide what to do. I will probably just need to take more iron or something. She did say that red blood cells carry oxygen and that is the reason I feel so weak and tired and get so dizzy when standing up and have trouble breathing.

Real quick before I go to bed, I have to mention that I walked to the window tonight! I was so excited and called Dad, and he started crying. It was the most amazing thing. It was weird using my legs again but so cool. I then was able to walk to the bathroom without holding my nurse's hands. I feel as if I want to run a marathon now! OK, maybe not that, but I am just so excited. I will do whatever it takes to convince the doctors I can go back to Davis this spring, whether it means lying a bit or not. I am going to make it happen.

February 17, 2009

Today was extremely scary and crazy all in one. I woke up feeling really good, and my body felt strong. Although my body felt great, my mind was racing. I couldn't stop thinking about how I would convince my parents and doctors that I would be ready for discharge in a few weeks and then could go to Davis for spring quarter.

Well, to make a very long story short, I will just talk about the highlights for the day. I had a nurse I love, but she was really busy and didn't know how to give me any of my meds or about my ability to stand up, get weighed, etc. I was feeling daring enough and agreed to try to stand up for my blood pressure and weight. I was also hoping to walk to the bathroom to pee since I hadn't gone since 11:00 the previous night. I stood up with tremendous difficulty for my blood pressure even though I didn't want to, and I ended up blacking out. After a minute or so, I could see again. A few minutes later, I told my nurse and my sitter I was ready to try to get my weight. I was able to stand on the scale and saw 67.7 pounds, but it wasn't accurate apparently because I hadn't gone to the bathroom. I ended up blacking out again. They really wanted me to pee, though, and after about 20 minutes, I decided I should and would attempt to walk to the bathroom, pee, get weighed again, and brush my teeth.

I very unstably made it to the toilet with my body sweating and feeling extremely light-headed. I was successful with peeing, but I wasn't feeling so great sitting on the toilet. My nurse and sitter didn't realize how big of a step it was that I made it to the bathroom in the morning. They were not listening to me begging them to slow down and help me as they were telling me to hurry up. They kept pushing me quickly as if I was fine (so scary!). I was feeling very unwell but had them stand me up. They were going to weigh me again. I was attempting to step on the scale really fast when my nurse started saying no. She wanted me to step on the scale backward. I'm thinking, "Are you insane?" Anyway, that's when I lost it, and everything went black. I couldn't take a breath in or get any air. I knew I was in trouble.

My nurse kept saying to open my eyes. I kept saying I need to get back to bed and lie down! I don't know why, but whenever I am upright I get terrible ear pressure and feel dizzy and sick. As soon as I lie down, it all clears up. Meanwhile, everything was pitch black, and my legs were buckling. My nurse and sitter sat me on a chair, but I still couldn't see or breathe. They thought I was OK enough.

I said, "No, I need to be carried to bed."

My nurse said, "Well, I would need to call a man," or something like that to lift me.

I'm thinking, "I need to lie down now or I am going to die!"

All I remember next is my stomach getting very upset and diarrhea pouring out endlessly. I hadn't even had any stomach problems in the last 24 hours. Then I remember hearing the chair being scooted and someone lifting me up into a bed. I heard someone say something about calling rapid response, and then I was completely out of it.

I finally started regaining some consciousness, and about 8 nurses were in the room. I was shivering uncontrollably and convulsing. I had an oxygen mask on, still couldn't see, and was lying in bed with nurses trying to talk to me. I was in and out of consciousness, but thankfully I heard Lisa's voice even though it was her day off. That made me feel better. It was the scariest feeling I've ever experienced, not to be able to regain full consciousness no matter how hard I tried. I felt as if I were buried underneath a pack of snow with no way out. I got rushed to the ICU. I remember Lisa was with me. There was a lot of commotion, and I really felt ill and was still trying to wake up fully.

My mouth was desert dry. After what seemed like an eternity, I finally was feeling a little better and saw my sitter in the room with me. She told me my lips and face turned completely white in the chair and that I passed out for at least 10 to 15 minutes. My blood pressure readings had been in the 40's. My blood sugar and temperature dropped extremely low. I don't remember too much now, but I do remember pleading to Lisa not to call my dad or anyone because I didn't want him thinking I was getting sicker. In reality, my muscles and body are better than when I was admitted. I don't want Dad thinking this was another setback and no Davis.

I spent about 9 hours in the ICU and saw a lot of doctors. The same doctor who talked to me about who would decide to keep me alive on a machine if I went brain-dead came to say hi. I told her how great I was doing as well as my discharge plan. I told her to tell my dad I am doing amazing and want recovery because apparently there have been plans of transferring me to UCLA after this program to continue refeeding, which no way in hell am I going to let that happen!

I had extreme stomach pain all day, but the GI doctor told me I could eat 100 calories of food tonight instead of increasing my tube feed by 100. She also said I could eat 100 percent food tomorrow and will take out the tube if my liver is OK. I really hope so!

I later saw Dr. Lucas, who at first was talking about how the tube would stay in for a long time. She said that I would eat 100 calories by food each day and do the rest with the tube. She explained how worried she was that I wouldn't be able to eat all my calories willingly. I, of course, was freaking out because the GI doctor just told me the tube could come out and I could eat all food! Dr. Lucas was firm and not going to change her mind. She then left to make some calls and look at her notes.

Thank goodness she came back a little later and said, "OK, fine."

She let me choose 100 calories today of real food, and so I ate a small plate of broccoli and celery. I was so happy to eat food again! Plus, it was only like 30 calories. I had my tube feed turned off for at least 3 hours and so hopefully I will lose weight. Anyway, Dr. Lucas and I had a great talk. If all goes how I hope, then tomorrow I will eat 1,380 calories of food and the tube will come out! That means I will also get to have more ice cups and gum again!

I am apparently having a severe problem with my hemoglobin or red blood cells, and my number dropped to 18. If it drops any more at all, I will need a blood transfusion. Yikes!

I got moved back to my room from the ICU late tonight and have a nurse I hate right now. She is making me stay up until 1:00 in the morning to finish my last Neutra-Phos dosage to spread them out because I am really behind tonight. Normally I would be happy to stay up later, but tonight I just want to sleep! Whatever. I am so tired now and can't remember anything more. I really hope my liver is OK tomorrow and the tube can come out. It's pouring rain tonight, I guess. I wish I could hear it.

February 19, 2009

Done with ED. Infections, brain fog, so hot. Sheryl prayed for me. Can't think. Want to walk, want 100 percent food, want memory back. 68.5 pounds. Everyone says I look better. Help. Can't think. So tired. Low red blood cells and hemoglobin. Getting blood transfusion soon. Love my mommy. Get better here in 2 to 4 weeks and go straight home and no Davis until fall. Go home after 2 to 4 weeks to Mommy and tennis and horse. I am sleeping all day and can't keep eyes open. Starting real food. Had 400 calories today and 1,800 calories total. Gain 2 pounds a week. Final goal is 2,000 calories by mouth and no tube. Angel, protect me and let me walk and think and remember again and not need tube and be able to think clearly and get energy back. Please let red blood cells and hemoglobin increase and make me feel the way I did when I could think clearly and journal and write. OK, good night. Can't think.

February 22, 2009

I got a blood transfusion last night. I can finally take a deep breath! I had a great day yesterday afternoon. I came out of my brain fog and was able to take a bed bath and walk a few steps. I was even able to sit in a chair 3 times for about 20 minutes without passing out! This morning I was able to stand for my weight, which was 66.5 pounds, and I didn't get dizzy. I then walked to the bathroom before having any water, and I still didn't get dizzy and could take a deep breath while I was walking. I am kind of scared because although I can now breathe better and feel more relaxed, I do still feel kind of foggy and overwhelmed with UC Davis. Am I OK to attend classes in the spring or not? When is discharge? I want to go straight home, not to UCLA or another program. I am completely done with ED and want life and never to be in a hospital again! I just feel overwhelmed with finding housing for Davis next year and all the people I was supposed to call and just everything!

All my IVs stopped today—hooray! I am having 2,000 calories per day now, but I still have the tube. The doctors are slowly increasing the amount of food I get by mouth and are decreasing the amount by tube feed until I am eating all 2,000 calories by mouth. I am kind of anxious because I am now eating a small breakfast, lunch, dinner, and snacks. I have to keep track of mealtimes as well as remember that I must eat 100 percent and not hide food like the old Brittany was used to. I am done with ED and want recovery. I can't wait to be myself again! Oh, I wish my memory would come back completely. Each day it gets better, so hopefully it will soon. Dr. Lucas even said

I would be ready for discharge in 2 to 3 weeks and could go straight home and see a dietitian and therapist. Well, OK, maybe I twisted her words into as optimistic as possible, but who knows? Please come back, memory!

I wanted to get up and walk around my room, but my sitter said no. At least I can probably go outside in a wheelchair tomorrow! I had lunch, and it was a huge bowl of yogurt (plain at least) and a mountain of tuna. I ate it all but can't stop obsessing over the calories now. I feel more alive and want out of this bed and hospital. I guess I should be thankful I am doing OK—and I am, even though I'm going stir-crazy. Apparently, I almost died 3 times, my vitals have been low, and I have had a lot of fevers and infections that have been affecting my hand, colon, brain, and heart. My hemoglobin ended up dropping to 6.2, which is why I got a successful blood transfusion last night and why I can now breathe! I guess I still must look pretty skinny. I know I am, and I know I look anorexic, but it's hard to hear everyone say I look better and for people to say I finally have a bit of meat on me. I know it's a step in the right direction for life.

I wonder where I would be on my UC Davis or home doctor's scale. When I got weighed there I was super water loaded and had shoes and 5 layers on. Oh well, hopefully I will get discharged soon, but I am a bit worried about the future because Dad is completely done with ED. Though I am also done with ED, he can't just expect someone with an eating disorder for 7 years to be over it 100 percent, though I hope I am. We are all optimistic and taking it day by day. I am upset at myself right now because I am feeling almost back to normal and am feeling the need to exercise and burn calories. I know I've been in bed for weeks and haven't been outside in a month, but do I want to exercise to burn calories or just because I am so ready to do some movement? Erg!

After lunch I sat in the chair for 3 hours! I even had my meeting with Dr. Lucas while sitting in the chair. We had a nice chat, and guess what? I have absolutely no brain fog right now! I am in shock and am so happy. Dr. Lucas told me my hemoglobin only rose to 7.8 after the blood transfusion and normal is 12–14, but I still feel amazing! I wonder how I would feel if it was actually normal? She said I might even need another transfusion if it lowers or doesn't increase. Oh, and more exciting news is that I am not orthostatic at all today, meaning my blood pressure is stable both sitting and standing. She also said my electrolytes look great.

I talked to her about being discharged, and although she was somewhat positive, she said she still wants to see my electrolytes stay normal without having to give me a million pills a day and for my hemoglobin to rise. Of course, she also had to mention that my weight is far too low. Erg! She said Dr. Schack is still going to recommend residential treatment afterward, but I really hope I can be an exception.

I then talked to her about the tube and how I couldn't sleep comfortably with it. She told me it is only being kept in right now for refeeding purposes, not because of my liver.

I said, "If it is only in for refeeding, then why was it not in at the beginning of my admission because my weight was lower? It was only put in for my liver crisis. Now my liver is in the normal ranges, so why the heck is the tube still in?"

She looked at me and said, "Yeah, let me go see if we can get it out tonight."

Oh my gosh, I almost died with excitement thinking it could be out! She then left and came back a little later and said, yes, the tube could come out now, but I would have to cram in 1,140 calories by bed. I said fine! Most importantly, Dr. Lucas said I will be able to have my gum once the tube is out. Only 4 pieces though... I will definitely have to find a way to get more.

Dr. Lucas then left and came back 20 minutes later only to say, "I'm so sorry, but the tube has to stay in 3 days longer. We will transition you to food fast, but the dietitian said if you eat that many calories that fast you will have diarrhea and not feel well."

I was crushed. No matter which way I pleaded to convince her to take out the tube, she continued to say no way. I was so upset because I wanted to eat food and obviously get this long painful noodle out of my nose!

I then said, "Fine! Let me drink the Isosource!" (That is the tube-feed formula.)

Dr. Lucas looked at me in disbelief, and after much contemplation she said OK! She told me that would equal 25 ounces of Isosource, plus dinner for tonight, and the tube can come out. I said great!

After all that, the plan was 3 cans of Isosource today and dinner, and then tomorrow I can have 1,000 calories of food and 1,000 calories of Isosource and then Tuesday transition to 100 percent food. She also mentioned that I probably would need 2,200 calories just to gain any weight because of my metabolism. I can't believe I am actually having 2,000 calories on bed rest each day and am not a balloon! Although I must say I can see the weight gain, especially in my legs. I also can see the fact that I am still very anorexic-looking... sometimes.

I had 8 ounces of Isosource, and then my nurse tried pulling out the tube, which was extremely painful. But then that pain became excruciating because the tube got stuck in my nose and she was pulling hard! She had to bring in 4 nurses. All of them tried to pull out the tube, but it was completely stuck. They had never experienced anything like it. They tried everything to get it out and were about to send me down for an X-ray to see what had happened. I even tried pulling it out, but it wouldn't budge and hurt a lot.

Then one of the charge nurses tried and pulled extremely hard for a long time. Finally it popped out, but I still needed to get an X-ray, and the tube was sent to the lab. It feels so amazing not having a tube. I got my gum tonight, and it has never tasted so good! Isosource tastes pretty nasty and is comparable to thick Boost Plus but not as good. It was hard having to consume that many calories as well as a dinner that was much bigger than I think it was supposed to be. I ate it all anyway. Mom and Dad were so happy when I told them how I was doing. I am so ready to be out of here.

I am drinking the last of my Isosource for tonight and want so badly to hide it, but I can't! I am excited because I can sleep with the bed flat from now on as opposed to the 45-degree angle required when I had the tube. I look as though I came from a war because my body is so beaten up. I have huge bruises on my arms from all my blood work and IVs. I have Duoderms all over my back, butt, and shoulders. My hands are chapped, and my arms are swollen. I have red dots all over my stomach. I have bruises all up my shins. My hair is falling out. I really hope eating food goes well tomorrow and doesn't overwhelm me too much. Yes, I want recovery, and, yes, I feel different. But it's still hard when I'm used to living a certain way for so many years. It's hard to deal with changes, but I truly believe I died for a second and have been given a second chance. I have never felt this alive, happy, and loving. I hope this lasts!

13

Survival of the Sickest

February 23, 2009

Sleeping without a tube was amazing. I was able to sleep on my side and move around. I was so comfy. My throat never hurt or got dry either. This morning I feel really strong and was able to get up, do vitals, go pee, and then get weighed. Today I got to see my weight (even though I saw it yesterday, which was 66.5 pounds), and today it said 74.2 pounds! However, I am thinking today's weight is the correct one because a lot of my previous weights were with the bed scale, which isn't as accurate, I think.

Anyway, the bottom line is I basically weigh 74 pounds, and this is not OK! I probably weigh almost the same as I did on my UC Davis doctor's scale because I had tons of clothes on and a bunch of water in my system. I am gaining weight ridiculously fast and still might be here another 2 weeks!

I called Dad. He's happy about my weight gain, yet he is pretty firm on me needing to weigh quite a bit more and going to another program. Erg! I can't think; I'm so overwhelmed with anxiety right now! I know I weigh more than when I left UC Davis because of how my legs almost touch. I should be discharged now and go to Davis in the spring! I have to complete 2,000 calories again today, and it's Dr. Schack's first day back, so she won't really know what's going on. I want to scream and run away!

Breakfast was a veggie-cheese egg omelet, fruit cup, and 7 ounces of Isosource—yuck! Too many calories! I am with a young and inexperienced sitter, so I was able to get away with throwing away some of the cheese on top of my omelet. I wonder how many calories are in Isosource? I have to have 20 ounces total today, but hopefully it will be reduced because of my weight? Yeah, right! Oh well, Dr. Schack knows about my weight, at least.

After breakfast I had a lot of diarrhea and didn't feel well. I then looked at myself in the mirror. I guess I do look pretty thin, though I can only see from my chest up. Snack is 4 ounces of apple juice and 12 rice crackers. I have to admit food tastes pretty good, but I'm just so overwhelmed with everything:

1. Hospital drama: discharge, doctors, health, weight, aftercare, rules, requirements, and food.
2. UC Davis: spring quarter, housing, dorm room, horses, doctor, requirements, and dorm friends.
3. Parents: requirements for home, weight gain, residential, UC Davis, calories, food, times, wanting to prove I am different, and freedom.
4. Friends: haven't called them, no Facebook, and wanting to show them I am different.
5. Future: will ED really be gone, tennis, horses, anorexia, life, college, home, aftercare, and my body.

I just can't stop thinking about all these things. ED is strong today.

Lunch was gross and large, and I was brought 1 percent milk as opposed to nonfat, which I thought I made clear to everyone. I was so uncomfortably full after. It's my first day eating this many calories in a long time, and I'm not even being given extra time to finish meals. I have to eat all the food at a sickly pace just to finish in 30 minutes.

I had a great session with the therapist I sometimes see here, but she told me she is leaving for the week. I am so mad! I form a relationship with Dr. Schack, and then she has to leave and I have to explain myself again and form a new relationship with Dr. Lucas. It's the same thing with the nurses and sitters. Each shift change it seems I must explain again what's going on with me. Now my therapist is leaving! This is so hard, especially because I have a deep down fear of people always leaving me. People just aren't worth trusting or getting close to because they always let you down.

I saw the hemoglobin doctor this morning, and my bone marrow or red blood cells stayed the same at 7.8. He said that's very good and that it could take 4 to 6 weeks for my hemoglobin to rise just one point.

For my afternoon snack, I got 1 cup of huge, fat grapes and 1 hard-boiled egg. My sitter right now is Valerie, who is this crazy kind of older lady who loves me. After pleading with her, I actually got her to throw away the egg yolk and 5 grapes for me! Stupid ED, but, oh my gosh, I can't believe she did! Then again, she is just that kind of lady, and there is no other way to explain her. You would have to see and meet her to understand.

She also told me she would visit me tomorrow, do my laundry, and bring me 10 packs of gum, though I doubt she will. Then again, she is just that odd that I don't really know? There are just no words to describe her.

I was allowed to go downstairs in a wheelchair and smell the outside air for one minute, but I couldn't actually go outside because it was too late and cold. Just being near fresh air was so amazing!

I met with Dr. Schack and had a decent meeting. She told me I am still very sick, though my blood work is improving. She also said that the magical 8-pound weight gain I had was all fluid. She argued that 1 pound equals 3,500 calories and that the weight gain I had in such a short amount of time is impossible. Still, I just know that 74 pounds must be my real weight based on how my thighs look. She said she doesn't know for sure which weight is the correct one, but the calories are still coming, and tomorrow I have to eat 2,100 calories! I have such an awful stomachache and am inhumanely full and uncomfortable. I later got very tired to the point where my eyes wanted to close so bad and sleep for the rest of the night. Maybe it's because I was more active today. I walked all around my room today and even organized it.

One of the nicest things about being able to walk and move better is that I am not as scared or fearful of whom my nurse or sitter is because I can do almost everything for myself now. I can also get in and out of bed by myself and get ready for meals. Everything gets done so much quicker and efficiently. Beforehand, just having to go to the bathroom used to be a huge task. I would literally need to be pulled out of bed, sit on the side of the bed hoping not to pass out, have help walking to the bathroom, help being pulled up from the toilet, help walking back, and then help getting into bed. Eventually, I formed little tricks to help me aid the nurses. Being able to do it myself now is so nice. It sure beats going to the bathroom on a bedpan and having the nurse wipe my butt for me—oh dear!

Dinner was enormous! It was a huge piece of salmon, green beans, lettuce, a container of kidney beans, a small container of shredded cheese, 8 ounces of milk, and 1 rice cake. After stalling and freaking out about the food and causing some drama, I didn't quite finish all of it by the time allowed of 30 minutes. My nurse, although I love her, is crazy-strict and paranoid about me eating 100 percent in the exact 30 minutes no matter what. It wasn't fair, though, because I didn't start eating until there were only 20 minutes left on the clock. I was waiting to take my meds first. Yeah, there was nothing stopping me from starting to eat, but every nurse should know by now that I must take my meds before I eat—I just must!

Anyway, my nurse still tried taking away my tray, saying, "Sorry, I will just have to bring you supplement for what's left."

I flipped out because I wanted to finish the food as opposed to supplement. I grabbed the food off my tray, and she kept trying to take it from me. Basically, after crying and getting upset, the nurse felt bad and gave me 5 more minutes to finish. Not only that, but she didn't even make me supplement all the food I left, which was 2 ounces of kidney beans, 2 ounces of milk, and all my cheese. Score!

I had a great talk with Dad. He told me I should be in a documentary because I am one of the skinniest and sickest people ever to survive and get back to functioning in such a short amount of time. Whatever, I don't think I am that sick. I later got to go outside—sort of. It was late and cold out, so even though I had a doctor's order to be outside for 10 minutes, the nurse only let me smell the air downstairs. It still smelled amazing! For my last snack I was supposed to get 7 ounces of Isosource and some food, but my nurse totally blanked and didn't bring the Isosource. Hooray! Oh boy, the nurses here certainly won't be forgetting me, that's for sure.

February 24, 2009

I had a good night's sleep and have a lovely nurse today. She isn't a regular on the floor, so I was able to get away with quite a bit. I was able to do a standing blood pressure and weight and use the bathroom to brush my teeth and walk around my room for an hour! That's way more standing and walking than I thought I could do. Eventually, I did start to get a little dizzy and sick to my stomach. Breakfast was 2 hard-boiled eggs, 8 ounces of blueberry yogurt, and the biggest, grossest orange ever to the point where it might have just been better to supplement it. However, I cut off quite a bit of the whitish skin left around it. I was also able to get my nurse to give me some paper towels in which I hid 1 egg yolk and some yogurt and then had her throw them away for me, completely clueless! Afterward, I was so tired and could hardly keep my eyes open. Lisa stopped by to say hi, and it was so nice talking to her. She said she would be my nurse tomorrow, which is great except for the fact that she is very strict as far as the rules and schedule go. I guess ultimately that is a good thing, though ED certainly disagrees.

I had Isosource for my snack and tried accidentally spilling some in my napkin, but I got caught. However, as much as I felt embarrassed and mad, no one ever did anything about it. I then had physical therapy to help me walk, and I got to take 3 laps around the fourth floor with this pretty hot guy, ha-ha! I am so much stronger and can balance a lot better. Next came lunch. Again I tried to hide some supplement under my ice cup, but the nurse found it when I stupidly accidentally spilled it. I then not only got away with taking a shower versus a bath, but I took one for 40 minutes and stood up the whole time and felt fine.

Shift change came, and I got a great nurse. She took me outside in the wheelchair, but it was freezing, so we only stayed out there for 1 minute. I then convinced her to take me to the gift shop. I bought 5 packs of Trident gum and was able to sneak 2 packs past the nurses. Unfortunately, they are mini packs (5 sticks per pack), but it is still better than nothing. Dinner was gross and lots of calories. It was 4 huge pieces of turkey, veggies, 8 ounces of milk, 6 ounces of blueberry yogurt, and 1 large apple. I cut off all the "bruises" on the apple and of course pulled off all the skin on the outside of the turkey. I had my Isosource for evening snack, but my sitter tonight is so cool and poured out about 4 ounces of it for me after I complained I was brought too much.

February 25, 2009

I had an all right sleep. Lisa is my nurse today, which is good. I was able to sit in the chair for all my meals, and I felt great! I do have to put my feet up on another chair when I sit for extra support, but it's still a step forward.

I saw my weight today, and it was 74.7 pounds! I hadn't peed yet, but I am getting so fat! Who knows when I will be free either?

Breakfast was 2 hard-boiled eggs, 1 orange, a huge bowl of cream of rice, and 4 ounces of milk. I chose to have the supplement for the cream of rice because it was only equivalent to 2 ounces of Boost, which is 60 calories, and I know the cream of rice was at least double. My sitter is a really young, sweet girl and hardly watches me eat at all. My chair was right next to the trash can, so I was able to pick up an old cup out of the trash, pour all my supplement and 2 ounces of milk in the cup and then silently put it back in the trash, letting it spill. I also grabbed a used glove from inside the trash and was able to throw away both of my egg yolks hidden inside of it! I guess that is a bad thing, but I do feel quite proud of myself for getting away with fewer calories. I am so scared about my discharge and when and what will happen as far as my parents and their decisions.

I can't stand my legs! They now practically touch at night when I lay down, and my thighs look huge. My left hand where my infection was has seemed to turn on me. I still can't fully twist my arm, but now I can't bend my thumb straight at all as of last night and all of today. Dr. Schack is going to have me see the orthopedic therapist, but this is just so weird. My thumb is stuck in the palm of my hand.

Snack was 4 ounces of grape juice and 12 rice crackers. Again, I was able to hide a glove underneath the blanket on my lap. Then I put 7 crackers in the glove and then in the trash. I also threw out about 2 ounces of juice by hiding it in a separate cup. Next was physical therapy. We had a nice 3-lap walk, and then the cute guy showed me some standing and balance exercises. Afterward, I went outside in a wheelchair and sat in the sun for a good 30 minutes. It felt amazing. I then convinced my sitter to take me to the gift shop, and I bought 8 packs of gum.

The one good thing about eating so many freaking calories is that I now finally get to choose my meals with a dietitian. When I was on a lower-calorie meal plan, the dietician chose all my meals for me without my input. I don't get much of a choice, but an option between 2 different fruits, veggies, and main dishes. At least it is better and I can make sure not to choose options with fluids so that I can have more ice cups and can hopefully pick the lowest calorie option. Of course, the dietitian said they make up for that. Lunch was 3 big turkey slices, 3 tomatoes, 4 ounces of cottage cheese, 4 ounces of apple juice, and cantaloupe. I again sat with the clueless sitter and was able to hide all 3 pieces of turkey in a glove and throw it in the trash as well as almost all of my cottage cheese. I was also able to pour almost all my juice into an empty cup. Hooray! My sitter just kept reading magazines and wasn't even really facing me.

I had a great meeting with Dr. Schack, and she told me I have really bad edema due to the refeeding process. My body is very fluid overloaded, and my ankles, calves, and legs are huge, swollen, and ridiculously puffy. She wants me to keep my heels up, and I am now on a low-sodium diet. Maybe she is a bit right about my suspiciously large weight gain being partly fluid because my legs are really swollen and puffy! She says she believes my true weight is really in the 60's, but either way she is going to keep pushing for 2 pounds of weight gain per week and says I will have to eat 2,200 calories tomorrow.

I now get to walk laps around the halls, which increases by 5 minutes each day. Today I get to do 10 minutes, tomorrow 15 minutes, and so on, but 20 minutes is the maximum. I'm also allowed to stay outside longer. The Isosource is thankfully being decreased by ½ a can a day, so by Sunday I will no longer have to drink any of it.

Dr. Schack brought in a paper release for me to sign so that she can call UC Davis and talk to my doctor there. I'm at least encouraged that she brought the paperwork in so willingly after I pleaded and told her about it yesterday. She said it would be good to talk to Davis now and know the requirements. Maybe she will let me go for spring quarter? My heart rate and blood pressure have been great, and I haven't been orthostatic at all lately!

I had to have 1 can of Isosource at afternoon snack (I figured out that 1 can equals 375 calories). I was able to pour out at least ½ in the trash. I had a new sitter. She didn't see me pour it out, but she pressed the nurse call light for Lisa because she had to pee. When Lisa walked in I guess the trash can must have looked suspicious because she searched it and found the Isosource and was really mad. I don't think the sitter even told ... gosh, I must have just looked guilty. She brought me another 4 ounces to make up for it. I got into a rage, saying she brought way more than the amount I threw out. I defiantly poured ½ of what she brought all over the table.

Lisa kept repeating, "That's why you need residential."

Oh, I just lost it on her! The psychiatrist came to see me during my tantrum. I guess he wanted to check in even though I was scream-ing at him and Lisa to get the heck out and leave me alone to journal. I yelled at the psychiatrist, and eventually he and Lisa both left.

Dinner was disgusting! It was 1 huge chicken breast, rice, peas, and grapes. The chicken was only worth 5 ounces of supplement, which equaled 150 calories. I wanted to supplement the chicken, but if I did, I wouldn't be able to have all my cups of ice with snack, so I painfully ate it all. I had yet another meltdown when Lisa came in to tell me she calculated wrong and I could really only have 1 1/2 more ice cups versus 2. I got to do only a 5-minute walk tonight when I know Dr. Schack said 10 minutes, but there was no order written so the nurses wouldn't let me, and again I got really upset. I had my last snack, which was 1 can of Isosource. I took a few sips and then told my sitter, whom I absolutely adore, I wasn't going to finish (even though in my mind I was).

She called the lead nurse in, who said, "Your 20 minutes are up." She told me I had 5 minutes to finish.

I said, "No way. I need at least 15 minutes!"

After arguing for 5 minutes, she left and called Dr. Schack. When she came back into my room she had a tube in her hand and said I was literally to pick up the cup and chug it in less than 5 minutes or get tubed, and she was completely serious! I mumbled and cussed the whole time, but, damn, she really meant it. So, I finally chugged the whole fattening shake. Then my sitter saw me eat 2 pieces of my gum that I had snuck and told the lead nurse, so I only get 2 pieces of gum tonight versus 4. Erg! Causing trouble never seems to work. My legs are so fat and swollen, but my total calories for today are around 1,600 versus 2,100 calories, so that is good, at least. I had a lovely talk with Mom, but she wasn't sure about me coming straight home from here and that is making me jumpy. Good night!

February 26, 2009

Last night continued to suck while I slept because my sitter wouldn't help me stand up when I had to pee! She responded with, "Do it yourself. You don't need help. You can walk." I honestly couldn't begin to even lift myself no matter how hard I tried. It freaked me out. She eventually helped me out of bed, but again she gave me the same response when I asked for help off the toilet. I was already feeling hot and a bit out of it, and so I pulled the help cord in the bathroom while continuing to plead for help until the lead nurse came and helped me up. Despite the awful incident, I did sleep quite well and didn't have to pee too much afterward.

I got to see my weight this morning. It was 75.5 pounds. I am getting so fat and want out! I hate it because even though most of the nurses say I look very anorexic, there are a few who say, "No, you don't look anorexic" and "You look better now and not sick," which really fuels ED.

At breakfast, I caused some drama again. I told my nurse before the time started all the things I needed and when to bring them. For some reason, I will not allow myself to start eating until I have everything I need, such as the right number of plastic utensils, ice cups, meds, and what I want heated. The list could go on and on. Well, first of all, she didn't bring my tray early enough for me to tell her what I would need and want. Second of all, she didn't even get the stuff I asked for until way after the time had started! I was surely not happy! I finally calmed down because a nurse I love came to sit with me and gave me extra time. Breakfast was a veggie quiche thing, but the top part of the quiche was sort of burnt yet completely edible. However, I complained that it wasn't. My nurse allowed me to leave all of the top burnt part, and it was quite a lot!

I took a nap because I was having terrible ear pressure, but when I woke up my ear clog, back pain, and shortness of breath were still there. It made my anxiety and panic rise because I can't hear myself talk very well, which only feeds into feelings of fear and vulnerability. It is just so weird, and no one has been able to give me a straight answer as to why my ears clog. Everyone does seem to agree it will get better with nutrition, yet they have never heard of what I seem to be describing. Every time I lower my head or lie flat all the pressure and clogged-up ears dissolves. Then as soon as I raise my head, bam! Sometimes it lasts for 20 minutes and sometimes hours on end.

February 27, 2009

I have a lovely sitter today, and Lisa is my main nurse. The morning began smoothly, and all was going well. Breakfast was huge: 2 hard-boiled eggs, Rice Krispies cereal, 4 ounces of milk, and an enormous bowl of cantaloupe. I tried to hide the yolks in a glove, but my sitter saw and told on me. Lisa was pissed! Then Mom and her friend came to visit briefly before my snack. It was so nice to have my mom hug me! The occupational therapist came to look at my left arm and hand today. She said my arm muscles were just tight, but that my stuck thumb stumped her. She was a bit worried about it and wanted to put it in a splint.

I then had snack, but it was more like a large meal! I had a lettuce bowl, dressing, celery, cantaloupe, and yogurt. I tried to spill the dressing in my napkin, but again my sitter saw and told Lisa, who was now extra-pissed. She made me drink some Isosource as replacement—yuck! Apparently Lisa even told housekeeping to check and search my trash cans before throwing them out. After snack, I had physical therapy, and we walked a good 7 laps. I was able to walk a bit quicker and even look straight ahead versus at my feet. I still walk like the Hunchback though. My legs and feet are so oddly swollen. They feel like anchors. I cleaned my room for bit and then it was time for lunch, which was rice, carrots, tuna, Italian ice, and strawberries. Too much! I was able to get my new sitter to throw out some tuna, thank goodness.

I met with Dr. Schack. She said she talked briefly with my doctor at UC Davis, who is sending her paperwork on Monday. Unfortunately for me, Davis requires ED students to be at least 85 percent of their ideal body weight when they return from medical leave. That would mean 105 pounds for me. No! I'm so angry because at Davis I did all my weigh-ins in the afternoon with layers of clothes and shoes, and now they are requiring morning weights with only a gown and no water, so I'm probably going to be heavier than I need to be! Dr. Schack said my electrolytes are still good, but that my white blood cells are still low. I am still on potassium supplements as well as taking 10 Neutra-Phos a day, which just isn't normal. I now get to do 4 5-minute walks, which is good. She was not optimistic about a 1-week or even a 2-week discharge.

February 28, 2009

I had a miserable sleep last night. I have a great sitter and nurse today, which is always a sigh of relief. I feel good and happy, but my legs are still insanely swollen and look so weird! They are so heavy, uncomfortable, and sore. My vitals are now perfect all the time, even in the mornings. My heart rate is good, but sometimes drops to 52 beats per minute—but that's still fine. My weight was 74.2 pounds. I'm sure it's actually higher because I went to the bathroom before-hand and usually I don't.

Mom and her friend arrived, and I had the best time with them! They took me outside in a wheelchair, and it was actually warm out. We had an honest and hard talk. We compromised on the conclusion that Mom will keep an open mind on me coming home straight after Torrance, and I must keep an open mind on going to UCLA for a few days or weeks afterward. Mom said I would probably only be at UCLA for a short stay, such as a few days or a week. Maybe I could handle that. I guess UCLA's program sounds kind of like Stanford, where people come for a brief period for stabilization? We then had to say goodbye, and Mom wheeled me back to my room. Oh, what I would do to follow her home.

March 1, 2009

I am upset because at breakfast, I now can't have a blanket, gloves, a trash can, or napkins to throw anything away. Just my luck break-fast this morning was huge! It was 8 ounces of low-fat plain yogurt (it's supposed to be nonfat!), 1 huge bowl of cream of rice with mar-garine, and 1 huge bowl of melon. I was beyond upset when my nurse brought a huge 5 ounces of Isosource when I chose to replace my cream of rice. Five ounces of that stuff has got to be at least 250 calories! With the yogurt and fruit included, I calculated about 600 calories just for breakfast! I absolutely lost my cool at that point and argued and questioned the amount of Isosource over and over. I'm not sure what happened, but I got really upset and spent at least 30 minutes yelling and throwing a fit like a 2 year old. Dr. Schack was apparently at the nurses' station and could hear my tantrum. I was even going to refuse just 1 ounce of Isosource because I claimed I had taken 4 bites of the cream of rice. Dr. Schack told my nurse to put down the tube, and she meant it! I finally gave in and drank it and then had my meeting with Dr. Schack. I cried and complained and was so upset.

I'm sick of all the rules, being trapped in a box, hardly getting to go outside, 20-minute walks only, having a new sitter every day and 3 times a day, no friends, no family, no privacy, not enough gum, etc. I am completely stir-crazy and want out! Dr. Schack was compassionate, yet unfortunately, because of my super-swollen feet, abnormal EKG, weight, and all the supplements I require just to keep my electrolytes normal, she said I wasn't going anywhere soon. She said if I wanted to go directly home after her program, it would probably be another 2 months. She said I would be allowed to transfer to UCLA today if a bed opened up, but that they don't usually want patients with an abnormal EKG like mine. She said UCLA would probably keep me there just as long, but she wasn't sure.

I called Dad very upset. He understood my frustration of feeling trapped. He said going to UCLA might be a better and quicker stay because their whole staff is equipped to handle solely eating disorder patients, whereas some nurses here don't know much about them. They just know the rules and how to keep me medically safe. He also said going back to UC Davis in the spring was unlikely but that I could hang out at home afterward. Dad shockingly exclaimed it would be a miracle if I even come home in a couple months because a week or so ago he was told I would be dead or at least in the hospital for about 2 years! He was so supportive and comforting, but he said he couldn't come get me until I was medically OK. He did say transferring would likely be necessary soon, because although insurance is still covering my hospital stay, it's not covering Dr. Schack and her program because it is separate.

After the huge morning ordeal and my phone call, I walked out of my room raging and started pushing the elevator to go down. The nurses had to pull me away and then even called security when I protested going back to my room. After security forced me in, I paced back and forth in my room until snack was brought 10 minutes later. Ugh! Thankfully, it was only a bowl of melon. I still threw all of it in the trash and covered it with some papers. My sitter wasn't going to tell and completely agreed that everyone was being awful to me today. I love her! Unfortunately, my nurse didn't believe I finished my fruit that fast. My sitter did cover for me and said I finished it, but my nurse and 2 other nurses could see through our lies and eventually found all the fruit! Thankfully, they did order me a new bowl of fruit as opposed to supplement after I pleaded with them. I really hope my sitter didn't get in trouble. As soon as they found the fruit, I started repeating to them that it wasn't my sitter's fault, but I still know it won't be good news for her.

Gosh, I have been in such a fury since breakfast, and my ears are full of pressure. I got extremely pissed because I wanted to go outside but had to get an echo of my heart. I was yelling, "I don't look anorexic anymore" the entire time and couldn't calm down. My nurse wouldn't allow me to push back my soon-approaching lunch even 15 minutes, despite the fact that I had just finished eating because snack and breakfast were late. I just kept screaming and screaming as if in a trance.

The sweet little lady who was doing my echocardiogram told me, "You look great and not anorexic anymore because of all the food."

I stopped screaming for a second and stared at her in disbelief. It only set me off even more. I spent the whole test being rude and pestering the lady about what she said and demanding her to hurry up. For the record, most people do think I look anorexic…even I do sometimes…yet there are those few now who say I only look thin and not anorexic. I know they intend it as a compliment, but it triggers me and causes my mind to go crazy with anger, fear, and…I don't even know. I really hope that all my yelling didn't affect the echo.

Lunch was fried tofu, rice, and carrots, but my sitter threw out all the rice and tofu for me. She flushed it down the toilet when no one was really around. Wow, I can't believe she did that for me even after getting caught earlier! My nurse and another nurse did a surprise room search and found all my gum! Oh, this day just sucks!

I am still in a rage, and it's dark outside now. This has been the most dramatic and worst day yet. I feel so unsettled and like my mind is going crazy! New rules: only 2 utensils of each, no blankets, no trash cans, security when I go outside now, no gift shop, no peeling my own fruit or potatoes, butter or oil is now part of my meal plan, no more Rice Krispies cereal, and random room searches. I hate life right now! At least my ears could stop being so full of pressure. Geez!

Somehow I ended up getting through the night despite my troubles. Valerie is going to be my sitter throughout the night. She started out OK, but now that she won't throw away food for me anymore and tattles on me when I hide food, I hate her! Then again maybe I only hate her so much because she watches me ridiculously closely and therefore I can't get away with even having 1 extra piece of gum. I guess that's a good thing though, right?

I took my last walk around the halls and had such terrible ear pressure. I need to go to bed. The albumin injection I got through my IV earlier has really helped the swelling in my feet. I'm also going to get an injection in the morning, which is supposed to make me pee like crazy and flush out the rest of the extra fluid. Oh well, I just can't think anymore. Good night!

March 2, 2009

I finished my snack, left my room, and started walking around the halls. The nurses tried to stop me, and I refused. They let me pace around for 10 minutes before they finally stopped me and said they would get the AMA papers and that Dr. Schack said I could sign myself out. Ah! They trapped me! Of course, Dr. Schack knows I would never sign myself out because I would have no place to go because my parents wouldn't get me. I reluctantly went back to my room. Another doctor came in to look at my swollen legs. Even one of the nurses said my legs were painful to look at, so I hope that means I really am skinnier than I look. Anyway the doctor looked at my legs—shocked at how swollen they were—and told me that it could be corrected in a few days with more albumin injections. She said it was a protein issue and that I needed a lot more. One interesting thing was that she thought my ear pressure could be a fluid issue. It actually makes sense because when it first started happening at UC Davis I was way overloaded on fluid and then after a few weeks at Torrance it went away for a few days and then came right back as soon as my legs got swollen. I wonder if that is the reason.

I am so annoyed because my nurse keeps saying how she is going to address all the "issues" she thinks I'm having with Dr. Schack, such as, "must wait 1 hour after meals to walk, I will supplement you for leaving 1 centimeter amount of green on your cantaloupe, I will consult her about mealtimes, document the sugar-free tea, and will be talking to Dr. Schack about them." Ah! I hate it! She doesn't even know how I like taking my meds. Lunch was gross. It was chicken, carrots, a baked potato, and olive oil. It was awful because I had Valerie breathing down my neck and watching my every twitch. On top of that, I had my nurse being a smartass and sarcastically threatening me if I didn't finish every little crumb as if she were Dr. Schack's best friend. I did get through the meal. I tried to hide some olive oil in a cup, but Valerie caught me. I had to drink the last few drops. That is just not right.

March 3, 2009

I had a good sleep last night. It is getting so much easier to move around more, which makes for a much better sleep. I can turn on my sides now and stand up out of bed on my own. This morning I opened my eyes to the one and only Valerie! Oh well. She really is a nice person, though a lot of things she does are a bit unreasonable. It is really ED who dislikes her, not Brittany, because she doesn't allow me to get away with anything. I guess in reality the more ED hates a person the better they really are. The fact that she follows every order really just makes her one of the better sitters, I suppose.

Lisa is my nurse today, and though I love her the most, I was prepared for a strict day. The first piece of devastating news for the morning was that Dr. Schack is only allowing me to have 6 ice cups versus my previous 11 cups! I now have to start drinking my remaining water in liquid form! I threw a fit and demanded Lisa call Dr. Schack to confirm this news was true. Lisa wasn't happy with me, but she did call. Sure enough, Dr. Schack wasn't going to change her mind. Lisa also made me change my mealtimes back a bit earlier and decided it was time to type up an updated treatment plan for me. She said I only get to brush my teeth 3 times a day now and took all my cups I've been hoarding from the bathroom. I know everyone is only trying to help, but I feel I have no control. Maybe that's the lesson—that I need to let go completely. I hate change.

I saw Dr. Schack. Our meeting was one big tantrum from me. I screamed just to send me to UCLA. Frankly, that is all I can really remember of the day. Dr. Schack showed me a letter sent to her from my UC Davis doctor stating the requirements for my return to college. I almost fainted. It basically said I need to be 102 pounds wearing only a gown and that I have to maintain that weight for 2 consecutive months before I could return. It also nicely explained that based on my current medical info, I could not return for spring quarter. Just kill me now!

March 5, 2009

I had an absolutely awful sleep. My mind is going absolutely nuts and I'm hot, uncomfortable, restless, and just overwhelmed. I also had to go pee a million times last night. I have one of my favorite sitters this morning. Hooray! I got to see my weight, and it is 67.2 pounds. That's good, I guess! Breakfast was 1 piece of gluten-free bread (so I thought), jelly, 2 hard-boiled eggs, and cantaloupe. I did well because my sitter watches me like a hawk, but I actually want to do well when I am with her because I respect and like her. I didn't even feel so guilty about completing my breakfast.

All too quickly lunch arrived, and this was a bad time! I had fish, crackers, and 1 baked potato. Right when I began eating, Dr. Schack and 2 dietitians barged into my room to tell me that there would be some changes to my plan. Dr. Schack said I would now have to eat gluten and would not be getting gluten-free choices. She also said I would no longer get to have my 6 ice cups and that I had to mix ½ a cup of ice with ½ a cup of water. (Little does she know I've been able to get away with straight ice by fooling the nurses.)

I am in pure shock! Gluten! I can't freaking believe it! I was just getting used to finishing 100 percent of my meals without cheating, and now she is not only taking my precious ice cups away but also putting gluten as an OK item for the dietitians to plan. Great, now I will have to be supplementing all the time.

Honestly, a big part of me wants to eat gluten-containing foods again because there are some really yummy and low-calorie foods like popcorn, low-calorie bread, 100-calorie pack snacks, cereal, and fiber tortillas. However, people have freaked me out by saying if I eat gluten it will be stored in my body and that if I ate gluten-free I would lose more weight. It also bothers me that my mom kind of believes in the no-gluten diet. Also, being gluten-free makes having an ED easier (as Dr. Schack probably knows), but I don't care! I just can't handle eating gluten right now! I also have to change my whole fluid schedule I had carefully planned out as well as my ice cups! I guess life is really trying to teach me to let go and allow myself to be OK with not controlling everything. I know there has to be a greater plan. As bad as things seem, I know everything happens for a reason.

May 7, 2009

Ugh! I keep repeating myself and have been since I was first admitted here. I don't know if it is just OCD or if it's my short-term memory since I really can't remember that I just asked for the same thing 1 minute earlier. Maybe I am just impatient? I don't know, but I think some of it has to do with the fact that I feel so vulnerable and am not used to depending on others. I fear I will be forgotten about or that someone won't be there to take care of my needs and me. It's frightening knowing you can't care for yourself and your basic needs even if it is as simple as wanting some Post-It notes. Ugh, and it's been decided that I am going to be transferring to UCLA's eating disorder program soon instead of going straight home. I just hate life right now!

March 8, 2009

My parents came to visit me before I leave for UCLA in 2 days. I had a really nice talk with Dad. He said I still look really sick and would probably be at UCLA for a while. He did mention that my stay would be shorter at UCLA versus staying here, though I can't see why, so I think he may be making that up. He told me the fastest way to get discharged is to follow the program 100 percent and prove I am ready and capable of going home. He also told me to consider taking some medication to help. Dad smiled and said he still can't believe I am going to live and told me just to keep thinking about playing tennis and Yosemite and my favorite beach trip when things get tough. He also choked out that he was planning my funeral and was going to bury me in Yosemite.

March 9, 2009

I met with Dr. Schack, and I still have to eat 2,000 calories. My potassium is only 3.7 even with a large amount of supplements, my hemoglobin is 10.8, my white blood cells are 2.7, but my liver is fabulous! She's worried about my arms and hands because I have a lot of muscle atrophy, or wasting, and you can almost see an indent on my underarm. It is so weird-looking! She told me to go to UCLA with an open mind and to commit to at least 2 weeks, which is the longest I declared I would stay. She told me my liver enzyme numbers were the highest ever recorded in someone who recovered and that I am still very sick. She also stated that if I slip back even a little, the refeeding syndrome would be way worse. She is so proud of me and wants me to keep going forward. She exclaimed that I am the most remarkable case and she is rooting for me. She smirked and said my feistiness is going to help me recover and that she knows a big part of me does want to recover. I gave her a huge, sobbing hug and thanked her.

14

TrappED

"Focus on all the positives. You have arms, legs, a voice, choices, can breathe, smile, and most importantly, create your own happiness." ~Britt

March 11, 2009

Today is my second day at the UCLA adult eating disorder hospital program, and I am not happy! My room, however, is amazing. It's almost like a luxury hotel room! It has a chair, whiteboard, private bathroom, shower, TV, and tons of shelf space...I guess people stay quite a while sometimes. The staff went through my luggage. We are not allowed to have gum, alcohol mouthwash, our own meds, mints, cell phone, and all glass items must stay locked in a cupboard in my room. We are only allowed to use electric razors. I even had to get my face cream sent to be checked and approved by the pharmacy. We aren't allowed to have ice, only 2 peppers and 1 salt packet per meal, and we can only brush our teeth twice a day. Dang...I don't know how I'll live with eating and not being able to brush my teeth afterward to get rid of the taste of food. Maybe Torrance wasn't so bad after all!

Lunch was brought to my room, which was chicken, strawberries, green beans, and rice. I was on 500-calorie meals and 150-calorie snacks, but I wanted smaller meals and bigger snacks, so they cut my lunch in half. I still wasn't able to finish in the 30 minutes allowed, and they even gave me an extra 15 minutes. I didn't drink the Ensure

Plus supplement either. They don't tube you here and apparently hardly ever kick anyone out. However, they do expect you to be here voluntarily since it is an adult unit.

The rest of my admission day is just one big blur. I am so over-whelmed, and it does not help that I am having the worst ear pressure again. I haven't made a good impression so far because I have basically told everyone flat out I don't want to be here and want to go home. Also, because of my fuzzy memory and because I am not able to think clearly when my ears clog (85 percent of the day), I am repeat-ing myself when I talk and have been asking nurses for things over and over again because my mind just can't seem to be able to store or process what I just asked for. I'm sure the nurses are sick of all my requests. I guess I am being difficult, yet honestly I feel that I truly can't stop myself...my brain simply gets too overwhelmed and crazy.

I always have a bunch of requests before each meal: must take meds, hot tea, hot black coffee, plastic utensils, salts and peppers, meal heated, napkins, etc. Perhaps part of the reason I keep asking for so much and repeating myself is because I can't physically do it for myself right now and so I feel really scared, vulnerable, and worried I won't be heard or taken care of. I fear I will be left alone and forgotten, which is a deep-down fear I have carried since before I can remember. In addition, because my mind is so fuzzy and unable to process things, I am talking like a 5 year old a lot of the time. Honestly, I have the IQ of a 5 year old almost all day. Wow, I think I'm repeating myself even when I journal.

Dr. Willis, who is the psychiatrist and doctor here, thankfully said my memory and ability to think more clearly should come back with time and better nutrition.

What happened to the straight-A honor student who got a partial academic scholarship to UC Davis and was accepted into their honor program? What happened to the girl everyone used to call wise beyond her years, more mature than 40 year olds, and so grown up? What about the elite athlete, happy girl, and talented horseback rider? Or was I ever even happy? Everything has just happened so fast that I almost don't believe it! It even took me 5 minutes just to remember my dog Kodi's name. I just can't explain the feeling. It even takes me a few seconds to recognize my parents and process that I know them and have known them for a long time. I am just so delayed in all respects. I am also having a hard time remembering nurses' names.

The scariest part is that my memory, mind, and thinking for the most part don't seem to be improving. Maybe part of the reason is because of the ear pressure. When my ears do unclog, I am able to talk in a more adult voice, process thoughts, and stay calm. I can actually remember things. At least I am still able to journal, so maybe I am not that hopeless. I am so scared and just want to be out of danger.

I feel vulnerable here because they aren't giving me fluid limits, labs aren't drawn every day, and if I don't finish a meal and refuse supplement they let it go for now. I almost feel in a way that there is a bit too much freedom in regards to how close they are monitoring my physical state. It makes me fear I am going to die.

I am on 1:1 monitoring because of a fall risk. Last night I took a late shower and took a good look at myself in the mirror before I got in. I was shocked. I look worse than airbrushed pictures of anorexics on the Internet. I couldn't believe it. At Torrance I was able to see my chest and a bit of my back but not much else. The mirror here is longer, and I am able to see a little lower than my butt—and whoa! Every bone sticks out—and just wow. I honestly can hardly comprehend that it is me I am staring at. I remember only just 1 year ago and even just months ago when I wished my legs were skinnier or wondered how certain girls could get so skinny but I couldn't. I was so upset that my body wouldn't be stick thin, especially my legs, but, oh boy, was I wrong. I have C. diff again, the colon infection. I have to be on contact isolation, and the nurses have to wear gowns when they come into my room. I am back on the vancomycin antibiotic. This sucks!

There are 5 other girls here right now. They all seem awesome. I haven't had much time to be with them though because I'm not doing groups since I've been feeling ill. I also haven't been able to eat with them because my eating rituals and behaviors are very triggering. I agree…they are quite triggering, I guess. Why am I having so much trouble? Is it because I know I can refuse supplement and because I know they don't use tubes?

My dinner with the group last night was such a disaster. I got the default meal because I didn't have time to order, and it was this tofu vegetable oriental dish. Well, after complaining that I needed plastic utensils instead of silverware, I began to dissect my meal. I spent the whole time saying, "I can't eat this, the sauce has gluten, too many calories," and on and on. I eventually took a piece of vegetable on my fork and rolled it around my napkin compulsively until I thought I had finally gotten enough sauce off.

This process continued until I had no clean napkin left. Then I simply refused the rest. Yeah . . . so that's why I am eating alone in my room now.

I am proud of myself for a few things though: being OK with having no gum, no ice cups, and none of my powdered teas, eating on their schedule and therefore earlier, understanding that rules are rules here and there is no bargaining, and eating tons of gluten!

With the way meal and snack planning here works, I could potentially get away with eating almost gluten-free, but that might mean having to choose a higher-calorie option. I have been living off Cheerios and am going to have saltine crackers today. I am also eating challenge foods and ones that have high fructose corn syrup; they taste amazing. I would even try some cookies or chips if I knew they were fewer calories than another choice. I guess I truly care more about the number of calories than whether or not the food I'm eating is considered "healthy" or not.

I am also proud of myself for not throwing out all of my Nutri-Grain bar last night when my sitter, who was very unaware and not used to our program, left me alone for a good 10 to 15 minutes! I hid ¼ of my bar, but that's better than all of it. I am also proud of myself for acknowledging the fact that I look awful and sick and need to gain weight. So, why is taking in calories and weight gain so hard and scary? I mean, I look at my body and think, "Shit! I need to eat 10,000 calories because I look so scary." Yet, I am so used to and comfortable restricting that I am still unable to act on my thoughts.

It's a step in the right direction, though, and hopefully my thoughts will soon turn into actions. Lastly, I'm proud of myself for trying to adjust to the new staff and rules. I seem to be able to accept things a bit easier and not be so obsessive over things like fluid amount, nurse needs, doctor questions, and even journaling.

The way meal and snack planning works is by exchanges, which I have never really heard of until now. The exchange system sucks sometimes, and it rocks other times. This is how it works: 1 grain = 80 calories, 1 fruit = 60 calories, 1 fat = 50 calories, 1 protein = 55 calories, 1 dairy = 90 calories, 1 veggie = 25 calories, ½ grain = 1 fat, and 1 fruit = 1 fat. So, for example, certain cereals = 1 grain, and Cheerios are 1. Now, 1 box of Cheerios is 60 calories, and it equals 1 grain. However, Total cereal is 1 grain, but it has 100 calories. In short, the exchange system is not determined by exact calories. The food item you choose may be a little less than an exchange or a little more.

I have been driving my already-starved brain crazy trying to come up with the lowest calorie combinations for all the exchanges. It took me days and a few hours, but I finally made all my snacks for the week. How it works for snacks is you choose acceptable options from a sheet of paper, and then you will have that same snack every other day. For example, I have snack 3 times a day, and I have to come up with 6 different snack combinations. There has to be 6 different fat sources, and for now my snacks have to equal plus or minus 30 calories of 300. So, I've been obsessively trying to come up with 6 different combinations that all equal 270 calories.

I haven't been forced to go to groups except for Melanie's group. She is like the head clinical nurse or something like that. It wasn't necessarily the best group. All the other patients were complaining how they feel neglected by the staff and that they are not sick enough compared to the new very sick and thin patient who came. They also complained how they feel that same certain patient is getting all the staff's attention and concern because she is so thin. Basically, they felt jealous and like they didn't need or deserve to be at UCLA compared to this new person. They didn't say my name or say this directly to me, yet it was plainly obvious they meant me but didn't want to hurt my feelings. Should I take this as a compliment? I'm used to being on their end and feeling the same way and comparing myself to new patients who are thinner and sicker than I. I'm the one who always felt I didn't belong or that I'm not that sick. I'm not used to actually being that sick and the thin one. Is it really possible I'm that ill? How on Earth did I get so low and bad off?

I always wished I could be and look like those anorexics I saw pictures of, thinking it was so glamorous and then being so mad that I couldn't seem to look that way. Yet, here I am...one of the worst and most severe anorexics! How did this happen? I am just still in shock this is actually happening to me. I had everything going for me! Now I can hardly remember my dog's name or recognize people. Oh, what I would give to be able to think clearly again and at least be able to sit up from the damn toilet by myself! Yeah, so glamorous, right? I am getting stronger each day but barely. The amazing thing is that after all these years and as bad off as I am, I can still get my life back and still have my amazing family, brains, UC Davis, tennis, and horses back. I just need to go for it and gain weight! How can something so simple be so impossible?

March 14, 2009

Erg! My meals just got increased from 350 calories to 400 calories. I really want to finish all of my meals, but I'm engaging in tons of time-consuming rituals. Besides, I'm not even sure I want to commit to this program knowing I could be here 3 months. I would almost rather get kicked out, but I know that's not an option. I thankfully got the best 2 nurses here. Each patient is assigned 2 main nurses for the day shifts and evenings are random. I have Nina for 3 days of the week and Ellie the other 3 and then someone random the remaining day of the week. Nina is awesome; she answers all my questions calmly and gives me time to breathe and feel better.

March 15, 2009

Late last night around 10:00 or 10:30, I called Mom and had the worst talk ever! I really was hoping to hear how proud she is of me for going through this, but all she could do was say "fuck!" and how I "ruined the family" and how she has no sympathy for me, that it's my fault I'm stuck here, and that she doesn't even know her own daughter anymore. She said my life is now just hospitals and giving her my lists. She basically doesn't have much hope in me changing and says she isn't proud of my hard work here because it's my fault I'm here to begin with. I can't tell you how much she hurt my feelings. She doesn't know how much guilt and shame I hold inside and how bad I feel. Just because I don't display it outwardly, it's tearing me up internally. I guess she was just ticked off because I told her I wanted to come home in a month and because I wanted to review and add 2 items to the list of things I need. We finally ended our conversation, and all the other patients were complaining because of the noise.

Today, Nina and I came up with a treatment plan to help me: only 1 utensil of each per meal, meds brought 15 minutes early, 4 hot packs every 24 hours, 1 warm blanket each shift and 3 at night, nurse asks me ahead of time about what utensils, drinks, etc. I will need at each meal and snack, if there are 90 calories or fewer left after time's up then I get an additional 5 minutes to finish, I get to cut all my food except fruit, plastic utensils only, and 1 napkin per meal.

Dr. Mitchell, the director of this program, came to see me briefly today and basically said I need to complete 100 percent of my food or I will be discharged this week. He also stated that he wants me to take some meds to help me sleep (because of last night). But I don't have any trouble sleeping, and I just choose not to. He then left and said he would talk to me tomorrow during treatment planning, which occurs 1 day a week where the doctors, therapists, and whole team discusses each patient for 10 to 15 minutes. I am so scared because if I get discharged I am screwed and will be homeless and dead because I am physically so not OK. I did better with lunch and snack and plan to do well on dinner and my last snack, but I am so scared. No, I don't want to be here, but I can't get discharged because of my fragile health and parents who won't pick me up. I am not feeling too well right now. I am tired, and my brain is all fuzzy, but I will try my best to make a brief list of a few things.

Accomplishments: I can get in and out of bed and turn more easily. My walking is much more stable, and I can bend down to the floor even though it's still hard. I can sit up from the toilet by myself if I use the railings. I'm not even thinking about or craving gum or diet soda. I am not going crazy with over-consuming fluids. I am eating on their time schedule without wanting it to be later. I am eating gluten and liking it. I am able to trust my parents with getting the rest of my belongings from my dorm room at Davis.

Overwhelming: UC Davis, summer school, classes, and registration. UC Davis housing for fall. UC Davis readmission. I haven't called or talked to my friends in months. I haven't had a chance to fill my parents in on UCLA details. Having to stay here at least 3 months and be 95 pounds. My health and fear of dying. My ear pressure, brain fog, memory loss, and shortness of breath. Discharge, home life, parents' expectations and requirements. My future. Length of stay here. Not being able to walk or move on my own. Weight gain. Calories. Gluten. Girls (patients) probably don't like me because of a bad first impression. When will I feel normal again? Low heart rate. Give up ED and identity for the past 7 years.

Goals: Recover. Discharged. Eat 100 percent. Eat meals with the girls and attend all groups. Brain fog to go away. Don't obsess over lists. Don't freak out if I miss a day of journaling. Relax and trust God. Get stronger and be able to move and walk around by myself and feel safe. Prove to parents and UCLA I am a changed person. Accept weight gain and being here awhile. Don't try to hide food. Go to bed by 10:00 p.m. Wake up by 7:00 in the morning. Be able to think, focus, and remember clearly again. Call friends. Do more artwork. Play tennis and ride horses again. Trust treatment team. Get myself out of danger zone. Don't think of weight loss until stronger. Have full function of left hand and thumb again. Be able to get into bed without help, and do daily tasks alone. Be able to bend down easier and put on socks by myself. Have normal blood work. Be able to run again. Relax. Compete in tennis and horses again. Take more acting classes. Listen to iPod and music more often. Find a job. Have calm and positive parent talks. Hike Half Dome in Yosemite with Dad. Go to Dewey Beach again. Go to In-N-Out Burger with Dad. Publish a book of my journals. Chase a tornado. Don't obsess over appearance and calories. Change someone's life.

March 16, 2009

A lot happened today. My weight this morning was 65.6 pounds, so I lost about 2 pounds since Thursday. It could just be water and fluid shifting, yet I also had a full enough bladder when I got weighed.

I met with Stella, my therapist here, for about 30 minutes, and we actually had a great talk! I started from childhood and gave her brief details up to my senior year of high school, but then she ran out of time. She has a stern, no-bullshit type personality, yet I still like her and think we could do good work. I like how she listened to me. After I met with her and before my next snack came, the moment of anticipation . . . meeting the whole treatment team with Dr. Mitchell! I was so nervous, yet it went OK enough, I think and hope. Dr. Mitchell reiterated our previous conversation that I need to start completing 100 percent of my meals, whether it is by food or having to take supplement, in the next few days or else I will be discharged. I then asked a few questions.

> Me: Can I not get a calorie increase until I am consistently eating 100 percent of my meals since I was only eating 50 to 70 percent?
>
> Dr. Mitchell: Yes, that is a very intelligent observation, and that will be fine, but not for long.
>
> Me: Can we adjust my calories so that I am gaining 1 to 2 pounds per week versus 2 to 4 pounds? That way I feel I am choosing recovery versus it being done to me.
>
> Dr. Mitchell: Yes, that will be fine for a few weeks, but then we will have to do more so that you aren't here forever.

[Meanwhile Stella keeps shaking her head as we talk and then says, "No more noncompliant days and weight gain rate must go up." Oh, what a bitch!]

Me: Is it possible for me to leave after 1 month or so if I really show I am committed and am doing well in the program?

Dr. Mitchell: We can reevaluate then, but I will still give you the same answer and that is that it won't be our recommendation. I want to leave you with this question that you won't be able to answer yet. What will and could your life be like without ED and how could things be better or different?

The meeting ended there. Dr. Mitchell is very smart, and I really like him, but I don't like how he talks as if he knows me. For example, he thinks just because I'm "so severe in my ED" that I will definitely need a long, intensive recovery program. I want him to understand I am not like all the other cases and can do it on my own. I will prove him wrong! Erg! How will I get out of here?

Snack was OK, but I left ½ of my ice cream. Dr. Mitchell said if I didn't eat 100 percent today, I wouldn't be kicked out, but that I need to show huge improvement and then be completing 100 percent shortly. I guess I took advantage of him saying that and purposefully didn't quite finish dinner either, but I did eat 100 percent of my last snack. Ugh, but why do I always have to push the limits into oblivion before surrendering?

I have to remember to go over some specifications and things I want added to my treatment plan: only my fruit gets to be cut by staff and nothing else, coffee at snacks and ½ cup of extra hot water with my coffee or cocoa to pour into in case my original cup gets cold, 2 tea bags allowed, may have an empty cup for milk as long as cereal gets eaten with milk, 2-minute pee break during meals (anxiety), allow me to open all saltine packets, cocoa package, tea bags, etc., knife allowed with eggs, mouthwash, and no meals until 15 minutes after I take my meds, even if it means starting the meal late. I hope all of these requests get approved!

March 17, 2009

Dinner was interesting. I had my usual meal. My nurse tonight (well, since 3:30) is Janet. She is a sweet Asian lady who is thankfully very forgiving and I guess a bit inattentive maybe? When she first brought my coffee and hot water for my cocoa, it wasn't filled to the top, so I freaked out and begged for more hot water, and she said later. My sitter for dinner didn't say a word the whole meal. To make a long story short, I basically spent dinner yelling for more water because I needed more for my cocoa, but Janet closed the doors to the dining room because I was disrupting other patients. To get to the point, I finally got more hot water, and Janet sat with me the rest of the meal instead of my sitter. Janet gave me extra time and I was able to hide my 2 egg yolks, 2 olives, and at least 2/3 of my cocoa packet. She thought I ate 100 percent! I'm feeling way better and more alive, yet I'm still feeling overwhelmed and crazy, as if in a panic... it's ED... and me freaking out about how to hide and reduce calories. Ah! Just eat the damn food!

March 18, 2009

I stayed up until almost midnight last night and had a restless sleep. Today hasn't been so great. I woke up feeling OK and then got the surprise of my therapist, Stella, eating and sitting with me for breakfast. I was so nervous! I had the plain yogurt today, and to my disappointment, it was 100 calories, not 90. I didn't finish my meal or Ensure Plus, but Stella was sweet enough and just kind of sat there and stared.

During lunch, I managed to hide and arrange my food in a way to make it look as though I ate everything, but 1 egg and 4 saltines, when really I left 6 saltines and 1 ½ of my eggs. I'm so nervous because treatment planning is today at 3:00 p.m. My morning snack didn't go well either. I had 4 ounces of cottage cheese (though it looked like 6 ounces), 3 almonds, 4 ounces of nonfat milk, and Cheerios. I had the milk and Cheerios, and I guess maybe 1/3 of the cottage cheese, but I tried to make it look like I had ½, so hopefully my nurse agreed.

Melanie came into my room and sat down to talk to me. She said she spoke to my therapist at Torrance (uh-oh!) and said that I was drinking supplement and completing meals in 30 minutes there. Melanie said either I complete 100 percent of my meals or else I'm out. She was really kind but absolutely serious. She said I can't stay here and get sicker and that if I do eat 100 percent, I should feel much better in a few days. Those were kind of the words I needed to hear. I guess you could say I was testing how long I could get away with not eating 100 percent before they put their foot down. But that's over now. It's kind of nice now to feel as though I, in a way, *have to*. It is less for my brain to think about. I won't have to think about which food items I won't eat. Now I just have to focus on what I can get away with hiding (just kidding!).

Dr. Mitchell spoke to me briefly and essentially said I must eat 100 percent of my calories and take the medication Seroquel. He said I had to take it because I'm up so late at night and he was firm. I don't know how, but with my thinking skills in overdrive, I was able to convince him to change his mind about the med (whew!). There was no way I was going to take a med that could possibly cause me to gain weight or change my relationship with ED. I told him to allow me to complete 100 percent of my calories consistently, get better nutrition, and be able to think more clearly first. Then, once I'm in a healthier state, I would love to talk about taking the med. He thankfully agreed. I need to be sure to be in bed by 10:30 p.m., though!

March 20, 2009

I am so much stronger and alive today and am getting so close to normal even at 64 pounds! Every day I feel more like a 20 year old versus an 80 year old with Alzheimer's. I had process group with Melanie and the other patients. I responded to one of the girl's comments and shared how I could actually see and feel ED next to me as a separate being/presence, and Melanie said that was very special and rare.

Dr. Mitchell walked by my room later.

Dr. Mitchell: Hey, Britt!

Me: Wait, I have a question! I wanted to say that—

Dr. Mitchell: What's the question?

Me: OK, I have to say something.

Dr. Mitchell: OK, what is your statement?

Me: I am doing 100 percent, I am going to recover, and I will be amazing and am going to leave in 1 month.

Dr. Mitchell: Not my recommendation.

Oh well, he enjoyed my spunk and said he would talk to me tomorrow. I am going to prove him wrong and make him never forget me.

March 21, 2009

I'm proud of myself for eating in the dayroom with the other girls, and they gave me great support. I also tried hard to work on my eating rituals, which was difficult, but I did quite well. I ended up having to stuff my face at the end of the meal to finish in the 30 minutes, but I did do it. The only downside to eating in the dayroom with other girls is that it's nearly impossible to hide food or get away with rituals. If the staff doesn't catch you, then one of the girls will and that would be very embarrassing. Oh well, ED doesn't like that, but Brittany knows this is the next step toward recovery and getting life back, as uncomfortable as it is to not restrict. It's like I get a high and feeling of reassurance and relief if I can restrict and get away with fewer calories (even if it is only 1 almond). Too bad, ED! It's now time to shift into recovery mode even if it means faking it right now. It is not only my best chance at getting discharged sooner but also my best chance at convincing and tricking myself into true recovery. It's like the saying, "Even if you're not happy, smile anyway and you will soon feel happier" or, of course, "Fake it 'til you make it!" It's so nice feeling part of the program now.

I'm sitting in the dayroom journaling, and everything seems easier and less obsessive now. I don't even feel as obsessive about being informed of the meal ahead of time because now I just go with everyone else. I even feel less compulsion about lists, journaling, needs, etc. It's incredible! Thank goodness it's the weekend and there are no groups, except maybe Dr. Mitchell's, so I can relax a bit. Snack was OK, I guess. I ate in the dayroom, but I am the only one who has an a.m. snack, so I ate alone with a nurse. I did eat 100 percent, but I was able to get away with a little less butter. I'm hoping Melanie approves all the orders I want when she comes later.

Well, lunch came, and it was difficult but not overly terrible. I ate 100 percent again, but I did manage to hide a small piece of egg yolk under my eggshell. My ear pressure got pretty bad afterward. It kind of makes sense because I've been so much more active now that I am leaving my room and sitting in a chair without feet support. The table is a different height, which makes it more difficult for me. In addition, I am dealing with a whole new environment, rules, audience, scenery, etc. I know it sounds crazy, but just walking into a new room and seeing a different picture is really hard for me and very surreal. It's almost as if my brain can't fully take in the new scene. It is very overwhelming and exhausting. It's draining just looking around and seeing a different view than just the inside of my room. I feel like a brand-new baby opening its eyes for the first time. Dinner was hard, but I got through it. I was able to hide 2 egg yolk pieces under my eggshells again. Oh, stop being happy, ED!

March 22, 2009

I am up early this morning! OK, so 7:25 a.m. isn't that early, but it's earlier for me. I'm already dressed and ready for the day and feel amazing so far. I am actually hungry. Yikes! That's hard for me to admit. Breakfast went well. I was able to spill some yogurt and hide probably what's equal to 1 of the margarine tubs. I have been going through all my old notes from Davis and Torrance. I found a quote Dr. Schack gave me, which is very special to me: "I take pride in what I've accomplished and look forward to what I intend to achieve."

Lunch wasn't that bad…I'm getting good at hiding egg yolk pieces under the eggshells, but my nurse caught me today. I went outside with the other patients on the patio for the first time. It was also the first time I actually walked outside instead of sitting in a wheelchair since Del Amo. It was so weird because I had to walk up a slight uphill slope to get to the patio, and I swear I thought I would fall over . . . it felt as if I were climbing Mount Everest.

15

Tricks of the Trade

March 23, 2009

I feel amazing and strong this morning, both mentally and physically. I am now able to get in and out of bed and stand up to walk to the
bathroom at night without having to be pulled up or without having
to raise the head of the hospital type bed. Today was weigh day, and
I weighed 68 pounds on the dot! That's about 3 pounds higher since

Thursday. However, I purposely held in my pee and drank about 6 ounces of water beforehand...so who knows. I'm probably closer to 67 pounds, but I wouldn't want them to know that!

I met with Stella briefly and shared with her the orders I wanted. She said they could be discussed soon. As patients, we are allowed to give our therapists orders or requests, such as "I want to be off dayroom status" or "I want to be able to have a pass to see a friend." Then, the therapist will discuss the orders at treatment planning once a week, and they will sometimes get approved. Let's just say I get quite carried away with my orders, and I spend almost all of our therapy sessions just talking and reviewing the orders I want rather than doing actual therapy.

A girl came to take a tour of UCLA's program today. She's 21 years old, very nice, and pretty. She's quite thin, but I still win the contest of thinnest, thank goodness. I had a good meeting with Dr. Willis and got him to approve my orders to get the next open room with a couch, to have more Lactaid, to have as much water as I want between meals and snacks and to get Duoderms for my feet because they hurt. I love Dr. Willis because he is so easygoing, and though he is clearly brilliant, he is not strict and writes orders too easily, I think.

March 24, 2009

It's my 2-week anniversary today. I had a wonderful sleep and got up around 7:20 a.m. today. It's so nice to be able to get ready in the morning so much faster. Tasks that used to take forever are now secondary. I remember when not long ago it was a huge effort just to have to put on lotion, underwear, or socks. Now look at me!

Lunch was good...I was able to hide almost 1 whole egg yolk because a student nurse was sitting with us. I was actually able to have normal conversations during and after lunch because I feel normal and like my old self. My ability to think and remember is also great today. It's a flippin' miracle!

March 25, 2009

Lunch came, and I was able to ½ of my egg yolk in the salsa container and ½ in my tea bag. I also was able to hide 1 graham cracker square. But Tina finished watching our table for Janet, and when I was done she checked everything! Tina is one of the staff who never takes her eyes off me to an unnatural extent. Anyway, she only found the yolk in the salsa container, but because it was squished, she estimated the ½ yolk to be a whole yolk and brought me Ensure Plus equal to 60 calories! I refused and pleaded it was ½ a yolk, but she wouldn't change her mind. Melanie then came over and told me to drink the Ensure Plus or sign the AMA papers she held in her hand! I begged and reasoned in every way that it was ½ a yolk. Melanie said it might have been, but that's the risk I run for squishing food and that it is then up to the nurses to decide the amount. I would have kept arguing but she was already pissed about my supplement refusal at snack the past 2 nights. She was completely serious and ready to kick me out, so I reluctantly drank the 60 calories. OK, so I honestly did hide 1 whole yolk and 30 calories' worth of graham cracker, but I was still pissed because she only found the ½ yolk and guessed it to be 1 yolk. I don't like people telling me I'm wrong. Anyway, that put a dent in my wonderful morning, and today is treatment planning for me also—yikes!

To make matters worse, Stella came to tell me I was getting a 150-calorie increase today, even after the fact that I had gained the maximum amount of weight for 1 week in only 3 days. That's not even ½ of a week! I just sobbed and sobbed. Soon thereafter, I got called into treatment planning for 10 minutes with Dr. Mitchell, Melanie, Stella, and a bunch of other people I didn't really recognize. It definitely didn't go in my favor, but at least no one yelled at me or seemed mad or anything. Dr. Mitchell explained that the 4-pound weight gain was fluid because I was dehydrated and that my calories must keep increasing despite the weight gain because I'm not on enough currently to continue gaining. I am now on 2,250 calories, though with my sneaky exchange system combinations, I am able to make it less. Then again, I should know that I would just keep getting increases no matter what my baseline calories are. Really, I'm only fooling myself.

The dietitian came to see me, and we did my menus together. I am now having 450-calorie meals versus 400 calories to accommodate the 150-calorie increase. But, of course, I'm a master of the exchange system now and was able to work it out so that most of my meals equal 350 calories even with them meeting all my exchanges in theory. I'm pissed, though, because I can tell I have gained quite a bit of weight. OK, maybe only a few pounds, but it's still a change and a change that happened too quickly for my liking.

March 26, 2009

My weight this morning is 70.2 pounds, which is an increase of 2 pounds since Monday and 6 pounds since last Thursday. I did, however, have 10 ounces of water in me and had to go pee. Stella told me I'm still on eyesight and that there have been no changes for me. Great, so I still have no private time for even a minute. She also left our therapy session early because I kept repeating myself and didn't want to talk about anything else besides the orders I wanted and my discharge date. One of the group leaders here said I look better and more alive today, which pissed me off. Too much weight gain!

Process group was amazing. I was so mature and insightful in the advice I offered that I got a huge round of applause from the girls and Melanie! I am proud of myself for eating all my food without hiding it. I am really going to try to continue. I am going to earn the trust of this place and prove I can leave here in 1 month. But I am so pissed because I have to be on contact isolation my whole stay here because I tested positive for C. diff, that stomach infection. Apparently it's a common infection to catch in hospitals, especially when you are on antibiotics and have a weakened immune system, which was certainly the case for me and still is. I suppose. Anyway, this basically means I have to wear a clean hospital gown every time I leave my room, have to sit in a designated chair for all meals, can't sit on any couches or chairs without a sheet on top of it, and can't really touch anything.

And if I do touch something, it either has to be vigorously cleaned or it just becomes mine. I hate this!

March 28, 2009

Triggers: Not being allowed to micro-cut food, not being allowed to eat yogurt and cereal with a fork, have to pour all of my yogurt into my cereal and not just 1/2, people rushing me or interrupting me, only 12 ounces of fluid at meals, no reheating foods, comparing myself to patients, having to make changes such as meal variety, orders being written and then not communicated to me, nurses staring at me obsessively when I eat, my belongings having to be locked up, having to be with someone all day (constant eyesight), being told constantly to sit down, having to eat at a separate table from the girls because of my triggering eating behaviors, having to finish every last crumb of food, nurses all having different rules/requirements/expectations of me, lack of consistency from nurses, theme... trust.

April 2, 2009

Breakfast was good. Right afterward, the dietician came not only to fill out menus with me but also to tell me I have a calorie increase and that my meals now have to be 550 calories versus 500. What? That's a total of 2,550 calories including my three 300-calorie snacks! I was really upset, yet I didn't complain... OK, maybe because I had thankfully only gained 0.7 pounds since Monday with a full bladder for a weight of 72 pounds exactly. The dietician told me I would need even another increase if I didn't gain 1.3 pounds by next Monday for a total of 2 pounds in 1 week, but Dr. Mitchell said 1 to 2 pounds would be fine! Hmm... anyway, this is where I am beyond proud and happy with myself. I completed 4 whole days' worth of menus with the increase, and I did it calmly, quickly, and actually quite pleasantly. In addition, I obviously didn't have any of my calculated combos readily available because I had made them all for 500 calories. I trusted the dietician and just went with the flow when she told me to pick a grain or said I needed this many more calories, etc. I even have some yummy but scary foods coming, like chips. I'm sure I could

151

have gotten away with fewer calories had I been able to prepare, but I just went with it and surrendered. It was such a relief. Everyone was shocked and amazed at how well I did. Stella even popped by for a second, and when she heard of how well I did she gave me a huge thumbs-up from the nurses' station.

April 4, 2009

I've been in a sad mood today...very emotional, tearful, and restless. I think a lot of it has to do with exhaustion because I haven't been sleeping nearly enough hours at night. I have been thinking a lot about my 1 ½ quarters at UC Davis and how painful, scary, and obsessive they were. Pure madness really. All those trips to farmers' market just to search for the tiniest fruits possible and then buying $100 worth of them. Eating the same thing every day at the same time and in the same ritualistic manner. All those days spent compulsively walking and exercising, spending my days at markets, and then paying a cab to take me to even more markets. The panic attacks, staying up all night until the sun came up, sleeping 2 hours before heading off to class, pacing around the dorm hallways, avoiding people, hardly being able to stand up, the trips to the health center, not being able to make it to the barn anymore, the constant excuses as to why I couldn't ever join anyone at parties, avoiding gluten, taking my heart rate at night, scared shitless as it dropped into the 30's, always being so cold that I would turn the heater on so high I think it broke my printer, wearing layers upon layers of clothes, spending all night on ED online chat groups and diet websites, practically overdosing on Pepto-Bismol and Lactaid, having so much artificial sweetener in a day I had a plan as to how to reduce it, and the utter and chilling loneliness. I have been having random crying spells throughout the day as I think back to those days and how ED abused me so badly. When I think about my life at Davis, I feel darkness all over and a trapped soul. I must remember that there has to be a greater plan for me...otherwise why am I still alive when I should have died?

April 5, 2009

Mom and my aunt came to visit me today, and I absolutely broke down sobbing in my mom's arms. We had an incredible visit. How could I have ever not accepted or loved myself? I am so special and clearly meant to be here for some big purpose because I have been given a changed life and a second chance. Well... I'm hoping I have changed. Mom and I had an interesting talk about what things need to change in general with ED treatment centers, media, staff, Internet, rules, schools, and treatment strategies. I have such great insight and would love to speak at conferences and someday to the world about how better to beat this disease. I mean, if I, of all people, could get as consumed and as sick as I did, even with all the good things going for me, then absolutely anyone can. On the flip side, if I can get out of it, then I really believe there is hope for everyone.

April 6, 2009

My weight is 74 pounds. That's an increase of 3 pounds in 1 week, and I only had to gain 0.3 pounds today not to get an increase, but I gained 2.2 pounds! OK, so I had a full bladder and 8 ounces of water, but still! I had a therapy session with Mom and Stella right after my weigh-in. It overall went really well, except for the part where Stella said realistically I would probably be here another 3 to 4 months. She also said that the treatment team will want me to reach my target weight range or at least very close to it. I almost choked with shock and could feel myself wanting to explode inside. I am beyond upset about having to entertain a stay any longer than a few weeks! I will just have to prove to Stella and everyone else that I am ready, even if it means forcing myself to eliminate my rituals and fake my progress. I, however, won't be faking my recovery because that is something I truly want, unlike all the years before.

April 8, 2009

I met with the dietitian briefly just to give her my menus and new snacks. She mentioned that she and Melanie were going to talk to me about not allowing write-ins anymore. You see, I've been getting the privilege of being able to write in certain foods, such as plain chicken, even when it wasn't offered that particular day, instead of choosing one of the main entrées offered on the menu. Well, now she is telling me I have to choose an entrée exactly as it is! She is crazy really. I mean, how could she possibly tell me such a thing? I will never do it! I am having a hard enough time just eating the chicken plain, so there is no way I could eat it with all the extra sauce and mixtures. I'm so nervous for tomorrow!

After dinner tonight I really wanted to take a shower, lie in bed, and forget about my dayroom status, but Melanie wouldn't change the order yet. I got really upset and marched into my room and laid down on my bed crying and refusing to leave. Melanie came in and told me I needed to go to the dayroom and that I wasn't complying. I said no and told her how unfair the situation was. I kept crying, and Melanie stood in my room perfectly still. I then reached for the phone in my room and called Mom with Melanie still in the room. I was really upset and told Mom what was going on. She felt really bad and wanted to talk to Stella or Melanie. Mom then put Dad on the phone, who told me he was sorry but that I needed to comply. I eventually calmed down and went back to the dayroom for snack, which went fine.

April 9, 2009

My weight today is 74.5 pounds. Well, I actually asked the nurse to weigh me again in a few minutes because I wanted to go back to my room to water load some more, despite my bladder about to explode from all the water I already drank. I got back on the scale 5 minutes later and was 74.9 pounds, which I told the nurse to record instead of the first one so I would be less likely to get a calorie increase. The team had my treatment planning today, and I'm still on dayroom status. Stella at least wrote an order that will allow me to have one hour to myself between dinner and the last snack, which I'm happy about.

Lunch was great in my mind, but I had a bit of a hard time eating according to their absurd rules. I had yogurt, fruit, 10 olives, 10 celery sticks, Italian dressing, and 2 graham cracker packets. It's one of my favorite meals, but I did too much spreading and spilling of the yogurt, although what was left on my plate was less than a replaceable amount, Ellie still said I must try harder. She said even though it wasn't much, it all adds up at the end of the day. The other nurse who was sitting at the table told me I was eating inappropriately and in a very triggering manner. I didn't think I did *that* badly, but I do understand how it could be triggering. I honestly was trying to spread around as many calories as possible; I just didn't want to be caught.

I must kill ED! Yes, I must kill my past identity. As much as I hate ED, this monster has still been a part of me for so long that I think I will have to go through somewhat of a grieving period, such as when someone dies: denial, anger, bargaining, grief, and acceptance. Right now I feel as though I'm bouncing back and forth between anger and grief…possibly some acceptance but I am not sure. The good thing is that I am getting close to acceptance, and I feel that's why ED's fighting so hard to hang on. The fact that things are getting tougher and more uncomfortable is a sign to me that I am doing the hard work and am really looking my fears in the face. Just like my mom always tells me, "You have to do the hard work before it gets easier," and on the other side, "Things are usually the hardest right before you are about to make a big change."

I can look at my situation in 2 ways. I can either get scared and obsess over the new rules and scary foods and paralyze myself, or I can step up to the challenge and take steps forward toward life and shock the heck out of everyone. I love a challenge and am shifting my mind to look at ED as one. I am going to rise to the occasion to fight and overcome this. It's the same in that I always played tennis or rode horses better when someone was challenging me because it intensified my focus and concentration. I love more than anything in the world to prove people wrong and to do the impossible. I get easily bored unless I am challenged and end up not working as hard or reaching my full potential. I need to look at this situation as something exciting to take away the boredom and as something that will intensify my focus and help me reach my full potential. I have to channel my energy down a different path.

One of the girls who got discharged a few weeks ago came and visited us tonight. I love her so much…she really kept me in line and motivated me. While I was talking with her, I got really excited about something, and she started crying. I was really confused.

She said, "Baby girl, I saw life in your eyes!" She was honestly in tears and told me to keep it up and that I look much better but still too skinny. I know it's a compliment, but it's still hard to hear people saying I look better. You could be the skinniest person in the world but doing better and therefore people can breathe a sigh of relief, or you could be thin but hardly eating and people will worry nonstop about you. Well then, it's not about the weight but about the sense of attention and being noticed. I must keep the reality of the situation in mind, and "I won't back down." Tom Petty, ha-ha! This is Dr. Mitchell's favorite song to share with us.

I spent all night until 1:30 a.m. trying to plan out the exact foods and combos I would choose for each meal during the week. I was able to sneak a copy of Friday to Monday's menu during a miscommunication last week with the dietician. I need to stop obsessing!

My heart is racing, and I don't feel well. It's probably the 16 ounces of coffee I snuck after snack when the staff left the room unsupervised. Worrying about calorie combinations is not helping. I need to let go and trust in the weight gain and foods. I really need to ask for support, vent, and accept recovery. Besides, if I gain extra weight, then I won't get a calorie increase. If I keep eating my meal combos, I could eventually start losing weight and would then get a calorie increase, which would be even worse because then I would have to redo all my snacks and meal combos again. Yet, now that I have a copy of the menu for the next few days, I am going to go crazy again. The same exact menu repeats itself every week, so I could technically plan ahead with meal combos for the new entrées I am now required to choose from. Ugh, geez! Why can't I just let go and sleep?

April 11, 2009

Dad arrived! It was an amazing visit, and I don't remember ever being so happy and excited. We talked about everything from how the Torrance doctors were preparing my family for my funeral to our ideas on eating disorders, treatment centers, strategies, and structure. We spent time crying with joy with how excited we both are for the future. One nice thing is that Dad understands and agrees that UCLA isn't the best program for me and that the program has some downfalls. He told me I look way better, and I was actually able to take that as a compliment. He still said I am much skinnier than everyone here and that I still take his breath away when he looks at me. He also said that it could be a few more weeks before I can come home but that he would almost certainly bring me home earlier than recommended and before I reach 90 pounds. He told me all I must do is comply, gain weight, and prove to the team and staff that I am ready. Yeah, simple enough, right?

April 12, 2009

Snack went well in my mind, but my yogurt had 1/2 inch of liquid on top to such an extent that I thought it was past the expiration date. Well, it wasn't, and the nurse watching my table said I had to stir all the liquid in. I did after complaining, but I guess I was a bit too aggressive and a bit of the juice spilled out. The nurse then got up and went into the snack room to talk to Ellie, I believe, and then came back. I finished my snack perfectly from there, but afterward Ellie told me I would now have to eat dinner alone and that she was supposed to supplement me for the yogurt juice but forgot. What the heck? How can you replace a millimeter of yogurt juice, and why would that result in having to eat dinner alone? Personally, my biggest problem with this program is that I feel very picked on and singled out. It seems as if everyone is just waiting for me to screw up so they can punish me. I am not blaming them completely; clearly, I do plenty of inappropriate things to get myself in trouble. However, I hardly ever get any praise, only criticism, and therefore I feel unwilling to want to please them. In addition, I truly believe I am often too harshly criticized. I really did eat my snack appropriately from any standpoint, and yet I am now going to have to eat dinner alone. Even when the other girls struggle, that would never be their punishment. Then again, the staff is usually too busy watching me to notice the off-limit behaviors the other patients are doing...but I notice.

16

Singled Out, Shut In

"Life works in mysterious ways, and I believe one of the biggest challenges and successes is to let go and let it be." ~Britt

April 13, 2009

I got up to get weighed and unfortunately wasn't able to water load beforehand. I did still have a full bladder as I usually do, and I hid a small mouthwash bottle in my underwear. Still, I only weighed 74.6 pounds, which is a 0.4-pound increase since Monday, yet a 0.3-pound decrease since Thursday. Erg! I am so frustrated because I feel as though my body definitely has gained weight, but the scale just isn't showing it because I didn't water load and because I've lost fluid through diarrhea. Shit! No pun intended!

I'm trying hard to look at all the unfair events and all my overwhelming feelings and turn them into positives. I need to keep encouraging and sticking up for myself rather than feeling sorry for myself and giving up.

I sat with my 2 favorite girls here for dinner, and we were having a nice time. Janet was sitting with us (she is now stricter than anyone with me as far as eating every last drop—what the heck changed?). Well, I had 2 Italian dressing packets on my tray, and, of course, I always seem to get a bit too much on my hands and then wipe them on my napkin. Janet is well aware of this and watches me like a hawk. She kept telling me to "get all the oil" and "stop wiping it on the lettuce leaf." I also had fruit and ice cream. I mixed them together, which Janet said no to even though the last time I mixed the 2 together I was sitting with Melanie, who thought that was fine! After some commotion, another nurse took my tray and made me eat alone!

After I finished, Janet brought over the lettuce leaf and plastic wrapper that was covering my veggies that had some dressing on it and showed it to the nurse, who finished sitting with me. The 2 of them went into the snack room, and then the nurse came out with supplement. She said she and Janet decided I had left about the equivalent to 1 whole dressing. Bullshit! I even offered to lick the lettuce before my time was up, and she still said no. I definitely refused supplement this time and was willing to deal with the potential consequences because I really felt the situation was unfair. I feel so attacked and picked on or at least singled out. As much as I hate getting in trouble and as much as I am sometimes in denial about my behaviors, I do have a good idea on some level as to when I deserve a consequence. Oftentimes, though, such as this time, I feel it gets blown way out of proportion.

April 14, 2009

Shift change came, and, unfortunately, Yasmine was working and, of course, is my nurse again. She is so strict with me and seems particularly to dislike me. I had 15 celery sticks and 15 carrot sticks in my upcoming snack, but the celery hadn't arrived yet from the kitchen. I was definitely panicked knowing my celery was late. I consciously tried extra hard to stay calm and simply wanted a few minutes to discuss my snack with Yasmine in case my celery didn't come in time. To make a long story short, Yasmine got upset at me, though I was able to eat my snack with the rest of the group. Yasmine sat alone with me during my last extra 5 minutes and told me how awful I behaved and how she "never wanted to work with me again" and that she would "make sure Stella heard about this." Heard about what? I was absolutely beside myself with disbelief because, honestly, I felt I acted appropriately and very nicely. I don't see how she could even twist such a scenario. I feel so targeted because other patients were freaking out about their snacks and obsessing, yet none of them ever seem to get in trouble or yelled at.

April 15, 2009

I met with Stella this morning and gave her a list of some orders, privileges, and changes I wanted. One thing she keeps saying that pisses me off is that "your parents aren't going to take you home until the treatment team says you're ready." I don't know why exactly; it just bothers me that she thinks my parents are basically slaves to their decisions. She also said I would probably have to be close to my target range before I will be discharged. Oh, shut up!

April 16, 2009

This morning was weigh day...oh joy! Thankfully, I was able to drink 16 ounces (I think) of water before getting weighed because the staff accidently left my bathroom unlocked. I weighed 77.3 pounds, which is a weight gain of 2.9 pounds since Monday. Yes, it's easy to blame it on the calorie increase, yet I really must remember how much fluid can affect weight. I also wasn't able to water load last Monday, so that makes a big difference. I guess I should be happy because the quicker I gain weight, the quicker I can go home. Think of it this way...the weight gain is unavoidable, so I might as well let go, enjoy food, and let it happen. I think sometimes I falsely believe that if I gain slowly enough, my parents will eventually just say I can come home because it's been long enough. I have to refocus and remember that I am done with ED and that I want to be athletic, healthy, energetic, and alive again. Yeah, alive...to truly be able to live without regret for sabotaging myself and health. Alive: still in existence, force, or operation. Still active in competition with a chance of victory. Marked by alertness or briskness. Yeah, that sort of alive is what I want because if I'm not alive then I guess I'm dead. If I'm not dead, I solely exist, and that has to be the hardest place to live in.

I'm so pissed. I was informed I have to eliminate almost all my celery, carrot, and Cheerio snacks. It was hell! All my snacks are now between 285 and 350 calories verses the 270 to 350 calories. I didn't even get to choose the order of them. Oh well, it's still better than the 400 calories they are supposed to be.

It was so difficult, and my brain kept circling with obsessive worry. It was honestly a good thing, though. Yes, it was very challenging, yet also a good test for me as far as letting go and trusting the team. I mean, yeah, my mind was going crazy, but I realize that I needed this challenge to continue my progress forward against ED. If it were easy, I would never improve or have victories. Success is always so much sweeter when the journey to reach it takes a lot of courage and hard work. It's like a tennis tournament. It's nice to win the tournament, but winning the tournament is always so much more satisfying if the matches you won were against highly ranked players who really test your ability verses an easy opponent who doesn't cause any stress. It sucks that I have an eating disorder, and beating it is not going to be easy. But each day I don't give in I learn something about me, about life, about other people, and I am better for it. There is always good in something no matter how bad it seems. It's sometimes hard to realize the good when you're dwelling on the bad, but it is there. Take this quote, for instance: "Anyone can give up; it's the easiest thing in the world to do. But to hold it together when everyone else would understand if you fell apart, that's true strength." —Anonymous

I had another frustrating talk with my parents. I asked Mom again when I could possibly come home, which always pushes her buttons. I also got really upset when Dad said I have to be around 90 pounds to come home and that he didn't know for sure, but it could be another 45 days here at the minimum. What? He said he would take me home before I reached 90 pounds. Sure, that's better than the treatment team's 3 months, but still.

ED went crazy with fear of weight gain, and Brittany went crazy with homesickness and frustration. I must think of the positives waiting for me once I eventually do get to leave and achieve my recovery. After that stressful phone call, I spent a long time rearranging the order of my snacks so that the ones with the higher amount of calories are also on the same day as my snacks with the lowest amount of calories. I don't even know if I will be able to change the order, though. Can everyone just scream "Ah!" with me?

April 19, 2009

After breakfast I had a bit of an interesting talk with Dr. Willis. He said it was reported that I drink too much water and am drinking my water before I even take my meds, which is complete bullshit! I honestly need a lot of water to swallow my pills. I'm convinced it's the night nurse who reported that because when she brings me my meds in the morning, she only brings me like 4 ounces of water at the most and expects me to swallow 4 huge pills. Ugh, whatever!

One thing Dr. Willis said really concerned me, I guess you could say. He said it was also reported that I was going into empty rooms to drink water, which is so completely not even possibly true. This is crazy scary! What is wrong with this place? I have honestly no idea how this came up. It worries me that either the night staff is very clueless and confused, or I really did go into a room? Yet, I know that's false because I would have remembered and so would the freaking night staff who saw it. I mean, really now? Could it have been that one night my bathroom was locked and the nurse had no keys so she told me to use the empty room's bathroom? Who knows? Anyway, Dr. Willis seemed a bit confused and completely dropped that topic, so I'm guessing it wasn't actually documented or anything.

I'm scared to meet with Stella and Mom tomorrow because of how this weekend's been going. It was so odd because last night I was awakened at 3:00 a.m. to do a surprise weigh-in (which Stella apparently ordered), but why at 3:00 in the morning? I've been doing so well, and now I feel as though this weekend is going to blow it for me. I hate walking on edge. I almost feel as if it's not OK to show you're struggling because then you get no privileges. At this rate I will never get my bathroom unlocked. I've been listening to a lot of music lately, and it has been flooding me with emotions, memories, tears, and smiles. Each song seems to have a distinct memory attached to it.

I want to share my progress now. I've kept a list of all the new things I accomplish as they come, and it's pretty long now! I am eating 100 percent. I am eating foods with gluten. I can flush the toilet easily by myself now, can get in and out of bed alone, and can take comfortable showers without feeling wobbly. I'm off 1:1 monitoring. I'm learning to accept being here. I've learned the exchange system. I'm allowing the dietician to deal with calories and combos (sort of). My ear pressure is gone. I can walk much more comfortably and normally. I can sit in a chair all day long without putting my feet up or having to lie down. I can stand up from the toilet without using the railings in the bathroom. I can dress myself. I am eating in the dayroom. I can jog in place. I am able to sneeze, blow my nose, and cough with more force. I am not as cold anymore. My labs are all in the normal range, I'm not orthostatic, and my heart rate isn't too low. My OCD is lessening, and I'm able to think more clearly. I am able to sit and lie in random positions without feeling weak or out of breath. I don't cut my food in to microscopic pieces anymore (sort of). I am standing up for myself, getting more patient, and taking supplement most times. I'm able to eat with Stella, and I'm choosing foods from the menu. I can lift my backpack up, and I can almost get up from the ground from a sitting position without help. I'm not staring at my body as much in the mirror. I'm trying to look at weight gain and calorie increases as positives, and I'm still alive and fighting against ED!

April 20, 2009

Today has been all right so far. It's Monday, and you know what that means. Weigh day! Yippee! Ha-ha, not! Well, my bathroom was, of course, locked, so I couldn't get any water from the sink, yet I had filled 2 cups of water the previous night during my 1 hour of free time in my room and hid them behind all my towels and washcloths on my shelf. So anyway, I drank 2 cups of water before getting weighed and hadn't peed yet. When I first stepped on the scale, it read 77 pounds exactly, but then I stepped off and tried again, and it read 77.7 pounds. I told the nurse to use the higher weight, which she did, so now my weekly weight gain is 3.4 pounds. Thankfully, I didn't gain too much from Thursday to today.

Afterward, I waited nervously for Mom to arrive for our 9:00 a.m. therapy session, but she was about 15 minutes late due to traffic. The longer I waited, the more I was filled with tears, anger, and memories. It made me feel not important enough for her to plan well in advance that there might be traffic. It also brought back painful memories of when she was always late to pick me up from school and tennis and how I would wait... sometimes alone in the dark for her, worried that something bad had happened to her, and/or someone would attack or kidnap me. Finally she arrived, and we ended up having a very emotional and good session. Stella definitely challenged how well I have been complying with the program and the strength of my ED. I had some good screams at Mom also and a lot of stuffed-up anger to release.

Snack was all right, and I managed to hide 3 cashews. I know I shouldn't feel good about that, yet I'm so angry at this program and uncomfortable with the weight gain that it's like me saying fuck you to the program and myself, too, because I'm only hurting myself.

Dr. Willis came in to see me before dinner, and we had a really fun time talking. He absolutely cracks me up! He asked me if I partied and if I ever "puffed the magic dragon." Ha-ha! I couldn't control my laughter. He is very relaxed yet uptight at the same time, and hearing him say that in his Japanese accent was just hilarious and totally out of character for him.

Here are some notes I took during a movie about "radical acceptance:"

- Radical = complete and total.
- Pain and nonacceptance = suffering.
- Radical acceptance is when you stop fighting reality.
- Accept mistakes and facts and move on; stop denying reality.
- Accept that every event has a cause.
- Everything should be as it is versus everything shouldn't be this way.
- Reality has causes whether they are good or bad.
- Radical acceptance is not always knowing the cause but accepting that there is one.

- People say, "Should not have happened," when they don't accept things.
- Practice saying, "Everything should be as it is."
- Acceptance is all about the word "yes!"
- Accept that life can be worth living, even if painful events exist.
- Accept that you can build a life worth living.
- If you want to change something, you have to accept it first.
- Acceptance is required to make a change.
- The more pain, the harder the acceptance.
- When you keep asking "Why?" you are not accepting.
- Choice, commitment, repeat.
- Acceptance does not equal approval.

April 22, 2009

After lunch, Stella took me down to the gift shop so I could buy a journal. I even got to walk to the shop without a wheelchair! On our way back up, we started talking, and we somehow got on the subject of going to UCLA's partial program when I was discharged. She mentioned she would buy me a journal when I go there, and I told her there was no way I would be going, that I didn't plan to stay here much longer, and that I would go home with my parents. She kind of laughed at me and then we said goodbye. The next thing I know I'm sitting in group, and Stella knocks on the door and tells me to come out.

She then says to me, "I just called your dad and told him that if you left in 2 weeks you would die. I told him how much you've been struggling, and he is not bringing you home anytime soon."

I literally almost fainted with disbelief. After somewhat collecting myself, I stormed off to my room to grab the phone and call my dad. A nursing meeting was going on in the dayroom with Melanie, and Stella made me sit on a chair outside of my room so that I could be seen through the glass wall to the dayroom. I absolutely cussed my brains out at her and told her to fuck off. I was screaming at the top of my lungs! When I got Dad on the phone, he was absolutely speechless with anger and disappointment. What exactly did Stella say? I was hysterical on the phone with him, trying somehow to convince him that I wasn't doing that badly and that he could still take me home in 2 weeks, but he was definitely not buying that and hung up.

I called Mom next, and she was angrier than I could possibly imagine! She pretty much said there is no way I'm coming home anytime soon now and that she didn't want to speak to me ever again. What the heck? Dad was still beaten down with immense disbelief and sadness. I don't think I've ever heard him so lifeless and hopeless. He told me it was now up to Mom and me to work out my treatment and future plans.

Finally, Mom and I were able to have a more mature conversation. I apologized repeatedly for everything and admitted to how big a mistake I made and how messed up I had been acting. She told me she was very proud of me for knowing how it feels to make a mistake and for trying to fix it. This is the first time I've really made a mistake unintentionally and am really feeling the pain and emotions associated with it. Before, I would make mistakes (such as going to the gym), yet I knew on some level I was making the mistake and that it would have consequences, but I made the mistake anyway. This time I made the mistake of not being completely honest with my parents with how I was doing here and the mistake of not trying harder to comply with the program. I wish I could have done the whole situation over. However, sometimes you don't get a second chance to redo something, but that doesn't mean you can't fix the situation or repair it.

April 23, 2009

Weigh day! I had about 3 cups of water before getting weighed from the cups I had hidden again. I weighed 78.9 pounds. I'm happy because I'm pretty sure it's enough not to get a calorie increase, yet I'm also mad because part of me wants the number to go down or at least stay the same. I feel so out of control seeing my weight go up without intentionally wanting it to.

I called my parents. That was a terrible disaster again. They mainly told me there was no way I was coming home in 2 weeks and that Dad wants me at 100 pounds. No way! Mom then asked to talk to my nurse, Nina. Nina talked to her for about 15 minutes. I heard Nina telling her that I was eating 100 percent but that I was also struggling with spilling things. I talked to Mom afterward, and she basically said, "Shape up and thanks for at least eating your food. Goodbye. Don't call me for a while."

After process group, I sat down with Dr. Mitchell and Melanie. Dr. Mitchell told me I needed to sign some papers giving my parents and them permission to talk and that I either needed to commit for a few more months or else be discharged from the program. I was actually very calm and poised despite their authoritative presence...not that I seem to have a problem with authority or anything. Geez. Dr. Mitchell said he would like to sit down with my parents and educate them about the nature of ED and the stages of recovery. I said no, and Melanie told me people pay big bucks to talk to Dr. Mitchell about that and so I should reconsider, but I still wasn't sure. I am too afraid he will convince them that I still need many more months of treatment when I feel I could be ready for life in only a few days or weeks.

April 24, 2009

It was time for process group, but I had to pee real fast beforehand, so Melanie just told me I couldn't come. Really, now? Well, that was fine by me because I wanted to journal anyway, but it was still kind of rude. I am so exhausted and tired. I had a very unpleasant surprise before afternoon snack. Melanie and the dietician came up to me with my menus for Saturday, Sunday, and Monday and told me I pretty much had to change them all.

Melanie said I could only have 5 olives a day and that I had to pick my entrées exactly as-is off the menu. She also informed me that I had to start using more fats, breads, and even different breakfasts. I absolutely went crazy and was in a world of rage and fear. I think I even slipped in a *fuck you*. How embarrassing! I hate you, ED!

April 27, 2009

Weigh day...yuck! I had to go pee so bad so I let out about 2/3 of my bladder, but then I drank 3 cups of my hidden water. I weighed in at 80.9 pounds, which is an increase of exactly 2 pounds from Thursday and 3.2 pounds since last Monday. No, I'm not happy with that number or my body and its changing appearance, but at least I won't get a calorie increase, which would probably only be more stressful because I would have to change my menus again as well.

April 30, 2009

Ah! Today has been the worst ever! I woke up and went pee because my bladder was about to explode, but I tried to hold at least some of it in because I was about to get weighed. I then drank the 3 cups of water I had hidden behind my towels and washcloths and then made my way down the hall to the scale. I was 81.4 pounds, so I guess that's a 0.5-pound weight gain since Monday, which, thankfully, I think is just enough not to get a calorie increase.

It was a pretty low-key day until Melanie and I had a decent talk in my room. As she was leaving, she looked over at my clear bin of drawers and I guess saw something I couldn't have. Then she looked through my drawers and found all my empty cups! I don't even know why I was collecting them since I only use the ones behind my towels, but she then left and came back with 2 other nurses to do a room search. Shit! They went through everything, including all my clothing one by one. I was sobbing as they turned my room upside down. My heart sank with guilt when Melanie found the 6 cups of water hidden behind my towels and washcloths. They also found my 5 pieces of gum, tea, and mouthwashes. They even took my stress balls! I was panicked with fear, guilt, anger, and frustration. I had to get a surprise weight and was 82.5 pounds. Melanie eventually left, and no orders were written for passes with my dad this weekend. I'm now back on dayroom status as well as my bathroom being locked 24-7 besides my 20 minutes to shower.

May 1, 2009

I feel so out of control and almost wild. Dad finally arrived for a weekend visit. I absolutely held on to him and sobbed harder than I think I ever had. I begged him to take me home. He wasn't too pleased with my whining. Melanie and Nina came into my room with us about 5 minutes later. Melanie told Dad about the cups with water, the teas, the mouthwash, and the rest. Dad was indeed pissed, but I guess it didn't go terribly awful.

May 4, 2009

This morning was weigh day, and I guess you could say it wasn't the greatest. I weighed 79.5 pounds with no water. I did put the cell phone in my underwear, though...gosh, that's so damn disturbing! Basically, I lost 1.4 pounds since last Monday. However, I'm almost positive it's all because I didn't water load. The dietician came to me to tell me I needed a calorie increase. I told her I'm refusing it until I see what my weight does on Monday because I feel it's all due to water.

Afterward I met with a substitute therapist while Stella is away. I did not like her or how she was approaching my disease and me. She pretty much flat out told me I would die if I left here early. She really made me feel vulnerable, as if I couldn't make it, and that I was in severe danger. My confidence was shattered after our session, especially because I was already feeling threatened. I asked Melanie about possibly getting off dayroom status and having a pass with my parents this weekend. She gave me a huge look of disgust and looked at me as if I were crazy and said, "No way!" as if I should have already known. What the heck? Anyway, I will have to wait until Wednesday I guess for the whole dayroom situation to be discussed.

Melanie also told me I needed a calorie increase. I told her no way until at least Thursday after weigh day to see what my weight was doing because of all the fluid decreases. She never really gave me an answer or response, so I'm praying like crazy that I won't get one at least until after I get weighed on Thursday.

May 5, 2009

I feel so vulnerable, unsafe, angry, and belittled here. I feel no one ever tells me what I'm doing right. I just want to be given the chance to show that I can be responsible with more freedom and privileges. We are almost playing tug-of-war. I will be more responsible but only if I get the freedom first. They are telling me to show I am responsible and then I can have the freedom eventually. But I'm impatient and think they should just trust me. I must keep going though...even if it means faking it just to get out.

May 6, 2009

I talked to my nurse, Ellie, after breakfast and expressed to her how it seemed no one ever told me good job for the things I am doing right and that all I ever hear is criticism. She said she would try to praise me more for the things I am doing well with. I told her that if I heard people saying good job more or praising me for progress that it would make me want to repeat that behavior. It's just as I learned in psychology...positive reinforcement leads to the intended behavior being repeated such as in the experiment with Pavlov's dog.

Mom and I had a long and great talk on the phone. We both mentioned that no one ever says anything positive or nice and that they only focus on the negatives or mistakes. I opened up to her about how I never hear praise and feel picked on and stereotyped by anorexia. I feel as if Melanie and Dr. Mitchell are somehow trying to convince my parents and me that we need them, as if I'm some sort of experiment. Even Dad said last night that he couldn't believe Melanie is still talking about the cup situation and that he feels she owes both of us an apology. Mom completely agrees with my feelings and is very unhappy with everyone at this program and says she isn't taking any crap from Melanie.

Well, Ellie informed me that for the next 24 hours I had to eat in my room—despite doing perfect at lunch. What? I then got called into treatment planning and had a good talk with Dr. Mitchell but no changed orders. Huh? He said he also talked to my insurance a few hours earlier and said they asked if I was taking medication. Dr. Mitchell told them I refused, and my insurance apparently said that was a problem and that they would question whether or not they still wanted to cover me. What? That can't be right. Coverage shouldn't be based on medication use. Dr. Mitchell also said that if I was that angry and unhappy with the program I should leave and come back later if I wanted to. Anyway, it wasn't the best treatment planning, obviously. I then had snack in my room with Yasmine and did perfect.

However, I did spend 2 minutes (Yasmine timed it) saying my celery was way too big (which it honestly was). So, she documented my snack not being appropriate and that my 24 hours in my room would now have to restart at dinner. What a freaking bitch! I still finished all of my snack and within the time allowed. She is absolutely beyond unreasonable to the point where it's laughable!

May 7, 2009

I went to bed much earlier last night yet woke up this morning so tired. I had my blood drawn and then had to go get weighed. The nurse found the phone I hid in my underwear but thankfully didn't tell (I think?). I weighed 79.7 pounds, but I tried weighing myself again 10 times. It kept reading 79.6 pounds and 79.7 pounds. I begged the nurse to write down that I weighed 80 pounds so that it would be an increase of 0.5 pounds from Monday, but she wouldn't. I ate perfectly at breakfast in my room, but I definitely caused a lot of commotion beforehand. I called Mom after snack. She told me I couldn't come home, and I flipped out! I was in a bad mood when lunch arrived and was in no mind-set to follow rules. I was so angry and distracted, and I was being noncompliant.

After lunch, I refused to leave my room, but eventually I did. I was so furious that I called my mom's good friend and told her to tell my mom I was signing myself out since Mom wouldn't speak to me. I was half-joking, but her friend took it seriously. I told her I would sleep on the streets if I had to. Then Dr. Mitchell came to talk to me. He told me I was being discharged tomorrow and that my mom is coming to pick me up. What the heck? Yes! He told me that he is very fond of me and welcomes me back when I'm ready. He even asked for my number so he could check up on me.

I refused my creamers at snack... I mean, why eat everything when I know I'm going home anyway? I refused my margarine, dressing, and creamer at dinner, but I was in my room anyway, so it wasn't as if I was triggering anyone.

I had an incident with showering tonight. I was supposed to have a staff member with me, but no one was available, so I just took one alone. Melanie absolutely flipped out! Come on, I'm going home tomorrow, why does she even care? She was ready to call security though. I refused my cream cheese at evening snack, of course. I then called Mom. Apparently Dr. Mitchell told her about the cell phone in my underpants as well as putting beanbags in my clothes.

Seriously? The phone may be true, but the beanbag story is 100 percent incorrect.

17

Home and Horrible

"Change, for the better, will never let you down if
you can have the courage to trust the unknown."
~Britt

May 12, 2009

I have been home now since Friday. Things have definitely been
rocky and quite good. Mom and my aunt picked me up in the afternoon after having a long talk with Dr. Willis. Melanie hardly even
said hello to my mom when she came. Mom talked to Nina for a
while, which was a bit uncomfortable for me because I didn't want
Mom to find out any more details of my difficult stay. We eventually
walked out those locked doors.

It was a very rough drive home. I was pissed because the first
thing out of my mom's mouth when we got into the car was about
the snack she had put together for me. She even went so far as to tell
me how many calories were in the snack. I got so mad. This is the
new me! I wanted to make decisions for myself, and the last thing
I wanted to discuss was calories. We fought awhile, and it was not
pleasant at all. Mom was furious and beside herself that I wouldn't
happily eat all the almonds, apples, and protein bars she brought. I
mean, I will admit the reason I was so mad was because I wanted to
get away with fewer calories and choose different foods, but I still
hated that it was her main focus. I know my mom is only terrified for
me and wants to protect me, yet it was the complete opposite of what

I had planned as the start of my new life. I chose to have the Balance Bar, almonds, and apple. I was so angry because Mom said my snack had to be 400 calories, which is technically correct; however, because of the exchanges system, I had been able to get away with 290-calorie snacks at most.

I ended up hiding the almonds in my purse not thinking anything of it. When we stopped at Starbucks, Mom said she wanted to check my purse because she didn't believe I had actually eaten all of my Balance Bar (which I had). She found all of the almonds, and, gosh, that was the end of me! She was so upset, and never had I seen my aunt get so angry in all of my life. I was speechless and absolutely in shock at how the afternoon had gone. As a punishment, I had to eat the entire second bar, which was 190 calories, so my snack turned out to be 500 calories versus 400! We eventually cooled off a bit, and the rest of the drive was better. We arrived home, had a late dinner, and went to bed.

Today I convinced Mom to let me go shopping alone in Ralphs while she waited for me in Starbucks. Disaster! Mom told me not to buy any drinks or diet things, but when I went in there I just couldn't resist the urge to buy some diet soda and sugar-free flavored water. I also spent about 15 minutes longer than I was supposed to. Mom was so mad at me when she saw what I bought. I also got 2 boxes of Splenda, some Lipton tea powders, and a bunch of gum. Because of all the drama, we were late to pick up Dad from the airport, but I still hadn't had lunch. Mom angrily drove me to Subway and sent me in while she furiously sat in the car. When I came out she had gone through all my grocery bags and told me I was to return every-thing. She would absolutely not stop screaming at me no matter how much I apologized. It was definitely the worst time to go greet and pick up Dad. It was so nice to see him, though. I told him what had happened. It was a rough car ride home as Dad talked about how I had to be 115 pounds and get weighed by him. I kind of brushed it off, but inside I was freaking out. I hate requirements.

Dinner was hard. Dad made BBQ chicken, a high-calorie rice pilaf, and zucchini. He served all our plates and told me I had to eat everything. He gave me so much chicken!

Right after dinner, Dad brought out the pink cookies. These are soft, doughy cookies with pink frosting and sprinkles on top, and they are 180 calories each. He told me I had to eat 1. I had a hard time but eventually choked most of it down. I ate a snack on the comfy new couches with Mom. Thankfully, Dad allowed me to eat about 100 fewer calories (300) for snack because of the cookie.

I don't remember much of Monday. I just remember that it was better, for the most part. Dinner was 1 huge and thick piece of salmon, baby potatoes, and broccoli. Again, it was a difficult dinner. Snack kind of sucked because Mom discovered one of my tricks. I had been telling her I was eating the flavored oatmeal for 130 to 170 calories, but that night she actually checked my package and discovered it was the original flavor and had only 100 calories. It was definitely not the best way to convince my parents to trust me.

May 25, 2009

I brought the space heater into my room last night because I was so cold. I'm starting to binge late at night before bed. I'm only binging on fruits and veggies, but it's still a lot. I guess I'm still eating much fewer calories than I should be, but it still bugs me. I feel I need to restrict throughout the day to allow myself to binge. Today has been OK. I told myself last night that today I would start increasing my calories, yet I've almost done the opposite! I honestly do hate how I look and do want to gain weight, but I just can't seem to be able to take the actual action. Why? I can tell I'm losing weight, and my hair is almost completely gone. I have to wear hats to cover my bald spots. It's Dad's birthday tomorrow, so I'm all freaked out because I haven't really done anything for him yet present-wise, and I don't know what I will do if there is cake.

May 26, 2009

Today is Dad's birthday. Last night I went crazy with a binge. It is probably because I'm not eating enough fat, so I never feel satisfied. I had 1 whole bag of mushrooms, 1/2 a tomato, 10 cherries, 6 huge celery sticks, and 3/4 of a bag of green grapes. I went to bed late and woke up early to go to my DXA scan appointment, which tests bone density, and then to get blood work done. I am so nervous for the results.

May 27, 2009

We celebrated Dad's birthday last night with dinner at Tahoe Joe's and it was amazing. Mom, Dad, and I got a huge piece of halibut. I ate almost all of mine as a present to him, and he was so happy. Then...the cake. I said I didn't want any because I was full and would rather have snack later. Well, it really upset everyone, and I walked off crying. I am so mad at myself. Why can't I just eat a small piece of cake? I was eating ice cream, cookies, and chips at UCLA. I'm such a failure.

Thankfully, today has been amazing in comparison to last night's birthday disaster. I had an appointment with my new doctor, Dr. Franklin, and my weight was 89 pounds! However, I had 32 ounces of water beforehand, as well as a cell phone in my pocket, a sweatshirt on, and UGG boots, but too bad! Guess what? My DXA scan results showed I have no osteoporosis or osteopenia! In fact, my numbers looked great. Dr. Schack had even told Dad it was 100 percent certain I would have osteoporosis, but I don't even have osteopenia—hooray! I had great blood work results.

May 28, 2009

Last night I had a crazy binge and ate 40 strawberries (yes, I counted), 1 bag of mushrooms, 1 mini peach, lettuce, and celery. I had a smaller snack that day, but still, I got awoken early this morning by Dad saying I haven't been doing well, I must have manipulated my weight, I can't have the car, etc. I was literally speechless. How could he say all of that when less than 24 hours ago I got the best news: great blood work, 89 pounds (even though it was fake), and no osteoporosis or osteopenia. Dad must have found and read my journal or something. To make a long story short and not to go into every detail, I have never screamed so much and never have I seen or heard my dad cry so much. He wanted to weigh me, and I refused to show him when I stepped on to look for myself (82.2 pounds with no water).

I finally ate some breakfast and went for a 50-minute walk. I am so mad and yelled some more at Dad when I got back. He finally said I could have the car, but I had to sign a contract saying I would weigh close to 91 pounds on Tuesday at my next appointment or no car. I hate requirements and threats more than anything. It only makes me want to rebel even more because I feel I am not doing it for myself but for someone else. That's no way to recover or ever improve. I have the same damn goals as my family. I just wish there weren't any requirements because it makes me feel controlled, which in turn makes me want to act out and give into ED as a way to take back control.

I wanted to cry and scream when Dad and I got home from going out to dinner. Mom wasn't in the best mood toward me, yet she and Kasey chatted up the nicest storm of conversation, and I almost lost it. Why can't Mom ever talk to me like that? Whenever we do talk, she always twists the subject so that we start talking about ED. I mean, I could mention the weather and a few minutes later my anorexia would be brought up. Why can't my parents—and Mom especially—understand that I have an eating disorder, but I am not my eating disorder and deserve to be treated like Brittany? It is a part of me...a big part, I understand...but if my family can't separate my identity from ED, then how the hell am I supposed to? ED is not my identity, and I'm trying so hard to rid that past life, but Mom won't let me escape it...I'm just a disease to her.

June 2, 2009

I had my doctor's appointment today. I went in to get my blood pressure and weight with the nurse, and she almost had me change into a gown! I told her I never change into a gown, and luckily she said OK. I was a little over 88 pounds but close enough to 89 pounds that the nurse said she could use that number. Whew! I had 32 ounces of water again, as well as a short-sleeve shirt, long-sleeve shirt, cashmere sweater, pullover sweatshirt, sweat pants, and UGG boots. I also had on a heavy necklace and my cell phone and rocks in my pockets.

June 13, 2009

Today is Mom's birthday. I was up really late last night so that I could put out Mom's doughnuts and balloons I got for her. I slept in late, but I did eventually get out of bed and went to a few shopping centers to walk around. I had ear pressure today! Ah! My left ear was clogged for a few hours. It is one of the scariest things I have ever experienced! Why is it back?

I had an absurdly late breakfast. Mom is really worried about me. I did a 65-minute walk around the neighborhood, then went to 2 more markets, came home for snack, and then did another 55-minute walk. Afterward, I went back out to more markets and then came home for my lunch. I gave Mom her cake slice, which she loved! Still, I had to go to yet another market and Starbucks afterward. Why can't I just take a break and enjoy my mom's birthday? I do feel good and happy now but probably for all the wrong reasons.

June 21, 2009

Happy Father's Day! I woke up late again today. I had a nice walk with Dad for 80 minutes. He told me I really needed to turn myself around. He doesn't care too much about my late eating and the weird foods I eat, but he does care about my weight and health. He told me he would pay me for every pound I gain. Hmm...

I went to a few stores, came home for breakfast, and did a 75-minute walk. I really wanted to skip my third walk and just take a nap or take Dad to Tahoe Joe's, but he had already eaten, so I went to another market and then did an 85-minute walk with my dog, Kodi.

The icy chilled air brought back a lot of intense memories of UC Davis. They weren't necessarily bad memories...just sad. I then had lunch and went to the market and Starbucks. I'm eating my lunch now around 9:00 at night! How can I reduce some of this chaos? Decrease my walks? Don't restrict? Just keep walking, but add a 200-calorie bar? Hmm...how about all 3 options?

June 22, 2009

I went to bed last night at 6:00 in the morning! I went down to my room earlier, but I just couldn't sleep, so I somewhat organized all the clothes I bought recently. I was so tired today that I decided to let myself sleep all day, skip at least 1 walk and not eat breakfast, lunch, or snack…not that they are that many calories anyway. I really am sick of eating and walking so late at night. I'm sick of always talking about what I want to fix and then never taking action. Well, that's it! I'm going to back up the talk with action for once! My life feels out of control with my sleep, calories, and activity, so I'm going to tackle it one at a time and my first one will be getting myself on a more normal schedule.

I ended up sleeping in until 5:30 in the afternoon. I honestly could have slept the rest of the day and night, but I figured I should get up for a bit. I took an 85-minute walk around 6:00, and it was such a gorgeous and warm evening. I was quite weak, tired, and slow, though. I went to some markets afterward and then hurried home to take my second walk, but I didn't leave the house until 9:00 p.m.! Thankfully, Dad came with me, and we had a nice time. I live in a very safe neighborhood, but it's still creepy to walk alone that late. I must change my schedule! I got into a fight with my parents afterward because Dad had thought I was going to bed earlier starting today, which I had hoped, but it will have to be tomorrow. My ideal schedule is this:

9:30 a.m.	wake up
10:00 a.m.	walk #1
11:30 a.m.	errands
2:00 p.m.	breakfast
2:30 p.m.	walk #2
4:00 p.m.	errands
6:00 p.m.	walk #3
7:45 p.m.	lunch
8:30 p.m.	errands

10:00 p.m.	journaling and Starbucks
11:30 p.m.	dinner
Midnight	shower
1:00 a.m.	snack and binge
2:00 a.m.	in bed at the latest

It will be harder to follow this exact schedule with appointments, but as long as I try to stick close to it, I will be happy. It's a start at least, but ideally I want to shift everything even earlier. My ear clogged again for a bit and my parents are really worried. Please help me shift my schedule tomorrow and for my blood work to be better and for my weight to at least be the same!

June 26, 2009

Wow! Last night was quite the night for me! After coming home super late from Starbucks and eating my "dinner," I went downstairs for my shower. I stood in front of the bathroom mirror as depressed as ever and the urge inside of me to say "fuck it all I want a new life" was as strong as ever. I could no longer try to pretend I'm OK, so I woke up my parents around 2:30 a.m. and declared to them that I was done and ready to try living because nothing could feel as bad as I do now with ED, not even my thighs touching. I sobbed in my mom's arms for a while and it was just such a special night. I then went upstairs and stuffed my face, including eating 35 mini apricots! Yes, my stomach is killing me! I went to bed around 6:00 in the morning and had to get up around 8:45 a.m. so Dad could take me to my appointment in Solvang with a hand surgeon that is going to look at my thumb that's still stuck in the palm of my hand.

I had a nice drive down to Solvang with Dad and a great appointment with the surgeon. He was quite baffled by my hand but said all my X-rays and tendons look great and that I was a perfect candidate to have surgery to lengthen the tendon, which he said should definitely help. He said the surgery could be done without anesthesia, which will be safer for me because of the anorexia.

June 28, 2009

I'm journaling for today and yesterday. Yesterday I slept in until 5:30 in the afternoon again and then took my walk. I honestly don't really know what happened, but Dad and I started texting while I was walking. I guess I didn't reply to his comments the way he hoped when he was talking about how I had to eat 2,500 calories. Pretty soon he was in a fury saying he was going to kick me out of the house. What? Anyway, he came looking for me while I was finishing my 100-minute walk. He found me, and we screamed and cussed the whole way up the hill to our house. My head was spinning. The next thing I know I lost my car, and my parents said I had to eat 2,500 calories in order to stay in the house and that they were going to watch me. Mom even packed a whole suitcase for me when I was resisting. I was honestly in shock, especially after coming into their room last night and pouring my heart out.

I eventually started pulling out some food with my mind in a trance. I got cottage cheese, 1 fiber muffin, 1 apricot, peanuts, and 1 egg because Dad said I had to eat close to 1,000 calories in that sitting...it was like 9:30 at night! He said 2,000 calories per day might be OK only for now because I lied and told him I was only eating 500 calories a day.

Now, that is completely false, but I figured my increase wouldn't be so big then. Anyway, I sat down, but no one even watched me eat. Dad left to go buy Boost Plus. I ate all of the muffin, cottage cheese, and apricot but ended up hiding and throwing out the rest...oh, there was also 1 string cheese.

July 5, 2009

Things are a lot different now! I haven't journaled the past few days, but things are changing and mostly for the better.

Here is my new life so far...

Good: Stopped all my walking, drinking less water, going to bed earlier; stopped freezing Jell-O; so happy and relaxed; tons of free time now; no more putting on walking shoes; I feel like 1 market trip is being active; having amazing dreams; am less obsessive.

Bad: Only eating between 800 and 1,400 calories at the most; getting weaker, harder to stand from a sitting position; throwing out the Boost Plus, milk, almonds, eggs, bread, meat, etc., that my parents believe I'm honestly eating; Dad is being my food servant and has been bringing my food down to my room, but I've been flushing it all down the toilet; I have been saving all of my calories for late at night and have been mostly just uncontrollably eating fruits and veggies plus sometimes cereal.

Dad is so proud of the new me and is happy, yet I have no life right now...I hardly get out of bed, I'm so weak. I'm losing a lot of weight...I think? The scale here has been reading between 73.1 pounds and 76 pounds. That's with no water or clothes, but that's still getting scary! Then again, I have never felt so happy and free. I just hope I will soon start eating the foods I say I am eating. I honestly believe this could happen.

OK, so I just ate a whole 18-ounce container of blueberries after all my other food, ugh! I did this last night also, only with 1 whole bag of grapes. I love and hate the feeling of being that out of control. Oh well. I guess I was a bit more active today? I went to quite a few markets, but they were all quick trips, and I didn't pace. I had about 1,250 calories today, but I feel like it has to be more?

Food plan for tomorrow: Water; vitamins; gum; sugar-free flavored water; diet soda; sugar-free Jell-O; coffee; mushrooms; peppers; 100 calories of fruit, yogurt, jerky, or cheese; 2 apricots; 1 orange; 2 yam cakes or 2 yam noodles (20 calories each); Powerade Zero; 1/2 apple; 2 more apricots; 10 mini meringues; and then bed! This should equal 650 calories, so I think that should be good.

July 6, 2009

Today was all right. I have been having terrible diarrhea today, which is not fun. I slept in until 3:00 this afternoon. I was so tired! I had Dad bring me my "food" throughout the day, which in turn went down the toilet and sink drain. I got on the scale, and it flashed 77 pounds. Whoa! I guess it was just a bit more than I expected, yet it was also before I had gone to the bathroom. I was quite active today and did feel slightly compulsive about it... perhaps it has to do with the weight gain? I must watch myself!

July 7, 2009

I had to get up somewhat early today considering I wasn't able to make it to bed until 4:00 in the morning. I went to pick up my blood work results, and they were not good! My sodium dropped to 123 from 130, and my white blood cells dropped from 1.9 to 1.8. Perhaps the most worrisome was one of my liver enzymes increased 10 points and another one increased by 30 points. I would say it is refeeding syndrome, yet I'm not eating enough for that to happen, am I? It's probably a result of not eating enough and eating it all at night. Also, my ferritin increased by about 100 points, which Mom said was my body's ability to store iron, I think. Can't I just get a break, please?

July 11, 2009

Well, it's been a few days since I've journaled, and things have unfortunately been awful. I had a lovely drive with my dad down to Santa Barbara to have my hand surgery, which according to the doctor went perfectly. My thumb is now straight. I have a big cast on my arm now, but it thankfully doesn't hurt that much. I felt really ill the rest of the day, and on Friday I had Dad bring me lots of food. I came upstairs later that day. Mom took one look at me and flipped out! Her reaction, of course, caused major drama. Mom accused me of weighing 75 pounds and throwing out all the food Dad was bringing me, which was correct, and she forced poor Dad to weigh me. It was a nightmare of an evening, and I had to eat 1 huge piece of chicken with Dad and rice and cottage cheese with Mom.

Today, which is Saturday, I was forced to consume Boost Plus, bread, and 12 almonds in front of Dad. The scale read 74.2 pounds earlier—yikes! Thankfully, only my eyes saw it. Again, it was a terrible day full of suspicion from my parents and screaming from me.

184

Dad is going to Yosemite to hike Half Dome with Kasey and her boyfriend, and I am so jealous. I've always been the nature lover and my dad's adventure buddy. Mom is so nervous to be alone with me while Dad is gone. If I don't weigh 76 pounds on Wednesday when Dad returns, I get shipped off to Stanford. I'm absolutely terrified! My weight is frightening, and I look like I did at Torrance. I'm scared for my life! I still only ate 1,260 calories today, even with eating all the stuff in front of Dad.

July 14, 2009

I went to bed late last night and really didn't sleep too well. I had Mom bring a piece of bread, 1 Nutri-Grain bar, 20 almonds, and 8 ounces of milk down to my bedroom.

I'm sure she questioned if I actually ate any of it...and I didn't. I always ask for those items because bread and Nutri-Grain bars are easy to flush, milk is easy to pour down the sink drain, and almonds are easy to hide in my room. I got out of bed quickly around 11:15 a.m. so I could eat my egg, drink my Boost Plus (full of water and almond milk), and make my sugar-free Jell-O before my appointment with my new psychiatrist. My appointment didn't go so well.

My psychiatrist looked at me concernedly and said, "I'm afraid you're going to die."

What the heck? Really? I couldn't help but stare at her. With a combination of butterflies in my stomach, anger in my mind, and sadness in my heart, I forced myself to shake my head and tell her she was crazy.

July 15, 2009

Well, today was my UC Davis deadline to weigh 102 pounds...I guess that didn't happen. Yet, maybe deep down I never want to go back...I just couldn't.

July 19, 2009

I ended up going to bed around 2:30 in the morning, but I was at least downstairs by 2:00 in the morning, which is much better! I am in bed again today but feel better and am being flooded with incredible memories when I was at my happiest many years ago. The antibiotics I have to take because of my surgery are not making me feel great. I have been having a good time with my parents today, which is a nice change. Dad says I look way thinner today, but my weight was 77.2 pounds, so I happily showed him. I do check my weight around the same time each afternoon, which is thankfully after I drink a ton of water—and a lot more than Dad thinks. I'm so happy, yet I wish I were honestly doing as well as my parents think, regarding the food part at least. I flush my egg, bread, milk, and bars down the toilet. I hide my almonds. I pretend to smear peanut butter on a tablespoon. I fill the Boost Plus bottles with almond milk and water. I throw my piece of meat, rice, and whatever else I say I binge on over our backyard fence at night while my parents are hopefully asleep. It's awful! I mean, I wait super late to eat my dinner so that everyone is downstairs, and then I quietly open the door to the backyard and throw all my dinner my parents leave out for me over the fence and into the creek. Ah! What is wrong with me? I hate it more than anything, but I do know that I have no desire to start the walking again and aisle pacing, which is some progress, right? Something in me is changing for the better, and I'm just hoping it's my calorie amount that changes next because it certainly does suck having no energy and going so long throughout the day eating nothing. Please help and protect me!

July 22, 2009

I spent the morning in bed again and flushed my breakfast. I did finally pick up my phone and officially called UC Davis to say I wouldn't be coming back in the fall. I guess it was a harder phone call than I thought. I did some laundry and weakly made my way upstairs to have my first Boost Plus with Dad around 2:30 in the afternoon. Gosh, my sister is so gorgeous, and I have to remember she weighs at least 40 to 50 pounds more than I do. I went back to bed for a while and then came upstairs around 5:00 to take my vitamins and drink my second Boost Plus (again, they are all full of water and unsweetened almond milk). Dad then took me to Starbucks and Ralphs. I found myself being a bit more energetic than expected, which was kind of nice, but it did lead me to be more active than I should have. I came home and pretended to eat some peanut butter while Dad walked the dogs. I then lay in bed for a little bit feeling incredibly angry. I wanted so badly to go to the yearly beach trip coming up, yet look at me. I'm a 74-pound freak! I just want to stuff my face and say, "Fuck! Bye, ED!" It also makes me want to say, "Fuck! I give up!" I can't let another year or even week pass of giving up my life, though.

I see my doctor tomorrow morning. Mom is driving me, so I will have to do my water loading in my room beforehand. I really hope I didn't lose a lot of weight.

Oh my gosh! I just finished about ½ a Ziploc bag of cookies and brownies! It was at least 300 calories!

18

Night of My Life

July 23, 2009

Last night was the night I killed ED! It started with that small bag of cookies, but I just couldn't stop! My sister had friends over for a sleepover. I was jealous that I couldn't eat junk food and enjoy myself like they were doing, so I decided I would! It was about 3:00 in the morning, but I was ready to go for it. I woke up Dad and told him to come upstairs to witness something significant. That's when it happened. I went mad, it seemed, and finally ate all the foods I had been craving and missing out on for 7 years! I called Mom upstairs a little later, and it was the happiest, most hopeful, and freeing night of my whole entire life! I ate Jell-O; mushrooms; veggies; fruit; yogurt; yam cakes; jerky; egg; 1 muffin; cookies; 1/3 a bag of peanut M&Ms; 6 mini Reese's Peanut Butter Cups; 10 handfuls of Doritos; 2 big chocolate-covered macaroons; ¾ a cup of mint chocolate chip ice cream; a whole huge deli sandwich with turkey, mayonnaise, cheese, and 3 slices of bacon on French bread; cotton candy pudding; 2 cottage cheese cups; 8 handfuls of honey-roasted peanuts; 1 whole cup of rice; 1 whole huge single slice of carrot cake and chocolate cake; and 1 protein shake. I did it! I did it!

I was very, very sick all day today. I probably should have gone to the ER, but I managed to make it through the night. I canceled my appointment with my doctor. Mom actually said it's OK for me to eat nothing all day today, ha-ha! I weighed 78.1 pounds on the scale without any water; wow! I guess all that food is still inside of me, though. I am so uncomfortable, my heart is racing, and I feel odd. I made a huge list of all the new and fun foods I'm going to allow myself slowly to eat and then check off. I can't wait to finally eat foods that were always off limits. It seems silly that I'm so excited about simply eating food, but the feeling is overwhelmingly wonderful. I've deprived myself for so long...I have 7 years of eating to make up for! I had about 600 calories today and feel so sick from last night still that I don't even want gum! I feel a little uneasy because last night was so fun and so significant, yet it was also so out of control and mindless.

Although I broke a lot of barriers, I just can't see myself eating normally from here on out...

July 24, 2009

I woke up feeling much better today. I stayed in bed throughout the morning and had Dad bring me some food, which I got rid of. I then went to the market quickly, and what a different experience I had. This time I took forever not looking at the low-calorie and diet foods but all the foods I did want and would eventually eat. It was so much fun, and I was so close to buying myself the German and lemon cake slice, powdered doughnuts, Teddy Grahams, Goldfish, and animal cookies. Tonight I will eat a Rice Krispies Treat and a Reese's Mini Peanut Butter Cup, I won't allow myself to go overboard. It's just remarkable how much more energy my body still has physically from last night's binge. I'm still not eating anything until nighttime today, yet it is so much easier to walk, stand up, and get out of bed. I guess those 10,000-plus or whatever calories I had are still burning off!

I still don't feel the best yet can feel myself wanting to go crazy and eat everything in sight again. It was just the most magical moment of my life, which I know sounds weird, but after living my life in pure deprivation and control, doing the opposite was like being freed from jail after being given a life sentence. I went upstairs tonight actually feeling quite hungry, but after just my Jell-O, coffee, and soda, I felt like barfing. All of a sudden food looked unappetizing. Dang! Earlier I wanted to eat the whole dang market. My stomach feels raw almost, and I can't tell if I'm starving or sick right now.

July 25, 2009

Hmm...well, it's certainly been an interesting day so far. I woke up with my stomach making noises I didn't even know existed. My body is quite unhappy with all the calorie shifts, new foods, and antibiotics I've been taking. I was really uncomfortable for a while because my chest felt like it was burning and like there was something stuck in it. Dad came in to check on me and brought me some peanut butter crackers, 1 egg, 1 piece of bread, and Gatorade. He put the scale in my bathroom so I could check. I got on the scale a bit later and didn't even really have that much water or anything in my body yet, and so I was almost prepared to see the scale read something like 72 pounds because I had a lot of diarrhea the previous night. I was quite shocked and almost confused when it still read something like 75.3 pounds! I guess I was expecting it to be lower, but is that really what I still want for my new life and me? The answer is no! I guess it's everyone's wish to eat whatever and as much as they want and not gain weight, but I guess I need to.

Dad came back into my room, and I told him I actually only lost 2 pounds. He was like, "Oh, OK, so you're like 80 pounds, then?" I said no...and he asked if he could see the scale read 80 pounds. Basically at that point I had to tell him I had been lying in the first place and that my weight was really around 76 pounds now. Oh well, it's much better to come clean versus creating another awful trap for myself. Dad was a little pissed but glad I was honest.

Later on I had Dad bring me some milk, a Nutri-Grain bar, and more Gatorade. Again I got rid of it all once he left the room. I got dressed and out of bed around 1:00 p.m. Mom saw me walking around with just a long shirt on, and she absolutely flipped out!

She was like, "Oh my gosh! You are not eating! You're losing weight." And she went on and on.

What the heck? It's not as if my body is going to transform magically in just a few days. I guess it also pushed her buttons because I was hoping she would take me to a few markets, and she told me no and that I look like I should be in a hospital. Her whole reaction to me was the complete opposite of what I was expecting, especially since I honestly had gained a couple of pounds—not to mention having the most memorable night of my life only a few days ago. Of course she then attacked my poor Dad and told him he needs to weigh me.

Dang it! Dad took me downstairs and saw the 76-ish pounds and said he would take me to one market only. I chose Vons but quickly went into CVS first and bought some Lactaid and sugar-free jelly-beans. I really should have known he would look at what I bought, and he got really mad to see I was buying "diet shit." I then went into Vons and went quite quickly with no pacing or anything and bought yogurt, peppers, carrots, 2 apples, and a York Peppermint Pattie candy for myself at the checkout—hooray! Dad and I had a nice enough drive home, but Mom again flipped out big-time when I walked back into the house. She accused me of eating absolutely nothing, lying, and being secretive. She said I must eat 2,800 calories a day in front of them from now on and how I am such a terrible liar. It was just absolutely awful! She then had Dad weigh me again, and I hadn't even had the chance to drink any fluid. Thankfully, and oddly, the scale read 77.8 pounds.

I was shocked! I had a lot of mixed feelings. I know it's a great thing to be gaining weight, but ED is trying to tell me it's the worst thing. Dad was at least decently satisfied. I then made my way sadly back upstairs and took my vitamins. Next I pretended to eat more peanut butter crackers and yogurt while my parents were away. I then went downstairs in a daze and ended up having a really nice talk with Dad in my room when he came down later. I explained everything to him and how I can't please or live with Mom, how I really am eating all those foods (lie), and I just honestly don't feel comfortable eating in front of others yet. He said he wouldn't mind if I woke him up, even at 3:00 in the morning, when I'm ready to eat my special treat, so maybe I will. I think I will have my Peppermint Pattie tonight.

I had a nice talk with Mom later on, and I think she might try to move out and live with my grandma, which unfortunately is probably the best for everyone at the moment. I hate how much tension is in the house right now, especially around me. I feel—and I am—responsible for it all, but I just can't help it. I don't want the attention, I don't want to be the cause of my parents' every quarrel, and I don't want ED to be my identity. For once I wish I could just be normal...it's not as if I'm some superstar tennis player, horse rider, or student right now anyway. I guess I should be thankful my weight is even as high as it is all things considering, otherwise I could be at Stanford right now. Ugh!

There is definitely a huge change and shift in me, but ED is still showing its ugly face! I'm quite proud of myself for one thing tonight, that's for sure! I not only followed through with agreeing to watch a movie tonight, but I actually sat throughout the whole 2-hour film and even enjoyed it! I had a really nice time sitting and snuggling on the couch with my parents. During the movie, Dad ate some Doritos and then brought out 1 bag of caramel popcorn. Although I did turn down all of it, I must say the urge to just say screw this and dive right into the food and forget the calculations was incredibly strong! The movie really brought up a lot of feelings for me (which I think is one of the reasons I avoid movies). Afterward I told my parents quite happily and emotionally that I am almost ready to be the Brittany I was meant to be. I'm so excited! Please help me break free completely. I'm so close. Ugh...I don't feel well.

July 26, 2009

Last night ended up turning into a "wake up parents, bring the camera" binge night! I went insane with the caramel popcorn, York Peppermint Pattie, Wheat Thins, pretzels, Doritos, and peanuts. I guess it all ended up to total 400-ish calories and 1,200 to 1,300 calories for the whole day, but still...I was so close to wanting to have another "go crazy, eat everything in the house" night, but somehow I resisted going that far.

Today has been all right. My stomach isn't happy this morning with all the junk food I ate last night. Ugh, my poor body! I really do have a great body, not only for surviving all the abuse but to actually be somewhat properly functioning amidst it all! The scale flashed 75.7 pounds with almost no water and then 77.2 pounds after getting dressed, but who knows what my weight really is right now with all the fluid and food shifts. It has been a really nice day so far with my parents at least. Dad and I went and rented the movie *Superbad* for tonight, and then I went to New Frontiers to buy vitamins and about 100 mini apricots. Dad then took me to Rite Aid, and we had fun choosing some candy. We ended up getting Milky Way Minis, Hot Tamales, and Mike and Ikes, and I bought some kettle corn popcorn. I had about 850 calories so far today, which I guess is better? Now I just better not let myself go back upstairs...

July 27, 2009

My gosh! I did end up losing it again last night and went nuts with food! I had about 2 cups' worth of rice, Doritos, popcorn, Wheat Thins, peanuts, and chocolate squares...and I just couldn't stop! Eventually I had to wake up Dad to have him help stop me. We even weighed me for fun last night around 4:00 in the morning, and it said 85 pounds. Crazy! Of course I had a ton of food and liquid in me at the moment, but whoa!

Today has been OK so far. Mom took me to some stores and to get my blood work done. We had a nice time for the most part, but I have to remind her constantly to butt out when it comes to food because she just can't help but want to give me advice. I'm super tired now and don't feel well either. It will be interesting to get my blood work results tomorrow after such a crazy week with food. Tonight has been nice so far. I'm about to go back upstairs to finish eating, and I pray I can stop myself from eating more than my 800 calories planned!

August 4, 2009

Oh my gosh, what the night I had last night! It was truly one of the most significant nights for me. Kodi was barking all night long, and I was restless, so after eating my usual food and lying in bed for a bit, listening to Kodi complain, I went upstairs only to give in to my craving for a cottage cheese cup and that last banana. Well, after scarfing down those yummy items, I lost complete control and had the binge of my life. It was fun, freeing, powerful, tasty, divine, exhilarating, significant, scary, painful, sickening, and over the top!

I had sugar-free Jell-O, carrots, peppers, 3 baby apples, 1 orange, 2 yam cakes, jerky, protein shake, muffin, pudding, 2 chocolate coins, 24 almonds, meringues, jelly beans, cottage cheese, Greek yogurt, 2 ½ eggs, banana, Fruit Loops, pretzels, 3 Milky Way Minis, 3 mini Reese's Peanut Butter Cups, caramel rice cakes, 2 peanut butter granola bars, 1 Nature Valley granola bar pack, 2 mini Zone bars, 2 waffles with peanut butter and jelly and honey, 4 whole Pop-Tarts, popcorn, TLC granola bar, 1 whole pepperoni pizza Hot Pocket, 2 applesauce cups, Canadian bacon, turkey, beef jerky, fiber tortilla with tons of peanut butter and jelly, and spoons of chocolate chip and mango ice cream.

It was quite sensational and amazing, however, I severely went over the top and have had the worst stomachache ever. I am honestly surprised I didn't throw up because I certainly felt as if I would. I had to cancel my appointment with my doctor again but with good reason! The receptionist at the doctor's office was definitely a bit suspicious, you could say, when I told her I was feeling too ill from overeating, ha-ha!

August 10, 2009

The past few days have certainly been eventful! Mom and Dad are both out of town, so it's just been the dogs and me. I ended up having another huge binge Thursday night and just kept stuffing and stuffing myself beyond the point of being overfull. Afterward, I had never felt so sick and somehow managed to grab the home phone and make it down the hall to our guest bedroom upstairs. I called Dad panicked because I had never felt so awful, and thankfully he picked up (it was 6:00 in the morning his time since he's on the East Coast). I was drooling uncontrollably, having diarrhea, and feeling ill in a way I've never experienced. Finally, I started throwing up all over the carpet, which was gross, but I had the worst stomachache imaginable! For me to throw up means something very serious and critical is happening. It's as if I don't have a gag reflex, and the last time I had thrown up I was 4 years old. Dad finally called my poor mom at 3:00 in the morning, who was in Santa Barbara, and she in turn called her lovely friend to come take me to the ER.

I could hardly speak or move because of the pain. Mom's friend stayed with me for a couple hours holding my hand. I got IVs and was admitted with low sodium of 120…wow, did it drop! Mom came home early from her trip to see me. Eventually I got moved to my own room and was given lots of Zofran and morphine, and I slept all day and night. I had an X-ray, which showed my stomach jam-packed with food, so one of my nice nurses put a huge (ouch!) tube down my nose like at Torrance. They put the tube in to try to suck some food out, but it didn't really work, so they took it out. The morphine made me itch like crazy and act really weird. I didn't really eat much at all during my stay. The doctor told me if I binged again like that my stomach could explode and I could die. What?

I was able to come home today because my blood work is better.

It's hard to be home alone with Mom, but OK I suppose. She told me she found and read my journal. Shit! So she knows about all the watered-down Boost Pluses and my dinners I throw over the fence. Oh well, things have been calm enough, and I slept the rest of the day. Erg! I'm pissed because the scale says I didn't lose an ounce, and my legs look bigger to me in the mirror. Maybe it's still from all the IV fluid and meds? I'm hoping so.

I'm so upset right now because I ended up eating 1 whole bag of grapes tonight. Ah! I'm freaking out! I went downstairs to my room but then stupidly came upstairs again and had another crazy binge. Help! I feel like I'm honestly dying now.

August 12, 2009

After feeling like I was dying the other night, I came downstairs and had terrible diarrhea along with lots of drooling, but I didn't throw up. I eventually called Mom into my bathroom around 4:00 in the morning. She held me for a while and made me feel so safe. She decided to take me back to the ER to make sure I didn't need an IV for my sodium.

The same ER doctor saw me. After I got lab work done and an X-ray, he told me he thought I needed to be sent to an ED center immediately but that first I needed to be sent somewhere where I could be watched. Apparently I had an open safety pin in my stomach and needed to be observed to make sure it passed through me. What the heck? How on Earth could I have possibly consumed a safety pin without noticing or feeling it? The doctor, of course, questioned me swallowing it on purpose, which couldn't be further from the truth. Mom was incredibly worried about me as well as the binging, and I could tell she wasn't sure if she believed me. The doctor was making phone calls to Stanford to try and get me transferred there, which I was furious about, especially because I binged out of wanting to kill ED and move forward, not go back into treatment!

The nurse came in to start an IV because my sodium had dropped back down to 126. I kept pulling off the heart monitor and threatening to leave I was so angry. Eventually Mom and I had a nice talk, and it was decided I could stay at our local hospital until the safety pin passed and then go home. Mom went home for a bit, and I was finally brought to my own room on the second floor. Mom came to visit later, and she brought me a few clothes and toiletries. The only thing that really sucks is that I'm on fluid restriction because of my low sodium and because they don't want me to get too bloated and nauseous and throw up the safety pin. They've turned off all the water in my bathroom, so I can't even flush the toilet or run the water in my sink. I'm also on a clear liquid diet and I can only have a tiny bit of chicken broth, Jell-O, applesauce, Popsicles, or juice, yuck! I'm not sleeping very well here. It's awful... I can't stop thinking about food and what I want to binge on next.

August 15, 2009

I wasn't feeling well the morning Mom and Dad picked me up from the hospital. I crawled into bed when we got home and had planned to sleep all day. But a few minutes later Mom and Dad barged into my room and started questioning me as to whether or not I ate my food while I was in the hospital. I said I did, but they just wouldn't leave me alone. They kept pestering me over and over again until I finally broke down—and I mean really broke down. I started balling and spilled everything! I admitted to throwing away all my food, the Boost Pluses, and just every little secret I had. I told them for the first time in my life I wanted help and really meant it. I told them I wanted to be watched and that I had to be watched. I pretty much threw my hands up and said that's it! I definitely caught my parents off guard, but they listened to me with open ears.

I then went upstairs and ate a ton of food. I wanted to eat even more, but my parents said I shouldn't eat past 2,000 calories. I ended up binging at night, though, up to about 4,000 calories total for the whole day. I didn't go to bed until 6:00 in the morning. Dad comforted me and helped me process what was going on. He came and talked to me after I binged. I told him that I felt guilty for ED being so quiet. I felt at peace. I felt guilty that I didn't feel guilty for eating so much! Dad totally made me feel great and reassured me that this was a good thing.

I slept until 11:00 in the morning and weighed 83.4 pounds with no water. I skipped breakfast and snack and washed my car. I had tons of energy. I noticed my hair and face are getting healthier looking, and Dad says I look better. I was quite active today, and I'm kind of scared ED will get louder and make me more active each day now. I'm so happy, yet also scared and not eating as much as Dad thinks, though still twice more than before. I keep going back and forth between being scared and wanting life and health. Shut up, ED!

August 19, 2009

I ended up having a huge binge last night. I had a slight binge, came downstairs and weighed myself. I was 91.3 pounds. I woke up Dad to show him, and it read 89.5 pounds. He was stoked and said he'd pay me for the weight gain. A few minutes later I came back into his room and said I wanted to go have another binge. Dad came upstairs with me for part of it and we had a lot of fun. He said he'd pay me right then! I finished my binge but only because Dad came back upstairs to stop me! I went down to my room and binged on about 2,000 more calories from the foods and bars I had stashed in my room. I have a whole dresser full of hoarded food. It was all my backup food hidden away in case, God forbid, the market was out of one of my particular brands or special low-calorie items. My stomach seems to be able to handle the binges better now, and I'm not sure how I feel about that.

August 22, 2009

I had a nice time hanging out with Kasey and her friends last night. Probably the thing I want most in life is to have a group of friends like she has and to be able to relax and have fun. I went to bed really late and did a good job controlling my calories. I really wasn't even hungry or tempted by food, but there was a part of me that still wanted to go on a binge. I came downstairs around 3:15 a.m. and woke up Dad and showed him my weight, which was 91.3 pounds.

I told him I needed to vent for a minute. I talked to him about my binge urge even though I was already full. I feel to truly kill this now almost 8-year addiction, I have to do it cold turkey and dive off the deep end, as Dad says. I feel the more times I binge, the quicker I can get my life back and get through the discomfort of physical change and weight gain. I know binging isn't healthy but neither is restriction. I wish I could find an in-between balance and do things the right way, but my all-or-nothing thinking won't allow it.

Dad and I went upstairs after talking for a while, and we shared 1 banana and 1 pink cookie. He then went back to bed and left me alone for a bit to have my fun. Dad had to come back upstairs again though to stop me because I was really overdoing it. I felt good and happy though and was enjoying it! Little did Dad know I went downstairs only to eat another 3,000 calories worth of food stashed in my room. I didn't finish eating until 6:15 this morning! I felt so sick, but my stomach is starting to accept the binges. I literally had about 7,000 to 8,000 calories last night! Dad is absolutely in heaven!

August 24, 2009

So much for having only 400 calories last night, which I had planned. I ended up completely letting myself go once again. I had 4,200 calories! I seriously don't even know how it started because I wasn't even having cravings or anything, yet stuffed my face with everything in sight. It started with just grapes, turkey, and some chicken. Then I came down to my room. But I felt as though I had already blown it even though I had only eaten about 1,100 calories at the most. I figured I might as well go for it and binge since clearly I don't know the meaning of balance. So, I started binging in my room and then quietly went upstairs so no one would hear and continued my binge and then came back down to my room and binged some more! It was crazy, but so much fun. I was quite proud of myself.

It is kind of scary because no food or dessert is off limits to me now when I binge, no matter how unhealthy or high in calories it is. What a change! I guess it's a good thing, though? It's really uncomfortable seeing my body change and watching the numbers on the scale go up, but I almost feel that each time I binge, the closer I get to my goals and get the discomfort over with. Also, I feel that at this point if I were to structure myself more normally throughout the day, it could cause me to become trapped again by ED by getting too rigid and compulsive about spacing meals, exercising, counting calories, etc. I feel I need to keep having occasional binges until my brain understands that ED is gone for good, just as my heart already knows.

My weight went up to 90-ish pounds this morning after my binge. My heart was pounding and I had tons of energy. I couldn't sleep, so I spent a while organizing my room. I then went upstairs around 7:15 a.m., made my Jell-O, showed Dad my proud work (all the leftover binge wrappers as evidence), got the newspaper, and collected all my wrappers from the binge to record my masterful job. I eventually decided to close my eyes for about 2 hours and have Dad wake me up at 10:00 a.m. so I could get ready to drive myself to Solvang to get my cast off.

Dad called me while I was at my appointment upset because apparently a few people have been calling to say they've seen me walking a lot during errands. Erg! I'm not walking to be compulsive or lose weight; it just feels so good to have energy again! Besides, if I'm gaining this much weight so fast, I have a right to exercise. What is wrong with this town? I hate that everyone seems to know me. Gosh, give me some privacy!

When I came home and showed my parents my arm without the cast, all my veins were popping out because I was really dehydrated. So, of course, Mom got mad at me and was accusing me of all this shit and even made Dad weigh me. I weighed 88 pounds, for goodness' sake! What the heck, Mom? I finally start binging, gaining weight, and eating foods I haven't eaten in years, and this is how you react? Eventually we had a really nice night, but I hate feeling like I always have to educate her on the same things over and over, such as having her live her own life, stop nagging, and let me make my own decisions.

Tonight after I had come downstairs for bed, the scale read 93.6 pounds! I was shocked and even woke up Mom to show her. It was after I had my coffee and food, but it is still the highest number I've seen in a while. Quite uncomfortable!

19

False Freedom

"Sometimes life doesn't make sense. Sometimes there is no good reason for the events that take place. But most times, you'll realize it will all make sense for a much better reason, if you're patient enough to wait." ~Britt

August 27, 2009

Mom started nagging and attacking me about food, but we finally had a good talk. Does she not understand how much weight I've gained in only a few weeks? I was still in the 70's at the beginning of August, and now I'm in the 90's! I need to keep restricting so my weight goes down and I can binge again.

August 28, 2009

Shit! I went on a ravenous binge last night again after promising myself I would restrict. I hate it because I'm now rebelling against myself. Before I would rebel against others and side with ED, but now I'm rebelling against myself and desire to restrict and therefore am doing the opposite and binging. I stuffed my face until 7:00 in the morning. I felt really sick. My plan is to restrict severely for at least 1 week and then have a fun binge.

August 29, 2009

Today sucked! I woke up and overheard my mom saying nasty things about me to Dad and how I don't want to gain weight, how I cause her tons of stress, etc. My weight is finally a little lower this morning at 81.5 pounds, but I was really dehydrated. It was nice to see, however, after it being in the 90's last night. I angrily told my parents I overheard their conversation, which caused Mom to get all pissed, and I ended up storming off to go hike the mountain behind our house. Dad ran after me and stopped me from hiking to the top, which was fine with me because it was so hot. We ended up doing a shorter trail on the mountain. We had a really nice chat about things, and I let him know all my honest thoughts. I then asked if I could drive down to Torrance alone to visit the nurses and Dr. Schack, and he said no, he would have to come the first time with me because it's a difficult drive. I got mad, stormed off again, and ended up walking around the neighborhood.

I finally came home only to hear Mom saying a bunch of other shit about me to Dad about how I was being destructive by walking right now. Well, fuck her. That's not true, and even if it were, who cares because I've gained so much weight! Does she not really know how many calories I consume when I binge? Not to mention I've been binging almost every night. We ended up screaming at each other again, and I stormed off and hiked the short mountain trail again. Dad caught up with me once again on my way home, and we had a good talk. He said Mom is going to butt out and perhaps even ignore me. Why can't she just be my mom? That's all I ever wanted. I can't express enough how much stress and responsibility I take on to myself because of my family. Erg! I wish everyone would just leave me alone! I'm going to figure it out eventually because now I truly want to, but I'm doing it in my way and my time.

September 4, 2009

Surprise, surprise, I binged like crazy Wednesday night...it was quite fun, and I finished the meat lasagna. I woke up this morning incredibly sweaty and really wanted to go hiking to help burn off the binge calories, yet something came over me...I went into Dad's office and asked him if he'd pay me not to hike today and instead have another binge day. He said yes and that he would pay me. I did it! It was one of the best and happiest days in both our lives. I was so excited to binge during the day as opposed to at night. I was quite proud of myself for binging again after having a huge binge only a few hours ago—not to mention I am binging instead of a 4-hour hike! I ate 1 big tortilla with a garden burger and ketchup, tons of grapes, and other stuff. Then Dad and I went to Trader Joe's to buy stuff for his dinner creation tonight. I was craving a cake slice, so we went to another market. We were disappointed to find none, so we had fun spending a while and eventually choosing 2 cupcakes, which we ate in the car together. I then came home and binged nonstop! Dad was even telling me to stop, ha-ha!

Dad and I then played tennis for 35 minutes, and it was the best I've played yet! I mean, I've only hit a few times now since coming home from UCLA, but it's a miracle I'm even holding a racket and standing on the court at all. On our way home from tennis, we went to Albertsons. I bought a bag of iced animal circus cookies, which have always been a favorite of mine. I opened and devoured them in the car. I then binged even more when we got home! Dad made artichoke cheese ravioli with spaghetti sauce, and I gulped down my huge plate and then started going for the leftovers. I was so tired afterward that I had to take a nap, and I woke up around 11:30 at night drenched in sweat. I stood up, but I couldn't keep my balance and kept running into the walls like I was drunk...kind of scary. I looked and felt pregnant, but I was so thirsty that I went upstairs for a drink and then automatically binged until my stomach was about to pop and went back down to bed. I had a total of about 6,700 calories, and the scale said 92.5 pounds—dang! I want to restrict until my weight gets down to 78 to 80 pounds, so I can binge a lot again without guilt.

September 6, 2009

Well, forget simply *wanting* to binge last night—I *did* binge! I had tons of cheesecake and other things, all the way up to 6,000 calories. I've been eating all day today, and I just can't stop myself. Why can't I ever eat normally? As soon as I go past 1,000 calories, I feel as if I've blown it and therefore need to binge up to at least 4,000 calories. What's so wrong with maintaining and doing this in a balanced and orderly way? I did do a 3-hour hike today, and it was so nice. I had lots of energy and even ran a few parts. Wow! I really am surpassing a lot of people's expectations, that's for sure! To think Stella told my parents I would die if I came home. Ha! I laugh in the face of danger, ha-ha-ha-ha! OK, just kidding about that part. The scale now says 99 pounds even before I've gone up to have my coffee. Dad and Mom say I still look anorexic but not that bad anymore. Ah! My legs are huge! I just binged on freaking grapes now and want to keep binging. New plan: hike every day and eat 1,500 calories a day for 1 month.

September 7, 2009

I woke up this morning looking pregnant all over and went upstairs early to get a drink. I saw Dad and told him I was sorry, but I'm going to lose a lot of weight, because in the past 3 weeks alone, I've put on 25 pounds. That's about 8 pounds a week of weight gain. I'm maybe OK with 1 pound a week. Anyway, I plan to lose at least enough so that the scale says 80 pounds in the morning, and so far that means I've got to lose 12 pounds. Dad completely understood and said that's fine. I know I will eventually regain the weight but not so fast this time. I want to lose the weight and then eat and pick at small amounts of food during the day and then eat something at night with the occasional tiny binge. I've had a terrible headache all day, and I have terrible indigestion.

My head really feels odd, and I'm so sleepy. I took a long nap and then went to a bunch of stores. My weight is slowly going down, but

I still have a long way to go. I'm so hungry and tired right now. My weight is 99.1 pounds tonight still!

Life continued on, and I slowly regained a lot of my strength. Dad and I began playing tennis every day, and I even went to the gym a few times for ½ an hour. My 21st birthday came on October 13, and for the first time in what seemed like forever, I actually ate my cake and enjoyed it! I weighed a good 125 pounds. The only problem was that ED was still as strong as ever, only in a different form. I kept struggling with eating a balanced amount of calories, and my weight was continuing to climb. I was at a healthy weight, but now what? I had no excuse to hide behind. I had nothing that made me special. I was no longer a nationally ranked tennis player or horseback rider. I was no longer a straight-A student. I was no longer an anorexic. Who was I? I couldn't just be me alone. My all-or-nothing thinking took care of that. I was so mad at myself for gaining so much weight that I thought I would never get back to my so-called goal weight of 80 to 90 pounds, so why even try? I failed, I blew it, I was weak, and I was fat.

Since I no longer looked the part for anorexia, I certainly couldn't go back to restricting and exercising to deal with stress...so I kept binging. I enjoyed finally being able to eat again, but this was out of control. I was binging out of fear of becoming so sick again I would die, I was binging to make up for the many years I deprived myself, I was binging as a fuck you to my parents for making me gain weight in the first place, I was binging to give myself an excuse not to perform my best and isolate, and I was binging because the word *balance* was nonexistent in my vocabulary.

20

Hi! Welcome to Fat Camp!

"Doors will open, but you have to be looking forward to see them and be thinking kindly of yourself in order to trust walking through them." ~Britt

December 6, 2009

Guess where I am? I'm at a weight loss camp in Marina Del Rey! It's called Live In Fitness Enterprise, or LIFE, as everyone calls it. Who would have thought that in the same year I would go from my deathbed with anorexia to a freaking fat camp? I'm staying for at least 4 weeks, and so far I love it! There are about 20 people here, and a lot of them are from out of state. All the trainers are awesome, and I have great roommates. I had my assessment today. I weigh 159 pounds, my body fat is 30 percent, and I'm on a 1,300-calorie meal plan. I'm so happy I'm finally losing weight and getting the binging under control!

December 7, 2009

Today has been great so far! It rained quite hard all day and was freezing. I first did 1 hour of circuit training, a 30-minute abs class, and then 1 hour of spin class. Next was lunch, which I saved for later, but my roommate told me people were noticing I didn't eat at lunch and might tell on me if I don't start eating. What the heck? I do eat my lunch...just later. I had group therapy and partner training, and then I did some cardio on my own. I definitely hate my body but already my stomach is so much smaller.

December 9, 2009

Yesterday afternoon sucked because I was hungry and the kitchen made all my meals wrong and put tons of cream on my salads when I wanted them plain. Well, I ended up eating them anyway. Then I ate a ton of lettuce and carrots, but I was then so upset that I ate my last 2 meals for the day and then 2 of my meals for the following day as well!

We all live in an apartment complex complete with a kitchen. The program delivers our 4 meals the day before, so I had my meals from today and tomorrow in the fridge. As if that wasn't bad enough, I also ate 3 protein bars. Ah! Probably 3,000 calories!

Well, at least that day is over with. Today has been OK. I'm really not feeling too great, though. I think I have strep throat or whatever my roommate had. I did yoga and circuit training and then had a nutrition meeting. I then did an intense spin class. One of the trainers pulled me aside to make sure I was OK because people had been saying I wasn't eating, which I told her I was, only later. I guess I need to eat earlier now.

December 10, 2009

Last night sucked again! I ended up binging up to about 3,000 calories on yogurt, bars, and 3 of my meals that were supposed to be for today. Dang it! I shouldn't have gone to the market across the street in the first place to buy the yogurt and protein bars. Usually it should be fine because I'm not eating many calories, but when I eat 1 week's worth of yogurt and bars, it's not OK at all!

Today has been good and bad. I was sick last night and this morning, but I eventually got to the gym around 10:00 this morning and did circuit training. Afterward, I had an intense meeting with the nutritionist, therapist, and my trainer. It was basically about me not eating when others do and just asking me how everything was going. The therapist talked to me for another ½ hour afterward, and we had a really good meeting. I felt better. I then did 50 minutes on the elliptical, a spin class, and then a volleyball class, which was fun—and I'm not bad at it either.

December 13, 2009

Today has been great! I worked hard for 2 hours in the gym and had the rest of the day to relax. I bought new tennis shoes with my roommate afterward and then watched lots of TV. I'm a little nervous because I have another progress meeting on my schedule for tomorrow with my trainer, so I hope it goes well and no one brings up the food issue. I'm also anxious because apparently there are a lot of new people coming this week, so I hope they are all fatter than me. Ugh, this is just no way to live. I mean I love it here, but it still simulates a treatment center... weigh-ins, meal plans, new clients/patients coming in who could possibly be triggering or a jealousy threat, and, of course, the gossip. Oh well, hooray for getting thinner!

I continued to do well in my workouts, but the binges became more and more frequent and more and more severe. I fell off an exercise ball while doing twisting crunches and hurt my shoulder, which was now in a sling. For safety reasons, the trainers limited my participation in activities, only adding to my anxiety, frustration, and rebellious tendencies. I was still having a great time and meeting lots of wonderful people, but I was caught in a nasty binge, restrict, and overexercise cycle with the binges slowly winning over. By January 23, I was 146 pounds... only down 1 pound since December 18. The big problem was I wasn't alone in most of these binges. The group of people I hung out with had been in the program many months longer than I had been and were enjoying treating themselves to junk food as well. It felt so amazing finally to eat real food with friends after avoiding social situations involving food all my life, but that still didn't make what I was doing OK. To complicate things further, my shin splints continued to get worse, and I developed bumps up and down the sides of my legs, which were diagnosed as anterior compartment syndrome. I started feeling sick, and blood work confirmed I had hepatitis A. I had just signed up and paid for 2 more months at LIFE when they asked me to leave and come back when I was no longer contagious. They put my training package on hold, and I left more out of control, confused, and terrified than ever.

Home quickly turned into a disaster. I told myself that I would return to LIFE thinner and better than ever, so I outlined my diet plan: 800 calories, 3 hours of exercise, and 135 pounds. I told myself I could not return to LIFE until I reached this weight. Big mistake. Every time I went over 800 calories, even if only by a few, I told myself I blew it and turned that 800 into 8,000 calories. I was still too embarrassed for anyone in San Luis Obispo to see me, so I locked myself inside. With my self-esteem running on fumes, I was ready to try anything to stop binging. I even stayed in a hotel in Santa Barbara for a week. Although I intended to get back on track there, I ended up binging every day on fast food and desserts. I came home and sunk even deeper into chaos. I didn't even recognize the girl in the mirror. What was worse was she was ugly, fat, a failure, a nobody, and someone I was now forced to live with. Sure, it was embarrassing being so obviously thin and anorexic, but this was the ultimate sin.

March 14, 2010

I can't believe this is actually happening. What the heck? I just arrived at Rosewood Ranch's step-down program. It is a residential eating disorder treatment center almost identical to Remuda Ranch Life. It's even in Wickenburg, Arizona. It was my choice to come here to see if it could stop my binging. I'm probably close to 180 pounds now, if not more; I'm going to bed between 3:00 and 5:00 in the morning. I can hardly stand up, I am sweating like crazy, I am blowing blood out of my nose, and I am starting to have a harder time breathing. Still, I feel as though I made a mistake in coming here. Sure, binging is an eating disorder, but no one wants to be "that girl." Treatment centers are for competitive anorexics...anyone else is silently laughed at and looked down upon, at least that's what my mind tells me is true. Everyone here is really nice. I'm just not sure if I'm ready for this again. I'm so fat—I just hate this! The only good thing about being here is I would start to lose weight, but I'm just so miserable.

March 19, 2010

I did a lot of crying today. So much pain came up as well as trauma from last year. I really haven't relived or thought much of those months when I was at my worst with anorexia. I just kind of pushed it aside as if it were someone else's life. I'm really struggling with food here. I know just how to restrict, fight, and act when in a treatment center, but the problem is my actions don't match my appearance this time. I'm sure everyone thinks I'm a fake or never had anorexia in my life. Yeah...if only they really knew. I refused dessert again tonight. I hate my body, yet at the same time, what an improvement with only 7 days of eating normally. I really want to binge, though, and am so hungry. I've been eating the same gross foods every day here...by choice, of course, because they are the lowest calorie exchanges.

I'm so scared of ED and getting dragged back into anorexia, yet look at me! Maybe anorexia would do me good right now. This has all just happened so quickly. I still feel as though just yesterday I was afraid of dying because I was so thin—and the truth is that it was only a few months ago—but I dealt with the fear in the wrong way. I binged to get as far away from death as I could, and it has now caused a whole array of new problems for me and hasn't cured the fear at all. I actually need to lose weight now, but that seems so contradictory to my mind since losing weight has previously always been my downfall. Ugh, help...someone please just help me! Let me start over! Take this all away, please!

March 29, 2010

A lot has happened the past 2 days. Today is Monday, but on Saturday we had just finished lunch and were all going around processing and giving each other feedback. When it was my turn, I talked about wanting to go home and that I once again didn't follow my meal plan. Well, the group started attacking me again and giving me feedback loops and trying to help. But then one of the older ladies stated, "Brittany, you are wasting everyone's time and money! You would be better off going home!" She said it extremely rudely. I got up and left and cried my eyes out for a long time. I packed up my suitcase and called Mom to tell her I was signing myself out, and she said fine. The staff tried to convince me to transfer to the main ranch, but I said no way, I was done. While waiting for my dad to call me back, I went to the Circle K down the street and bought junk food and ate it in my room. I then got a cab and went to the hotel down the street.

After I put my suitcase in the room, I walked to the convenience store across the street and bought a ton of binge food. Ugh!

Sunday (yesterday), I woke up and went to the market and bought really healthy food even though I really wanted the doughnuts and cookies. After eating the healthy food, I lost it and went to Circle K and bought a ton of binge food. Then I got a call from Mom saying my aunt and uncle who live in Arizona about 2 hours away were coming to pick me up. Before they arrived, I ate a ton more junk food from the vending machine at the hotel.

They arrived shortly after, and we had a nice drive back to their house. Today (Monday) has been nice so far. I have to take a plane home tomorrow alone, though—yikes! I am scared to death of flying. I used to love it so much. When did I become so paranoid about everything?

I arrived home feeling even more like a failure. I was trapped in my own misery. I was too fat to leave my house for fear of running into someone I knew, too fat and embarrassed to go back to LIFE because they would be so disappointed I gained so much weight, too fat to exercise because my body hurt so much, too fat to wear any clothes but my dad's...and too fat to live. So fat in fact, that I spent the next 3 months in my house eating everything in sight while watching TV and old videos of me riding and playing tennis, wishing that was still my life.

I kept gaining weight steadily until I was at my limit. I could hardly sleep, was snoring, was sweating, and was out of breath. My joints ached. I had trouble standing up from a sitting position, and my back screamed with pain if I sat for too long because I was carrying so much extra weight on my stomach. I was as lost as ever. No one knew how out of control my life was. Everyone thought I was still anorexic...and I let them still believe that. Out of pure desperation, I started searching the Internet in a frenzy looking for some type of weight loss program similar to LIFE. I landed on Premier Fitness Camp's website and wrote down the contact number. I begged my parents to let me go, and they agreed. Nothing was working, and they were probably sick of watching me slowly kill myself with food and crying every day.

21

PFC, Please Save Me!

June 28, 2010

Yesterday I boarded a plane and flew to Utah. I am here at Premier Fitness Camp, which is a live-in weight loss program. There are 10 of us here right now, and everyone is so nice. The house we stay in is unreal. It has 6 huge bedrooms, 2 huge kitchens, a pool, and a movie theater. It is drop-dead gorgeous. I could definitely see myself living here...I mean permanently. It feels so amazing to be out of California. This place has way over-exceeded my expectations, that's for sure!

Today has been so-so. I had my assessment this morning with the head trainer, Wayne, and that was...well, difficult. I weigh 221 pounds, my body fat is 45 percent, my BMI is 37, and blah, blah, blah! I know I look like shit and incredibly fat and all, but 221 pounds? Is this for real? I have to be in a nightmare! I plan to stay at least 4 months, which I hope will get me close to my goal weight. Ugh! I really hope I don't have loose skin after losing all the weight. How did this happen? How does a person gain 165 pounds in 16 months?

We had boot camp this morning, and it was brutal! I really thought I was going to pass out or throw up. It was tough mentally and physically. I couldn't even jog for 5 seconds! Me? Me, the elite athlete, the overexerciser, the one who could out-sprint anyone? Oh boy, was that a difficult thought to process. Sure, I'm proud of myself for taking charge of my life now, but how on Earth did I ever let things get this bad? I would do anything to be 120 pounds right now when that used to seem obese to me...yeah, what did I know. I am now obese, and I have so much more respect and sympathy for all walks of life. However, I sure am not going to live this way...time to find that happy medium!

We had breakfast after boot camp, which was great. We have a personal chef here who prepares all of our meals, and for being so healthy, they taste great! We went for a walk next and then had weight training at the gym. After lunch I talked with the trainers for a bit and told them about my history with anorexia and stuff and my goals here. They are amazing people! I'm sure it's hard for them to believe I ever struggled with anorexia looking at me now, but, oh well...I'm certainly a rare case, and I'm not lying, that's for sure. We all went back to the gym a little later for cardio. It was hard being there and seeing really skinny and fit people and then looking in the mirror at myself. I struggled to do 10 minutes on the cardio machines I used to abuse for hours. I couldn't even think about attempting the StairMaster. Well, I'm staying here until I'm perfect!

July 2, 2010

What a day! I did my best yet at boot camp, had breakfast, and then went on a gorgeous hike, but my shins were crippling me! It sucked because I wasn't even tired but had to keep stopping because they hurt so much. Then was weight training at the gym. I can tell I've lost weight, but again I'm still just so fat. After lunch, Wayne, a few others, and I went on a short walk/hike to a little waterfall. Again my shins were throbbing, but Wayne stayed back and walked with me. Next up...tennis! It had to be the worst I have ever played, but it was so windy, the balls were flat, the court literally had mini hills on it, I haven't played in a while, and I've gained 80 pounds since I've really last played, but it was still embarrassing. I played with Chris, one of the other awesome trainers and owners of PFC. He has a minimal tennis background but was still able to hit the ball over and get my shots back because he's so fast and in incredible shape. He even beat me 4–3 in games. This will be the last time! Just wait until I'm fit! I hope Chris doesn't think I'm terrible now or that I made up being a nationally ranked tennis player. I suppose the only thing to do is prove it but that could mean patience, which is one of the hardest things for me. I haven't been eating too much...the past 2 days I've really only had fewer than 1,000 calories...

July 5, 2010

Today was OK...I lost 12.5 pounds in one week—hooray! I really hope I don't end up with loose skin, though. I didn't sleep at all last night. I just feel awful. After lunch Chris mentioned to me that I really need to eat all my food and that he's got his eyes on me. He was super nice and chill about it, but I better make sure I do better so that I don't create a problem. Erg...some other people here don't always eat all their food...in fact, one girl purposefully always leaves her carbs. Why is everyone focusing and picking on me?

July 21, 2010

Things are going great! I'm still struggling a bit with food but am making progress with eating all of my meals. Chris and Wayne keep bugging me about needing to eat all my food and how much they believe in me. It's weird...I mean, how could people actually accept, like, and treat me so nicely when I'm so fat and ugly? It doesn't make any sense to me.

August 7, 2010

I had my first tennis lesson today at the Sports Mall with a respected coach and it was phenomenal. I played great considering my shape, and he is a fabulous coach. I can't be any more excited. It's official...I must move to Utah!

My plan: eat meals but no grains, only eat carbohydrates from vegetables, 2 packs of gum a day, 16 ounces coffee a day, no Crystal Light, try not to eat snacks, burn 4,000 calories a day, may have string cheese and a piece of fruit only before bed.

August 13, 2010

Happy Friday the 13th! I guess you could say today isn't very lucky for me. I've gone twice now to this lady who does colonics because I have been having terrible constipation problems. It has become such a concern of mine that the program thought this might help. The colonic lady told me my digestive system was totally whacked! It did help me get some stuff out, thankfully. I ended up going to Urgent Care today. The doctor took an X-ray, which showed my stomach still completely backed up! What the heck? I've never had constipation problems in my life. After talking with my GI doctor I'm now seeing here, he prescribed the strongest laxative for me, which is this gallon of liquid stuff. I had to drink it every 10 minutes, and, boy, did it make me feel awful! Ugh! All it did was make me pee out of my butt. I don't even think it worked! Blah...I only ate 600 calories today. I guess that's good?

August 14, 2010

Last night sucked, and today so far is worse, if that's possible. I felt terrible this morning, so one of the trainers took me to the ER. I had another X-ray taken, which showed I was still completely backed up! Seriously? The doctor also shared with me that the results of my HIDA scan my GI doctor ordered last week were very abnormal and that I would need my gallbladder removed soon. What? I called my GI doctor's office yesterday, and they didn't even have the results. This is getting really confusing and frustrating.

The ER doctor discharged me with a prescription to repeat the liquid jug laxative I did yesterday. Again! Ah, that stuff was the worst! He gave me the name of a gallbladder surgeon and said to get in with them as soon as possible. I called my parents afterward. They are really worried and want me to come home and go to Stanford hospital, but no way am I going to leave Utah. The doctors here should be fine enough, right? My stomach is killing me right now, and I'm only on my fifth glass of the laxative. I'm sure I will start peeing out of my butt soon, or maybe barfing. One weird thing I noticed is how low my heart rate is getting. Ten times while I was in the ER the alarms were set off because my pulse was dropping as low as 38 and averaging 45 beats per minute. I'm not even skinny, so what the heck? On the bright side, literally, I'm getting a nice tan from sitting outside in the sun.

August 16, 2010

Ugh, another hard day. I felt really odd all day and wasn't even able to complete any workouts each time I attempted. I met with the PFC doctor later today and that was...not good. She told me my body is shutting down and that I'm in a very serious situation. She said given my medical history she wants to be extra cautious. She told me my body can't take all the compulsive exercise right now and that I'm going to have to modify my plan in the program. Thankfully, she said I wouldn't have to go home, but that after I meet with my GI doctor and surgeon, she, Wayne, Chris, and I will need to sit down and create a reduced schedule for me until I'm 100 percent OK. As much as I wanted to scream and hit her for threatening to take away my compulsive exercise, I have to say I completely agree with her. She is by far one of the most thorough and intelligent doctors I've ever had, and I really trust my health with her. I guess I should be thankful that PFC is even allowing me to stay through all this. LIFE would have had asked me to leave by now. I know if I left PFC right now I wouldn't do well at all. They are saving my life mentally and physically, and their genuine support is really altering my faith and trust in humanity.

August 18, 2010

Chris took me to my surgeon appointment today, and the physician's assistant told me my HIDA scan results were the worst they have ever seen in their office. Normal functioning is 35 percent, and mine is negative 68 percent—what the heck? The surgeon came in and wanted to do the surgery this Friday but then decided I should wait another week because of my constipation issue. He prescribed me more laxatives. I swear I've tried every laxative on the market now and honestly am not getting results. I feel so sick and have terrible back and radiating shoulder pain. I had an appointment later to get a colonic. A ton of shit came out, and it was all undigested. The lady told me to eat nothing and come back Friday. I started crying because I couldn't just not eat, but I'm scared, exhausted, and in pain. I only ate about 600 calories of food today.

August 27, 2010

Surgery day! I arrived at St. Mark's Hospital and was taken to room 8. At 9:20 a.m., a really cute guy wheeled me to the pre-op room. I met my anesthesiologist, who was so nice and near 7 ½ feet tall! I talked to my surgeon briefly and was then wheeled off into the OR. A mask was placed over my face, and I was out within one second. I later awoke feeling not so great. My stomach hurt a lot. My heart rate was again really low, and the guy monitoring me told the nurse it was averaging 40 to 43 beats per minutes. I was later taken back to the fourth floor and room 8. A wonderful staff from PFC came to see me and take me home. I was in so much pain! Getting up to go to the bathroom made me cry, and I felt so light-headed and sick. I spent about 2 more hours in my room. The nurse took my blood pressure, which was 70/44, yet still discharged me. What?

I felt so sick. As I was being wheeled to the elevators, another nurse said I should not be going home and should go back to my room, but oh well. We stopped at the grocery store on the way home to get some broth—and what a disaster! My stomach started to bleed again from the incision site. I was seeing black, shaking uncontrollably, so hot, and so not OK. I made it home, took my pain medication, and lay in my bed for a while. Chris came and hung out with me later and turned on a DVD for me. One of the other clients and I had a blast joking and laughing (ouch!) in my room. Every time I stand up I feel so nauseous and as if I'm going to faint. The incisions on my right side hurt so bad...almost too bad.

August 28, 2010

Wow! Where even to start? I felt awful when I woke up. I was in a lot of pain with some nausea, light-headedness, and sensations of blacking out. I slept in until 11:00 this morning and then got up and ate some Jell-O and broth. I spent pretty much the rest of the afternoon in bed. I came out to the kitchen around 5:00 p.m. and ate some more as well as 1 whole bag of celery, zucchini, and egg whites. Well, within the time span of 1 hour, my stomach literally tripled in size, I could hardly breathe, my shoulder and stomach were killing me, and I was freaking out! I called my surgeon, who told me to go to St. Mark's ER immediately.

One of the lovely clients took the van keys and drove my pregnant stomach and me to the ER. I had a lovely nurse and doctor, and he ordered a CT scan to check for a bile leak. I had to wait 2 hours after drinking the CT contrast before they could actually do the scan. I finally got the scan done and waited for the results.

The doctor finally came back in to tell me I was being hooked up to monitors and being admitted because the CT scan showed internal bleeding in my back and my hemoglobin dropped from 15 to 10. He said he was 99 percent sure it was due to something being nicked during surgery and that I could need a blood transfusion and exploratory surgery to stop the bleeding! Can this really be happening? I called Dad and told him what was going on as well as assuring him he didn't need to fly out although he was worried. I was moved up to the fourth floor and had a really nice nurse. I got absolutely no sleep despite feeling miserable and exhausted. I guess the bleeding explains why my pain was so much worse than I expected!

September 3, 2010

I've been home from the hospital now for a few days. Today sucked! What is it with Fridays lately? I feel absolutely awful and sick, ugh! I guess I should mention that last night another client and I kind of binged. The good part was I hated it and I have no desire or cravings ever to do it again. It could have been about a 2,000-calorie binge, and the day's total was around 3,000.

September 11, 2010

What a day! I had a fabulous tennis lesson and really pushed myself to the limit physically. When I got back to the house, something was not right. Wayne and Chris were both there...on a Sunday...making lunch. Chris then told us all that our personal chef never woke up this morning. He overdosed on pills and left a suicide note. It doesn't really surprise me. He was so severely depressed and hooked on drugs, but the news hit me hard. I cried for a long time, realizing how precious life is and thinking about Torrance, my family, and how I got a second chance when I wasn't perhaps supposed to. I love life and myself and need to take care of my health now and always. I went for a hike alone, feeling sick to my stomach and numb. It was such a weird day, and I feel a bit anxious right now.

September 12, 2010

Late last night another client and I ate some food—to put things lightly. I succumbed to the anxiety, and it was his last night, so he didn't care if he splurged. It was only a small binge, thank goodness, but a freaky night nonetheless considering the earlier events. The phone rang at 9:30 p.m., all the doors were unlocked, Wayne texted me at 10:00 p.m. out of the blue, and we kept hearing weird noises and seeing weird shadows. We were freaked out as if something bad were going to happen to us because we were cheating on our meal plan. I reluctantly asked the other client if he would sleep in the empty bed in my room because I was scared. I ended up getting almost no sleep because he snored so loudly and because I was sweating so badly— from the binge, I suppose. Ugh! Well, at least tomorrow is Sunday so I can sleep in a little and be lazy.

September 13, 2010

I slept so well last night and had a great weigh-in. I lost 3 pounds, gained 3 pounds of muscle, and lost 3 percent body fat—sweet! I am now in the healthy range and weigh 164 pounds. Geez, I even binged a few nights and still had good results . . . maybe I can keep doing so? It was a good day of workouts. I encountered one of the trainers I worked with once during weight training when I first arrived, and he didn't even recognize me today when I said hi. He couldn't believe how much I've changed, which was nice to hear.

22

Panic in Park City

"I think the most successful and accomplished people are those who can show courage and admit they can't do it alone. It's pointless to struggle silently behind a fake smile." ~Britt

September 25, 2010

Ah! I binged last night. What makes me think I have the right to eat late at night when everyone else is in bed? Fuck this eating disorder! I had about 5,000 calories for the whole day. It was all healthy foods but still so much. I had a terrible stomachache, sweated all night, and was filled with so much guilt I just wanted to scream and cry. It was my best body image day, and I was in a great mood as well...what happened? Oh well, I learned...right?

PFC moved their location and the program now resides in beautiful Park City, Utah. It's wonderful here, but a different setup, living situation, and schedule. Change, good or bad, is just so hard for me and I always seem to turn to ED to help me cope. Things aren't starting out well for me here. I was hoping I would feel safer and less tempted to binge with the move, but now I fear the opposite is happening. I've been so bloated and mad at myself today. I'm really freaked out for Monday's weigh-in now.

September 29, 2010

Why is it that on the days I'm happiest and work out the hardest I keep having huge binges to match it? I was so happy on Monday because I still lost 4 pounds even with that one binge, but why am I still falling into this trap? I ate about 4,000 calories for the whole day, which I've burned through exercise, but I ate about 2,500 to 3,000 calories at night. I sweated all night, which I guess is a good thing because it means my metabolism is working well. I surprisingly and interestingly had tons of energy and endurance today and didn't even look bloated! I did about 7 hours of exercise—whoa!

October 2, 2010

Ugh, I binged last night and had about 4,000 calories for the whole day again. I am just so stressed out lately. I slept in this morning and did absolutely no exercise, which was a nice break, but why do I need to binge to justify letting myself relax? I guess because I have a reason to give myself permission to chill as opposed to doing something more productive.

When I binge I get so self-conscious that I *can't* do productive things because I don't want people to see me. I'm so nervous for weigh day now.

October 3, 2010

Despite planning to refuse my weigh-in since I ended up binging the following night as well, I stepped on the scale. It turns out I should have refused...I was 155.6 pounds, so I gained 2 pounds, ah! I did still have lots of food in me and was retaining water, but still, how embarrassing to gain weight at a weight loss program! My body fat actually went down 4 percent, though, which was great, and I did lose a few inches.

October 14, 2010

Last night kind of sucked, you could say. I binged very badly. In fact, it was my worst binge since arriving. I weighed in yesterday and was 150.6 pounds. It was also my birthday. Somehow I must have justified that this gave me the right to binge.

October 18, 2010

Today was good and bad all blended together. I decided to get weighed despite the previous binges because I felt thinner. But when I stepped onto the all-mighty scale, it read 153 pounds, which is a weight gain of 3 pounds just since Wednesday, ah! This seems crazy, but I did have 2 huge binges, didn't exercise much, and my hormones are all screwed up...I did lose a lot of inches, and my body fat went down 2.6 percent to 23.3 percent now.

November 6, 2010

Talk about a roller coaster day. I was all over the place emotionally and had awful body image. It didn't help that I started my period as well. I had a tennis match in the afternoon in the open-level tournament I entered. My 2 friends in the program drove me to my match. I played the number-one seed, and she wasn't even that good, but I played terrible. I felt so weak and had limited preparation, but still I should have won easily. Instead I lost in a third-set tiebreaker. I just gave up. Afterward, the 3 of us went out to dinner, which certainly was not on the PFC meal plan. I, however, ordered an egg-white salad.

The 2 guys were splurging with burgers and fries, but I wasn't—nooo! I have the utmost control. Though it's a rather lonely place to be...so heck, I played tennis earlier, and I deserve a little treat right? One night can't hurt. We mutually decided to split a thin-crust pizza afterward. "We?" Not "them?" Well, go me! Screw that anorexic mentality, and let's have some fun, baby! Why not have dessert as well? With each bite of pizza and the taste of frozen yogurt smothered in candy, I became more and more out of touch. As I finished off the night eating an entire bag of white chocolate-covered pretzels, the slight guilt I felt at the start of an innocent night became overpowering.

November 7, 2010

Ugh! Well, after my poor performance on the tennis court yester-day and the burden and bloat lingering from last night, I defaulted my consolation tennis match. I ended up spending the whole day with one of the guys in the program close to my age. We went to lots of stores and cafés and shared tons of yummy (and sinful) foods and bakery items. We then went out for dinner, which most certainly included dessert. What is wrong with me? Why can't I just be normal? I am either too strict or too reckless. How can it be that hard to find a happy balance?

The day's total came to 6 apples, 3 egg whites, beans, 1 large chicken wrap, 10 coffee creamers, 1 protein shake, sweet potato fries, veggies, peppermint mocha, 2 huge muffins, 2 huge cookies, 1 scone from Starbucks, 1 protein bar, 1 cookies 'n' cream candy bar, 4 mini Reese's Peanut Butter Cups, 4 Peppermint Patties, 1 bagel with cream cheese, 1 peanut butter and chocolate cookie, 1 extra-large frozen yogurt smothered with candies, 1 bag of chocolate-covered Cinnamon Bears, 1 huge cinnamon sticky bun, 10 servings of white chocolate-covered pretzels, 1 bowl of Special K, and 1 yogurt. It was a pretty fun day minus the small fact that this was the worst binge for me in 6 months.

November 10, 2010

What do I want to do? Who do I want to be? What do I want to have? I want to be a leader and role model for others. I want other people to benefit from my life experiences and learn to love and accept themselves. I want to be a person who is respected and looked up to, a person who changes people's lives for the better. I want to continue loving life and myself, never taking a breath for granted. I want to have solid relationships, support, love, security, success, happiness, health, balance, and opportunities.

November 14, 2010

It's been a few days since I journaled now. Thursday was good... at least up until the afternoon. My friend and I ended up going to a café again later on. We had a nice time hanging out... and eating. Friday was, uh, well, I don't even know. I was extremely sore and mentally exhausted. I slept in and didn't work out all day—first red flag. I then talked with one of the trainers about being burnt out and wanting to take 1 week completely off and then go 100 percent my last 4 weeks, and he agreed—second red flag. After confirmation from a few other people that it would be beneficial to take a break... bam! I gave myself confirmation to binge—and what a binge it was. This was just after my huge binge Thursday night, too.

Saturday was interesting. I was so bloated and felt so gruesome. I slept through breakfast but ate lunch and dinner with the group. A bunch of clients went out to a bar to watch a big fight on TV, but my friend and I stayed behind. I had a nice massage after dinner and then chilled in my room and worked on an article I was writing. I finally went to bed, but I didn't sleep. In fact, it was one of the worst nights yet. I took a little bit of castor oil, which can work as a laxative and all night I had severe cramps and diarrhea—and I mean all night. It got to the point where I felt so dizzy and nauseous I thought I would black out or throw up! Then again, I did take it on purpose...

November 15, 2010

"Love, appreciate, accept, enjoy, respect, and be kind to yourself. Stop wishing you looked different, were better at something, or more successful. It's good to have goals to keep pushing yourself forward, but enjoy who you are now. The fact is you can never be anyone else but you. So make yourself the best person you can possibly be and honor yourself for who you are, not what others say you are." ~Britt

23

Back to LIFE

"But why are you so hard on yourself? Why do you
think you have to walk this life alone? Why do you
believe all your struggles are your fault? Why do
you believe everyone else deserves help and support
except you?" ~Britt

December 3, 2010

I am back home now in San Luis Obispo. I left PFC 2 weeks
early with the plan to come back January 1st and complete my last
2. I also put a deposit down on an apartment in Park City because
I just can't be without PFC in my life. Yep, you heard me right. I'm
planning to move to Park City. Thankfully, I now have 1 month at
home to lose even more weight and wow everyone when I return. The
first couple of days home have been amazing. So many people are
thrilled to see me looking healthy rather than anorexic, but it's still
weird. I really want to get down to 140 pounds here at home. I'm not
exactly sure what I weigh right now, and honestly I'm afraid to know
as I'm probably close to 160 pounds after all my previous binges. I
know 140 pounds is a big goal, but I can do it as long as I don't binge
anymore...I hope.

December 6, 2010

The last 2 days sucked. I absolutely binged my brains out and felt
so sick. Today has been OK. I went for a 45-minute hike, but there

was so much water retention in my legs that my shins felt as if they were breaking. I'm considering getting another colonic. I have everything going for me now, and besides, I learned from those binges, so it's not going to happen ever again!

December 14, 2010

I have a surprise to share...I freaking binged again...badly! I am so bloated and mad at myself! I've been so down lately. Either it's just me or the fact that I'm back in my triggering hometown, same house, same environment, no friends or people to support me other than my parents, I'm lonely, I don't have any commitments or reasons to wake up for, Mom stresses me out, and my body is all out of whack from the binges. Phew! Maybe I should give myself a break and stop hurting my body, stop binging, and start loving myself. I'm so overwhelmed with everything I need to do before moving to Utah. This is going to be a huge change for me. I will be living alone in a new state, with a new job and new responsibilities. I'm starting to get addicted to colonics, which can't be a good thing. Sometimes I think I justify a binge because then I can just go get a colonic (expensive!) and undo the damage. Of course, realistically I know that all it does is dehydrate me, not get rid of the calories or promote weight loss, so really I'm just screwing myself over.

December 17, 2010

The previous 2 days were just awful. My sister had a bunch of people over for a party, and it included lots of junk food. They made a chocolate cake, and there was a bunch of leftover Thai food in the fridge. I was doing perfectly with food that day, but I had to wait for what seemed like forever for them to leave the kitchen so I could eat alone and in peace. I ended up eating just a tiny bite of cake and Thai food and then bam! It triggered a huge binge, which lasted all night long despite Dad trying to help. It was just dreadful.

Yesterday was not a fun day either. I got up around 1:00 p.m. and talked to Chris on the phone. PFC is starting to get a lot more attention now, and it only makes me more excited to return and look great. However, I must get going on this weight loss. I'm moving in the opposite direction right now and am freaking out. Yeah, it's one thing to tell yourself to lose weight, but it's another to do it. I ended up binging all damn day yesterday. It was an upsetting day for everyone. I need to grow up, take responsibility, stop binging, and make my life happen!

December 31, 2010

I haven't journaled in about a week, so I'm just going to recap what I remember because so much happened! I once again (ta-da!) binged Wednesday, Thursday, Friday, Saturday, *and* Sunday. It was absolutely ridiculous! I don't know what got into me. Hormones? Feeling lonely? I don't know. Anyway, I've been contemplating a lot and have decided to go to LIFE again now to finish up my 2 months that they put on hold and won't refund. This is my best opportunity to use my weeks especially because I actually need it right now anyway.

Sure, I guess I'm justifying that the binges are OK since I'm now going to be entering a strict weight loss environment. When am I going to finally realize that I can't keep depending on external sources to fix me? Well, on that same note I am really getting sucked into the dependence of colonics. I really love the lady I see because she is someone I trust and can be honest with, so partly I think I just enjoy her support. I've decided to do 6 colonics in a row to get rid of all the toxins from the junk food and hopefully prevent more binge urges.

January 7, 2011

A couple days ago I ended up binging on apples and bananas, which isn't the worst, but it left me feeling bloated and uneasy with myself. I woke up early the following morning still really bloated, hungry, anxious, and craving a real binge where I could eat whatever I wanted without caring. So...I did. I had 2 heads of cauliflower, 5 eggs, 1 protein shake, 6 Subway cookies, 6-inch Subway sandwich, 1 huge cinnamon roll, 3 bagels with cream cheese and butter, Lucky Charms cereal, Cinnamon Toast Crunch cereal, 1 whole jug of milk, cream cheese cake, lots of pancakes with syrup, 1 whole can of whip cream, 1 coffee Frappuccino, 3 protein bars, chocolate almonds, 1 huge cookie, apple, bean salad, 2 Arctic Zeros, and 1 large pastry. So what do I do next? Immediately schedule 2 colonics as if the binging could be erased like a pencil.

January 19, 2011

I've been at LIFE for almost a week now, and so far things have been going well. I've had the few occasional binges, but for the most part have been eating fine and busting my butt in the workouts. I wrote my mission statement in one of our classes, which is as follows:

I am creating and living a balanced, healthy, positive, and fun lifestyle. I make decisions that are best for me, my well-being, and my future. I manage, treat, and respect myself and my body with the utmost amount of care. I think positively, believe in myself, accept myself, and love myself uncondi-tionally. I am always striving to learn, make improvements, and be a role model and leader to all. I'm OK!

Some notes I took during the same class that I really need to get through to my head:
- Food is fuel...nothing else!
- Food creates false emotions if I let it.
- Binging is a temporary escape to feel or not feel.
- Food does *not* control me.
- Eating junk food or overeating needs to be a conscious choice.
- I do not need to fear dying at night.
- Food is not a friend and is not there to comfort me when I'm lonely.
- Food is not a hobby or something to use as entertainment when I'm bored.
- It's perfectly fine to treat myself once in a while as long as it's a choice.

- Food is used when I'm hungry, not as an all-or-nothing purpose.
- Know what's important and what's not.
- I am defined by my qualities, not by my weight, image, money, job, tennis, and achievements.

Trust: Trust means a person has my best interest in mind and will stand true to their word. It means putting faith into someone else and giving up all control. Trust is so important because it means someone is looking out for me and will commit to their actions and words. Without trust, there is no safety.

Unconditional love: To me, this means a person will still accept, care for, and appreciate someone, including their flaws, positives, negatives, strengths, and weaknesses. This is so important because nobody is perfect and nobody should feel the need to be perfect or change himself or herself for someone. Everyone is unique and should be loved regardless of their faults or past.

January 31, 2011

I am back in Park City right now at PFC for a project, but just for 1 week. It was so amazing to see all my favorite trainers and people again but also very overwhelming. Unfortunately, I probably look the same weight-wise as when they last saw me in December. Obviously, I was hoping to wow them by losing a significant amount of weight while at home, but clearly I set my standards so high they backfired altogether. My second night there I ended up binging. Out of desperation, I took 5 Dulcolax laxatives even though the maximum amount is 3. This is definitely not starting the week out well.

February 3, 2011

Ugh! I am so struggling yet I am so OK at the same time. Today started off great with a difficult boot camp that I did well in. Next was a quick circuit class, but I had no energy or motivation. I began feeling weak and sick. After lunch I went downstairs for weight training, but my energy was nonexistent. I chose to go back to my room to take a much-needed nap. I woke up late and missed dinner, so I ended up binging on protein shakes, yogurt, apples, and protein bars. I then had a great massage, but I was already in that anxious, bored mode, so I walked across the street in the freezing snow to the gas station to get some more food. I eventually went to bed but woke up at midnight, drank ½ a jug of milk and then took 5 laxatives, erg! I have to—but hate to—admit that these laxatives are becoming a frequent part of my diet. I wouldn't say I abuse them, such as those who take around 20 a day, but I need to stop. I just wish I didn't always get so bloated every time I eat or drink anything.

February 5, 2011

I hate today. I woke up in one of those moods. Those moods where you feel the whole world is against you, your mind is spinning a million miles per hour with anxiety, and you strongly disapprove of yourself. I ate about 2,000 calories yesterday, which isn't that bad, but it consisted of lots of apples, and they always make me bloated. So, when I woke up today still feeling bloated, it led me to want to binge today and unfortunately I have been…badly. The positives are I found a lady who does colonics about a half-hour away and tomorrow the binging will stop. I hate that colonics and/or laxatives are the only way to end a binge. It's like some sort of mental symbolism that I'm starting over new, which I'm sure links back to my all-or-nothing thinking. I feel so gross and disappointed in myself. For the heck of it, I Googled the dangers of binging and if it was possible for your stomach to explode—and it can! That really scared me and brought me to an aha moment. I still have an eating disorder and am using eating disorder behaviors when I binge. Just because I'm not skinny or fat, it doesn't give me the right to use ED secretly. I pride myself in recovery, so I had better damn do it all the way—not to mention quit this laxative shit. No more denial!

February 6, 2011

Erg! I'm just down today. I guess you could call it a post-binge hangover. I slept in and then got a colonic that wasn't that great. I'm so out of whack right now and emotional. I just can't even comprehend myself right now. Not only am I at PFC—the place where I am supposed to be the superstar—but I also undid much of my hard work over the past weeks by binging. I just want to disappear, yet I keep growing bigger.

February 19, 2011

Things have been going OK lately. I did 8 colonics in a row when I returned to LIFE and started feeling better about my appearance. I've also been taking laxatives on a more regular basis, which I can't say I approve of. Today started out awesome. I felt good about myself and performed wonderfully at beach boot camp. Since today was only a half-day, I decided to go see a movie to kill some time. It was pouring rain, and I decided to get my nails done afterward. While waiting for a cab to take me back to the apartments, I went and got a frozen yogurt next door to the nail shop. No big deal, but the cab ended up taking 1 hour to show up! So, I kept getting more and more frozen yogurt while waiting. When I did eventually get back to the apartments, I felt frantic and anxious. I started thinking about UCLA and my time there in the hospital. That only made me feel more vulnerable. In reaction, I found myself taking the elevator of the apartments down to the ground level where another serve-yourself frozen yogurt shop sat. Like a puppet, I got 2 of the largest cups full of frozen yogurt and littered them with candy. I ate them both, getting my drug fix, and then as predictable as the sun rises, the guilt, anger, and hopelessness settled in.

February 20, 2011

I woke up and did 45 minutes of cardio but was in a very unstable mood. I was not planning to binge today, yet before I knew it I had eaten all my meals packaged for the day, plus 1 chai latte and 3 enormous muffin top cookies. I had a nice talk with Dad, and he made me feel better about myself and assured me I'm just going through the ups and downs of life. After Dad justified my struggle, it was as if it gave me permission to keep on struggling. I found myself at Panera Bread next eating 1 turkey sandwich, macaroni and cheese, plus 1 large apple muffin. I then ventured next door and jammed in 2 milkshake smoothies before heading off for my colonic. Oh my...

February 25, 2011

Today is hard. I got weighed and was 154 pounds! Apparently I am down 1 pound, but in 10 days, ugh! I thought I would have lost more. I did have a lot of last night's food and coffee in my system but still. I'm sure I must have gained some muscle, too, because I feel thinner. I want the scale to go down, though. I wish I now had a longer stay here. My calves have been killing me today, and I'm just so stressed right now. I did pretty much no exercise today. After lunch I ended up hanging around in LIFE's community kitchen because it was raining outside, and I still wasn't in the mood to work out. A few other clients stayed in the kitchen as well, enjoying a lazy Friday afternoon. There was a lot of peanut butter protein shake left in the fridge, and we all ended up having most of it. Uh-oh.

What a setup. Rain + canceled tennis + laziness + disappointing weigh-in + sore calves + boredom + stress = leaving gym early to go binge. I still have 2 weeks left here, and I want them to be binge-free! Why is that too much to ask? Today's binge consisted of yogurt, walnuts, almonds, berries times 2, salad times 2, 3 cups of peanut butter shake, 1 apple, 1 egg, 1 protein bar, 1 chai latte, 1 frozen yogurt with candy, 6 extra-large cookies, 1 huge banana bread loaf, 1 vanilla latte, 1 large ham and cheese sandwich, 1 extra-large bag of almonds, 1 java chip Frappuccino, and coconut water so far. I'm caught in a lonely and frustrating in-between stage right now. In the past few years, I haven't had a permanent residence or home life. I'm so ready to settle down and live!

March 3, 2011

I haven't journaled in a few days now. After the ridiculous Friday binge, I ended up sleeping in the next Saturday. I felt awful when I woke up, yet binged again and badly! On Sunday, I had a colonic but then ended up binging again afterward, just not quite as bad. I then had a second colonic later in the same day! Ugh, $230 down the drain! On Monday, I slept in and had another colonic and then chilled. I ate about 3,000 calories, which is still awful, though not as bad as the other days. I hate my body so much! On Tuesday I again slept in a little bit and then had an appointment with world-renowned Dr. Habib Sadeghi at Be Hive of Healing. I just went in for comprehensive blood work. It's an expensive test, but it checks absolutely everything, including heavy metals and hormones. I took a nap later and then had an afternoon colonic.

March 8, 2011

My goodness, what an amazing day! I had an appointment with Dr. Sadeghi himself after he received all my blood work results. I don't even know where to begin. He is the most incredible man I have ever met! It was as if he knew everything about me without me even opening my mouth. It was almost eerie. As I began sharing things about my life, so much raw emotion came over me: anger, sadness, guilt, loneliness, and confusion. Dr. Sadeghi said everything I went through was perfectly planned to create who I am now and that there is no regret, blame, or missed opportunities. He kept saying over and over how proud he is of me and that I have so much courage and will help so many. Next, we moved on to my blood work results. Here comes a shocker. He said I have the best genetics he's seen in 12 years! He was in shock at how perfectly put together my body was and said that is why I survived the impossible. He stated I did no irreversible damage and that I am a phenomenally created human. He told me to relax because my life is going to be so beautiful and I am perfectly guided.

Some notes I took after our session: I was the caterpillar who needed to cocoon for that period of time to become the butterfly I am today. I had to go through that golden darkness. All of this was for a reason. There is no regret, blame, or mistakes. The issue is how I handle the issue. I didn't miss out on anything. I am going to help so many people (caterpillars). I have the most amazing, capable body and genetics that Dr. Sadeghi has ever seen. I need to be the best parent to my inner child. Yes, I was reborn! I need to heal myself now. Wow, I feel like I just had a personal meeting with God. There is something so divine about Dr. Sadeghi and I've never felt more connected and comforted by another person in my life.

24

Confusion and Delusion

"You think you're lost. You think you're headed for disaster. But this isn't true. Quiet your mind. Be patient. Let go. Quit overthinking. You're on your way and you are headed for a beautiful life full of meaning." ~Britt

March 21, 2011

I haven't journaled in over a week now...never a good sign. Dad picked me up from LIFE early to go home last Sunday, and we had a nice drive. The problem? I had binged severely the previous 3 days. I binged again once at home and started back up with the colonics in San Luis Obispo. On Tuesday I binged severely again. It was fun, yet oh-so desperate, shameful, lonely, and harmful. I created a contract with Dad not to binge, hoping it might put some restraint on me but without luck. Later in the week, I fell hostage and binged again. The binges are only getting more insane. As I finished a gross binge, I stayed up all night researching eating disorder/therapeutic treatment centers. Oh, déjà vu or what? Sigh. Why is it I'm always bouncing from one program to the next looking for answers that can only come from within? Yeah, I'm comfortable in treatment and am, in a way, good at it, but I can't live the rest of my life like this. There is going to come a time where I won't be able just to ship myself off to treatment to undo the weight gain from binges. I'm going to have to face the consequences and myself sooner or later, but right now I'm hoping on later.

On Saturday morning I had a nice talk with my parents, and then we got sandwiches for lunch. I then went out afterward and binged all day. I knew I would, though, as I had already made up my mind last night. My parents are being so great and removed all the food from our house except for my food for the day. I hope it works, but part of me feels I need a treatment center to really focus on me and heal the core issues. Ugh…and to think I only came home for a few weeks to get ready to move to Utah and be this fitness star…good gosh, look at me now.

March 26, 2011

What the heck, Brittany? Four days binge-free, then 2 nights binging on gross home food like eggs and beans, and then bam! Today turns into one of my most disgusting binges. I've been doing great mental work lately. I've really been piecing together my life and childhood. Why does that make me think I deserve to binge then for all the hard work? I guess I just know no other way to cope with the pain I don't want but have to face. One realization I did have is that I cannot do this (lose weight, recover from ED) at home. I finally have all the pieces to the puzzle, but I don't know what the finished picture is supposed to look like. I need guidance, healing, professional support, and time. I know with confidence that I need to check out from the world for a few months or so to heal myself…physically, mentally, and spiritually. I'm ready; I'm truly ready. I want this done right. No restricting, no binging, no bargaining, and no excuses—just balance and patience. I have to trust that my opportunities will still be there even though Dad threatens I could blow them. Mom is being supportive and agrees with me. Lately, I've had so many options, but I wasn't sure of the right choice. Now, however, I know the right choice, yet I don't seem to have many options…or shall I say money. Why does treatment and receiving help have to bankrupt a family? I am at a loss right now. I'm not giving up or giving in, but I am surrendering. I feel so lonely and sad. I feel as if I've lost touch with people again. It doesn't help that I feel like crap and look pregnant with 12 kids right now.

Today's binge consisted of 4 doughnuts; 1 huge streusel muffin; 1 biscuit with pie filling; 1 oat cookie bar; 1 breakfast burrito; 1 granola bar; 1 whole box of Cinnamon Toast Crunch cereal; 1 whole carton of milk; 1 croissant, ham, and cheese sandwich; 1 mango smoothie; 1 protein bar; 2 Sausage McMuffins with Egg; 1 vanilla iced coffee; 4 huge peanut butter pancakes with syrup; 1 rice and bean burrito; lots of peanut butter; 10 Reese's Peanut Butter Cups; 1 extra-extra-large frozen yogurt with candy; 1 orange juice; 1 Double-Double In-N-Out burger; french fries; 1 milkshake; 1 pint of Ben & Jerry's ice cream; 1 Rice Krispies Treat, 1 banana, and 3 oranges.

March 27, 2011

Help, help, help times infinity! I have never felt so sick…OK, actually I didn't feel that sick, but the binge side effects have never been so severe, such as bloating, soreness, sweating, swollen glands, and edema. I'm really scared. My clothes are starting not to fit, and my body and face are starting to look as they did when I was creeping up to 221 pounds. No, no, no! I'm also seriously thinking my heart still lies with PFC and that I made the wrong decision to cancel my move to Utah and take an opportunity in L.A. instead. But honestly, I'm so conflicted that I'm not sure I should take either opportunity. I'm incredibly stressed and am still out of control with my eating disorder…moving to a new state or city would be a recipe for disaster, wouldn't it? I'm so uncomfortable right now yet am semi-binging today. Ah!

March 29, 2011

I am having the hardest time recovering from these binges. I feel so out of it. Dad has been starting to cry at night now…how has it come back to this? Today hasn't been so great. I overheard Mom crying hysterically on the phone with Dad earlier. It was so sad, and my dad is so depressed. I did have a nice talk with Mom later. She basically told me I need to go get help and then not come home for a long time. She's right. I left the house and have been eating junk food for the rest of the day. I'm too far gone to care anymore.

April 1, 2011

Oh goodness. It is rather hard to believe that only 3 weeks ago I was the envy of many and in the best shape of my life. I guess after 2 weeks straight of eating 10,000-plus calories I should expect exactly how I feel and look right now. I look pregnant, am always sweating, have awful body odor, puffy face and eyes, double chin, swollen glands, sore joints, edema, headaches, am exhausted, am irritable, my clothes don't fit, I have trouble breathing, and I have foggy thinking. I suppose I'm lucky my stomach didn't explode, in complete honesty.

Thankfully, my dad now has my car keys and there is hardly any food in the house. I'm going to try to do a mostly liquid diet for the next 2 weeks. I just hate my appearance now and can't believe Miss Perfect Anorexic would eat such things. These next 2 weeks I hope to get reacquainted with Ana, aka anorexia, and then continue at a treatment center. Why is it that I can't just do this in a healthy manner, aka recovery? Why would I even want my identity to be an anorexic again anyway when it ruined my life? I suppose as much as I hated anorexia it at least shielded me from having to have the identity of Brittany. But my gosh...what is so wrong with me? How is it that I have no idea who I am? I'm having an identity crisis at 22 years old! This is all just so hopeless.

April 2, 2011

Well, Brittany, you just found the tub of hidden almonds along with a little bit of peanut butter and 1 English muffin, so what do you do? You eat all of it, of course! I'm honestly scared for myself...I don't even have a gallbladder anymore, so how the heck is my body supposed to digest all that fat? You like challenges, right, Brittany? You like proving people wrong. You like doing the impossible. After spending hours looking at all my old, healthy, and pre-binge photos, I want to kill myself knowing how I look now, but I also want the old me back more than anything. It will take a lot of work. I feel so out of touch with the world now, as if 3 weeks ago I was never even a part of LIFE or working out. I am completely consumed by ED again, and it's twice as bad because it's binging and not anorexia. It is time to get obsessed again. I need to create a new problem to help get rid of the binging. Rules: 3 protein shakes a day, asparagus, sugar-free Jell-O and popsicles, and 1 apple. Work out in the house. Hardly speak. You are only allowed to stop hard-core restricting when someone says you look anorexic!

Interesting observations:

ED treatment centers: Always pointing out what you're doing wrong. Always high anxiety about new admits and potential competition. Always competition with who is the sickest, skinniest, can hide the most food, or exercise the most. False flattery from patients to other patients. "Oh, you are so skinny!" Even though in their minds they are either truly thinking, "I wish *I* was that skinny, you bitch!" or "Yeah, right... *not!*"

Addiction treatment centers: All about being positive, motivating, and pointing out the good in others as well as small victories—30-day chips, 60-day chips, etc. "Keep coming back!" AA (Alcoholics Anonymous) is very much about acceptance and that people can inspire others, break free, and live their best lives. Everyone is encouraged to work with a sponsor as well, which is someone who has been in solid recovery and serves as a role model and gives support and accountability for those just beginning their own recovery journey. All addictions are treated the same. There is no judgment as opposed to ED centers, where it's all about certain weights, calories, and requirements.

There is no "healing"—only rules when it comes to EDs, in my opinion.

Fat camps: Acceptance at any size. All about tiny victories (I jogged for 5 seconds today!), genuine care, support, and lifestyle change. Less competition. No punishment.

April 5, 2011

I binge... for the thrill, for fun, out of fear stemmed from anorexia, because food once saved my life, one of my happiest moments was my first binge at 75 pounds, out of self-sabotage, stress, boredom, loneliness, success, failure, bad body image, good body image, hunger, happiness, all-or-nothing thinking, to stay stuck and hidden, as an excuse, as punishment, for attention, to reward myself, to make up for all the years I ruined with anorexia, out of trauma, to say fuck you to anorexia, to say fuck you to my parents, to say fuck you to myself, to say fuck you to all the doctors and treatment centers who gave up on me, to let go, to zone out, to socialize with friends I avoided, and because I know no other coping skill besides anorexia or the gym.

April 7, 2011

I'm essentially living my worst nightmare. I went from a relationship, or shall I say prisoner, of anorexia so strong that I was on my deathbed to months later being clinically obese. Not only did I lose anorexia and my identity, but I also became my biggest fear. But wasn't my biggest fear death? I came face-to-face with death but never died. Maybe the world wants to show me that I lived my life around the wrong fear (gaining weight). I was so afraid to gain weight for fear I would never stop eating and overdo it and yet that's what I did. Almost as if a self-fulfilling prophecy. Hmm...it's OK. I'm OK. I'm calm. I'm patient. I'm forgiving. I'm determined. Do we subconsciously become our biggest fear? I will not give up. I will not give in. I hate the mirror. I hate my reflection. It does not show my true perfection.

April 16, 2011

I am so angry and so obese! Even Dad said that a few days ago I looked obese referring to the fact that I now am looking better, but come on...a few days ago! I have fat rolls everywhere and want to scream. This is so hard to do on my own—and not to mention at home where all my triggers reside. My life is completely on hold, and that is OK, but it's just hard when I run into roadblocks and take steps backward. In the past 3 days alone, I've consumed 16,000 calories. I'm not even done eating yet today.

April 27, 2011

I dreamt of Scandalous last night. I hated waking up this morning from that dream. What is it about horses that ALWAYS can make me cry when crying is so impossible for me? Scandalous was my best friend. When I was with her (I'm sobbing right now)...when I was with her I had a FRIEND. I've never had a best friend my whole life. I had lots of people who maybe wanted to be my friend, but I wasn't so sure. Besides, I had ED. I definitely met lots of people who could have been close friends, but we were never in the same city long enough for that to happen.

Being with Scandalous REPLACED all the negatives in my life. I didn't worry about homework, getting top grades, winning tennis tournaments, my unhappy and worried parents, feeling lonely, my body, and ED. Being with her made me feel free and my mind at peace. She was the ONLY thing that could take the place of ED. She had that power. We were such a TEAM and got recognized every show we went to because of the amazing chemistry we had together. That horse and I loved each other so much that it was evident we were ONE when I was riding her. She loved me UNCONDITION-ALLY, listened to me, and didn't judge. I could DEPEND on her, and she was all MINE.

I chose tennis over horses because of what I thought looked better to society. Tennis was more social, less expensive, and produced more opportunities, but horses are my true love. In fact, I take that back. I chose ED over horses, not tennis. When I'm with horses, all the pressure I put on myself goes away. She was my baby, my RESPON-SIBILITY, my best friend, my COMFORT, and my reason not to give up. No wonder just saying her name makes me cry....

Interestingly enough...the words I capitalized are words I once used to describe what my eating disorder gave to me. I don't have either in my life right now...although I wish I had Scandalous back, or any horse really. Wait...did I just say I don't have ED right now? I do. Just not in a form I know and certainly in a form I hate. I don't know how yet, but once I make a decision about what I'm doing with my life in the next few months, I will find a way to incorporate horses back in again. Anyway, I just felt the need to write about her. I love you, Scandalous!

April 29, 2011

I met with a lady named Erin today. She is an eating disorder psychologist who has impressive reviews and quite the résumé. My review? Oh my goodness, she is a gift from heaven! She is a brilliant psychologist and a wonderful person. She is kind, yet firm and blunt in a compassionate way, which I need more than anything. I need her to have that authoritative role. She is very supportive of the idea of me going to an inpatient facility, but she feels that it should be a very long stay and I should not come home until I am finished in all respects. She concernedly told me how dangerous it was for me to be binging when I was at such a low weight. She didn't understand why my parents didn't interfere more during that time. I told her how angry I am that when I was anorexic my parents smothered me with help, treatment, doctors, and worry, but when I was binging they couldn't care less even though it's equally as dangerous physically and psychologically. My dad even paid me to gain weight. Wrong message, parents! Why the heck didn't you help me? From 75 pounds to 221 pounds? Come on now!

May 1, 2011

Happy May! I'm so overwhelmed right now, but it's mostly from Facebook stalking. I'm so caught up in who placed how in dressage shows, who's showing what horses in jumpers, which friends are at treatment centers, what's new with PFC, what's going on in the world of LIFE, and who's winning what in tennis. I should just delete Facebook. It only makes me feel worse about myself, and I'm living vicariously through others, it seems. There is this one girl I went to UC Davis with who I always thought looked somewhat anorexic. Well, now she looks awfully anorexic. It almost pisses me off with anger, regret, and jealousy. Why? OK, I guess part of me just hates I couldn't balance anorexia with a social life and health, which led to

UC Davis asking me to take a leave. Obviously, I was much worse off than this girl, but it still pushes my buttons and makes me sad.

May 2, 2011

No, no, *no*! I binged last night to about 5,000 calories. I was doing just fine until Mom came upstairs because she couldn't sleep. Somehow that triggered me into deciding to stay up late and binge. I don't have to have a problem to justify living at home, so stop, Britt!

I had a tough meeting today with Erin. She basically told me that I'm just as sick and stuck right now as with the anorexia and that I am in possibly as much danger. She said I make it seem as though I'm in recovery and talk about future great things but that recovery is hard and slow and I'm not fully doing it. Erin reminded me that I must learn to eat all food groups in moderation, even if it means I struggle at first. So, guess how my eating disordered mind twisted that statement? ED convinced me to go to New Frontiers and spend $250 on food, and I've binged badly. Brittany heard what Erin said, but ED heard, "Go eat any food you want because it would be a good thing for your recovery." Yeah, well not in this manner, ED!

My size large shorts now fit like my mediums used to, so I'm guessing I have about 10 to 15 pounds to lose to get back to where I was, but after last night's binge, it could be more like 15 to 25 pounds. Dang!

May 5, 2011

I did an intense 30 minutes of exercise consisting of hallway sprints and running up and down the stairs in my house. It felt amazing and was much easier than I expected. I've been seeing a crazy amount of the number 11, which is my little symbol of encouragement and good luck.

Tonight I had finished my last snack and was very full but still in that mode of looking for food. It's a habit I've had for such a long time. Even when I was anorexic, I used to look for a little treat at night and didn't feel too guilty about it after the normal 3-plus hours of exercise I would do. It also used to make me feel safer going to bed, as if that little extra snack would help raise my heart rate enough to prevent me from dying in my sleep. Anyway, I told Mom as she was getting ready to go downstairs to bed that I wanted a treat, very well knowing I didn't need one nor did I need to put her in that position.

She said, "I do, too!"

"Well, you have all those gluten-free cookies and bars I bought that you locked up in the car."

"I guess I do, but the chocolate chip ones didn't taste that great."

"What about the big cookie that was individually wrapped?"

"Oh, that's right!"

She goes out to the car while I stand in the kitchen telling myself that it's fine that she eats it, but I won't be sharing.

"Want to split it with me?"

"I can't. I've already eaten too much."

She opens the cookie, and I stare at it, wanting so badly to share it with my mom. It's something I longed to be able to do during anorexia. I ended up having some and loved it!

I then was tempted to keep eating. I wasn't in full-blown binge mode, but I did want to eat the cottage cheese, the gluten-free bread, and the Arctic Zero ice cream. I wanted to have fun with food as I did when I was really little and would have "hunts," which was when I would be allowed to eat anything I wanted late at night and alone.

Mom told me to have some slices of turkey and go to bed when I expressed wanting more.

"You should have protein to help your brain not feel so crazy."

"Whatever, Mom."

"Here, have 2 slices of turkey and go to bed."

"It has too much sodium!"

"The sodium isn't going to hurt you!"

"It will make me retain water!"

I ended up taking 1 slice of turkey, rinsed it under the sink water, ate it, and went downstairs to bed. Looking back, I'm proud of myself. I ended up having about 1,800 calories for the day compared with the 1,300 I planned out to eat. However, I was able to eat a little extra at night, including a trigger food, and stop eating at a decent amount.

Honestly, I'm so much more comfortable restricting or binging. It's actually when I eat in the normal caloric range such as this night that are the most difficult and therefore essentially positive in regards to recovery.

May 6, 2011

Today has been fine so far. I got up and ate my breakfast even with the house cleaners in the kitchen, so I was definitely proud of myself. Dad has to go to a funeral this afternoon. It's for his friend's wife who died of liver and kidney failure from alcoholism, among other things. I couldn't help but think I'm so glad I'm still here and my parents didn't have to attend my funeral. I still remember my dad telling me he planned to have it in Yosemite because of our great memories there. I'm now crying...it's just too real and too unreal at the same time. I'm so incredibly afraid of death...I was terrified of it growing up. During the anorexia, I was afraid, yet almost numb to it, and now I'm terrified again.

I worry about the 15 CT scans I've had and hope and pray I never get cancer. I worry that I did somehow harm my body and that as extensive of a workup I've had with perfect results, that it will only be temporary. I worry that something bad will happen to my family or me. I love them *so* much, and it makes it so hard to love them fully because I don't want to get too close. I also worry I will have loose skin once I get to my goal weight. I worry I'm now too old for certain opportunities. I worry I will never find a boyfriend or true love. I worry I will never get another horse opportunity. I worry I won't get back the tennis talent I once had. I worry I will go back to anorexia. I worry I will never have true friends. These worries occupy my mind...not obsessively but much more than they should while I am bored at home or before going to bed. I can counter all those fears with positives, but it doesn't eliminate them.

More than anything I can't wait to start my life. I know that is future talking, but I'm trying so hard to put myself in a position where I can truly live freely and take every opportunity instead of just thinking about it. I want so badly to see Dr. Schack, Dr. Lucas, and all the Torrance staff. I want to visit UCLA basically to give them the middle finger and hug a select few. I want to go on the yearly beach trip to Delaware this summer, and I want to get back playing tennis at a competitive level. I want to visit PFC and show them how damn well I'm doing. I want to have horses in my life again and create an opportunity where I get to show and compete a talented horse. I want to publish a book, and I want to be a certified personal trainer through the National Academy of Sports Medicine (NASM).

I watched some of my old show tapes with Scandalous. Oh, if only I knew how lucky I was then. I had so much talent and really could have done some cool things with my life.

Even then, as much as that horse meant to me, ED was already starting to win. I would do *anything* to have horses back in my life. The minute I feel somewhat OK with my body and my riding pants fit is the day I go back out to my old barn and start riding. Part of me is still having so much trouble growing up, just as much trouble as I did when I was 13, 14, or 15. I always had this belief that I not only had to be number one but also the youngest to be number one. If I were just number one, I risked there being a younger person coming up behind me trying to take my spot. All the attention would be on them because they were younger. Instead of doing my best every year, I stepped backward, unwilling to grow up and take risks. I retreated with ED so that I could think about all the things I could have been instead of trying and failing. I guess ED shielded me from failure in a way or at least a way to place the blame on not living up to my high expectations. Then again, ED also shielded me from all successes and ultimately life. What the heck is so bad about trying my hardest without self-sabotage and falling short of my expectations? Maybe I wasn't the best, *but* I would be so proud of myself for giving it my all and committing... something I was never able to do. I can now—or maybe I'm still caught in delusion.

Everything happens for a reason and I *had, had, had* to go through what I did. No one goes through the complications physically and mentally as I did and comes out with perfect health and a mind-set to be free from all disorders. I have a gift—a second chance—and I know that I went through the pain and isolation to bring me to where I am now. I'm really trying to look back at my life with a positive attitude. How could someone not, honestly? I'm not lucky; I'm doing exactly as I was intended to do. Life sucks right now. However, I'm taking the action, and I'm doing the work. As Erin said, recovery is boring, not blog-worthy, and hard. She insists recovery is worth it, and sometimes I think challenging ED is somewhat fun and not always *that* boring. I like fighting, I like winning, and I like overcoming the odds. So, in a way it feels great to eat breakfast, go to bed before 11:00 p.m., read, get off Facebook, and exercise even though my life isn't perfect yet. But geez—why do I always feel the need to wait until everything is "perfect" to live my life? Appropriately enough, the iTunes song that's playing right now is the Pussycat Dolls song "I Hate This Part."

Mom is in Santa Barbara with her friend all day today and is coming home tomorrow to bring Kasey home from UC Santa Barbara for prom in San Luis Obispo. I've been having a nice day with Dad. I feel so much more responsible and confident when Mom isn't here. I think when she's around I feel as though I have to take on the role of the daughter and let her take care of me in regards to house chores, cleaning up, etc.

I did 35 minutes of intense exercise again in the house, which was composed of hallway sprints and nonstop stair running. It felt great to sweat, and it's getting easier. Afterward, though, I sat down to watch more of my horse tapes, and when I stood up a little later I was so dizzy I thought I would faint. I wasn't dehydrated and felt OK beforehand, but it freaked me out, which in turn gave me anxiety, which only caused me to become more short of breath. In my state of fear, I gave in and ate 8 ounces of cottage cheese and a few blueberries. I felt awful about eating unplanned calories, and it didn't even help that much. About 2 1/2 hours later now, I feel perfectly fine. Assuming all goes well the rest of tonight, my total calories would be 1,500, which I guess isn't terrible, but I don't know if it's few enough to lose a lot of weight.

May 7, 2011

It's 11:45 in the morning now, and I'm eating my breakfast of strawberries, blueberries, and Greek yogurt. Mom is coming home today with Kasey this afternoon, which I'm not really looking forward to. I really hope Kasey doesn't have any of her friends over. I know I should exercise, but I'm just not into it today. My body is slightly sore, and it's one of those days in which I try to motivate myself, but all I want to do is sink into the couch. Oh well, I will take today off so that I can do 40 minutes tomorrow while my parents take my sister back to UC Santa Barbara.

I was so hungry and emotionally tense that I ate an extra 8 ounces of blueberries, 3 strawberries, some snap peas, and lettuce. Because of this, I chose to get plain coffee with 4 ounces of unsweetened almond milk versus my usual nonfat venti cappuccino from Starbucks. I saved about 70 calories that way. I also threw out the yolk of the hard-boiled egg I was planning to have.

I went into the office tonight where Mom was on the computer and told her I wanted to have a "hunt" in her car because she had lots of good gluten-free treats stored away that I had mostly bought on Monday. She said, "No way... how do I know you won't binge?"

I know she was only trying to look out for me, but I got really upset mostly because I was asking really nicely and she had that supercritical tone of voice that really pushes my buttons. I truly didn't want to binge, yet I also knew I didn't need any of it. I went into the pantry and opened up the fridge and stared at the gluten-free bread, the tuna, and the cottage cheese. Then I opened up the freezer and stared at the Arctic Zero. Mom came in and gave me a huge hug and told me she loved me. I was then able to convince myself to go downstairs with her and to bed. My total calories were about 2,100 at most. Not good, but I guess I'm happy I was able to stop from eating anything else since it would have been emotional. Mom said she would love for us to each get a rainbow sprinkle doughnut for breakfast tomorrow... oh, how I wish I could say yes.

May 8, 2011

Happy Mother's Day! I had a nice afternoon. Now it's 5:30 p.m., and I'm home alone while my parents drive Kasey back to UC Santa Barbara. I'm so bored and am going crazy right now. I tried watching TV, playing on the computer, and sitting outside. Nothing interests me. I did 10 minutes of exercise before I just decided to stop. I wish this weight loss process was quicker. My stomach is just enormous! Of course, because I'm bored and alone, I want so badly to eat. I really am not hungry at all.

Actually, I probably should be hungry given what I've had to eat so far, but I've had so much water to drink and am so bloated that I don't feel hunger. I would love to eat the gluten-free bread, the Arctic Zeros, the cottage cheese, and some protein shakes. That's just my mind talking, though.

I got coffee with my unsweetened almond milk versus my cappuccino again, so I saved some calories there. I'm also going to throw my egg yolk out again. Off-plan, I've had frozen strawberries (80), lettuce bag (40), 32 ounces unsweetened almond milk (160), other (70), for a total of 350 calories extra. However, I saved 70 calories with the coffee and, let's say, 30 from the egg yolk, so 350 minus 100 = 250 extra. So, if I can stick to the rest of the day perfectly that will be a total of 1,550 calories.

Ugh, so I'm not binging but definitely having somewhat of a "carefree" day. So far I've had 1,650 calories, and I'm hoping to keep it fewer than 2,200. I guess having 1 or 2 days a week that aren't perfect calorie-wise is OK. I have to find a way to occupy myself on days I have no appointments. I somehow need to get out of the house... maybe drive and sit by the beach and study? Drive to Coffee Bean? I just don't know. I don't want to get weighed tomorrow at my appointment with Erin now because of what I've had to eat today. I stand on the scale backward so it's not like I will know my weight, but I still feel embarrassed for what Erin will see. I seriously *hate* that issues like food and weight are what give me the most stress and consume most of my time.

May 12, 2011

I came home after my appointment with Erin and made my snack, which I ate at 5:00 in the afternoon, so much too late. Mom was out shopping all afternoon with her friend. My mom and sister are so similar in how they live. "Do it for me. I need your help. I don't want to. This is too hard." Of course, my mom and I are very similar in our need for control, our intensity, and our enthusiasm; however, I definitely reflect qualities in her I think she would wish to excuse. My mom is such a freaking worrier, too! No wonder I get anxiety over pointless things sometimes. I've lived my life with her nagging at me over everything and anything and *all* the time! "Make sure you floss your teeth at night. Are you flossing your teeth in the morning and at night? Thank you so much for flossing your teeth. I trust that you are flossing your teeth." Seriously, she will say something like that 5 times, 5 different ways, in 5 minutes! How old am I? 2? Seriously!

And then there was her whole freak-out over the protein powder: "I think we should switch to Dr. Mercola's protein powder because I read that whey protein isolate is dangerous." Oh boy, well, I let her have it. Not in a mean way, but I firmly told her she was crazy in a nice way. "Don't eat too much gluten. Make sure you're getting enough protein. Are you eating every couple hours? Maybe you shouldn't eat so late. It's better for your metabolism to eat breakfast. I read that soy is terrible for you, so make sure you never eat it. That's really high in carbs. I think you're having too much artificial sweetener. You ate 6 Jell-Os? That's way too many! You should try to eat unprocessed foods. Want to take a survey to find out your nutritional typing? Coconut oil is so good for you, did you know?" The list is literally endless. I mean, now that I think about it more, I can remember her nagging me about nutrition-type shit since way before ED. And after everything I've been through, how can she still talk about and make such comments to me and think they won't bother or trigger me? Ahh! Just shut the heck up about food!

Dad and I had the *best* time playing tennis today. It just feels so amazing to be back on the court, and I'm so proud of myself for going out in public even though I make sure to choose less populated courts.

Dad teased on the drive home, "Maybe your mom will have dinner already cooking and ready for me when we get back."

Yeah... definitely not; we both already knew that answer. I wish my mom would appreciate my dad more.

25

Psychological Paralysis

"Confidence comes from discovering you can overcome the unimaginable." ~Britt

May 13, 2011

It was no surprise really when I opened the fridge 1 hour after
breakfast. From there I proceeded to eat about 8 ounces' worth of
chicken and lettuce, which then led me to eat 1 apple and blueberries,
which ultimately led me to go have a talk with Mom. I told her I was
having a hard day, was sad, and will need help distracting myself this
weekend since I was making today my "carefree" day as far as my meal
plan went. Of course, my carefree days tend to turn into full-blown
binges, but ED tries to trick me into thinking otherwise and that I'm
still in control. I really am not planning to binge today, but in a way,
if I eat 3,000 calories once this week, oh well, although I hope I eat
under that. Mom told me it's perfectly fine to feel the way I do and
that she would love to help me this weekend.

Surprisingly, food doesn't even really interest me. I had thought,
oh, today will be a day I just want to eat, but no. I've eaten off-plan
and at different times but have no desire to binge, overeat, or even
really eat at all. It's weird but wonderful. I've already got plans for
the weekend to keep me busy so that I stick to my exact meal plan.
I actually have to force myself to eat right now. Part of me kind of
wants to binge because I feel this is my "once a week eat a little more"

day, but for sure the desire and obsession to do so is dramatically decreasing, which is such an incredible step forward.

Ugh! Well, it is 12:40 a.m. now, and as far as food goes, today is one to forget. Did I binge? I can confidently say yes. Was it like previous binges? Definitely not. Well, today's total calories are around 5,650, so indeed there is nothing to be proud about.

Damn it! I hate you, ED! I know exactly what you are doing! I'm making tremendous progress, am starting to deal with the issues that created you, am playing tennis, and feeling better about myself, so what did you do? You decided after breakfast that sitting on the couch and relaxing just wasn't an option. You decided I needed to be jealous of people on Facebook, you decided I looked fat in the mirror, and you decided it had been much too long since I spent some time with you. You have now left me alone at 1:00 in the morning with a stomach that looks pregnant and a guilty conscience. Well, ED, you must be pretty proud of yourself! You might have even done enough damage to prevent me from playing tennis tomorrow. Guess what is going to happen next? I'm going to go to bed, all 5,000-plus-plus-plus calories and all, have a great night's sleep, get up tomorrow morning, and follow my meal plan perfectly. I'm not going to think about my pregnant-looking stomach or the damage you did. I'm going to relax, I'm going to do some activity, and I'm going to be OK. You, ED, are about to experience what it truly means to be alone, rejected, and not good enough!

GOAL: 4 weeks of following meal plan ranging from 1,300 to 2,000 calories, tennis 4 to 7 days a week, and 1 day per week at most of 2,500 calories. Do it! Good night!

P.S. Eek! Make that 7,200 calories now. I'm so over this!

May 14, 2011

I slept terribly! I went to bed around 3:00 in the morning after taking 7 Dulcolax...bad, I know, but I could not have cared less, to be honest. I got out of bed around noon today and certainly did not touch breakfast. I had a colonic at 1:00 p.m., thank goodness, which made me feel better physically.

Mom and I went to get coffee a little later. So, we are sitting in the car, and Mom is trying to decide if she wants something.

"I can't decide if I want something with calories or not."

"Why not? What's wrong with getting a fun drink?"

"Well, I don't know if I want to use my calories with the drink or get a plain iced coffee and eat ½ a protein bar."

"What the heck! Why not have a fun drink and the bar? Are you hungry?"

"Yes, I'm really hungry, but I don't want to spoil my dinner."

"Mom, seriously, you are talking like a crazy person. I know you don't have an eating disorder, but you are being an absolute freak. Are you trying to diet or something?"

"No, it's OK. I want the bar."

Ah! I honestly find it humorous because I can handle these situations better now, yet at the same time, no wonder she and I used to fight viciously during my disorder. It used to be that if she mentioned one thing about food, health, or supplements, I would snap at her violently. Now it's just a joke.

May 15, 2011

Sometimes I truly wonder about my life, especially about what Dr. Sadeghi had to say: "I had to cocoon to become the butterfly I am becoming. Everything happened just as it should. I was chosen to go through what I did because it was known that I would be able to survive the experience and do something meaningful with it. I was the lucky one to be given this journey. My life is beautifully guided." I want more than anything for these to be words of truth. I believe them in my head, just not in my heart.

May 16, 2011

I had a great meeting with Erin this morning. I shared a little bit about my indecisiveness with tennis, work, living location, and some other things, but really those questions are to be asked later and, as they always seem to do, will answer themselves. I'm scared. The binging is subsiding for the most part, which is awesome, but what about the rest of the days? I am eating during the day and consistently spacing my meals apart, which is great. However, I'm eating the same thing every day! I'm not even getting tired of it as I used to. I'm just as comfortable and safe eating this meal plan for a long time with minimal variations just as anorexia convinced me to do.

What if someone asked me to go out to lunch? Well, either I would say yes but make the rest of my meals carefree, or I would say yes but eliminate my other foods as much as needed to equal the calories I want for the day, or I would make an excuse and say no. Sound familiar? Damn it! What if I had to change my meal plan, such as having a turkey sandwich at lunch or having chicken for dinner? Even that brings on anxiety and wouldn't be something I could stick to. Once I find the yummiest and safest foods, that's it, they are golden and can't be replaced unless I can find another item close in nutrition facts that possibly takes longer to eat. I still make my protein shakes with massive amounts of ice to make them last longer, I still eat with plastic spoons, I still use gum to pass time, I still only allow a few veggies or fruit extra if I'm starving. I've eliminated my cappuccino and egg yolk. And who knows what next. I'm starting to exercise now and feel a need to do it, not just a want. What happens when it turns back into only a *need*?

I want to say I'm doing well. If anyone looked at my life from a whole they would say, "Wow, you are a miracle, an inspiration, possibly even recovered, and OK." Yet, that's not good enough. This is my life, my journal, and this is where I will look at the darkest parts of my life. Let me tell you, I am far from OK. I shouldn't say far because actually I have great confidence in living my life without any eating disorder, yet it will be tricky. It's one thing to maintain your health and weight, but it's another to do so freely. How awful would it be to get to 120 pounds and be in awesome shape but be trapped in my isolation and romance with ED again? Never going out with friends, always eating alone, always making an excuse, and always wondering, "What if?" That's the problem I'm realizing—eating disorders really are all about your mind...my changing shape is merely a symptom of my behaviors that stem from my destructive thinking.

I want to believe once I achieve a healthy weight I'll magically be free and recovered, but again, that so clearly won't be the case unless I address the underlying issues.

I am eating my almonds in the morning now, so I'm really proud of myself for that. I am playing tennis even though I'm overweight, so that's huge. I'm eating slightly earlier today. I'm also quite aware of my actions and the pull ED still has. Basically, I'm not in denial and am taking action, but what does it take to *kill* ED? What does it take not only to recover but to stand in front of millions and say I *beat* ED, not just I survived. I will figure this out. Recovery isn't perfect, and frankly my idea of "OK, I will be the best recoverer" is bullshit as there is no such thing. But I'm a very curious, rebellious, and out-of-the-ordinary person and feel that recovery could be a fun challenge to occupy my mind. I may have beat out a lot of people with my low weight and medical complications, but there are plenty of people who have beat me in how many times they've been in and out of treatment centers. I know some people who have gone more than 20 times, so heck. Hello, all-or-nothing thinking, I can't be the best in all aspects of eating disorders, nor is it a thing to strive for anyway. What I can do is write the next chapters of my life...differently. Sometimes I get lonely. The ED world, as artificial and Internet-based as it was, certainly was a way to feel competitive, have company, and occupy my time. What a sick little world and bubble it creates...but a toxically addicting one at that.

What do I miss most about anorexia? I miss the attention (any attention), the games (having to get smarter and smarter to hide my behaviors), the excuse ("I could have been great but..."), my bones showing, being able to fit into any size clothes, not having hormones, the look of shock on doctors' faces and then freaking them out even more by not listening, the safety in knowing my routine would not change, knowing I was skinnier than most people and that was something they didn't have. I miss the friends I made in treatment, I miss the safety I felt in hospitals knowing someone was monitoring my health 24-7, I miss being a threat to other anorexics, I miss the gap between my legs, I miss being indecisive about an outfit for fear I would look too thin not too fat, I miss people telling me I was sick (I had a label; I was something), I miss having company in my head, and I miss the feeling of surrendering always to ED...no effort or decisions were made by *me*. It is quite obvious (now, at least) that the list of negatives that came with anorexia far, far, *far* outweigh those so-called positives. But there are still certain needs that ED fulfilled and took care of when I was too young to understand my misery and so ED has made me believe that I can't get my needs met without it. This thinking though has only strengthened my false negative beliefs, low self-esteem, and deadly relationship with ED. I need to break free and live a new way of life and a new way of thinking, but now it seems so impossibly foreign.

Ultimately, I want to inspire, help, and work with all varieties of eating disorders. I certainly can relate to both anorexics and those who are obese struggling with binge eating disorder. At the moment, though, I don't think I could handle working in an environment with anorexics. I hate to admit the reason why it would be so difficult for me, but it's because of the triggering environment, the competition, and the life or identity I gave up. Obviously, recovery is better and I don't want to go back to my old ways, *but* anorexia was stripped from me, stolen, forced without a goodbye, a warning, or a choice. Sometimes I see anorexics and a strong sense of jealousy comes over me. "Why do *they* get to stay that way and I didn't?" is the screaming voice inside.

May 17, 2011

Mom and I had a nice drive to get coffee together. I mentioned how I stayed up late last night reading all my medical records I just got from our local hospital. Wow! In every single note it basically says the same general thing: "She's a really nice girl, but there is absolutely no hope for her." Oh boy, did that make me smile reading it. The look on doctors' faces if they could only see me now...

May 18, 2011

Last night after I finished my last snack, I was still hungry, so I asked Mom if I should have some almonds or broccoli. Her answer certainly wasn't what I was expecting.

"Have 5 almonds."

"Five! Who the heck has just 5?"

"Well, you had 14 this morning, so all you really need is 5."

"Mom, you're crazy! Most people have at least a handful and don't count."

"Well, you could have 10, but you certainly don't need any more. Like 30 would be way too many."

"Even 30 would only be about 200 calories, which is no different than having 1 protein bar."

"Well, you are about to go to bed and you don't need those calories sitting in your stomach because you won't use them."

"Mom! I have a freaking eating disorder!"

She then got up and went to bed ignoring me. I ended up binging on 17 strawberries and about 10 ounces of blueberries right before bed. Oh great. Even as I was doing it I knew why. I told ED to shut up. I told myself I didn't need to be eating them, but I wanted to say fuck you to my mom so bad and in turn only hurt myself.

May 19, 2011

I'm having a really hard time with forgiving myself. I feel as if my life has forever been labeled like a tattoo I can never erase. It's weird. I am so overwhelmed with embarrassment and am having an identity crisis. I no longer have ED (at least I don't feel I do since I'm overweight), and I haven't had enough years away from ED to reestablish who I am and create a new life and identity. It's like a drunken person waking up and wondering, "Oh shit! What did I do last night?" Except for it's not just last night for me, it's 8 years of my life.

26

The Truth Will Set You Free

May 20, 2011

These past 2 days I've been almost paralyzed with shame, embarrassment, and guilt. I don't know why. I don't have ED to hold my hand, nor do I have a new life. I also don't have any friends around to say how great I am and how worth it I am and to help me realize everybody has difficulties in life. I have to do that validating on my own, and that's something I never could do in the past. ED always told me how I was doing as a person, but before ED? Before ED I was an insecure, *angry*, and sensitive child bottling up all my plummeting self-esteem and constant ridicule from my peers. So now that I've awoken from my 8-year coma, I am left facing my old insecurities and feelings of rejection. I feel haunted by ED. I feel damaged, different, and disabled. I am actually letting myself feel for once, which is a great thing, but I *hate* it! I just want to go home, but I have no home in a metaphoric way... I've never felt safe or as though I belong anywhere. Everywhere I go brings back a memory. Unfortunately, almost every memory is of ED, of killing myself, of overexercising, of spending hours in markets, of hating high school, of people I once knew, of hospitals, doctors, gyms, places where I would binge, and, ah, just everything. Every gosh damn thing is a reminder of some fucked-up idiot who supposedly is *me*! I don't know who I am anymore. I can't hold on to who I was before ED because I didn't even know me or like me then. I am embarrassed by the events that took place with all forms of my eating disorder. Currently I'm isolating and uncomfortable with myself and not working toward my purpose in life—so, shit!

I asked Mom her personal intuition on whether I should stay in San Luis Obispo or move to Los Angeles in a few months. Let's just say it turned into a huge fight. Long story short, it ended with me losing it. I eventually left the room, but I had so much more I wish I could have said to her...

I *hate* you! I'm sick of you telling me I'm not good enough! You are a health freak! I hate you for being late to pick me up at school! I hate that you treated Kasey better! I hate that you blame all the problems in the family on me! I hate that you yell at Dad when you're unhappy. I hate that you didn't explain to me how life worked and why I had a little sister. I hate that you sent me to preschools. I hate that you never came to watch me play tennis because you had to take Kasey to dance. I hate that you used to criticize my school outfits. I hate that you gave up on me! I hate that I would always overhear you on the phone talking about me and how awful I was doing. I hate that you could never separate me from ED. I hate that you left me with babysitters. I hate that I lost my alone time with you when Kasey was born. I hate that you always nag me as if I'm deaf or stupid.

I hate that you told me I could be just like Anna Kournikova. I hate that you wrote awful e-mails to your friends about me. I hate that you threatened to divorce Dad! I hate that you told me I was crazy and how embarrassed you were that the neighborhood was calling worried about my appearance and my obsessive walking. I hate that you didn't trust me. I hate that you said goodbye to me when I was dying. I hate that you never believed me when I would call you hysterical from UCLA. I hate that you always sided with the doctors. I hate that you never gave me a chance. I hate that you never believed in me and you had accepted ED was my life and who I was! I hate that you blamed me for failing every treatment center. I hate you for not living your own life. I hate that all you ever do is go out with your friends. I hate that you got so mad at me every time I gave you a list of things I needed when I was in the hospital because I "deserved it." I hate that you told me I would die. I hate that you don't accept me. How can I accept myself if you can't? I hate that my horse and only friend got sold. I hate that Kasey was sick and got attention for it. I hate that you don't make dinner. I hate that you never hugged Dad or acted like you appreciated him. I hate that you worry about everything. I hate that you're so close with all of Kasey's friends now and when they were growing up. I hate that you would watch me eat all my food. I hate that the scale was the most important measure. I hate that you would yell at me one moment and then talk super sweet to Kasey the next as if to rub it in. I hate that I couldn't have a conversation with you without it somehow turning into something ED-related within 5 seconds *every damn time*! I hate that you told me that girl got the coffee job over me because she doesn't look like sick. *I am so angry with you that I don't know how to forgive you and in turn don't know how to forgive myself.*

Wow, that felt really good to get out. I definitely started crying, but I do feel better. I always blame myself for everything. My mom is honestly one of the most amazing people I know and I feel beyond lucky and blessed to have her. In my mind she is a huge part of why I am still alive today. But it doesn't mean I can't get angry or feel hurt about past events even if they weren't her fault or intention to make me feel bad. It's hard for me to understand that I can be upset with people without blaming them. I always feel I have to internalize all the terrible feelings in order to protect others out of the fear they might leave or hate me. I have to learn that it's OK for me to feel the way I do and to get angry or sad over certain situations. It doesn't mean it's anyone's fault. It just means I perceived something in a certain way and it's healthy for me to let out my emotions instead of stuffing them silently inside until they come out in destructive ways.

I place so much shame, blame, and guilt on myself when in reality it doesn't even belong to me and never has. I was not replaced. I was not rejected. I was not bad. I was not a defect. I am good enough. I had a mental illness in which I couldn't help my choices, words, and actions. I *love* the person I am today and would not trade places with anyone. Unfortunately, I just don't know myself very well yet and have no past to look to for guidance. I am haunted by a place so dark that the light can only eventually shine when I can love and forgive myself unconditionally. Only when I believe I am OK, acceptable, and perfect just as I am is when I can look upon my previous life and move on. I am going to share my story. Not because I want to but because in doing so it will set me free after so many years of isolation and telling everyone I was fine with a fake smile.

I am ready to tell the whole damn world the pain I suffered through every day. I want people to know that it's *not* their fault, they aren't alone, and that they have a better life to move on to.

May 22, 2011

I have the worst body image today! It's crazy because when I look in the mirror at my stomach I actually look thinner, but for some reason I feel fatter than ever. My shirts that fit me so loosely at LIFE are still tight on me. I know I have at least 10 to 20 pounds to lose to get to that size, so in reality I shouldn't panic too much, but I'm just getting impatient and irrational right now.

I decided to skip eating my asparagus today because I had eaten too many blueberries. I was getting ready to go out to the market today as well as Coffee Bean and asked Mom for her credit card, which she gladly gave me and asked me to get her a nonfat latte as well. After harassing my mom with the usual "How fat do I look?" I went upstairs and asked Dad the same. He told me I don't look fat but about 10 pounds overweight.

With me already being in one of those moods, I got really upset and threw my market list at him and said, "Please go for me. I can't go!" About 1 minute later Mom comes upstairs.

"I want my credit card back."

"Why? You came all the way up here because you don't trust me, huh?"

"Well, since you're just going to Coffee Bean, I will just give you some cash."

"What's the difference? You've always just given me your credit card. You came up here because you think I'm going to binge!"

"Yes, I do think you might binge."

"What the heck! You don't trust me! You always do this! You never even give me a chance to prove myself first! You did the same with anorexia! I didn't even have the thought of binging, but now I want to just to prove you right! What? Do you think I'm that dumb? That I can't think things through or work them out myself? I hate you! I hate you! You don't trust me and must think I'm stupid! I hate you so much!"

I ended up throwing the container of pens on the floor and storming out of the house to drive to Coffee Bean. Ugh! I don't even feel bad for how I reacted. She's done this my whole life! I'm not 2 years old anymore. I don't need to be reminded 15 times, in 15 minutes, and in 15 different ways about appointments, errands, or tasks. She did this with anorexia, too. She always just assumed she couldn't trust me with certain things and never even gave me a *chance* to prove her thoughts wrong. So, if I'm not given the chance, the trust, and the belief, then screw you, of course I'm going to do what you thought.

For example: I'm about to eat my snack of peanuts and cottage cheese. "I want to watch you eat your snack."

"What the heck, Mom? Blah, blah, blah!"

266

After a large argument, she backs off and says fine, she won't. Well, what do I do? All along I wasn't even planning to restrict one bit, *but* because of that argument and question of trust I *do* restrict. Dang!

Story of my life and how a person gets to 56 pounds! Obviously my rebellious attitude and ways of acting only hurt me, but it seems to be an impulse that always gets the better of me.

If I wasn't so smothered by her I might have actually been able to be proud of myself for certain things. Every time she intervenes when I could have made a positive choice, it takes the victory out of it. For example, let's say I didn't restrict my snack after the argument. Well, I wouldn't feel proud of myself because she took that power away by forcing me to watch out, if that makes sense. I swear if my parents (mostly Mom) would have backed off while my anorexia wasn't that severe, I most likely could have overcome it or at the very least never gotten to the point I did. It was such a game with them (her). They made it such a big deal— weighing me, watching me, taking keys, canceling gyms, etc.—that it only drove me to get worse. They highlighted my eating disorder so blindingly bright that it made it seemingly impossible to let it go, escape it, or be someone else in their minds. I just wanted to be Brittany, but there was so much attention and commotion around ED that I feared I had to keep it up in order to keep my family close to me. I am so intelligent, so rebellious, and so ready to do things my way and on my time that this was an equation for disaster, and that was exactly what happened.

I can't promise the same outcome wouldn't have happened, but I can assume it. Again, I don't blame my parents for me starting to binge and then becoming obese, but I also have *no* right to blame myself, which I do. I hate this! Watch me become anorexic again! It's easier to recover from BED (binge eating disorder) in a sense, but recover from anorexia? That was never my choice, that was never in the plans, and that never happened. Well, Mom and Dad, you're screwed if anorexia comes back into my life, and *this* time you had better handle it right! You had better trust me, believe in me, support me, give me freedom, not watch me, forget the scales, and let *me* come to terms with what I want. I never got to do that. I never got to say goodbye to anorexia by choice, and that means a *lot* to me ... that means *revenge*. I don't even know where these words are coming from right now, but they are so intense. This challenge of becoming anorexic again genuinely excites me and horrifies me at the same time.

May 23, 2011

I guess if anything I'm thankful to be alive right now to write this. The past 2 days were a living reoccurring nightmare. I will start with Monday. It was the perfect setup. I had been eating my meals later and later each day, my hormones were probably going crazy, my mom was giving me the usual stress, I had been doing great for 1week straight, and the chaos in my head was just too much.

Sunday night I got caught in the trap late at night eating pointless foods, that is, excess amounts of egg whites, 1 package of turkey, tons of fruits—anything I could get my hands on. I also went to bed around 3:30 in the morning and got hardly any sleep. I awoke around 7:00 a.m. restless and ready to eat some so-called real food. This same exact scenario has a 10 out of 10 success rate for ED, and it got me again. Almost in a frenzied daze, I got up out of bed almost excited I was going to binge. My rational thinking had been shut off and the blinders put on ... ED was in complete control. I was supposed to have a parent meeting with Erin, but there was no way that would be the case after the binge last night and my anxiety over the binge day I knew I would have.

I told Mom I was going to go to the market to get some things I needed especially because she wouldn't be able to drive for a bit because she has an upcoming knee surgery. I asked if she wanted to come with me or if I should just go alone, assuring her I didn't mind. She said I could go alone and gave me her credit card. *What!* The first thing I said to her and Dad individually when I woke up and as I was making a shake at 8:00 a.m., which is *highly* uncharacteristic of me who is so rigid with my schedule of foods and times, was, "Today is going to be an awful day, so just let me be." Hello, red flag! Well, I was given the credit card with a smile from Mom, and Dad knew I was going but mentioned nothing. *How many times have I rehearsed setups just like this for you guys to intervene properly and take control and contain me?* Whatever, screw you guys. ED gets the control today, and you will be sorry for your mistake.

I left for the market and had quite the shopping spree. I did of course stick only to gluten-free items, but I certainly didn't hold back. The day was just awful. I baked a lot of junk from some supposedly healthy recipes I looked up online. It all came out gross, but I ate it anyway. I had around 15,000 calories, without exaggeration, easily. I did have a colonic at 4:00 p.m., which was great and helped me lower my binge drive at least slightly and prevent the use of laxatives, though I thought about it.

May 24, 2011

Hello, early Tuesday morning! I had to get up around 7:00 a.m. to drive my mom to her surgery appointment. I knew she would be fine, but I think a part of me was worried about her because she spent the past month saying how terrified she was of the anesthesia and her fear that she wouldn't wake up. I got quite the surprise when I opened up my wallet. I had told Mom yesterday that I didn't want her credit card for any reason for at least a month and figured she grabbed it like she always does, but *no!* It was there!

I struggled for some time thinking about just handing it over to her or Dad, but again the setup was too perfect for the binge: worried about Mom, early morning, already in a different town where I can binge more anonymously, Dad is gone all day at work, Mom will be out of it for a while, I'm already bloated, so, hey…why not go for it? Well, damn, did I. I even forgot about eating only gluten-free, also. By 10:00 in the morning, I had consumed 2 large carrot cakes, 1 venti Mocha Coconut Frappuccino Light, 1 foot-long Subway sandwich with egg whites and sausage, 1 whole pint of Ben & Jerry's Peanut Butter Cup ice cream, 1 whole bag of kettle corn, 1 apple, and 1 large bag of peanut M&Ms.

Once I arrived home I proceeded to make 7 pancakes, eat 1/3 of a carrot cake, and then sit in partial disbelief. I felt just awful. I had just taken 10 Dulcolax. I've never taken that many before, especially at once, but at this point I figured it really was my only hope.

I texted Dad around 5:00 in the afternoon saying Mom and I wanted pizza for dinner. I also asked him to buy me low-fat ice cream. He said fine. At this point I didn't care that he said fine because I was much too far gone, but in retrospect, what the heck? Well, he came home later but without the ice cream because "there was no low-fat."

"Well, damn it! Call me at least or get a different kind!"

Ugh! This was only the beginning of our—or more like ED's—fight.

I was hysterically angry, and a lot of nonsense words came out of my mouth as well as a tug-of-war with Dad over the peanut butter, honey, and sugar cookies I made because there was no ice cream. I ended up winning the tug-of-war and ate all 8 *huge* cookies filled with about a jar of peanut butter, but only after I had eaten 2 slices of pizza, 1 apple, and a lot of berries. I crashed around 8:30 p.m. I took a fast shower and went to bed. It was another night in hell.

I have *never* felt so sick in my life. I have debated many times whether or not to go to the ER but always decided against it out of pure embarrassment and shame. I drank some water for the first time before bed, and that only made me feel worse. I couldn't pee at all anyway, so it only increased the pressure in my stomach. I spent the night moaning every breath, half throwing up, with severe nausea, a severe stomachache, a huge headache, confusion, inability to walk straight, and just pure fear. I remember thinking to myself at one point that this whole binge-restrict cycle really is and can be as bad as anorexia. OK, no, I don't really believe it can be as bad, *but* I did acknowledge that the disease I have currently deserves a little more respect than I'd been giving it. With binges of this magnitude as well as the symptoms it causes, it really is like a drug. It is a temporary high and then a violent crash where I *can't* even think straight or speak correctly. I will be glad to have this crutch put behind me. I just can't help but wonder what will take its place.

May 26, 2011

I had such an incredible meeting with Erin. *Finally*, ED has met his match. I didn't even really know where to start when I sat down for my session. I honestly just felt like passing out and never using a brain cell again. I keep setting up perfectly lighted pathways for my parents to follow into parenting me the way my younger self lacked and needed. Time after time I test my parents. I put myself in crisis and wait for their response. Well, they would make the worst EMTs because they always—and I mean *always*—arrive at the scene too late. Erin helped me to see that they are truly incapable of containing me and being the parent model I need in my life. It makes so much sense now. My parents are handicapped when it comes to protecting me and keeping me safe from my own self. ED took over as my authority figure, but ultimately it's me and me *alone* who needs to learn how to take care of myself.

When I think of it that way it puts the issue at rest. I know how to take care of myself, and I know how my inner child needs to be parented. I have to adopt my own self because I will never get what I need from my parents. I actually feel as though I can start to move on now, which is such a sigh of relief.

Another interesting thing Erin said is how I somewhat "idolize" my dad when, really, is that true? My parents truly are phenomenal people, but that doesn't mean I have to protect them or believe that they are the best parents. ED loved my dad during anorexia. My dad turned his head away from doctor after doctor after doctor to give me "one more chance" because "I'm so glad you aren't like those other girls" (in regards to Remuda Ranch family week).

Well, Dad, guess what? You weren't there for me! You didn't protect me! You didn't keep me safe! You let me down! There were so many fabulous doctors at Stanford and each told you personally I needed to be conserved, I needed not to be allowed to play tennis, I needed residential treatment, etc., and each time you said no and that I was different. What length of self-suicide, if you want to call it that, did I have to go to before you woke up and took on your role of my dad?

It wasn't enough when I had a heart rate in the 20's. It wasn't enough when I was hospitalized in the ICU during Christmas break with doctors trying to "5150" me as well as have me conserved by the court. *No,* you drove me back to college saying I needed to find a doctor to monitor me. Back we drove to Davis—all 75 pounds or so of me bundled up under 7 layers. What was it going to take? If it weren't for the grace of God and a highly educated doctor at the UC Davis health center I would have died right on campus. It took the head of the school to force me to leave until I had completed a refeeding program? *Pathetic!* Come on, Dad, really?

You come pick me up from Davis, and you and Mom don't know how to act. I can tell you guys are angry, yet Mom then treats me extra nice as if she expected those to be our last days together. Well, no problem, just drop me off at Del Amo treatment center. Now guess what? Now I'm at Torrance Memorial and you're getting phone calls telling you that I'm nearly in liver failure and weigh 56 pounds and you need to get your butt down here to say goodbye to me. You plan my damn funeral, and that's it? How does your daughter lose close to 50 pounds in a year on an already anorexic body? Major fail!

Then you hardly visit me at Torrance anyway, and after a few months of torture at UCLA, I'm brought back home, and I'm *not* fixed. Here you are once again responsible for an 80-pound girl who is now 90 percent bald and walks like the Hunchback. I went right back to eating only after midnight and once the family was in bed. I went back to walking over 3 hours around the neighborhood. I went back to running errands compulsively. I went back to playing all my old games, and guess what? I got back down to 69 pounds at one point! How the heck does that happen again! *How?* For a mixture of crappy reasons, I start binging. Your reaction? "That's wonderful! I will pay you for every pound you gain!" So, I keep binging. I get hospitalized twice with dangerous electrolytes and a stomach doctors said was at severe risk for rupturing. Oh well, no worries. I get discharged and keep binging. "At least she's gaining weight and getting out of the danger zone," you believed. *For goodness' sake, if lying on my deathbed isn't enough for you to step in and take charge, then nothing, nothing, nothing is, and I must come to terms with this and mourn what you can never give me.* Ugh! I hate it! I hate it! I hate it!

Do you know what it's like to know that you're never safe? To know that no matter what walls of protection you put up, I can always tear them down? To wake up to a stranger every day? To not be able to lift your arm, let alone walk? To be asked if you want to be resuscitated? To have a blood transfusion in the middle of the night all alone? To watch your heart rate on the monitor drop into the 20's with the alarm sounding? To have a tube shoved down your nose? To not be able to wipe your own butt? To have to wear diapers because your C. diff is so bad? To have to think for 5 minutes just to remember your dogs' names? To lose all your hair? To start to lose your vision? To want more than anything to be able to look out the window at the rain if only you were able to walk? To be so cold even a Bair Hugger can't keep you warm? To be told you're hopeless? To be told you're the worst case ever known? To be asked to leave college? To be so alone in a school full of thousands of people? To sit by the space heater at night trying desperately to get warm? To go to bed afraid you're going to die? To have a voice inside your head holding you prisoner? To have to exercise like crazy each day even with chest pain? To have to relearn how to walk? To have to relearn how to run? To have your finger pricked every few hours for low blood sugar? To have ear pressure so bad you can't think? To be so thin you have to wear padding because your bones stick out? To look in the mirror and see a dead person? To drink so much water you think you might pop just to fake a weigh-in? To spend each birthday/Thanksgiving/Christmas/Halloween alone while everyone else enjoys themselves and food? To miss out on your favorite summer vacation? To be told you're the reason everyone's lives are ruined? To be told everything is your fault? To be told you're stupid, hated, and selfish and that you deserve to be miserable? Do you know what it's like to be said goodbye to? To be stuck sitting alone on your dorm room floor because you don't have the strength to get up? To be bribed to eat your brains out? To explain to an ER doctor that at 80 pounds you feel like death because you binged and to be looked at like you're insane? To eat so much you can't keep your eyes open? To look in the mirror and see a stranger? To enter a fat camp only months after being discharged early from UCLA? To lock yourself in your house in embarrassment with food being your only friend? To enter an eating disorder treatment center being legitimately obese in a room full of anorexics? To be so fat you can hardly walk up a flight of stairs without getting out of breath? To finally like who you are as a person but have no recollection of your reflection? To be haunted by your past? To be so scared of dying you binge to save yourself, yet to be so afraid of being fat you constantly come up with new diet plans?

Do you know what it feels like to want to be loved so bad that you will go to any length to get it? Do you know how it feels to know that the 2 people who are supposed to love, protect, and keep you safe are less capable than you? Do you know how it feels to know that ED is so much smarter and stronger than the 2 people who are supposed to save and shelter you from everything? Alone, alone, alone, so fucking alone!

No wonder I'm so afraid to truly live! I have no friends, I have no happy memories, I have parents that ED can overpower. Who do I have to fall back on if it gets too scary? If I succeed too much? If I fail? If I need help?

I have so much mourning to do. Mourning over my sister being born, my parents' failing, never having a good friend, losing tennis, losing my horse, losing my life, and losing my eating disorders. I finally feel as though I can start that process now. I can separate enough from my parents to know that I don't need to practice insane setups anymore. Definition of insanity? Doing the same thing over and over again expecting different results.

Erin is right when she says the time I need the most support is when I'm doing well and when my parents are happy about it. In a weird way, I hate my parents being happy about how I'm doing. That makes me believe they think they succeeded or they won. I'm not one to take losing lightly, therefore, it's really going to be important for me to be OK with their satisfaction. Partly, I feel it's unfair. I somewhat believe they contributed to my eating disorder, and therefore (as I've given them so many chances) they should be responsible in destroying my eating disorder. But the fact is only I can. In reality I know it's going to have to be me who saves myself, and that's what scares me the most.

27

Hooked on Colonics

"What's more appealing...staying in the struggle where things are safe, predictable, and small or taking that struggle and turning it into a powerful resource and triumph? It seems like a no-brainer answer, yet there is something distortedly luring about staying stuck." ~Britt

May 27, 2011

I had a great colonic appointment! My appointments with my colonic lady are such a 2-for-1 deal for me. I get a colonic as well as awesome therapy/venting/processing with someone I trust. We talked about my patterns: running away and not finishing and committing. I go into crisis mode, go off to a treatment center (anorexia as well as fat camps), and then leave early. This gives me a perfect excuse to come home and struggle.

Come home too skinny? It gives me a reason to struggle at home. Come home too fat? It gives me a reason to isolate and once again struggle. She said I'm up against my shit right now and I can choose to handle it differently this time. Every time I'm up against a wall and break through, I grow. I'm right where I need to be, and this is what doing the work looks like. She said I have to stick this through because I will bring ED anywhere I go if not.

May 30, 2011

I had an appointment with Erin, and I did reluctantly step on the scale. Supposedly, I actually lost a tiny amount of weight, as in most likely less than 1 pound, but that is better than gaining or maintaining. Then again, my mind would have played tricks with me either way. See, by losing weight, ED has the same theory as when I was at the fitness camps. "See, Brittany! You got to binge and eat anything you wanted and you still lost weight!" Therefore, it validates that the binge-restrict cycle is semi-effective. If I would have gained weight, ED would have blamed it on the binges. No matter what I just can't win it seems.

June 3, 2011

Ugh! Where to even start? After having a great day Thursday, I struggled later that night…not too surprisingly in retrospect because I have consistently binged on my most so-called successful days for some time now. The game I was playing with the box of pancakes…well, I was outplayed Thursday night. The box had been sitting in the cupboard for about 1 week now. Each day I acknowledged it was there, but I resisted the urge to give in, which made me feel in control. Anyway, I wasn't even hungry, but I was wide-awake and perhaps a little anxious? So, like a zombie I proceeded to the lower cupboard where the pancake mix had been hiding. I only had a little at first, but there was no way I could just stop. I had the whole 3/4 of the box of pancake mix as well as an additional apple, pear, cottage cheese, Caesar salad, and jelly. I took 6 laxatives afterward for the heck of it.

Unfortunately, as predictable as the sun rises, I didn't sleep, woke up Friday morning super early, and wanted to binge for real. I had thought about binging the whole night and where I would go since I only had about $30. I started eating around 7:00 in the morning: 2 cartons of egg whites, 1 apple, ¾ a cup of gluten-free oatmeal, 1 protein shake, almond milk, unsweetened cocoa powder, 1 yogurt, 1 carton of strawberries, some cottage cheese, and about 1cup's worth of almonds. I told my dad how badly I wanted to binge and how difficult resisting the urge was. He understood, but what more could anyone do or say? He also wasn't aware that I had any money on me. Mom left for an appointment, and Dad was working. I left the house around 11:15 a.m. to eat as much as I could before my 1:00 colonic appointment.

I drove to Arroyo Grande and made my first stop at the doughnut shop that apparently makes their doughnuts with palm oil or something supposedly healthier. I bought 5—2 very large cinnamon twists, 2 regular, and 1 jelly/cream-cheese-filled croissant. Cheap, good, and damaging. I then was going to stop at Starbucks because I have my Starbucks card with about $20 on it, but I decided I could do that later, so I stopped at Yogurt Creations. I sat in their parking lot and finished all 5 doughnuts and then I made my way into the yogurt shop and got their extra-extra-large-size cup, of course. I put peanut butter and yogurt chips on the bottom and then overflowed the cup with vanilla and banana frozen yogurt with rainbow sprinkles on top. I was actually surprised I didn't put more toppings on it as I usually do. I wish I did now since I probably won't get to do it again for a while, but I suppose after 5 doughnuts it doesn't sound as appetizing.

I then drove back to San Luis Obispo for my colonic, which was good but not the best since I was so bloated already. I then drove home feeling a little better and ran into Dad driving down our street. He asked me if I got his funny text and I said no that my phone died. He then asked me if I was OK and I said no, I'm not. He then asked if I binged, and I said yes, I did. He replied by saying something nasty and then drove off in a bad mood. I mumbled, "Fuck you," and drove up the street to our house. Dad ended up turning around and driving back to the house. Dad screamed at me once inside, saying things like how the heck could I have gone out and binged, how mad he was, etc. Then he tried grabbing the keys from me, saying the car was his. I screamed at him and said I have an addiction and that I can't help it and hate it! Ugh, it was just awful, and he was *so* angry!

I eventually went back outside and locked myself in my car until he left for a meeting. I then went back inside and ate 1 apple and tuna. Mom came home about 20 minutes later and found me sitting on the couch crying. She gave me a huge hug and held me for a while as I sobbed. It's times like this where it's my mom who understands me the best and is exactly what I need. I told her I can't do it at home and that I needed help... *so* much help. She agreed and said she knows and told me to ignore Dad. She explained to me how hard it is for her to live with him as well sometimes, because he just doesn't understand certain situations. Mom said she and Dad both had such different views on how to help me when I was anorexic and basically her way of helping me would have been more of what Brittany needed, but ED hated, whereas Dad's approach was the opposite. No wonder I butt heads with Mom so much in the past... ED knew she was the biggest threat and had the ability to make decisions that would severely threaten its existence.

Dad came home a little later. When he did, I went back out. I made my first stop at the same doughnut shop and got 1 huge cinnamon roll, 12 doughnut holes, 1 ham and cheese croissant. I then drove to the Starbucks, but it looked crowded so I sat in the parking lot, ate all the items I bought, and left a message for an outpatient treatment center for the heck of it. I feel my binges are more justified while I'm searching for treatment centers online or, in this case, actually calling them. I mean, might as well binge all out until treatment starts, right? Ugh. I then stopped at 2 different Starbucks, getting 1 chocolate smoothie and 1 Strawberries & Crème Frappuccino Blended Crème... both so not worth it. I then stopped at a drive-through McDonald's and got the 20-piece Chicken McNuggets.

Only having $6 left after the McNuggets, I decided it was time to drive home. I felt so sick that I could hardly keep my eyes open. The weirdest thing happened while I was eating... I started having trouble swallowing. I almost choked at first; it was so freaky! I came home in a complete trance. I had just been severely abused by ED, so I guess I had the look of someone who had just been beaten up. Mom and I spent about 1 hour in the office searching the Internet looking for different treatment options.

Transitional living? Residential? Back to PFC? Find an apartment and therapist? We explored every possibility. Mom even asked me if I wanted to go back to Remuda...an option she never would entertain before. She even asked me if I wanted to go back to Utah, whether at PFC or just to live.

It was nice to have Mom helping me and realizing the seriousness of my eating disorder because Dad only ever looks disgusted and disappointed when I tell him I need a higher level of care. To him, it's as simple as just working harder and changing, as if it were all in my control. I know he knows how serious and difficult addictions are, but sometimes it's hard for him to think of me that way. He doesn't realize that binge eating disorder is as difficult and really the same as severe anorexia. It's only my appearance and behaviors that have changed, not my mind! He sees me looking OK, playing great tennis, having so many opportunities and thinks, "Get over it."

The truth is both my parents love and care about me—almost too much. I can't fault them for that...if anything it just shows what incredible human beings they are. But the problem is that they love me *so* much and fear losing me *so* much that they instinctively went to any length in an effort to save and fix me. Sometimes my parents unknowingly perpetuate and fuel my eating disorder. All parents want is for their kid to be happy and healthy and I'm sure my parents blame themselves and believe it's their job to save me. But in their effort to save me...they've sometimes only enabled my disorder more. If only I could make them believe that this was never their fault, that they never could have prevented my development of an eating disorder, and that only I hold the answers. If only they didn't have to suffer with me. If only they knew how much they've already done. If only they knew that they have already played a huge part in my survival. If only they knew that just being there for me is enough.

The truth is I'm struggling just as much now as I was with anorexia, just in a different way that isn't as obvious to the eye based on appearance. I'm living my life identically to how I was with anorexia. As Erin brilliantly made me aware of, I am repeating and reliving the trauma of anorexia and dying every single day by isolating, sleeping way too much, chewing excessive gum, eating more at night, getting sad on Facebook looking at people living their lives, etc. No wonder I keep binging! Erin has been wonderful in helping me in general, of course, but through e-mail, too, which is *so* nice to feel as if I still have my main support even without a face-to-face session. She replied to one of my e-mails as follows:

> Please read this a few times:
> Every time you restrict your food intake like you have, exercise without sufficient calories, isolate yourself, and spend 14 hours in bed you are *replicating* the trauma of anorexia. Binging will continue to be the response your body has if you continue to have the mind-set that you need to exist on a restrictive diet (under 1,800 calories) while exercising in order to shed weight quickly. You are not able to escape these facts. In 4 to 6 weeks, you will take off significantly more weight by following the meal plan while exercising moderately most days per week than you will by restricting heavily and then binging. I know ED doesn't want you to believe this, but ED has been wrong over and over. Reread your journals from this week to see how ED tricks you.

I really needed this e-mail from her. I took 8 laxatives and finally called it a night. A total of around 8,500 to 10,000 calories on average for the day. Oh dear.

June 5, 2011

I got up around 10:30 a.m. and Mom dropped me off for my colonic at 11:00. I was not feeling well. I was so tired, had a headache and stomachache, and just felt dizzy and odd. I had a great colonic, though, and did a lot of good talking. "By being ordinary, I become extraordinary by piecing together my strengths." This was a great topic we talked about during my colonic. I'm so concerned about being extraordinary that I keep myself *less* than even ordinary! By allowing myself just to "be," I can then build upon what I have to offer, which can in turn lead to extraordinary. It takes hard work, it takes patience, it takes belief, and it takes acceptance and confidence in oneself. My life has been dictated by fear of failure, fear of success, self-doubt, and low self-esteem. This is where ED conveniently comes in handy to predictably and consistently *control* the outcome through sabotage and excuse. Well, no more of that! I get to be ordinary first and discontinue basing my worth on expectations and externals. Don't hypothesize! Judgment keeps me isolated and in a world of "Well, I'm so amazing, but I'm too afraid to experience it and live." I must decide to use my talents for a positive purpose as opposed to allowing my talents to control and destroy me.

June 6, 2011

I really wanted to binge today, but there really wasn't anything in the house. Mom came home around 4:30 in the afternoon, and I told her I was starving and asked if I could have money to go to Coffee Bean and Subway. She was very reluctant, but after I told her I just needed it, she gave me $10. I decided I would make this my supposedly last binge, since I had $6 in my wallet, a loaded Starbucks card, and a free frozen yogurt stamp card.

I got a frozen yogurt first and then proceeded to Starbucks, where I bought 1 yogurt parfait, 2 small Frappuccinos, 2 mini cupcakes, and 1 mini caramel square. I made sure to mention that I was buying for a bunch of people. I then debated what to do with the rest of my money. I decided I really wanted doughnuts again, so I went to my favorite doughnut shop and bought 3 large doughnuts, 1 huge cream-cheese-filled doughnut, 1 huge cinnamon roll, 1 cream cheese/jelly-filled croissant, and 1 extra-large croissant. I ate 5 of them while sitting in my car by the ocean. I texted Mom and told her how sad I was, and she urged me to come home so she could hug me.

I came home and cried harder than I think I had possibly in my whole life! I let out some of the deepest pain I carry with me. How I spent all of middle school and high school completely alone with no one ever to talk to, not ever sharing anything with my parents growing up, never getting to go to prom, never having friends period, that I have no say in my disease and how serious it is, how badly I want my life, how much trauma and near-death feelings are starting to come up, how hard it is to see my class graduate this year when I had to drop out, and how badly I want and need help. Dad gave me a huge hug and just listened as I cried to Mom. They were both so incredibly supportive, and even my dad really seemed to take this eating disorder seriously for once. Not that he doesn't, but with the binging, he tends to get more annoyed than concerned. But now he seemed to understand how powerful a grip ED still has on me. I gave Dad every last dollar I had as well as the Starbucks card with $7 left on it and breathed a small sigh of relief.

June 7, 2011

Despite taking 8 laxatives last night, I didn't go to the bathroom at all. So, I upsettingly took 4 more. I slept in until 4:00 in the afternoon and then got up in a really bad mood. Mom was in her room on the phone with Kasey. I was trying to ask her if she could take me to get coffee, but she was busy talking. About 20 minutes later, I had a major breakdown or temper tantrum, whatever you want to call it. I haven't been that out of control since I was little. I mean, it even caught me off guard. I was acting like a spoiled 4 year old. I don't even know *what* was pushing my buttons, but I just kept screaming for Mom to take me to get coffee and saying that she loves Kasey more. I was *so* losing it, and so many old feelings came up. It felt as if all the anger I ever had bottled up my whole life was bursting out.

Mom was *so* angry and screaming at me. I even broke a candle-holder and picture frame. Mom was so upset at me and told me I make her hate God...she apologized for that comment. All I really wanted was for my mom to come hug me and hold me when instead she just ignored me and said she wouldn't come near me or talk to me until I calmed down. This is exactly what she did when I was growing up. The louder I screamed, the more I wanted her to come hold me and pay attention to me. She always did the opposite. I never wanted to give in. Kasey was always the good kid, and I was the wild one. The only way I knew how to get attention was to scream louder and louder, usually just to be ignored or given in to. All I want is for my mom to notice *me*!

28

Chronic Chaos

"Maybe you don't have to do anything. Maybe you don't need the answer right now. Maybe the very thing you have to do is just be with yourself just as you are. Maybe the answer is waiting in the quiet. Be still. Slow down. Listen." ~Britt

June 13, 2011

Happy birthday, Mom! Ugh, the day after a binge. An 11,000-calorie binge at that. I ended up taking 13 laxatives last night. I didn't even have anxiety over taking them this time, considering it's on average 5 more than I've ever taken. I would have slept through my appointment with Erin today if Mom hadn't woken me up. I quickly got dressed, and Mom drove me to my appointment.

I was so not there today. ED controlled every word, and the session was chillingly familiar to many of my previous therapy experiences. Head down, miserable look, quiet, no eye contact, pissed, etc. It was definitely not the fondest of memories as I was always *really* struggling with anorexia when I acted that way... but this time... this time I am not dangerously skinny and in any type of health danger. Do I really want that, though? To be honest, it's a little compelling to go back to my old ways. It was a lot easier to be miserable and curl up in a ball while watching my family, doctors, and therapists squirm with concern.

Realistically, I can understand that living life, being healthy, working, playing tennis, and making friends is *so* much better than a life dictated by anorexia, but the memories are so powerful and familiar that they draw me in like a magnet. My positive intentions of losing weight, staying healthy, being happy, and looking great always seems to attract negative behaviors, health problems, isolation, and a psychological trap. It's such an enticing illusion though, I tell you! It's like I fear reaching this "destination" of health and recovery so much that I keep sabotaging my efforts to get there because then what? What if I reach my goals and am not happy? What if I'm not success-ful? What if I don't have lots of friends? What if there is too much pressure? What if I still hate myself? Then again, is it worth hiding behind ED to shelter me from the "what ifs" after so many years of misery? I might as well at least give truly living a try.

I felt so bad for being in the state I was during my session. I was a little caught off guard at Erin's reaction toward my behavior this morning. I guess I would have thought she would have been a little more disapproving and lecturing at how I was acting. All I can think back to is previous therapists sitting there in pure silence or me getting angry and walking out, or, in the case of my therapist at UCLA, just saying, "OK, see ya later, bye!" and walking away. Erin said she missed me more than she was worried about me...quite the opposite approach of all my previous experiences. No one ever cared for connecting with *me* before...it was just about my eating disorder, requirements, and medical concern. That was really nice of her to say.

June 14, 2011

I had a really nice phone session with the dietitian I just started working with. I feel bad because I'm always half-asleep during our sessions. She is really smart, straightforward, and compassionate. I wish she lived in the area so I could put her face to her voice, but I will have to make do with what I do have. Anyway, we talked a little bit about the past week as well as my upcoming plans. She mentioned how strong I am and that she doesn't buy for a second that I can't stand up and defeat my eating disorder. That really made me feel good, and I know she is completely correct. It's funny because my own strength scares me. I know without a single doubt I can walk all over my eating disorder and never entertain it again, *but* it's still providing certain needs in my life. It's also easier to fall into ED's trap than say, "You know what? I'm not going to listen to you and challenge this thought or action instead." Of course, that means doing something different. That means change. That means taking a risk, which means the possibility for rejection or failure is high. I think I'm so afraid to be left alone that I find myself siding with ED's ideas so that I know I'm at least accepted somewhere...by someone...or *something*.

My dietician also mentioned that I should look at my weight. She said not knowing only gives ED more power. I told her I might be willing to ask Erin if I'm close to a certain number but that I don't think I could handle knowing the actual number yet. She said it's important to talk about and get support around seeing the number. She also brought up that I should process and get in touch with how awful it felt to see my highest weight for the first time and how awful it felt to *gain* weight at a weight *loss* camp. Hmm...

I stayed in bed until 2:45 in the afternoon and then got up and left for Coffee Bean at 4:45. For some odd reason, I actually feel just as thin if not thinner than before I binged on Sunday, which is really weird especially because I didn't even have a colonic yet. This intrigues me slightly. I have a friend who is extremely underweight and regularly binges up to 20,000 calories a day, yet purges constantly as well. She claims that she *loses* weight on her binge days, and others have said the same thing. Well, I can't purge, unfortunately, but it raises my attention toward the laxatives. Do they work better than I thought? Why do I feel thinner? Is having 1 binge a week when gluten-free foods are eaten accelerating weight loss? I'm a little confused. It's probably just all in my head.

Sometimes I wonder why I can't throw up. I've never really tried, to be honest, because it scares me. That form of purging is one of the most deadly forms of an eating disorder. So, no, I'm not trying to become that kind of bulimic, but sometimes when I want to binge I wish so badly that I could just throw it up. Ugh, honestly I should be thankful I can't throw up because knowing me, it would have killed me by now. OK, stupid topic... moving on.

June 16, 2011

I woke up around 6:00 this morning to Dad crying. I was still kind of asleep, but it really bothered and saddened me. It was his usually crying, moaning, "I can't do this anymore!" deal. He sounded just like a little boy, and it kind of made me mad... he's supposed to be my dad! I guess all people are entitled to cry and be upset and all, but I just wish he could be happy because he is one of the greatest people.

June 18, 2011

I hate my life right now! Yesterday was just awful. I woke up earlier than usual for my appointment with Erin. I actually thought I looked slightly thinner, which only encouraged me more to step on the scale and ask Erin if I was close to 160 pounds. I told her "close" could mean within 10 pounds. When she said no, I pretty much went into shock. When I asked if I were closer to 170 pounds or 180 pounds and she answered 180 pounds, my heart absolutely stopped. I spent the rest of the session lifeless, destroyed, somebody else. I've always *overestimated* my weight... this was something new. Erin said since I started working with her I've lost a total of about 1.5 pounds and that I was the same weight as last week. How is this possible?

It's now the following day, and after processing things a little more, I guess it makes sense. When I started working with Erin my size medium shorts did not fit nor did any of my shirts. Now my size medium shorts fit snugly and my shirts continue to get minimally looser each day, so you would *think* I was losing some weight, right? I thought because of these factors I must be within 10 pounds of 160 pounds given my starting weight at LIFE was 162 pounds. Knowledge is power, as Erin pointed out, and I guess I do feel more in control. *Not* happy... in fact, way less happy, but now I know. I suppose this is what I should have expected, right?

Perhaps I should be happy that I have not *gained* weight in the past few weeks considering my lifestyle. Yes, Brittany, yes...you can have your 1 to 2 days of binging and then hard-core restrict without gaining weight, *but* you will not lose weight and you can't expect to see changes. So, now what? ED let me down; ED betrayed me and lied to me! *I hate you, ED! I hate you, I hate you, I hate you!*

A lot of things changed that day for me. Utah was no longer a near future option given how much I actually weigh, and once again I felt glued in crisis, failure, and embarrassment. I cried for a while in the car. When I came home I broke down with Dad, and it was just awful. Knowing that all I needed to do was eat "normally" to promote weight loss and knowing that I couldn't and that I *still* won't be able to is such a conflicting way to live. I *hate* restricting the way I currently do! I don't eat anything really until 8:30 in the evening every day. No wonder I binge after 5 to 7 days and yet, whenever I try to eat like a regular person throughout the day, it turns into a binge! I tried to gather my strength and triumph over the news I just heard by eating before noon. It felt so good to allow myself to eat as I was starving. Predictably, though, the day soon turned into a binge.

Once I start eating I can't stop because I won't leave the house given my weight. Therefore, I have nowhere to be to go, no friends to see, and no activities to do. I am left trapped inside 4 walls containing food. The food becomes my escape, my friend, my distraction, and my activity. So I ate, finished, and then decided to numb the overwhelming feelings of guilt for breaking my routine by eating some more. Then, since I had already blown it, I continued to eat even more until I had consumed a ridiculous amount.

June 18, 2011

I slept in until about 5:00 this afternoon because my colonic was canceled, which sucked, but I was too out of it to give a shit, no pun intended. I came upstairs and cried harder than ever in my life. It was the most genuine sadness I think I've ever felt. Wow. No life, no friends, no college, no tennis. I hate my body. The highlight of each day for me is getting coffee and spying on people I'm jealous of on Facebook, which in turn only makes me feel more envious and inadequate. I cried hard for about 30 minutes straight. My parents felt bad, but what else could they do? I just kept saying I don't want to live anymore. The worst part? It's kind of true. I want to experience life, love myself, have fun, make friends, and truly know what it means to be alive, not merely exist. I can't seem to do that right now, and I don't see the answer into making it happen.

I mentioned in one of my e-mails to Erin that staying at home is making me suicidal or something like that, and she freaked out and replied that I needed to go to the ER and basically start the inpatient process of going to a psych ward. Am I really suicidal? The sad part—and I suppose ultimately the good part—is that I'm too chicken to actually hurt myself in that way. I'm too hopeful even amidst the bottomless pit I seem to be trapped in. Maybe I'm not hopeful. I am just intelligent enough to know this doesn't have to be the end, to know I am amazing at my best, and to know there could be help, change, and healing somewhere.

Then again, I honestly would be better in a psych ward right now. The thing is, I am a danger to myself. It wouldn't come in the form of purposely intending to kill myself or hurt myself but in a much more unassuming form. The fact that I—the most cautious, self-disciplined, and responsible person—am not only struggling with severe, out-of-control binging but am now impulsively taking up to 15 laxatives is just one of the examples demonstrating my reckless and unpredictable decline. I remember not that long ago reading about people who struggle with laxative abuse and thinking what idiots they were—and now look at me. The next time I binge I'm almost certain I will take 20 Dulcolax. These are no gentle solutions. Damn!

June 20, 2011

Today has been awful, to say the least. Last night I once again was placed under the binge spell, and today has continued with me in binge mode, though I have absolutely no urges of going out to get any food now knowing my true weight and appearance. I binged on all the food in the house (think protein shake after protein shake) and then went ballistic asking my dad to get me things at the market. It was like I wanted 1 last binge before changing my life, 1 last smoke before quitting, 1 last drink, you know? I don't know how to explain it, really...it is truly a chemical and/or brain imbalance and something I *cannot* control.

Anyway, it made for one very large argument with my parents, which resulted in me going to the medicine cabinet and taking a handful of about 30 Advil while telling my parents I was going to take them all. Do they believe I actually would? I want them to. They came and literally pried them all from my hand. The thing that scares me the most is I am not truly suicidal and would never actually plan to kill myself, but in moments of rage, I act *so* impulsively that a part of me honestly could see myself in the blink of an eye swallowing all those pills...similar to the laxative abuse now. Again, it's not that I want to die or that I am suicidal, but I do *not* trust myself anymore and could potentially see myself making a detrimental decision out of impulse. Sometimes I think I should check myself into a hospital or something just to breathe for a second behind safe doors.

June 22, 2011

Last night I felt really weird, which scared me, and I wrote Erin an e-mail telling her so. I was taken by surprise to find 2 e-mails from her this morning instructing that I should go to the ER or some type of walk-in clinic to get a basic evaluation or blood work done. What? I have without doubt experienced some very disturbing symptoms, but I'm alive right now and I guess OK, right? I'm trying my hardest to look at my disease from an outsider's view. It's not pretty. Here's what it looks like:

This individual has binges totaling a *minimum* of 10,000 calories (without means of vomiting relief), overdoses on 15 to 20 stimulant laxatives, drinks no water, and then awakes to the IQ and physical functioning of a severely intoxicated person. This same individual then proceeds to eat nothing until 8:45 in the evening. The next day this person, along with getting a colonic, goes to the bathroom at least 30 times, thanks to the laxatives. The young lady sleeps most of the day, goes to bed well past midnight, takes daily diuretics, does not show her face in public, body-checks compulsively wondering how she got so fat, eats in a hopelessly antisocial manner, has spontaneous mini-health scare alerts, has awful flashbacks of a former life, has become noticeably more depressed, and is starting to shut down.

Well, objectively speaking, I first of all would *not* want to be this individual. Second of all, I would say some sort of medical monitoring needs to happen. And lastly I would say there *has* to be some sort of intervention. "No! No! No! But I'm *not* sick!" I scream. "I'm fat; my body can handle it. It's OK that I restrict because I don't exercise. I feel better now. I don't care; plenty of people do worse things." How have I been able to fool myself into thinking things were and are really OK?

I fear that because I don't *look* sick nobody will take me seriously. This was especially uncomfortable when I was in Utah and had all those health problems. Each time that I would eventually end up in the ER I had to explain my significant history to the doctor and how "I struggled with severe anorexia for almost 8 years and just 1 year ago I was 56 pounds. But hey, you know I'm now 190 pounds because I binged my brains out." Totally believable, right? Ugh ... I felt the same way at Rosewood explaining to the clients and staff that I actually struggled with the opposite disorder for a predominate part of my life. At least with anorexia, as fatally stubborn as I was, I knew when it was time to ask for that extra level of help. The difference is I wasn't embarrassed. My ego didn't play a part. I figured, "OK, well, if I go to the ER and they look at me like an idiot because everything checks out fine then at least I look believably anorexic and was just being smart." Now, though ... now it's embarrassing enough to look the way I do and even more embarrassing to admit to having an eating disorder without being thin. It's just not worth the anxiety of being seen for symptoms that could be nothing. Yeah, I'm an idiot—I know.

It scares me to think that after everything I've been through, I'm *still* struggling...more so than ever at that. Will I ever be free? I feel as trapped as I was with anorexia at my worst. *Just make it go away!* I don't want a true emergency to have to take place for me to wake up. I can't live this lifestyle anymore. Even without the binges, the plain act of sleeping in and eating nothing until 9:00 at night is *not* OK. Got it, Brittany? It's not OK, and it doesn't have to be this way.

29

The Reality of Recovery

"Even something as frightening as a tornado can have a nice surprise that brings lots of joy." ~Kasey (5 years old)

June 28, 2011

Erin wrote me an e-mail last night in reply to some of my questions and overall feelings of hopelessness.

Insights: We all have a limited amount of energy to use to take care of ourselves each day. Currently, you are using a great deal of yours to counsel people about fitness camp decisions and replying to people seeking your help via e-mails and other online inquiries. You are spending energy you need for yourself. If you continue giving that energy away, there will continue to be nothing left for you to use to pull yourself out of this big hole you are in. It is your choice to either give this energy away or use it to help yourself.

What you are learning is that when you choose to engage in behaviors like counseling others about weight loss, recovery, using your story as a motivator, etc., you are given a lot of praise and positive reinforcement from others. However, your body, mind, and spirit are not at all appreciative, since all 3 are being neglected. And your body, mind, and spirit rebel by binging, trying to take back the energy you have given away.

Furthermore, your body, mind, and spirit know the truth and are not appreciative of any bending of the truth. You are more vulnerable to binging every time you present yourself as one way in recovery when you are in fact in another place.

It is not uncommon for someone in recovery from anorexia to go over his or her ideal body weight via binging. What typically happens is with some non-dieting based treatment for binging, the weight stabilizes in a healthy range. I suspect that had you never gone to the first fitness camp, this would have happened. You would have peaked at the weight you were prior to the first fitness camp (between 150 to 160 pounds, right?), and then with treatment would have lost weight and stabilized in a healthy place.

Treatment would have helped you realize that to avoid binging and more weight gain, as well as anorexia, you had to embrace a non-dieting, non-weight loss focused lifestyle. You would have learned to set boundaries so that people knew to never discuss weight loss or dieting with you. You would have wanted a career in anything other than fitness. You would have been very cautious when interacting with anyone with an ED, likely opting not to engage in any online conversations with people in the thick of recovery. You would have found shows like *The Biggest Loser* and weight loss camps to be extremely triggering and would do everything possible to shield yourself from these destructive shows/programs.

But instead you attended the fitness camp and ED and got to be a superstar. The same ED that got to 56 pounds became the star weight loss patient. Not surprising. ED became obsessed with the fitness camp idea and still has you convinced that it's a good idea to work for one of these organizations. These organizations will make a lot of money off your ED, but when ED gets so bad you need to be hospitalized from binging and laxative abuse, they won't cover the bill or be there to support you.

These days, you spend the bulk of your day either

engaging in ED behaviors or engaging in relationships that ED adores like the relationships with people in recovery or people wanting to go to fitness camps or the employees at these facilities. No wonder you are in a deep hole of despair! A drug user can't expect to get sober by working for drug dealers. You are trying to build a future in an industry (weight loss) that is also killing you via binging and laxatives.

This is a hard truth to see, and I hope you can hear what I'm saying. Once you are able to see the truth, a whole new and more fulfilling future will open up.

Really interesting thoughts...sometimes I do wonder what would have happened had I received intensive treatment once I came home from UCLA and then started binging. Of course, I was much too embarrassed at that time to comprehend the idea of treatment. If only I would have known that it would have saved me the trauma of gaining an additional 100 pounds over my healthy weight range and thousands and thousands of dollars.

June 30, 2011

In a rock-bottom type of state, I e-mailed Erin basically saying, "I'm done. I'm sorry. I can't do this right now. I will contact you in the future." What the heck, Brittany? The one person I trust more than anyone? Erin told me how much that affects her as well and how I'm always looking to flee.

Recovery is *unbelievably* difficult! It is the most boring, grueling, painful, saddening, and frustrating process I have encountered and believe I will ever encounter. There is nothing special about recovery. It doesn't come overnight, and although there are likely mini aha moments, it's nothing ground-shattering. Recovery is something I'm learning takes the commitment and patience I don't want to give it. I want to be moving on with my life and on to bigger and better things, but I've never given recovery a minute of my time. Because of that, I *always* (no matter how many times I tell myself it will be different) fall back into ED. So, this time I want to try something different.

I've made plans during the past 4 months living at home on several occasions of fleeing, but the difference is I haven't followed through this time and am really starting to come to terms with the fact that I am not going to, for who knows how long. I want to put an end date on my recovery, but the truth is I'm just going to have to sit with the unknown for a while.

One thing Erin mentioned is that the biggest reason Oprah is so famous and well-liked is because of her vulnerability. I'm good at sharing my vulnerable moments but only when they are part of my past...not my current struggles. Erin is right in that—when I am able to let go of putting on a perfect image at all times is when the pressure will decrease and people will become more available.

July 1, 2011

Why do I always blank about what Erin and I talked about? Hmm...we talked about how things were going at home as well as the trap I tend to lead myself into. Part of me feels as though I can't leave my dad because I mean so much to him and he gets so sad when I am away. So, a lot of the times I plan to leave the nest, but I end up sabotaging myself so that I have to stay. In a way, my dad feeds off my eating disorder as well. He *hates* it more than anything, yet he has failed *every* single time in giving me the protection I need from all the way to the point of literally fueling ED (allowing athletics against doctors' advice, buying binge food, buying laxatives, etc.). I want and I need to move on, separate, and be almost forced to start taking care of myself. However, there is a big part of me that so badly wants the childhood I never had and that I stick around trying to give my parents one last chance type of deal to do it right.

How is it that I'm now 22 years old and it's time to grow up? When I think back on my childhood, all I remember is performing, never resting, and always pleasing. Tennis training, tennis tournaments, tennis academies, horse training, horses shows, straight-A honor student, traveling, gym sessions, OCD, people pleasing, severe sleep deprivation, etc. No friends, no fun, no relaxing, no movies, no hanging out, no prom, no nothing! I wouldn't trade my life with anyone, though, in all honestly. As difficult as it has been and continues to be, I do see the light at the end of the tunnel, and I do see myself being that much more desirable in all aspects in life once I kick these eating disorders to the curb (and run them over multiple times!).

Anyway, it only makes it harder for me to take the first step toward moving on. Once I move on, the "cocooning/hibernating" is over. Time to get back to work. Time to be an athlete. Time to train. Time to think about the potential of college. Time to schedule appointments, keep commitments, make friends, be responsible, and create a successful future. I *love* all of the above mentioned, but I have 2 switches... overdrive and system failure. I am not good at pacing myself, balancing my life, or saying no. I eagerly push myself because I *like* the challenge and I *like* the busy work and I *like* the *power*, but I *must* learn to a) not turn to ED when I'm stressed, b) learn to ask for help and/or take my power to turn back the throttle and workload, and c) allow myself to make frickin' mistakes and move on. A lot of the time I am so terrified of messing something up, making just *one* wrong move no matter how miniscule, that I don't allow myself to be a human being!

I somehow need to keep myself safe as I learn that I can exist in the world in a social manner without having to perform and stand out. Good health and no struggles does *not* equal go-out-and-win-something-big. Ugh! Again, Brittany, the definition of insanity is doing the same thing over and over again and expecting different results. A really good warning sign Erin pointed out is when I put something off. The minute I tell myself I can reschedule something a week or so later is the minute I sign up for a binge session. In fact, many times I've wanted so badly to binge that I will postpone appointments and such so that I have enough time to binge and then put a shit ton of pressure on myself to lose the weight. The whole "I have time" theory has now affected big-time decisions... dang!

I came across some notes I took after my colonic session last week that helped settle my mind a little. "Each rung of the ladder to freedom is equally necessary, important, and with purpose to reach success. The first rung is as important as the last. The little steps can lead to that single profound person, moment, event, or sentence. If I don't do the hard work and use my courage to take different and uncomfortable steps then I won't recognize when everything is OK. If I wait 'til everything is perfect, it will never come, and I won't recognize it when it's there."

July 2, 2011

I got on Facebook and saw that a girl posted she was possibly going to Remuda. My heart sank with anger and jealousy. Maybe I'm just overprotective? Remuda was the start...a place that I first found true friends, safety, and boundaries. I begged to come home almost every day, but that was my beginning. I was an innocent girl who hadn't ruined her life yet. Not saying I've now ruined my life, but I really found a person I liked and I lost her again all too quickly. As much as I hated the events that happened to me in the moment...their reminiscent memories haunt me in a much too compelling way. When you're sick and wanting to stay sick, your only job is to fight and be taken care of. When you're healthy and wanting to stay healthy, your job suddenly becomes insurmountable...balanced meals, balanced exercise, work, athletics, relationships, appointments, errands, appearance, finances, judgment, etc. At least that is how my all-or-nothing, overachieving, perfectionistic mind believes.

At Remuda, I was too much of a people pleaser to *ever* come close to breaking a rule. At Stanford, I knew that if I put together enough consecutive days of noncompliances I would be conserved and tubed. At Torrance, I had the fight but lacked the physical strength to challenge the authority. At UCLA, I knew I was locked up, without a voice, and too afraid for my life to believe I would win if I fought. Remuda aside, I pushed every single treatment center to their limit. I tested their walls, their boundaries, and their intelligence, and each time after quite a war, I gave in with a sigh of relief knowing, "I have no choice but to surrender." I loved that surrender more than anything. It was something I always allowed myself to do knowing that once I was discharged I could play with the rules again. It was like a mini vacation from the constant torment and miserable lifestyle ED forces me to endure.

I want to be my own authority and to make my own decisions, but I also want to feel as though I have a safety net of people I can fall back on no matter what. Not just to catch me but also to treat me in a way that I know they are as competent and strong to match my ability. I want to know I have people in my life who will not give into or up on me no matter what! Who do I have in my life like that? Erin. End of story. This is new for me, though...to actually work simultaneously with someone who isn't intimidated by me. I've gotten remark after remark from doctors and therapists regarding my intimidation factor. However, because of this, professionals tended to loosen the reins rather than the opposite. Similarly to how my parents used to give into my temper tantrums growing up, leaving me feeling as if I had too much power and control at such a young and impressionable age. What I really needed was the opposite—boundaries and a feeling of safety and direction.

I just feel so let down by my parents...by my dad...because you can't protect me. So, you said goodbye to me.

I am forever haunted by my past. No one will ever understand. I don't know who I ever was or the monster I turned into.

All I want to know and to feel is that I am important enough for you to stand your ground.

30

Sleepless in San Luis

"I don't believe we hold ourselves back consciously, but rather are so afraid of the success we can achieve and the power we hold, that it's easier to never know." ~Britt

July 4, 2011

Happy 4th of July! Last night I struggled, though not badly compared with previous experiences. My parents were out with friends until close to 11:00 at night, and I was already having an uneasy day. After consuming a ton of fruit late at night, I decided to open up the special de-fatted powdered peanut butter called PB2 that I had bought on Amazon a few weeks ago. It's only 45 calories for 2 tablespoons, but I started getting a little carried away. I had maybe 5 or 6 servings before I put it away (I *did* put it away, though, which was good). I followed the directions and mixed the powder with water, but it didn't taste that great.

My parents finally came home, and my mom freaked out! "Is there *peanut butter* in the house?"

I told her yes, I've had it a few weeks, it was low-calorie, and I wouldn't order anything else again.

Basically she just freaks out! "I can't believe you did this! How awful! Blah, blah, blah!"

I was a little stunned. I mean, what the heck? I've *never* ordered anything I wasn't supposed to, and I just really wanted to try this product.

Meanwhile, Dad is just standing in the kitchen texting and not seeing the big deal. Mom finally left, saying, "Anytime you want to jump in and take over now, Lee!"

Dad flashed Mom a look of confusion. Mom replied, "I guess we just have such different parenting styles!"

I just kind of sit there, Mom goes downstairs to watch TV in her room, and Dad starts washing the dishes.

July 5, 2011

Sleeping is such a difficult thing for me and always has been. I *hate* the loss of control and the unknown. One of the hardest things for me was transitioning from Torrance to UCLA to home. I had a sitter with me 24-7 at both places even throughout the night, so I felt I could hand over control to them. The fear is so intense! I feel I need not only to protect myself but my family. They are soundly asleep, so who is going to be the one who saves the day when that extremely unlikely and unthinkable event happens? Ugh!

Sometimes I feel so mature, so ahead of the game, so smart, and so lucky with the opportunities I have. Other times I feel so held back, left behind, uneducated, and inexperienced. The truth is I am. I did a lot of my growing up and learning in treatment centers. You ask someone their most vivid memory, and they might answer with prom, graduating college, or some epic party. Mine? Mine would probably be losing my life at Torrance, hiding food at UCLA, the day I was able to run a few steps. It's just something I have to accept and come to terms with. I need to understand that I can move forward now in a different manner. Things can change. I can choose to take hold of the new memories I want to make and look back on. At the moment I'm really not making any memories. I'm doing great work, but I'm also putting my life on hold for now. Once I start going out into public, getting together with friends, playing tennis, and visiting horses, then the memories can start being made. Why must I always wait?

July 7, 2011

Are you in physical pain? Keep going. Are you tired now after working out? Go until you can't physically move anymore. Do you feel sick from binging? Eat more until you throw up. Are you starving? Drink water. Are laxatives uncomfortable? Take more and make them worth it. Are you lonely? Lose more weight. Blood pressure of 80/50? Heck, that's nothing. Heart rate of 40? Whew, still just fine. Liver enzymes 200 now? *Please*, try close to 3,000. Chest pain? Eh, once it's gone you'll forget about it.

This is my life. It's like I believe I receive some sort of admiration if I keep going when all other (sane) people would quit when in reality all I am doing is playing Russian roulette with my life. It's OK not to feel stuffed or starving. It's OK to work out and feel energized afterward. It's OK to rest when my legs are throbbing. It's OK to take a day off when I'm really tired. It's OK to eat something yummy and let it sit in my stomach naturally. It's OK to feel good. It's OK to be social just as I am. It's OK to *feel*. It's OK to be *healthy*.

July 12, 2011

I turned off the lights at 2:15 in the morning and actually slept pretty well. I woke up on and off but actually felt tired and groggy as if I actually slept for once, which was nice. I got up at 12:30 in the afternoon because Dad and I had planned to play tennis at 1:30. I came upstairs anxious about going out in public and playing. I began to have one of my OCD weight talks with Dad:

"Do I look obese or fat?"

"Uh, neither. You look great..."

"Why do you say it in that tone of voice like you aren't sure?"

"You certainly don't look obese...maybe just a little overweight."

"What? So are you saying I am fat then?"

"You are maybe 5 pounds overweight. That is all I mean."

"How can I trust you when you keep telling me different things?"

"You just look a little bloated from all the fruit you eat—that's all."

Then Mom butts in and told my dad to just walk away and for me to knock it off. Dad got up and left, and Mom followed Dad out.

I then overhear him say, "I can't do this anymore!"

Mom replied along the lines of, "Well, don't!"

I thankfully had a great session with Erin later today. I explained to her that I have this weird OCD around fruit. I always eat the bad fruit first and then leave the fresh fruit for my family. Erin said that eating the bad fruit was actually a commonly documented symptom in once-starving people. Whoa! I never would have known or thought that. I think it goes back to wanting to save the food and not waste it, which would make sense to a brain that was conditioned to starving. It's also probably because I feel so undeserving of anything good that I believe if I punish myself enough, or leave enough good for others, I will be accepted, loved, and forgiven. Ah, this is all such nonsense! I just wish I could have had friends growing up. I wish I were never bullied or made to feel so terrible and rejected. My peers haunt me just as much as ED.

31

Fighting the Feelings

"Keep pushing forward. You never know when the walls that cage you in are going to crumble." ~Britt

July 13, 2011

I had a fabulous meeting with my new psychiatrist, Dr. Guimaraes. He is extremely sweet and has an accent. He went over my basic history and how I was doing currently. He confidently prescribed me a combination of the medications Prozac and Topamax. He said for the Prozac to work effectively, the dose needs to reach at least 80 milligrams. He also explained that taking Topamax in combination should help with cravings and binging urges, which I am most excited about. I said OK to everything despite being such an opponent when it comes to medication, but I am at the end of my rope. I fear taking medication will somehow change me or cause me to lose control. However, I am drastically out of control right now and not in a way that I like, so I'm willing to try anything. He is having me start on 10 milligrams of Prozac and then is adding the Topamax next week at a dose of 25 milligrams. He said he will increase both each week and that the goal would be to get Prozac at 80 milligrams and the Topamax at 200 milligrams. I thanked him and drove home.

Mom came into the kitchen where I was because we were getting ready to go get coffee. I mentioned how upset I am today and that I was really having a hard time. I told her I ate way too much fruit and vegetables, how anxious I am, and that I'm so frustrated with the scale.

She then proceeded to lecture me in her critical voice: "You're eating too much fruit. Your portion sizes need to be adjusted. That's why you don't lose weight. You need more protein. Eat 6 small meals a day. Anyone who eats as much fruit as you do in one sitting wouldn't lose weight. You need to eat earlier instead of eating so late at night."

I was almost in shock and tried to tell her that I am eating much earlier than previously, that I'm eating enough protein, that fruit can't be *that* harmful, and that given how I used to eat while binging, the fruit diet should be OK. She continued to say how there is way too much sugar eating as much fruit as I am, and she just kept going and going.

I finally said, "Mom! I have an eating disorder. What do you expect?" How can she think I will just eat normally after all these years with a deadly disease? It's as if she had completely forgotten all that I have been through.

I then went to the bathroom, looked at my stomach in the mirror, came back into the kitchen, and said sadly that I would now have to cancel my scheduled appointments for tomorrow. Mom looked at me and asked what appointments I had. I answered that I had an appointment with Erin and a facial.

Mom gave me an awful look and said in an analytical, disgusted voice, "Well, then I guess you aren't a very strong girl and aren't working hard enough" or something like that.

And I *flipped* out! I felt as though I had just been shot, literally. I, who agreed to see a psychiatrist, agreed to meds, went 2 weeks without binging, attend therapy 3 times a week, go to bed earlier, stopped taking laxatives, started playing tennis, started exercising…I am *not* working hard enough? I am *not* a strong person? I was absolutely *crushed*!

Mom then followed up with, "Yeah, you should *want* to go to therapy."

Well, duh, of course I want to go to a certain extent, but am I supposed to jump up and down and clap my hands because I get to go talk about all the trauma, tears, fears, and dysfunction I have in my life? *No!* I don't think so!

I screamed at her while crying so hard I could hardly make out the words: "Why don't *you* check yourself into a hospital for a few months while losing all basic functions, including the ability to wipe your own ass while strangers watch you 24-7 and your parents hardly come to visit you as you're dying? Why don't *you* get forced to leave college? Why don't *you* lose your horse that means the world to you? Why don't *you* live your life without a single friend? Why don't *you* live your life a slave to your own mind with exercising and starving? Why don't *you* relearn how to walk? Why don't *you* get a blood transfusion, have a tube shoved down your nose, have your liver enzymes reach almost 3,000, and get asked if you want to be resuscitated while in the ICU?

"Why don't *you* stare at the heart monitor dropping to 27 beats per minute while being told you're going to die and that you're the most hopeless case ever encountered? Why don't *you* binge so severely you gain 80 pounds in 3 months then enter a fat camp in hopes to like yourself again but continue to binge? Why don't *you* agree to go to Rosewood Ranch despite being obese in a facility full of anorexics? Why don't *you* go to Premier Fitness Camp weighing in at 221 pounds and 48 percent body fat only a little over 1 *year* after weighing in at 56 pounds? Why don't *you* finally return home decently healthy only to binge again and regain 30 pounds? Why don't *you* look into the mirror only to see a stranger?

"*But to not give up!* To stick it out here at home when I wanted to flee to treatment, to invest in therapy, a dietitian, a psychiatrist, and think of ways to stop my binging. To give you all my money, have you lock the pantry, and to pick myself up and exercise in the house. To hold on, to believe in something better, and you think *I'm not working hard enough and that I'm not strong!* Are you *serious?* [I am sobbing hysterically right now.] Do you not know what I've been through? And yet her I am *still* alive and trying to help myself. I *hate* you!"

I went and sat in Mom's car and cried harder than I have ever cried in my life. I have never ever, ever experienced such sadness, loneliness, and gut-wrenching insult. I could not even begin to comprehend what just took place. I've been through *so* much! I'm still *alive*! I'm still trying my best every single day to like myself, to help others, to find peace, to smile, and to keep myself safe. My parents are all I have. I don't have any close friends. I don't have anyone who has stuck by my side through all of the chaos. I know I can't expect my parents to be perfect, but I guess I just never would have thought they would say and react in certain ways that they do.

Mom came out to the garage and opened the car door about 5 minutes later and said, "You had better shut up if you want me to drive you to coffee!"

I told her how much I hated her and just kept crying and crying uncontrollably. She then left and slammed the garage door behind her. Pushed over the limit by her insensitivity, I honked the car horn until she came storming back out into the garage. She then opened the car door and threw all her keys at me as hard as she could! They hit my hand really hard. If they had hit my head I honestly could have been in big trouble. I was absolutely stunned and beyond hurt to even comprehend everything that had and was taking place.

I hysterically made my way into the house a complete out-of-control mess. Dad came into the kitchen where Mom was, and I threw lemons at her feet while sobbing that I couldn't believe she threw her keys at me and that she could have seriously hurt me. Mom left the room, and I experienced a state of emotional frenzy. I couldn't think. I couldn't feel. I cried and cried and kept repeating to Dad that Mom doesn't think I'm strong and working hard. Dad tried to hold me and tell me I am working hard and I am doing amazing, but I just could not calm down. I kept trying to reach for the scissors saying I wanted to kill myself, but Dad did his best to restrain and calm me down. I eventually broke free from him, grabbed the scissors, and locked myself in the bathroom where I eventually settled down.

I cut myself on my arm with the scissors. It really caught me off guard as well as brought up some very old and dark memories. When I was about 10 or 12 years old, I actually did harm myself, although minimally. I used to scratch myself on my arm and leg until I had a huge, red, and noticeable mark. I did it with the intent to get some-one's attention…any kind of attention. I always told my parents I fell off my bike or I told others that a rose bush scratched me if they did ask. I had forgotten all about that brief time in my life until I was staring down at a huge bleeding line I had just created with the scissors.

I began remembering back all the way to when I was just 4 years old. At that age, I would play with my toy horses and beanie babies. The story was always the same. There was one character that was pretty, skinny, had blonde hair and blue eyes, and was loved, perfect, popular, famous, and successful. That character was like superwoman, and I was that character. It was the only way I could pretend my life was better. This story line continued for years. I used to pray every single day during elementary school to make my life better and for me to be like my fantasy character. In a lot of creepy and bizarre ways, *all* my prayers were answered, just not in a positive way…

July 16, 2011

I played tennis with Dad, but I was angry the whole time, criticiz-ing each shot. I need to remember to be grateful that I'm even holding a racket and standing on the tennis court. Dr. Schack informed my parents that the best case scenario for me *if* I survived the 5 percent chance she gave me would be to live in a hospital for a few more years and/or live the rest of my life with brain damage, with osteoporo-sis, and in a wheelchair. Hmm…well, clearly I'm defying some odds here, but that doesn't always help me see the bigger picture. I still can't quite come to terms with the fact that I'm even alive, let alone fat now. Since I'm OK now, I keep living my life as if nothing ever happened and have expectations that are too high for the time being. Why can't just waking up every day be enough?

July 22, 2011 (written July 25)

I don't want to journal. I don't want to do *anything* right now. I actually have a lot of words and emotions to let out and say, but I just don't want to go through the effort. Well, here goes nothing.

Friday... Friday was great including a positive session with Erin. It was so great in fact, that I was literally almost out the door headed to a public gym 45 minutes away. I chose to take a nap instead... damn body image! Damn all-or-nothing thinking!

My parents went out for dinner. I got ready to work out in the house and put on my headphones to my iPod... but I never turned it on. What was it that lured me to the fridge? What was it that made me open it as if something could have magically placed itself there in the hour since I had last opened it? Well, there was nothing new in it. No cheesecake, no pizza, no peanut butter, no... nothing new at all. There was, however, that ½-full bag of cheese, a little bit of turkey, the possibility of making dessert-like quinoa, and a hint of insanity brewing.

"Just eat some of that cheese! Just have some! You don't want to exercise! If you take 1 bite of cheese maybe I will let you start your workout. Trust me, Britt, just have a little bit first."

` "You're right, ED! I've been doing so well lately and haven't had much fun lately. You and I haven't spent a night together in a while. I'm feeling kind of down for aborting the gym earlier anyway, so I'm glad you are here to keep me company and cheer me up.

"What if I *had* gone to the gym and made a fool of myself? Worse... what if it all went OK? Then I would have to keep going. I would have to commit, keep it up, and start living again. I *hate* exercise right now anyway! ED, you remember better than anyone all those hours I slaved away at those damn fitness camps. Ha! The fact that I even *needed* such a thing! Well, screw exercise! Screw it!"

"Oh, I know, Brittany. There you were, surrounded by obese people, and they probably never even knew the success you once had in the weight department. You are better than they are. You don't need to work hard. You're the exception. You're the expert. It's OK; you can give yourself a break. You have *me*, and that is the difference. I will take care of you... they don't have *me*. Yeah, that's right! Doesn't that cheese taste good? There is only a little bit left... why not make an egg-white omelet with it? Have a food night; forget the exercise. You're tired and burned out. It's OK!"

"Shit, what am I doing? I've been making so much progress. I've noticed positive changes in my mind and body. I thought I trusted myself. Well, too bad. No exercise, no meal plan, and no gym this week. I hate you, ED!"

"That's what you *always* say…'I hate you, ED!' Yeah, that sentence really works for you, huh?"

Before I knew it, the day's calories totaled 5,000-plus. I surprised myself. The exercise was getting increasingly harder for me mentally, but I kept pushing through. I hadn't thought out what my backup plan would be if I didn't do a workout or what my OCD would think if I altered my routine. Knowing my all-or-nothing ways, it would have been an easy 'A' to answer that ED would come to the rescue and sabotage me. And so that was my Friday. Miserable.

July 23, 2011 (written July 25)

I woke up late today, but I had planned to resume my meal plan and work out. However, I figured after all the food I ate yesterday I really should skip breakfast. This led me to feel mentally deprived. The rest of this day is a blur. I was doing just fine up until my parents left to go out to dinner and I put on my sneakers to work out.

"Come on, Brittany, wouldn't it be more fun to see if you can find where Dad hides all the food? You know it must be somewhere downstairs. Let's look harder this time. It will be fun!"

"Yeah, but it's already past the time I should have started working out, and even if I do find the food, I shouldn't eat it."

"Look at you! You are already so bloated and gross and come on…you are probably the last person on the planet who has a desire to work out tonight."

"Ugh. You're right. Besides, it's almost *too* late to start my workout. Maybe I could go look."

I find the stash, which thankfully only consisted of 1 large handful of raw almonds, 1/4 cup of salted almonds, and the 3/4 jar of PB2 Powdered Peanut Butter. I actually found the stuff and didn't take any. This only lasted about 5 minutes before I thought of what I could do with the PB2. I could put it in quinoa! I ran back downstairs and got it. I ate the whole jar in a matter of minutes before I could even make the quinoa. Next I was on to making the whole entire box of quinoa to eat, then the cottage cheese container, the yogurts, the almonds, 3 apples, 6 eggs, the stale bagel, and 1 long-lost can of Spa-ghettiOs. *Why* couldn't I have just decided I didn't want to exercise? Well, because I couldn't sit with the guilt of choosing to give myself a rest. I needed a reason, an excuse, and a catastrophe to justify my decision. I needed a way to feel self-hatred and anger... those are easier to feel than guilt.

Ugh, it was such a rough night. I didn't go downstairs to bed until 5:00 in the morning. I had a nice dream. I was at a treatment center or something, and a *very* sick young lady was complaining about never going to be able to recover to some professional. I remember getting butterflies in my stomach, and I couldn't hold myself back any longer. I blurted out that I, too, was once that bad with xyz complications and that "Look! I'm completely recovered and healthy now!" I was so excited to share it with her. Was I talking to myself?

32

Psych Wards Are for Crazy People

"Forests thrive the most after they've been burned down to nothing. Maybe a crisis is healing and growing in disguise." ~Britt

August 3, 2011

Monday:

Oh my goodness, where even to begin? Monday was just awful. I had an OK appointment with Erin and my psychiatrist. I had a really hard time when I came back home, though. I was tired, bored, and drained from getting no sleep the night before. I was feeling unsettled and was still hungry even after I finished my snack. Mom and I got coffee earlier than usual and later in the day I wanted even more coffee, so we went back to Coffee Bean and I got another coffee plus 1 small sugar-free blended vanilla drink. Uh-oh... the blended drink was certainly not part of the plan. We arrived home safely, but the seed of destruction had already been planted.

"Don't open the fridge, Britt. I know you are still hungry, but it's almost 5:00 and then you can have your gum."

"Yeah, but you are *so* hungry, and you still have at least 30 minutes before you can have your gum. Besides, you are already feeling miserable right now. You can eat a little extra to calm yourself down. Just go check out the kitchen fridge."

"OK, fine, ED. I will at least look. Hmm...just as I thought—the tortillas and salmon. Ohhh, salmon, hmm..."

"Eat it! Salmon is good for you! At least eat the pieces that are broken off. You know your OCD can't leave those scattered pieces. You don't have to eat the main large piece...just a little bit."

"Yeah, salmon is really good for you. Oh geez, look! A bunch of little broken-off pieces I *must* eat. Nooo! I'm eating too much now, and I can't stop!"

"Ohhh, you started into the big piece now, huh? I knew you would! Keep eating it! Might as well finish the whole plate now."

The rest of the night was a blur. Basically, I started binging, and the night ended with me in hysterics. I wasn't screaming nor was I fighting...I couldn't stop crying, and I just wanted to die.

Tuesday:

I made a last-minute appointment with my psychiatrist today at 11:45. I told him how depressed and hopeless I was feeling as well as the continued binging and such. He told me it would be a good idea for me to be admitted to Cottage Hospital psychiatric ward for a week to help stabilize myself, increase medications faster, break the binging cycle, and because I was suicidal and wanting to hurt myself. Well, just because I said I didn't want to live anymore doesn't mean I'm really suicidal, does it? Anyway, I reluctantly agreed.

He called Cottage Hospital, and they did have an open bed. He told me to go down to Santa Barbara, where the hospital is, that day, and he said he would work with the team there. I called Mom from the car after my appointment to tell her. She was really supportive, but I know it took her a little by surprise. Why can't she ever take it seriously that I might be or am suicidal? I *never* thought I would be at a healthy weight. I *never* thought that I would be obese. I *never* thought that I would be 56 pounds. I *never* thought that I would abuse laxatives, and I *never* thought that I would cut and self-harm. Who knows what's next? I don't trust my impulses or myself anymore. Along with the severity of my depression, might I actually kill myself by mistake? I arrived home, began to pack some things, and sent Erin an e-mail.

I got a call from someone at the psych hospital who was really nice. When I asked if I could come down the next day instead of today she said that would be fine because they weren't full. She was 99.9 percent sure it would be no problem. That was a huge relief for Mom, so that she could figure out who could take care of the dogs and she wouldn't have to drive at night, which scares her. Mom and I were getting ready to go out to do our usual coffee run when I saw a missed call from Dr. Guimaraes. I listened to his voice mail, which was confirming I was on my way down. I called him back and told him I was planning to go tomorrow. He got very upset and told me I *had* to go right *now*! He said it's impossible to get a bed there and the fact that I have one is amazing. He upsettingly told me I have no good reason not to go this minute and that we shouldn't even be having this conversation. He followed up that he would call 911 and put an involuntary hold on me if I don't go now. I then gave in and consented to his request.

Mom gave me an awful and panicked look and told me to hurry up and pack all my clothes.

During the drive, Mom would not stop pestering me about how angry she was and how she couldn't believe this was happening. She gave her "every August you end up in a hospital" speech. *Come on, Mom!* I am doing the best I can and am trusting in my team. I told her either to support me or get out of my life. I'm fighting a disease, and I can't predict when I will be OK. I could be all better and done with ED in as little as a few months or this battle could be a part of my life for who knows how many years! She's either in it with me to the end or not, but I can't have her stressing me out and making me feel like shit every time I need help. I already feel like a big enough failure for not being able to fix things on my own, so give me a break!

Without my eating disorder, all the pain, depression, anger, and emotions I have tried so hard to suppress are able to surface. ED was only a temporary cover-up, a bandage over all my real unhappiness. To heal myself for real means getting rid of ED, sure, but the next required step is getting help for *why* I needed ED in the first place to drown out the underlying pain. Maybe this is a positive and expected step. The fact that these raw emotions are coming up could mean ED is no longer working efficiently in my life. Mom felt really bad and gave me a huge hug after she got my coffee and said how proud she was of me.

We walked into the Cottage Hospital ER around 7:30 at night. Everyone was so nice! I was really upset and almost numb. I got called back and gave Mom a big hug goodbye. I went back to a section of rooms that seemed designated for the psych ward only. I shared the room with this boy around 20 years old or so. It was very clear by his conversations with his mom and staff that he was a regular on the psych floor. Overhearing some of his conversations with his mom was hilarious.

> Mom: "You know, I didn't realize that a lot of people take twice the amount of X than you. I'm surprised you haven't tried upping that."
> Son: "I will pretend to be the doctor, and you pretend to be me. *So*...what meds are you taking?"

It was quite comical. I first met with a medical doctor and then soon afterward the admitting therapist, I believe. The mother-and-son duo left to be admitted before me, and I could hear the nurses cleaning up the bed for the next patient. About 20 minutes later, I hear a doctor having a conversation with another doctor exclaiming, "This is the *third* time!" Then a lady takes the bed next to me. The curtain is pulled, so I can't really see her, but then she stands up and walks toward the paper towel dispenser, which is slightly reflective. She walks up to it unusually close as if she's trying really hard to look at her reflection. She did this a few times before I figured she must have mental issues. Then the doctor comes in to see her.

> Doctor: "Hi, I'm Dr. X."
> Disturbed: "Hi! Please, can you tell me first—are you a *real* doctor?"

Doctor: "Yes . . . I am a real doctor."

Disturbed: "You're an actual medical doctor?"

Doctor: "*Yes.*"

Disturbed: "Oh, wonderful, thank *goodness!*"

Doctor: "You've been here quite a few times recently. I understand you were transferred last time to the county psych ward. [In annoyed voice] So, tell me . . . what *is* your goal of coming to the emergency department *this* time?"

Disturbed: "Well, a lot, actually. I was discharged yesterday from the psych ward, and I'm afraid I've been poisoned. Whenever I look in the mirror at my abdominal section, it looks loose, and I'm afraid I've been poisoned with a muscle relaxer. Every time I take one sip of coffee, I start peeing uncontrollably all over myself. I'm also experiencing some paranoia about being outside as well as hallucinations."

Doctor: "I see . . . and what do you think we could do for you?

Disturbed: "Well, it was by the suggestion of my father that I come. My symptoms come and go. I would like you to do a physical examination as well as check to make sure there is no poisonous substance in my bloodstream."

(Doctor does exam.)

Disturbed: "Oh, see? It's contracting!"

Meanwhile, this lady is talking in a very calm and adult voice . . . it was just so bizarre. I then finally got taken up to the fifth floor around 11:00 after a 3-hour wait in the ER.

August 3, 2011

I got called to talk to my psychiatrist, Dr. Easton, along with a student staff member. The student asked me a bunch of questions while the doctor listened, and then he asked some. According to the doctor, I said quite a lot of profound things. I don't want to get well because then all the pressure and responsibility comes back. Dr. Easton told me my perfectionism really gets me in trouble because I set unrealistic and unreachable standards (well, duh). I then end up subpar, whereas if I just tried to be average, I would end up being extraordinary by nature. Yeah, yeah, yeah... easier said than done.

I've been in my room most of the day lost in my own thoughts. Since this is specifically a voluntary psych ward, it means the rules aren't as strict as a locked unit would be. I can have my phone, iPod, and most of my other belongings. I did some journaling and played Tetris on my phone. A few patients keep pacing slowly up and down the hallway in a daze with headphones on. This is certainly a new experience for me. Then again, I would think after a few days here I would be going crazy, too.

August 4, 2011

I had a good meeting with Dr. Easton today. He asked me what getting well looked like. I told him I would be happy, love myself unconditionally, and would allow myself to do the things I enjoy and am good at with no pressure. He then asked me what would happen if I purposely had to play an awful tennis match. I said I would freak out! He then asked what responsibilities I would have once I'm well. Gee, umm... I would *have* to get back into competitive tennis, I would *have* to decide on job opportunities, I would *need* to start working out at the gym, I would *have* to enroll back in college, I would *have* to get out in the real world and make friends, I would *have* to find a successful career, I would *have* to find the right guy and have the responsibility of committing to a relationship, and I would also *have* to somehow recover and be free from my eating disorder. Whew, what a load!

Dr. Easton then asked me what I would say if I could never do any of those again or if I could only choose 1 or 2 to do after 1 year of being well. Hmm... what a concept. I agreed that I can't overload myself, but am I even capable of finding and maintaining balance in my life?

Dr. Easton laughed quietly and said, "No wonder you don't want to get well, because getting well means jumping right back on that sprinting treadmill that got you here."

I have to change what I was doing before. I have to allow myself to be imperfect.

I went to a process group later. We talked about how we have a choice to change the way we think about situations and fears and how to reframe our minds. Then we wrote down the worst case scenario of doing certain things we were doing before the hospital and the best case scenario of doing that same thing. For me, the worst case was death, and the best case was having comfort in a familiar routine. Obviously, life has so much more to offer for the best case scenario to be familiarity. Then again, maybe I don't really believe that deep down life can be wonderful because apparently my fear of truly living outweighs the very real possibility of death. Ugh! What is wrong with me?

I had an OK rest of the day, but uneasiness was building inside of me. Toward the end of the day, I cut myself on my leg with a plastic knife. Why? Well, stress sums it up simply. I'm stressed about finding a program to go to afterward as I really can't and don't want to go home. I'm overwhelmed that I'm in a hospital, and past traumas are flooding my mind. I'm stressed about food and have been eating as little as possible here, as I absolutely despise my body. To top off my list of issues, I really don't want to get discharged here...at least not as soon as most people tend to stay here. I'm just not ready. I told a nurse whom I formed a bond with about the cutting incident. She said if I do it again, I would have to be transferred. Huh?

August 8, 2011

I am so depressed. It's an effort just to keep breathing. I've hit rock bottom physically many times before, but this is the first time I've hit rock bottom mentally. Maybe just maybe, the ability for me to find lasting change is on the horizon. I am going to dedicate myself to recovery, help, and healing. Claudia A. Howard sums it up perfectly with one of her 5 principles of unconditional human worth: "Externals neither add nor diminish worth. Externals include things like money, looks, performance, and achievements. These only increase one's market or social worth. Worth as a person, however, is infinite and unchanging."

August 9, 2011

I heard today that I could be getting discharged tomorrow. What? I can't be discharged. I have nowhere to go. I'm really starting to get overwhelmed now. I'm starting to feel out of touch with reality. When you isolate long enough and abstain from normal functioning routines, you start to feel that much sicker than perhaps you really are. Ugh, this is such a mind trip! I have to trust that I will be lead toward the path of recovery, health, and healing as well as discovering my true passion and purpose in life.

August 10, 2011

Today hasn't been so great. I met with Dr. Easton as well as a case manager, and what I had feared and assumed is true. My insurance will only cover partial hospitalization programs, meaning there are no residential programs I can go to. The case manager mentioned a place called Sovereign Health, which is a partial program yet provides housing and has 3 different tracks, including eating disorders, mental health, and addiction. I could give that my best effort, I suppose. Ugh! Stop being so stubborn, Britt! Don't wait 'til every detail is perfect to start. Just find the buried desire and make it work!

I had a long talk with one of the staff members. We were processing my fears of moving on to the next step and recovery. To make a long story short, he mentioned ill gain, where some patients in a twisted way would actually rather stay sick and stay in the hospital or treatment rather than face the scary real world. I lost it after he said that. Well, sure, there is an element of truth to what he just said, but come on! I was a shut-in the past 4 months; was 56 pounds and nearly dead 2 years ago; was 221 pounds and obese 1 year ago; and have plenty of athlete issues, school issues, work issues, ego issues, depression issues, anxiety issues, trauma issues, and friend issues. You name it! I'm done!

You think I *like* this? I should be out playing tennis, going to school, and having fun with friends. I started sobbing. He apologized and walked out the door, and the charge nurse came into my room and asked what happened. Damn!

33

You Have No Rights

"The brightest rainbows are found after the roughest storms." ~Britt

August 11, 2011

Today has been rough, to say the least. I got my blood drawn early, sat in the lounge, drank my coffee, skipped my breakfast, took my meds, and went to community meeting where I shared my struggles and suicidal thoughts. Uh-oh... I've been so out of it today, so numb, so distant, so sad, and so hopeless. I talked with a lady from CARE (whatever that stands for) later today, and after a brief conversation, she said she was going to 5150 me and put me on a 72-hour involuntary hold at a lockdown psychiatric unit called Vista Del Mar in Ventura. What? She trapped me! All I did was answer her questions honestly. I had no idea people had the right to put you on an involuntary hold based on words alone. I'm definitely on the fast track to understanding mental health 101, whether or not I wanted to sign up.

An ambulance came to get me, and I arrived at Vista Del Mar around 9:00 in the evening. I was taken to a room behind the nurses' station, and some rules were explained. No gum, no iPod, no items with strings, no pens, no cell phone, no tweezers, no hair straightener, no dental floss, no perfume, no jewelry, no shaving, no hair clips, and on and on and on... ah! What *is* this place? Apparently there is a *big* difference between the voluntary unit at Cottage Hospital and a real-deal psych ward. I had to get weighed and was 174 pounds, but it was at night after all my liquid and food, so maybe it's a little lower? I had to do a full-body check and then sat down with an older nurse to answer some questions. I was in utter shock when I lay down on my so-called bed. The pillows might as well have been doormats and the mattress as well. I hardly slept, and after about 1 hour of staring at the ceiling, I heard some of the most disturbing screams and words being yelled, or rather chanted. I got up to take some Benadryl, and, oh my goodness, the screams coming from the backroom! This lady was basically channeling the devil and having an exorcism or something in the lockdown room. It was the most disturbing thing I think I might have ever heard! Good gosh, get me the heck out of here!

August 12, 2011

I got up around 7:00 in the morning, having gotten almost no sleep at all. They weighed me again, and I was 169.4 pounds—hooray! I didn't eat any breakfast…just 2 cups of coffee. Most of the staff here are really nice and well-grounded…then again, I suppose you have to be to work in a place like this. The whole living environment, lounge, etc. is very uncomfortable, cold, and small, but I'm no demanding princess, so whatever. The couches are actually made out of a plastic-like material, and there isn't anything sharp or shiny to be seen. There are maybe 3 groups a day, and they are so boring! It is definitely a different crowd here as far as patients go. I've talked with a few, and they are nice, but we aren't in here because we've got our lives together—with some of the people here being quite extreme.

I met with my psychiatrist, and he seems all right. His name is Dr. Statler, and he spent a lot of time with me gathering my history. He was very interested in my story and life events. He increased my new medication that replaced Prozac to 80 milligrams and my Topamax to 200 milligrams. Whoa! Doubling the dosage of both of my meds in a day? Umm…OK, then. I felt so down and depressed all day and pissed about not being able to have gum. I really might as well forget about wearing makeup, too, since our bathroom mirrors are nothing but blurred plastic. For lunch and dinner, I ate about 6 to 8 ounces of cottage cheese and 1 plain salad with veggies. I also had 1 apple before bed.

My total calories for the day are under 1,000, but I still had too much. One lady here keeps crying on and off. Between her wails and the staff opening my door with a flashlight every 15 minutes to do room checks, it's going to be another really long night.

August 15, 2011

I got put on a 14-day hold by a substitute psychiatrist who saw me over the weekend. *What?* This is unbelievable! I feel as if the only way to be released from these places is to lie and say you feel great, are happy, and have no intentions of harming yourself. Obviously, that isn't true for me, so yeah, I told him I'm depressed and hate my life. But staying in here certainly isn't making me any better.

I met with Dr. Statler, who is back today for the week. We were having a lovely talk until he said, "I want to decrease your Topamax because the staff say you're not eating much, and I want to try adding an antipsychotic like Abilify, Seroquel, or Geodon."

What? I said *no way* will I ever take any antipsychotic and that I really didn't want the Topamax to be decreased.

We fought back and forth for a bit, and then he said, "Fine. I will just go to court and force you."

Oh, yeah? Well, that started another argument, and 2 staff members pretty much had to drag me out of the office. What the heck? *Court? Force me?* Ha! I feel like I'm on an episode of *Punk'd* or something.

August 16, 2011

Well, today is court day... at least, so I thought. Dr. Statler called me into his office early, which I already found strange. To sum up our meeting, he told me he was really sorry about yesterday, that I don't have to take antipsychotics, and that he would like to try a mood stabilizer with minimum side effects called Trileptal and keep the Topamax at the same dose. What a sigh of relief! Now, *if* I had gone to court and *if* they had ruled in favor of the doctor, I could be literally held down and injected with the antipsychotic. Wow…talk about having no rights.

On another note, there are quite a few *crazy* patients here right now. Yikes! We've got the one screaming at the top of her lungs sporadically, the door-slamming champion, the food-and-book-stealing hoarder, the one staring off into space while on 24-hour watch for thoughts of killing others, the world-record crier, the one who hasn't taken a shower in weeks, the I-regularly-have-conversations-with-myself one, the one warning that the aliens are coming, the one sitting in the middle of the hallway cussing and harassing staff members to release her right the fuck now, and then the few depressed, suicidal, and/or drug abusers. This circus is a 24-hour event, and the admissions price is unsurprisingly affordable. Maybe I'm not so bad off.

August 21, 2011

I don't have words to describe how I feel right now. Today has been just a blur and I still can't comprehend my life and situation right now. To sum things up, earlier I was lying in bed getting angry and needing a release. What to do? The only way I know how to express anger is through self-destruction: eating disorder, overexercise, binging, laxatives, cutting, etc. Well, I have limited options here, so I chose to bang my left leg/shin against the furniture a few times. Ouch! I finally gave in and walked to the nurses' station, saying I'm going stir-crazy and that I hurt myself. I got put on line of sight, meaning I have to be in the sight of a staff member at all times, and I had to rest in the "time-out room," which is an isolated, padded room with a bed in the middle and cameras watching you. Long story short, I even had to sleep there because I scratched the surface layer off my skin on my arm with my nails. I almost got put in restraints. I tried escaping a few times as well but with no luck. It felt good and familiar to rebel.

August 23, 2011

I confessed to Dr. Statler about feeling suicidal if I were to leave. But wait…why am I always so honest when I want to get the heck out of this prison? Do I really feel suicidal? I don't know. I do know that I would be destructive toward myself and unsafe. I suppose that's important enough. It's easy to say I want to die and not really think about the consequences. Sometimes I think it would alleviate all this confusion in my head. Why did I survive what I wasn't supposed to survive? Why keep fighting what seemingly can't be fought? Why keep believing healing and help is just around the corner? Why keep staring at a reflection that I want to disappear? Why pretend everything is OK only to find myself back in crisis? Why not give in? Or would that be giving up?

August 26, 2011

Oh my goodness, where do I even start? If I thought I had already seen crazy, well, apparently my new roommate, Meg, was going to show me otherwise. So, I'm in bed, and she comes in after the 9:30 p.m. smoke break. She goes into our bathroom and starts cussing and mumbling and saying all this weird shit. (Now, she does talk to herself sometimes, and I thought maybe she was on the phone.) Then she comes back into our room, and I still can't tell if she is talking to me or to herself, but she mentions something in the bathroom about ammonia, bottle of pills, failed pregnancy, paying rent, bitch-bitch-bitch, Asian lady, and tons of other nonsense. Then she said something about how I better hold my breath all night.

Finally I ask, "Are you talking to me?"

"Yes, I'm talking to you, you stupid fucking bitch!"

"What the heck?"

"You threw up in the bathroom. I saw you take those pills from that lady."

Insert 30 minutes' worth of Meg cussing at me, accusing me, and bitching about random stuff that didn't even make sense let alone happen.

After that little ordeal, I went to tell the nurse what was going on. She told Meg to be quiet and that we would be separated in the morning. Well, around 2:00 in the morning, I hear Meg loudly whispering again…something about being on a 14-day hold, fucking bitch, if you step any closer I will stab you with this knife. That's when I got up and got a nurse again. While they were cleaning a bed for me in the back to transfer to for the night, I went to use the bathroom real quick back where Meg was. She then started flat-out screaming at me and cussing, which led to me saying, "Don't speak to me like that."

And then she says, "I'll get put on a 14-day hold, bitch, and sock you in the face!"

Then the nurses come in, and Meg sits there and talks in almost a sweet, baby-like voice and says, "Well, I was in here early at 8:30 tonight sleeping, and then Brittany came in and just started screaming, and I'm in here for anxiety, and she's just here for suicide and bulimia."

I almost fainted. Can you say the complete opposite! Not to mention it totally triggered childhood memories of a friend lying when we would get in fights and then placing the blame on me. I always felt picked on and wrongly accused. I ended up walking out of the room with the staff and into the back room. I certainly didn't sleep well, but at least I feel as though the staff respected me when I explained my side of the story. I know I didn't feel safe in my room, so at least I got out. I spent forever staring at the ceiling not sure what to think. I can't say if I was confused, traumatized, paralyzed, or if the whole situation was just laughable.

August 27, 2011

I woke up restless today and skipped breakfast as usual. I went to my old room to gather up my few belongings because I was going to be moving rooms. Meg was in there, and she came up to me and asked, "How did you sleep last night?" in a really sweet voice as if she genuinely had no recollection of last night.

"Terrible," I mumbled.

She then gave me a huge hug and kiss...umm? She said she was really sorry about last night...that she just had really bad anxiety and snapped. Yeah, snapped OK...well, I'm not one to hold grudges or judge people, so of course I forgave her, but that doesn't mean I haven't learned a lesson. My safety comes first, so though I will be friendly with her, when the staff asked me if I still wanted to move, I quickly packed up my stuff and gave her no second chance.

I had my meeting with Dr. Statler but didn't know what to say. I didn't want to lie, and I didn't want to be honest either. When you're honest, you have nothing left to protect you; you are completely open, judged, and vulnerable. It's risky; it's different and unfamiliar. I don't like change! I eventually started talking, which spiraled into hysterically sobbing, but it felt so good and so out of control at the same time. I could have cried forever.

I finally let out such a rare and protected emotion of mine. Life isn't fair! Why am I still alive? Why was I even born when every single day I suffer? An angry childhood, a depressed school life, an over-pressured athlete, no true friends ever, an eating disorder at 13, pulled out of school for treatment, playing Russian roulette with death.... When people my age look back on their life, I'm sure most think about high school memories, prom, vacations, college, graduating, friends, drinking, relationships, parties, and relatable things. What will I tell new people I meet if we ever started talking? My whole growing up is shaped and structured by treatment centers, in and out of relapses. My stories of friends are the crazy patients I met in treatment, my memories are trying to hide food, and my vacations are hospitals. My college memories are nothing more than panic attacks and utter loneliness.

I can't relate. On the other hand, I have glimpses of brilliance. Yet, how do I build on the glimpses from hell? I'm done, I'm done, *I'm done*! I'm sorry world, I'm sorry. Take my journals and learn from them, but I feel like taking my life like my eating disorder should have taken 2 years ago.

August 28, 2011

We all watched *The Lion King* tonight, and I was excited because it's my favorite childhood movie. I must have watched it over 100 times! So, why was I having a panic attack watching it? Why did I have to look away as Mufasa died? I was 7 years old when I saw this movie multiple times in the theater with my dad. It was also around that time I began having intense fears of death and intense fears I would lose a parent. Even Dad confirmed that that movie traumatized me, but I couldn't stop watching.

August 29, 2011

I woke up feeling kind of down. I sat out in the hallway early in the morning on line of sight but escaped back to my room when no one was looking and scratched my arm...again. I got put in the time-out room and then was allowed out and sat numbly through group. I then met with Dr. Statler in my room, and he didn't have good news. First, he was looking through all my colorful and positive pictures I drew that were taped to my walls. He said that some kids at a young age do a thing called "splitting" where they preserve their good feelings through an outlet such as art or imagination but then everything else is negative (all-or-nothing). He said I have to find a balance and integrate them together. He believes in me and said that over time, I will do it. On another note, he said that my insurance says I have to leave tomorrow. What? I'm still on line of sight, cutting, and suicidal, and now I have to leave? Don't get me wrong. Of course I want out of this circus, but where would I go? I'm not ready to take care of myself and going home would be a disaster.

The rest of the day has been tough. I've been handling it OK, but I've just shut down. I got put on a 1:1 with a staff member in the time-out room because I kept scratching my arm. I then stormed out into the hallway with my poor nurse following me as I screamed at her, "Get away from me! What am I supposed to do in the real world? Hire a babysitter? I'm being discharged tomorrow, and I just want to take a shower!" (Hmm...sound familiar? UCLA.) I proceeded to go into my room and close the door behind me, not letting anyone in. The staff threatened to call the escort service and eventually did. One of my favorite staff members showed up, talked to me until I calmed down, and convinced me to go back to the time-out room. I reluctantly went and sat in the room sobbing hysterically.

34

Rules and Regimens

September 2, 2011

I was awoken in a hurry from the time-out room. Apparently, some new guy was hysterically out of control and needed to take the room. I got thrown out into the lounge and was greeted by the usual welcoming faces as well as a new, quite large lady in much distress. She couldn't sit still and kept flapping her arms as if trying to fly away.

She kept trying to escape the room as well but with no luck obviously. Then, from across the room, she waved at me. She then walked over to me and got *really* close to my face.

Twice she asked me my name, and twice I answered with Brittany. Next, she announced to everyone in the room while pointing at them one by one that if anybody messes with me, God would get them. Whoa! She then sat right next to me and asked if we could be friends and sisters. I answered with of course we can be friends. She kept staring at me lovingly and smiling. She told me she was Jesus's wife and pregnant with babies and needed to get to a hospital. Hmm...I kept assuring her that she and her babies would be OK, and she was so comforted. Every time I had to get up she would freak out. She kept saying she and her babies were bleeding. Um...true? Not true? I don't know, but I got to be an angel in her life for the time being. She was specifically drawn to me. I hope she is going to be OK.

I got called in to see Dr. Statler, and we had a nice meeting. We were disturbed halfway through by a staff member saying my dad was here and ready to pick me up. What? Ahh! Well, sure enough, he was there. We gathered up all my things and checked out. It was really so amazing to see him, though. It was decided that I would be going to Sovereign Health after all.

We had a wonderful drive together. Dad and I arrived at Sovereign's clinical building in San Clemente, California, around 3:00 in the afternoon. I did my admission paperwork, got my luggage together, took my meds with the nurse, gave Dad the biggest hug, and was greeted by a bunch of welcoming people. I am being admitted into the dual-diagnosis track. Even though I have no history whatsoever with drugs or alcohol, I specifically requested to be in this track because I want nothing to do with my eating disorder or others with eating disorders. I fear doing Sovereign's ED track would just be redundant and trigger me. I got in a huge van with 8 other girls, and we were off to the gorgeous residence about 15 minutes away from the clinic.

I ate 1 huge salad for dinner with lots of veggies because of my "gluten allergy" and being a "vegetarian." With the Topamax and now Wellbutrin I hardly have an appetite anyway. I told all the girls what I was here for, and they are all so supportive and wonderful. Most of the girls are struggling with drugs, alcohol, or both. Some are fat, some are thin, and some just look great—but they all eat tons and whatever they want, including junk food. It is so refreshing to see!

September 3, 2011

Today is Saturday, so we only have 1 group at the clinic today. We ended up watching a movie called *What the Bleep Do We Know!?* and it was actually really interesting. We didn't finish the movie, but it's kind of about the power of thought and the power to see matter and molecules differently. One scene showed a picture of water and then a picture of the same water after it had been blessed. It looked like a snowflake; it was beautiful! One man then said, "If the mind has the ability to change a molecule of water, imagine what our thoughts could do to us." That sat with me. I love myself, I love myself, I am healthy, I am strong, I am worthy, I am capable, I am meant for great things far beyond my comfort zone, I will be shown the way, I trust, I won't give up, I am loved, and I love me!

September 8, 2011

Today started great and ended in chaos. I had my first meeting with my therapist, Chloe, today, whom I really like. However, about 20 minutes into our session, the head of the dual-diagnosis track and the head of the eating disorder track barged in. They basically had come to tell me that I couldn't stay in the dual-diagnosis track and house because of insurance reasons since I don't technically struggle with those issues. I absolutely went crazy when I heard this news. I explained all my reasoning for needing and wanting to stay in the DD house, but no-go. I stormed out of the room hysterical and sat outside picking at the scab on my arm. I felt like hurting myself...and I even felt almost impulsively suicidal, but I kept it together. So much for my first therapy session.

I met with the doctor later that day and weighed 168 pounds on his scale. *Shit!* It was after a ton of water, but still, dammit! I took an

ED schedule home with me and decided it really would probably be a better program for me. However, I do want to continue living in the DD house since I love all the girls so much and don't want to live with other ED patients. To make today even crazier, the power went out in all of San Clemente, so everything had to be done by candlelight once darkness fell. Oh man, what a day. I am so ready for bed.

September 9, 2011

Ugh, bed! Why couldn't I have just gone to bed? It was just one of those nights. No electricity, drama in the house, craziness in my room with a new roommate, I was hungry, and I was pondering having to move into the ED program or else go home. So, what do I do? I say, hey, it's late at night, pitch black, and my anxiety is sky high...time for just a few almonds. Now, no almonds were left in the jar of mixed nuts, but who really wants to count out 1 serving of 14 almonds anyway? Everyone was asleep except for 2 others, and I could not have cared less if they saw me eat. My hand kept going in and out of the large mixed nut jar. Before I knew it, I was mindlessly grabbing at the nuts in a more frantic manner as ED was assuring me, "It's OK, just this once...only 1,500 calories...only 2,000 calories...you worked out today." But then I never stopped. Nuts, *just* nuts, I told myself as I hung out with the 2 other girls in their room. One of the girls went to bed, and the other snuck out of the window to go have sex with her boyfriend of 2 weeks, leaving me alone and still emotionally hungry.

I went back into the black kitchen with a lantern and sat on the couch in the TV room in the flickering light. I then impulsively got up and figured, "Oh well, this is my last *free night* anyway before I will probably have to move to the ED program." ED gave me the green light. I got a bowl and filled it with about 1 cup's worth of Skippy peanut butter and inhaled it with a spoon as if it were a bowl of soup and I was a starving person (well, maybe I was). After my throat and chest were glued with peanut butter, I proceeded quietly to stare at the gluten-free cheese ravioli leftovers in the fridge that no one had touched. The problem was there was a huge container left, it was about 8 cups' worth, and I don't like to leave things half-eaten. Did

I eat it all...um, yes...ouch. But what was missing? I really wanted cereal, but the damn gluten! Then again, I really wanted to harm and punish myself at this point, so I went ahead and had 1 huge bowl of Special K with milk and then a 2nd *huge* bowl of Honey Nut Cheerios with soymilk, ugh! I felt so sick, so bloated, and so constipated. I eventually sat on the couch in bewilderment and successfully vented honestly to my journal all the reasons for shying away from the ED program and deep down why ultimately it meant I had to move over to it in order to truly heal myself. In the area of mental work, it was a very successful night. I just hate how I often binge when I do my best work. It's as if my emotional work is so powerful and capable of connecting the dots toward a better life that I need ED to help me cope with the overwhelming new feelings. And I'm sure ED jumps in to make sure I don't actually act on all my positive new thoughts and insights.

I can't say I got any sleep last night, but today went well besides poor body image. I told the head of the DD program I would consent to move to the ED house. One concept really stuck out to me in one of the groups. The instructor brought up the topic of inner peace, which was really eye-opening for me. Without inner peace, you can have all the fame, money, and external validation, yet be the most suicidal, depressed, addicted, and messed up person in the world. Ring a bell? Tennis. "If I'm not the number-one ranked tennis professional, famous, beautiful, and successful, I am nobody." Umm...no, not true. Inner peace is the key to true happiness and success. After group, we went home for lunch. I packed up all my belongings.

My transition to the ED house was great. There are only 3 others in the program right now, and they are all older and larger than me, which was a surprise. It's actually a pretty laid-back program. There is way more freedom than I could have imagined. I ate a total of only 200 calories today, yet with the binge I had last night, I think it's acceptable.

September 14, 2011

We are getting a new admit today in the ED program. I'm so nervous to see the competition. Not that I'm anywhere near thin or anything right now, but I at least hope she isn't skinny or anorexic. The new person arrived—and much to my distress, I might add. She looked to be about 85 to 90 pounds and around 5 feet 6 inches to 5 feet 7 inches. It triggered a side of me I hadn't had to look at in about 2 years. For a second, I was staring at my former self. No, she doesn't look anything like me, but the possessed anorexic ED returned in blinding force like a flash of lightning. I started shaking, and before I knew what was happening, I was crying hysterically and sobbing, "That used to be *me!*" That was my identity for 8 years. I've only been "Brittany" for about 1 year...well, wait...who says ED isn't still in my life, just in a different form?

No matter who I am now, I do know that I need to find a way toward a healthy, balanced self. Frankly, looking at this new girl, Sasha, only drew me more toward an old familiarity.

One thing that did please me about this event was that my healthy voice was stronger than expected. "Her hair is short and brittle, she is boring-looking, she looks too thin, and she smokes and drinks." The one interesting thing that shocked me the most was that she eats...a lot. She eats all her necessary exchanges to gain the weight she needs and performs no eating disorder rituals...what? Maybe I can deal with this and learn to cope with real-life triggers. In fact, maybe it will trigger some trauma I need to get out anyway.

I'm so proud of myself and how I'm working through this new situation. However, I am still restricting severely, and although I'm coping with Sasha, I'm performing eating disorder rituals badly enough to count for 2 people. Ugh...yeah, I want and need to lose weight, and, yeah, I certainly don't look anorexic, but behavior-wise I am as bad as ever. I did have a good meeting with the psychiatrist today and he's taking me off Trileptal and Topamax, thank goodness, because they've been making me feel like a zombie!

September 18, 2011

Things haven't been going well. First of all, the house managers who supervise us in the residence still haven't gotten me plain nonfat Greek yogurt, unsweetened almond milk, egg whites, and celery stalks. Come on, really? Things in the house have been going very poorly for me as well. All the other ED patients and house managers love Sasha, and, as a result, I keep struggling more and more with food and rituals, which is pissing everyone off. Everyone is kind of over me, and no one really even talks to me right now because I've been such a downer to be around. I hate Sasha. I feel so left out. So replaced. So unloved. She has ADD (attention deficit disorder) and never stops talking, so I can never get a word in. She always interrupts and over-powers me when I do talk. I liked helping the house managers with the dishes, but now Sasha is always doing that, so why even bother? I was the one who entertained the other ED clients here, but now she butts in. I used to be best buds with one of the ladies in the house, but now she and Sasha are bonding. I loved our little group. Everyone gave me so much support, and now it's as if I don't exist. Yet, what's left for me to say when Sasha literally talks every second?

I feel alone again, just like at school... I feel replaced and unloved again... just like when Kasey was born. I need a friend. I need my mom. I need to belong. I need help, and I don't know how to take care of myself because I was never given those social tools growing up.

Oh, man! We were all drinking coffee and I asked a question.

Me: "Does coffee have calories?"

House Manager (HM): "Oh yeah, just like everything else that has *zero* calories."

Sasha: "Coffee has *so* many calories *and* fat! There is so much oil from the beans. There are calories in everything, even your gum!"

Me: "I know that!"

HM: "If you don't eat anything, your body will just hang on to everything."

Sasha also said something rude to me earlier. Fuck her! Fuck the house manager because she actually started playing along sarcastically as well. I mean, come on; this *is* an ED program! I went up to my room and sobbed for about 30 minutes. I've been in my room now for about 1 ½ hours, and no one has come to check on me, so what am I going to do? I'm going to let this be an emotional day, but tomorrow I'm taking back my power. I am a strong, confident, positive, talented, accomplished, and highly capable person. Yes, I may still struggle with eating enough food at mealtimes, but enough with the ED voice of a 2 year old, enough with the tantrums, and enough with the complaining! That's not me; that's sick, and it will get me nothing but a cold shoulder—so grow up, Brittany, if you want to be heard and get your way!

Oh my goodness, Sasha changed my life! OK...so maybe those words are a little strong, but here's what happened. I went over to the men's ED house across the street for dinner as usual and entered while everyone else was eating their pizza. It was a normal night to begin with. I sat down with my frozen cottage cheese in a plastic bowl with a plastic spoon, 1 whole bag of cooked broccoli, leftover stir-fry veggies, and 1 head of lettuce.

Calorie-wise it wasn't much, but yeah, of course you could call it binging on vegetables. I sat down at the table with my smorgasbord of veggies, and Sasha yelled at me.

"I can't take this anymore! How can you allow her to binge on vegetables every night! This is an ED program for people who want to get better!

"Why don't you go somewhere else! The fact that this is happening in an ED program is ridiculous...just ridiculous! All the veggies are gone because of *her*! We all shared our opinion and agree! I'm sick of watching you not even try!"

She then went out for a smoke, and I sat there frozen, partly shaking, crying, and finishing my food. I left shortly after and went back to the women's ED house feeling numb. I took a shower and then angrily made myself a new meal plan containing hardly any veggies. The house manager came over later flustered and dug through the

337

fridge for veggies. She was pissed and said the veggie binging needs to stop and that I'm triggering people. I apologized repeatedly, gave away my personally bought veggies, and said I won't be touching them anymore.

Later that night I was eating snack, and Sasha, Kara, the other lady client, and the house manager were sitting at the table. Kara and I slowly started talking and got on the topic of food. I mentioned how the whole veggie thing was insane and that I really need to get back to eating breakfast and the whole egg yolk, how sorry I am, and how I need help. Bam! I don't even know how to explain it, but Sasha said some things I really needed to hear. She told me she wants to get to know Brittany, not ED, who's been taking over. She went on and on about how much she understands, how much she wants to get to know me, how hated she feels by me, and how much she wants to support me. This led to us having an amazing talk. I told her how I didn't give her a chance when she first arrived because I was triggered and how inspiring the way she eats is to me. One pretty incredible thing was that as we kept talking, Brittany came back. My strong, positive, confident, and mature voice gradually returned. My sentences were clear and intelligent, I held myself high, and I felt in control. It was the most remarkable experience, and everyone in the room was so happy and amazed at the change. Ah, what an important night! Success is peace of mind.

September 20, 2011

I had a great session with my therapist today. We talked about boundaries and why I feel the need to test treatment centers before I comply. I made an interesting realization. I like pushing treatment centers to the limit for these reasons:

- I want to know their boundaries.
- I want to know how safe they will keep me.
- I want them to realize how much I am struggling so they will force me to comply and take the anxiety of choice away.
- I am so used to always saying yes to everyone no matter what

(e.g., letting classmates cheat off my homework) that for once in my life I want to say no when in treatment.

- I want to make it known how powerful my ED is and stand out from the rest of the group. That's my all-or-nothing personality again... taking me to the extremes.

September 27, 2011

The morning started off pretty routine, but unfortunately lunch was a little more overwhelming than I would have liked. Our house manager was explaining that Sasha and Kara were going to be moving to the townhouse next door because we were getting new admits and were maxed out of space. The house manager said those 2 got to move because they were on the higher level (we earn levels based on our compliance). I caught myself starting to get insecure, on the verge of tearing up, and emotionally overloaded.

The house manager talked to me briefly upstairs, and I vented to her how I felt left out and left behind as well as missing the relationship Kara and I had before Sasha arrived. I suppose a part of me is assuming Kara and Sasha wanted to both move out because I am struggling so much.

I had my therapy session after lunch and that was... uh, well... tough. Chloe told me that despite unanimous feedback that I was improving tremendously, I still wasn't approved for level one because of the Facebook incident (I went on Facebook in the computer lab knowing it wasn't allowed) and talking longer than 10 minutes on the phone to my parents. I absolutely lost it and started sobbing. I've been here almost 1 month. I am still on level 0, and most people are on level 4 by now! I only went over time on the phone once this week, which was yesterday, because I miss my parents and love them so much. Not to mention it motivates me that much more to focus on recovery when I talk to them. I only got on Facebook because I wanted to delete negative people and let everyone know I was still alive. I came from 6 weeks of hard-core psych units with no cell phone or computer, so, uh, yes, it *is* a big deal that I want so badly to communicate. I'm not manipulating the damn program. I'm just lonely and homesick.

Anyway, it's really not a big deal, but it triggered memories from being at UCLA where I always felt singled out, picked on, never praised, and only punished for the bad things. Come on, I've made huge progress and am following my meal plan better, and it's only phase 1 anyway! It's making me feel as though I have to be perfect to be praised and advanced. OK, now I'm really just making all this a bigger deal than it needs to be, but I am just so fed up and angry, especially because I know it's partly because of my housemates who are tattling on me about the phone time even when it's clear I'm just having a happy and motivating talk with my parents. *Come on!*

When we got back to the apartments, our house manager mentioned that Sasha and Dena (another ED client) were going to the new apartment. Kara immediately and firmly said, "No. I'm going with Sasha. That's what our other house manager decided. Just leave it alone. It is all under control." She spoke so forwardly that it made me feel insecure...do you *want* to get away from me? She hasn't talked much to me either. Why is it that I always seem to get in these funks where I believe everyone has something against me, is whispering behind my back, or avoiding me? I mean, I've caused drama all week, but I have challenged myself immensely. I need to focus on me. If I'm doing what I'm supposed to be doing, I imagine I would feel a lot less of a victim.

35

Making the Choice

"When things get hard, get excited! It means you have been given an opportunity to become that much stronger and knowledgeable." ~Britt

The Great Change (written June 2012)

The beginning of my turnaround certainly came as a surprise. I think I finally hit a breaking point while at Sovereign Health. I had been exerting so much energy toward blowing up over the small stuff and focusing on others that I had been neglecting myself and neglecting to look at the uncomfortable things in my life. I guess you could say that I've grown up a bit lately. The difference with Sovereign is that it is really up to you to make the program work. Now, one can argue it is up to you anywhere you go, and this is true, but only to a point. The freedom at Sovereign is one of the main aspects that set it apart from any other facility I've been to. It offers PHP and IOP treatment, however, the fact that it provides complimentary housing makes it run more like a residential program with a house manager on-site and all meals eaten together. In this respect, it has proven to be the right combination for me.

I always test treatment centers. I push them to the limit and see how much I can get away with before authority draws the line. I am such a people pleaser to a fault, bending over backwards to say yes to everyone no matter the cost. My eating disorder proved to be a way for me to say no for once and rebel. Of course, I was only ever hurting myself, but I was so angry at always pouring my heart out to others without anything in return that my anger and resentment had to come out somehow. I kept pushing with Sovereign, but authority never stepped up in the manner that I was used to. It became pretty exhausting rebelling against myself. I mean, it was either work the program and improve or else I was just wasting my time. No one was going to make a dramatic deal about it or provoke the response I was used to receiving. I suppose you could say I realized how silly and childish I was acting and embarrassedly shaped up in some form.

The other thing about Sovereign is that it offers 3 separate programs simultaneously. There is an eating disorder track, a drug and alcohol track, and a mental health track. Each of these programs is separate, but we do all go to the same treatment clinic each day and share some groups together. This was a refreshing aspect for me because I was in the presence of others who really could not care less about their weight or how much food they did or did not eat. It opened up my small little world of eating disorders to a taste of diversity and reality.

September 30, 2011

Today has been great! I've really turned my attitude and behaviors around. All the groups were wonderful, and while I was waiting outside to go back for lunch, one of the therapists who leads some groups came up to me to tell me how incredible I'm doing, how remarkable my turnaround is, and how all the staff keep mentioning my name. She gave me a high five and said again how astounding it is. At that same time, one of the intake staff came up to me to thank me profusely because I had talked to a prospective eating disorder male client. Apparently, the client decided to come to Sovereign because of me. The intake staff was so thankful and said that I am helping to change people's lives.

October 2, 2011

I had a lovely talk today with another client about treatment centers and making your own recovery. I went to some of the best treatment centers in the world, and they didn't help me. Now, however, I could go to one of the worst treatment centers in the world and recover because I am ready and will make the most out of every day and opportunity. I had an amazing talk with my parents tonight as well. I don't know how to explain it, but I'm a different person. A shift has come over me. Here are some ways:

- I'm working through my childhood. I'm not bad. I am loved. My misperceptions of the world were OK.
- I'm eating breakfast, lunch, dinner, and snack.
- I am going to bed and waking up at a consistent time.
- I can now sleep wonderfully and fall asleep without any fear.
- I'm adding new challenge foods each week.
- I'm living in the present! I do not fear the future and am letting go of the shame and regret I have around my past.
- I'm growing up, dealing with people my own age, and participating in a school-like setting with the normal drama.
- I'm learning my boundaries, my values, and how to say no.
- I am starting to believe in myself, love myself, and know my priorities and passion.
- I have made the commitment to have a strong support team for a long time, even when I am doing my best down the road.

My greatest success is carrying out this journey I feel I have been chosen to experience because it was known I could use it in a way to positively influence others. I am living the greatest success possible, and it's not fame, not money, not popularity, not beauty, and not genius. I have gone from despair and rock bottom to turning my life completely around and healing my inner child and myself. I am becoming whole again. I am becoming spiritually connected and feel my purpose and passion in life is that I can one day inspire others for the better. Faith has been an empty spot in my soul for far too long.

I have been chosen for this task. That's why I've been through it all, leading up to the ultimate triumph—recovery of myself.

October 5, 2011

What makes me special without ED? Without ED, I have freedom mentally, physically, financially, socially, and spiritually. I have the ability to live in the moment, feel, and make decisions from the heart. Without ED, I can be Brittany's (*my*) best self, which means I can follow my passions without self-sabotage. I am an incredible tennis coach and trainer with just the right blend of compassion, patience, and demandingness depending on the client. I am naturally positive and upbeat and always have a smile on my face. I go out of my way to make people's days, even strangers. I have a heart of gold and am always looking for ways to improve myself and learn. I have a fantastic memory and really listen to every detail that others have to say. Without ED, I have a story. I am a role model and leader with inspiration to flood the world. I have a spark to me. I am mature and responsible. I am accepting of all but know how to set boundaries and make healthy, safe decisions. Without ED, I respect myself and have an overflow of magnetic confidence. I am so honest and inviting with nothing to hide when I am free of ED. I can be a mentor and counsel those struggling and actually do as I say without feeling like a hypocrite.

Without ED, my mind and creativity is brilliant. My brain becomes a sponge and is clear to take in and use knowledge. I am physically able to use my athletic talents to their fullest potential without ED. I am able to play tennis at remarkable levels and enjoy my natural harmony on horses. People are able to rely on me free of ED and trust my behavior and good health to be consistent. Without ED, I feel good enough just for being me. I am accepting this journey to use my passions to heal.

October 8, 2011

Epitaph (with ED)

Here lies Brittany Leigh Burgunder. She was someone with so much love, ability, talent, and creativity to offer. Brittany wanted nothing more than to impact the world in a positive way and to be remembered as a life-changing role model and courageous influence. It is a shame she could not find the inner love and strength for her own self to defeat a vicious and all-consuming eating disorder. Brittany always put on a smile and assured everyone she had things all under control. She told everyone not to worry as it became clearer she was the one with no control whatsoever. Brittany kept trying to focus and remember how good her life would be if only she could be free and get better. A once nationally ranked tennis player and horseback rider, she had many opportunities and dedication. She attended UC Davis on a part academic scholarship and decorated high school career. Her eating disorder made for a rough college experience. Brittany kept searching for a solution or the magic compromise between perfection and freedom. Unfortunately, eating disorders only give you 2 choices: life or death. There is no compromising. It is a tragedy that the pendulum swung too far to the wrong side. I pray she is now at peace and has true happiness with herself.

Epitaph (without ED)

Here lies Brittany Leigh Burgunder. What a miracle she was to this Earth and everyone she encountered. After battling an eating disorder that brought her to the brink of death, she found a way out through inner strength and purpose. Brittany continued fighting her eating disorder and with her tenacity and perseverance, she was triumphant. This was the greatest success attainable according to Brittany—finding inner peace, self-worth, purpose, and unconditional acceptance. She continued on to fulfill her passions and touch people's lives. Brittany returned to the competitive tennis scene, this time playing with love and fearlessness. She spent much of her free time with horses and animals. She wrote straight from her heart a memoir that changed people of all backgrounds and struggles for the better. Brittany went back to college and faced her biggest fears. Everywhere Brittany went, she carried a rare and hypnotizing smile that radiated happiness and love. The light and confidence inside her glowed like the moon and shined liked the sun. There was not an unloving cell in her. She spoke to all, helped, all, shared with all, gave to all, inspired all, and was a leader and role model to most. Always noting that her parents and family were her greatest support, she was also a firm believer that people create their success, environment, and happiness. "There are no lucky situations. Only the ability to say yes to making the best of your current situation and yourself." She believed everything happens for a reason and that in due time the reasons would be made clear. Brittany will be greatly missed but lived a long, happy, healthy life to 111 years old. Her influence and positive leadership will go down in history. She will never be forgotten as one of the most courageous, loving, and good-hearted role models.

October 11, 2011

Today has been quite a life-changing experience. I've been struggling lately, and this time, unfortunately, it hasn't been with restricting. I actually pulled the house manager aside and admitted to all the binging I was secretly engaging in. The townhouse I sleep in is full of food, and oftentimes I'm in there with no supervision during the day as well as at night. I was so stuck in restricting mode that none of the food tempted me until more recently. I wasn't going to tell anyone because I was so ashamed and was hoping I could get things back under control without anyone ever knowing. Yet, I know that doesn't work and that secrets only fuel ED, so today it was time to tattle on ED. I asked my house manager for help keeping me accountable. She gave me a huge hug and told me congratulations for taking this step against ED. I felt so proud and a sense of relief!

I then sat through group sweating...the day-after-binging sweat. I had a fabulous session with my Chloe after lunch, and she was so proud of my honesty. Tonight at ANAD (anorexia nervosa and other associated disorders) group, I shocked myself when I shared with my whole ED peers about my binging. They all tried to assure me I really wasn't overeating, but I assured them right back that ED is sneaky beyond measure. Oh goodness, does it feel good to be honest!

October 17, 2012

I had a great session with Chloe today. I gave her a recap of the week as well as some insight as to just how bad and hopeless I previously was. Why am I so stubborn? I don't want to be the first to give in. My whole life my mom has nagged me so often and so prematurely that it's made me feel as if no one trusts me and that I wasn't going to make a good decision even though I was planning to do so all along. For example:

Mom: "What are you having for lunch? Don't forget you have to eat in 1 hour. I want to watch you prepare your food so I know you are following your meal plan."

Me (in my head): What the heck? I was planning to do all of the above anyway, but now that *you* told me to/decided for me, I am not going to because I want to feel proud of myself and like I decided on my own. *You* will get the credit because *you* made me!

So, I would end up restricting out of anger and revenge. Why won't you just trust me?

Me (out loud): "I know, Mom! You didn't even give me a chance to do it right! Quit smothering me and leave me alone. Only I can cure myself, not you!"

October 25, 2011

Check out my progress so far. I am:
- eating a real breakfast,
- eating lunch,
- eating frozen yogurt once a week,
- allowing myself to get a light Frappuccino occasionally,
- walking,
- working out,
- reducing water from 6 bottles to 3,
- reducing gum,
- reducing coffee,

- reducing Crystal Light and Splenda,
- using real utensils, plates, and bowls, and respecting all house rules.

October 29, 2011

I had probably the best visit with my parents ever while being in treatment. We sat down together outside and had an incredible 1-hour talk. We then drove to Dana Point and ate lunch at Five Guys Burger and Fries. I was going to order the veggie burger, but when the lady said it was only veggies on a bun I said without hesitation, "No way! I will have the burger!" Dad was so proud and shocked. I seemingly easily ate 1 big burger without toppings or a bun as well as lots of french fries and peanuts. What a wonderful, cool lunch! We then went to Peet's Coffee, and Mom and I got drinks. Next we took a wonderful walk around the Dana Point harbor and had fun goofing off and enjoying each other's company.

November 3, 2011

The whole ED group went out to dinner at P.F. Chang's tonight. I actually did amazing! I split chicken appetizers with the house managers and had tofu, veggies, and three-fourths of a sesame sweet-and-sour chicken, which tasted phenomenal! I know it has tons of calories, yet I ate calmly and was nowhere near overstuffed. I got 2 scoops of fat-free Baskin-Robbins ice cream afterward as well. It was all really fun though. I had about 3,500 calories for the whole day, but it did not trigger me to keep binging, feel guilty, or want to give up. This is such an important and huge step forward for me. The days I eat around 2,000 to 3,000 calories and can stop are probably the most important because it means my all-or-nothing thinking is subsiding.

November 8, 2011

I had a fabulous therapy session today. What stood out to me the most was the way I was processing information. If I don't commit to recovery and continue to revert to treatment centers/familiarity/

safety, I will be doing this 'til I'm 40 years old, never achieve my dreams, always live in fear, and be miserable. Usually these kinds of words go in one ear and out the other, but wow! I actually heard it this time...I mean, really heard it! It's life, risks, adventure, unknown, mistakes, failures, growth, success, joy, health, friends, work, athletics, and freedom that make a difference. I can't keep magically thinking I have time to change and put off living. The time is now.

November 15, 2011

It's been about 1 week now, and things have been a little rocky. I got brought into clinic today 15 minutes early...uh-oh. As I had presumed, it was a meeting with the nutritionist, the therapists, and the director of the ED program. They wanted to meet with me out of concern and to figure out how to best help me. They all gave me the most amazing compliments, though. The director even said I am the most determined individual when I put my mind to something than anyone she's ever encountered. Now to put it to the correct use is the challenge. The team informed me that normally they would just let a client get denied insurance or ask them to leave, but they said they made an exception for me because they love me so much and see how much potential I have. Bottom line from all of them, including myself, is just do it! Quit holding back because life has its ups and downs and stressors with or without an eating disorder. I know how to do failure, and my treatment team is going to help me do success. I can have any destructive thought I want, but I just can't act on it. I need to talk about it instead. They are here for me as Brittany...not Brittany with ED. Game over. Time to shine and push myself to the limit without expectations of perfectionism. I know how much I can achieve in a blink of an eye when I want to. Well...I want to. I can and will once again show how strong I am by taking on this challenge headfirst. Yes! It's showtime!

November 24, 2011

Happy Thanksgiving! I have to say it was the best Thanksgiving I've had in about 10 years. I did end up overeating, yet I didn't go binge-crazy. I allowed myself to eat all of my favorite foods. I did go a little overboard with the crackers and dips, but it was a lazy day, and we were pretty much stuck in the townhomes with appetizers lying around. Besides, Thanksgiving is a day where almost everyone overindulges, right?

At dinner, I had lots of turkey, some stuffing, 1 bread roll, sweet potato casserole, salad, and 2 slices of pie with Cool Whip. We then saw the fourth *Twilight* movie, and I got some Dippin' Dots. It was a pretty great holiday!

December 1, 2011

What a day! I got a touching message from the Blue Cross case manager I have been working with. She said she was so proud of me and that she noticed a huge change in my voice and words and that Blue Cross recognizes my progress with Sovereign and they are all rooting for me and will give me the time I need to continue healing. I then had an amazing talk with Chris from Premier Fitness Camp. I am going to meet him at the La Costa Resort in Carlsbad, California, which is Premier Fitness Camp's new location on Thursday—hooray!

December 5, 2011

I enjoyed my cognitive behavioral therapy group this morning. If you change your thoughts, you can change your feelings, which can change the outcomes of negative behaviors. CCC: Catch it. Challenge it. Change it. The main message that hit me the hardest was: "The reasons you are here should be so powerful it brings you to tears." Process group was next, and it was a difficult one. My peers starting confronting me about eating too many veggies again. I was already feeling down. I took the feedback well, but then I just broke. I had to leave the group because I started uncontrollably crying so hard. That out-of-control feeling and raw emotion hasn't happened to me in a while. The therapist found me after group and made me feel so much better.

Ugh, this is it! I am sick of following the same old meal plan I put together for myself versus eating what the other clients eat. I want to eat what the group eats and what the house manager prepares instead of making my own separate meals. It's just so hard! With other addictions, you can live a normal life without using the substance ever again. However, for people with eating disorders, they have to face food multiple times a day. You can't just abstain from your drug of choice, so to speak. It's like an analogy that one of my group therapists made: with addictions you can lock up the tiger and throw away the key. With eating disorders, you have to learn how to take the tiger out of the cage and walk it multiple times a day.

I suppose I could be experiencing an extinction burst... where things get worse before they get better. As I get better, ED's voice gets louder. I start getting scared of being healthy, living life, and opportunities that may arise, so ED comes to the rescue. This time, though, I can't give in.

Oh my goodness, I did it! I ate dinner with the whole group and ate what was served. Everyone, including me, was so proud! As I get better, ED's voice gets louder, and in return my voice breaks the sound barrier. I am in charge.

It's funny how opportunities and doors open right and left when you take care of yourself and embrace the good that enters your life. After finding a part of myself that had been lost for so long and making some lifestyle changes at Sovereign, I was presented with some unexpected decisions. I was offered a full-time job working at Sovereign Health that would allow me to stay in San Clemente as well as a full-time job offer working with my beloved Premier Fitness Camp in Carlsbad about 1 hour south. Wow! Really? With ED in my life, there was never any room for opportunity or growth. It's funny how great things come into one's life when the negatives are let go of.

36

Welcome to the New Age

"Remember: External beauty is a matter of opinion. Internal beauty is far too great to be measured. When basing your self-esteem on beauty; choose wisely." ~Britt

February 19, 2012

After 3 months of taking a journaling strike, I feel the desire to share this new beginning of my journey. It's now nearing the end of February, so there is some backtracking to be done. I chose to take the job offer from Premier Fitness camp and I moved into my beautiful, 2-bedroom, 2-bath apartment in Carlsbad where the hawks sing to me every morning. I started my sales training, my new position at PFC, January 20. Only a few days later, 4 ladies who were being featured on the TV show *The Balancing Act* arrived at Premier Fitness Camp as part of their weight loss journey. It was great publicity for Premier, but it was a chaotic week with cameras following the ladies' every move and the trainers being stretched thin trying to cater to the cameras as well as Premier's regular campers. All of PFC's staff were a little on edge with all of Premier's owners present, along with a clientele over 40, which is past the maximum to ensure a small trainer-to-client ratio. Needless to say, I was really thrown into the deep end given I had no previous sales experience or time to observe how Premier's new facility operates. Heck, I hadn't even met the new trainers or coworkers yet!

I was a little disappointed to learn that I wouldn't be involved with the clients or on site much at all given that my job was done primarily by phone and computer. My first 2 weeks working in sales was rough. I was seemingly always on call and glued to my laptop. I'd be in the middle of grocery shopping or a gym session and would get a sales call. It was practically impossible to plan any designated time for myself. I was a little rusty at first on the phone, but I quickly gained confidence. Fortunately and unfortunately, I didn't make many sales. I gave it my best shot, but being the people pleaser I am, I was pretty upset feeling that I had let Premier down. To be honest, working in the sales business isn't my calling anyway. I'm a people person and a hands-on individual, honest and compassionate, not a behind-the-scenes worker. And being in the business of sales requires a type of confidence and language I just don't naturally speak.

After about 2 weeks doing sales, I had another meeting with Chris. He apologized for throwing me into such a high-pressure position with minimal training. He told me there is a position opening up as an administrative assistant to Mary, one of my favorite coworkers, and that he believes I should take it and wean back into sales with more training. I was relieved and devastated at the same time. I was relieved I would no longer have a pressure-filled job that seemingly never allowed me to relax but also devastated in that I felt I had failed and wondered how I would pay the bills given the salary differences.

Thankfully, my parents were visiting during this time and were so supportive and made me realize all the positives and bigger possibilities that could stem from this new position. I confirmed with Chris that I would take the position. On Sunday night, the night before I was to start my new position, I binged to numb my hurricane of feelings. This was not the first binge of my move, though. A week ago I had a nightly binge that led into the usual next-day-all-day binge, but at least I could hide and isolate afterward, whereas my job now requires me to show my face at Premier's facility. The worst part about tonight? I took 6 laxatives, and the next morning before work I took 4 more. Great, so now I get to start my first day of work bloated and running to the bathroom. Bring it on...

353

On a more positive note, I have continued to work with my therapist, Chloe, from Sovereign on an outpatient basis. We've continued to have good sessions as well as some breakthroughs and new realizations. One of those realizations was that binging is the only way I can give myself permission to relax or take a break. Since I'm seemingly so incapable at saying no or setting boundaries, binging forces me to say no because I feel publicly unacceptable. I've also begun playing tennis at the La Costa Resort, and it's been incredible! I am known as the "celebrity" here around the courts, and everyone is so nice, really enjoys my company, and watches with their jaws open when I play. I even have to admit I've been playing unbelievable. It helps that there are so many great players and top coaches for me to utilize as well.

I joined 24 Hour Fitness in Carlsbad, which happens to be the headquarters of the company. It is the largest gym I've ever been in, that's for sure. It's littered with top athletes, former Olympians, and fit people, so the energy is motivating and intense, just as I like it. I've already made my mark with all the staff and trainers, and they all seem to genuinely like me. I've been training twice a week with a personal trainer, too. He is such a sweet, knowledgeable, and correct trainer, as well as level-headed, which I need. I feel safe with him, too, which has allowed me to open up about my very personal past.

It's been 1 ½ weeks now since I binged that Sunday night before I started my new job position. Apparently that's 1 ½ weeks too long according to ED. I tried so hard to find a healthy and safe meal plan but without success. There were a few days during the past week where I consumed 2,500 to 3,000 calories but didn't full-out binge. Things were still progressively getting out of control, which led to my next massive binge.

It was a Monday—a rainy day, a day I had woken up early, a boring day, and a day I felt bloated and wanted a break. Bam! I binged. I mean, what else is one supposed to do to entertain themselves when they are in a new town with no friends or family? I suppose eating not only numbs out the roller coaster of feelings but also gives me a hobby or way to pass the time. The damage had been done, but that didn't mean I was done. I took 11 laxatives this time. I did so partly out of magical thinking that it would undo some of the calories, partly out of punishment, and partly to symbolize the end of my binge and a way to start over new. Still, as much as I know they don't really help, they did make me feel better, and my stomach looked artificially acceptable. The optimum word being *feel* because the scale slowly moved upward, so there was no real canceling out the calories.

Working in my new position alongside Mary has developed into such a rewarding experience. I've now had 7 clients approach me to ask if they could speak to me in a private 1:1 setting after one of the trainers shared a bit of my story during a group. I also got to fill in as a trainer during a couple of the classes, and I did an awesome job, especially at the beach boot camp. One of the clients told me afterward that I'm going to be a dang good personal trainer, and one of the trainers grabbed me and was ecstatic at how amazing I did. He said I *have* to become a trainer and get my certification.

March 9, 2012

I feel like so much has happened in such a short amount of time. I've been here only 6 weeks, but it feels like 6 years (in a good way). I'm now working about 40 hours a week and am starting to help as well as lead certain classes for the clients, such as cardio tennis. It's been almost 3 weeks since my last binge, and I can finally notice some positive changes in my appearance.

May 15, 2012

Where to even begin? Life has certainly had its ups and downs lately, and it's time to be more honest with myself. Since moving to Carlsbad, I haven't been living completely alone. ED doesn't pay rent but walks in uninvited occasionally, which is always one time too may. I've been holding it together well... a few binges here and a few laxatives there. I kept showing up to work, tennis, appointments, and the gym despite my secret struggles. I can't believe I've been in Carlsbad for almost 4 months now. It seems like much longer because I am so happy in certain ways, but I've had so much thrown at me since leaving treatment. Living in a new town. Living alone. Paying bills and taking care of an apartment. Managing my eating disorder while trying to manage a normal life. Getting to know my new coworkers. Learning how to be a salesperson. Don't know or have any friends here. Had to learn multiple new computer programs specific to PFC. Had to learn how take people's blood through a finger prick and then run it through a special machine. Working 40 hours doing many different tasks. Being in charge of running tennis cardio classes. Having to wake up at 5:00 in the morning every Monday. Finding time to go to the gym for myself. Fitting in grocery shopping, appointments, and other basic household chores. Then there is having to drive 1 hour north for all my therapy sessions with Chloe. Additionally, there are tennis lessons and matches I enjoy fitting in and working with an editor on my book. I'm trying to handle insecurities with other star clients along with mentoring a few other clients as well. And then, of course, I can't forget my increasing binges and laxative use to the point of taking 30 Dulcolax at once. Needless to say, a lot has happened!

On top of the list above, I've been having problems with my legs. I've had shin splints since I was 12 years old, but the pain and pressure in my lower legs has now reached an unbearable point. I have had large bulges running along my lower legs for about 2 years, and no one has really had an explanation for that until recently. I went to see an orthopedic surgeon, and he did exploratory surgery on both of my lower legs, believing the bulge was a cyst or some sort of fatty tissue. He was wrong. I awoke from surgery with him telling me the bulge was my muscle that had literally torn through the fascia that normally encloses the muscle. The surgery was ultimately pointless, but it turned into a nightmare.

I got a freak, life-threatening infection, called Streptococcus in the surgical site on my left leg. I was hospitalized for 1 week while being treated intravenously with all sorts of antibiotics. It was an eerie feeling to be back in the hospital. Flashbacks flooded my mind with almost identical feelings of when I was in Torrance Memorial Hospital. It was as if I was reliving a nightmare. I never did mourn or accept the seriousness of my anorexia. I couldn't. It was as if it happened to someone else and I just so happened to remember every day and detail of it. It was easier to just distract myself and push the memories away, which I believe is partly why the binging got so out of control from the very beginning.

Toward the end of my hospital stay, the doctors decided that I needed a PICC line (a more permanent IV) because I would need to continue the antibiotics for another 30 days and a regular IV would destroy my veins. I was sent home with the PICC line and a little black purse that carried a machine pump, which administered the antibiotics 24 hours a day. It was miserable and not something I was expecting, let alone having to deal with all alone. I met with a home health nurse once a week who checked on me, and I had to change my bag of antibiotics every 2 days. My fridge was packed full of penicillin bags. This PICC line also meant no tennis or gym for 1 month. What was I going to do with myself? Exercise not only was a big coping skill for me but removing it took away a part of my social life and left me with too much boring alone time, which is always dangerous. ED freaked out having no exercise, and the binging and laxative use progressed.

Despite all of the challenges and difficulties thrown at me, I really am happy, right? I mean, I love my coworkers, the clients, my job, my gym, my trainers, the tennis, this town, my apartment, and my support network. I even got 2 other job offers! This is great, right? So, why is it that all too many lonely nights I succumb to Olympic-sized binges followed by lethal doses of laxatives? The smile is real this time, but its purity isn't confirmed. What's going on? Well, for one thing, I don't know how to eat. This is the part I never quite reached during my stay at Sovereign. Heck, to be honest, I was struggling with following their basic meal plan at all, so forget intuitive eating. I never let go of the false control, the manipulation, and the pieces of ED that kept me stuck. I never fully ate normally and certainly didn't have a healthy mind-set. I get an A+ for effort, though, in trying my best to figure it out. Since living on my own, I've tried multiple meal plans, new foods, having food in my apartment as well as having no food in my apartment, cooking for myself, incorporating frozen yogurt, eating with the clients, and continuing to go to therapy.

I'm at a new transition. I'm ready for more in my life. Don't get me wrong. I love Premier more than anything, however, I feel there is so much more I could offer to this world by using my talents and passions in a different way. Of course, this is a conflicting statement for me to make. I want more, but I'm not ready for more. I want to move forward in life, yet I continually hold myself back. In fact, the more I strive for new responsibilities, the more ED puts up debilitating boundaries. I don't want to be 90 percent recovered—I want 100 percent. My head is spinning with choices as to what to do next, especially since I feel I've maxed out the growth of my current position at Premier. Should I go back to Sovereign? I gave them a call around midnight during one of my binges.

After a week or 2 of indecisiveness, I finally told Mary I needed to take a leave and get more help, even if it meant risking my job. Thankfully, things went better than I expected. Mary was so supportive and understanding. Most of the trainers and clients think I'm just taking a leave to have more surgery on my legs, which is partly true. Yeah... I forgot that lovely detail.

I have to have a fasciotomy on both of my legs soon for chronic exertional compartment syndrome. I met with a well-known orthopedic surgeon. He performed a pressure test on my shins to test for the compartment syndrome, and my results were alarming. My numbers were so high at rest it was almost considered an emergency. It's going to be a slow and painful recovery, which is in part why I feel being at Sovereign during the surgery and recovery is a smart move. I can't imagine sitting alone in my apartment with limited movement and nobody to support or supervise me. ED would have a field day with me. Anyway, I'm actually pretty excited to go to treatment this time because I want it more than I ever have. I also don't feel as triggered by outside sources and people, which gives me an added boost of confidence entering back into a world surrounded by eating disorders.

Yesterday I drove myself to Sovereign and arrived around 2:00

in the afternoon. It was so nice to see the familiar faces of the staff. They were all so happy to see me. Quite a few thought I was there because I was going to start working for them, so I kind of had to say, "No…I'm here to get some extra support, but life is great." I suppose that is pretty much true minus the fact ED has been trying to kill me. I do wonder sometimes what would have happened had I accepted the job offer from Sovereign instead. Well, everything happens for a reason, I suppose. I finally arrived at the new ED residence, and the program has changed in quite a few ways for the better. There are 6 other girls here right now, and 5 of them are around my age, which is already a big change compared with being with mostly adults last time. The program feels more similar to Remuda Life now, which I think I like better. It's not without drama, and I was heavily warned by multiple sources of the "excitement" in the ED house, but, oh well. I guess I just can't let it affect me.

I was given my first taste of the dysfunction in the ED house at dinner. Two girls here don't really eat, to put things bluntly, and mealtimes are full of ridiculousness from them. I was so proud of myself, though, because I ate a normal portion from all the food groups and without any weird rituals. For the rest of my peers, dinner didn't go so well. One girl was upstairs refusing even to come to dinner, another girl was talking about nonsense and playing with her food, which in turn pissed off 2 of the other girls, who left the table in fumes, and the other 2 wouldn't even attempt to eat in the dining room with this one triggering girl, so they ate outside. Meanwhile, the house manager left to go talk to the girl upstairs, leaving me sitting alone with the girl who is triggering people the most. I didn't want to stay, but I also didn't want to leave her alone. She is a nice person if ED would only leave her alone. It was kind of a surreal experience sitting with her actually. Although I thought her comments and actions were bullshit and fake, I did emphasize with her and tell her that I understood the struggle, that it's OK she's at a different level, and not to worry about others' issues. The girl took 1 tiny bite from 1 meatball and then declared, "That was a valiant effort!" Are you *serious*? I wanted to shout from the top of my lungs with disgust. This is a life-ruining, life-threatening, and life-altering disease. She was practically mocking it.

Anyway, I like all the girls here for the most part, which is good. It's weird because I feel so much older and more independent than them all, yet we are all about the same age. It will be a good test here to focus on myself and not get caught up in the chaos. My 2 roommates are the 2 girls who are struggling here the most. Gee, I wonder why the only open beds are in their room? Lucky me. It took me such a long time to fall asleep mainly because the 2 girls were up well past midnight with music on, looking at Facebook and YouTube, and just being generally loud. Come on, seriously? Then one of the girls asked the other if she wanted to do push-ups. The reply was that the 2 of them would make such a great support system for each other. Oh, help them, *puh-lease!*

I did eventually fall asleep and slept well. I had a good breakfast with some of the girls while one of my roommates skipped it and the other exclaimed that ½ a banana was all she could manage. My goals so far for my stay are:

- eat correct portions at all meals,
- eat regularly and not save up my calories for night,
- eat intuitively and don't calorie-count,
- eat fear/trigger foods without feeling the need to binge or that I blew it,
- trust my hunger cues, not my head,
- add more variety and eat meals prepared by house managers instead of my own,
- recover from my surgery and work through anxiety from not exercising,
- reduce gum chewing, and
- fill the loneliness still inside of me.

May 25, 2012

I had an interesting therapy session today. When I was talking, I made 2 contradicting statements: "I accept everyone" and "No one is good enough/equal to me." It seems I accept those who are below me and/or not a threat to me in regards to looks, tennis, or accomplishments. It's hard for me to accept help because then I feel as if I'm below that person, and I don't want to be anything but better than others, which stems from my overly competitive nature. I need to learn and learn quickly that I can accept help and support from others without being less than them or considered a failure. I'm so used to putting on a strong face after so many years of being a target of bullying that sometimes letting down my guard makes me feel helpless and like a victim again.

Oh man, I binged tonight...badly. I *hate* you, ED! What did you *do* to that little girl? That sweet, innocent little girl who was so vulnerable and valuable. You kidnapped her! You lied to her, and you stole her soul. So dark, so alone. The memories are haunting. A bone-chilling wind beneath 8 layers of clothes a girl walks...alone, possessed, obsessed, and lost. Unable to see through her own eyes. But I'm still *here*! I'm alive, and I am a fire that can't be put out. A tortured existence. A deeper purpose. A life so distant. I endured it relentlessly. To know you're trapped and believe there will never be peace and calm. To the depths of death and the angels who sang. My eyes open. So many scenes I have seen. The survival and revival of the sickest. Enclosed in a room...the heart monitor capturing a rhythm too slow and a disease progressing too fast. A room full of art, full of color, full of shadows. The voices never stop: too many calories, you have to hide your snack, just refuse, water load, you ugly fat failure, why can't *I* be the skinniest? I'm not sick enough. I am worthless. I'm fat. I lose....

May 27, 2012

I am trying to forgive myself right now for binging Friday night as well as yesterday. I thought this would be a safe place to come to but that doesn't mean ED will obey. It doesn't help that the house is full of a lot of my trigger foods. Peanut butter, cereal, leftovers, and bread, just to name a few. There is always a house manager with us, but I still find it too easy to binge secretly. No one seems to suspect that I'm struggling, partly because I am more advanced and mature than the rest of the group. But, oh, can people be deceiving.

I'm having such a hard time with weight and body image right now, and, of course, binging only helps to further enhance the circular cycle. My dissatisfaction and preoccupation with my body is partly heightened because all my housemates are thin, if not too thin. It only makes me focus more on my flabby, bulging stomach, oversized boobs, squishy upper arms, and touching thighs. I do forgive myself and know this is a process I must be patient with, but it's just so damn difficult! If recovering from an eating disorder was a true job in a business sense, then I'd be a billionaire... it is that difficult, stressful, and selective. Am I scared *not* to have a problem in my life? How would life be different? Hmm... so very different it would be, and good or bad, it's the change I can't seem to face. I want, and frankly I need, to commit to myself the act of self-love without self-sabotage or this eating disorder will kill me eventually. I will see the positive changes both physically and emotionally if I can just be patient and trust in a process other than my own.

May 29, 2012

Fuck this! Fuck you, *ED*. Fuck you! Do you hear me? I *hate* you! You are a liar, a thief, a bully, a predator, and you are *not* an ounce of me! You hurt me, you make me feel like a loser, you are killing me, you make me cry, you hold me hostage, you make me feel alone, and you are destroying my family. Don't touch me. I am stronger than *you*.

When all is quiet and I'm alone, I don't know how to be my own authority and trust my own voice for direction, reassurance, and comfort. So, ED, *you* come in and take over, which results in a predictable binge. Well, no more! I trust myself. I can be alone with myself and myself only! I am my own best friend and would *never* treat anyone, even my worst enemy, the way you treat me, ED. I don't regret you being in my life because I believe there are no mistakes or accidents. You see, ED, because of my strength to overcome you, I now in turn get to help millions of others overcome you as well. It is *you*, ED, who will be left eternally alone. You have no power. You have no power over me. In fact, you have no power over *anyone* and you know that, which is why you will do anything in your power to convince people relentlessly otherwise.

I am strong. I am healthy. I am loved. I am capable. I am courageous. I am intelligent. I am beautiful. I am whole. I am forgiven. I am independent. I am honest. I am brave. I am happiness. I am good enough. I am supported. I am safe. I am making a difference. I am blessed. I am at peace. I am a leader. I am confident. I am a role model. I am a success. I am on the right path. I am joy. I am hope. I am a fighter. I persevere. I don't give up. I am a survivor. I am deserving. I am giving. I am creative. I am compassionate. I am a gift. I am accepted. I am patient. I am valuable. I am irreplaceable. I am learning. I am growing. I am healing.

I believe in me. I believe in Brittany. I trust myself. I love myself. I am proud of myself. I am a ray of light. I am possibility. I am *Brittany!*

I have broken free from this enemy.

No longer trapped, my strength is fact.

I have destroyed the chains. I have control of the reins.

I now can be me, a soul forever free.

May 24, 2012

I had a really incredible session with my therapist today. Our conversations led to a lot of aha moments. I had too much power growing up. All I had to do was yell loud enough and long enough and my parents would give in. I felt I could eliminate any boundaries that were ever put in place and that is a scary feeling, especially for a little girl. ED became my authority figure and provided the boundaries my parents, nor I, could give myself.

ED was and is different from humans, though. No matter how hard I tried I could not overpower ED. This frustrated and intrigued me at the same time. ED was a mean parent/authority figure, and I grew up believing lies from ED as well as the unrealistic standards that were demanded. However, if I/ED set goals so unrealistically high such as, "I am only good enough if I'm the number-one professional tennis player in the world," then I would also never have to make any *choices*. Choices are hard, and what's worse is what if

I make a *mistake* and a *wrong* choice? Well, are there such things as mistakes anyway? No! My therapist then shared with me her inspiring education experience and proceeded to ask me the same question someone asked her.

"If I could go back and take a past year out of my life and replace it with school knowing that the school year would be better and more successful, would I?" Well...no, because every year, no matter how difficult, was all a piece of the puzzle that has made me who I am today and has brought me to this place in time. So, it is OK to make so-called mistakes because I learn. Also, I am not abandoned and never have been. I might have been invalidated but never abandoned because *I* am always here for myself.

June 3, 2012

Ah! I am so frustrated right now! Maybe I just want a place to call home. I binged last night—surprise, surprise. I had just returned home after a short stay in the hospital from surgery complications. I was slightly hungry, sure, but mostly just consumed by overwhelming emotions of not feeling well, pain from my leg, and fear. I handled those emotions by having an uncomfortable and unfulfilling binge. Physically I was stuffed, yeah, but emotionally I was still raw and empty. It was a binge more out of needing comfort and out of trying to make my head and body feel better, but all it did was put me into a food coma. It ultimately resulted in swallowing 30 laxatives I had hidden and saved for moments like these. I hate that I even had the laxatives waiting for me, as if I knew I would eventually binge, as if binging was an OK thing to do.

- To think about a binge puts me in an all-over cringe.
- Stuffing my face full of food, hoping to temporarily change my mood.
- I numb out with guilt, trapped by the walls I have built.
- A secretive destruction, my stomach ready for eruption.
- I swallow the laxatives whole, knowing the effect will take its toll.
- A sleepless angry night, knowing what I did wasn't right.

- Heal me from this monster within, a battle I know only I can win.
- This journey I will begin, knowing it's far from the end.
- But I will find my true self and live in abundant health.

37

Beauty and the Feast

June 7, 2012

After 2 binges and 50 laxatives in 2 days later, I found myself drooling and then...drum roll...majorly throwing up. Yes, *me*, actually throwing up! It takes something insane to make me throw up given my gag reflex seems to be nonexistent, which I suppose is its own blessing. Thankfully, my favorite house manager was there with me during my episode but talk about being stuck, depressed, and miserable. After many phone calls later, it was decided that I should be taken to a psychiatric hospital to get better stability, both mentally and physically, as it was clear I was a danger to myself. I arrived at Mission Hospital in Mission Viejo and was admitted through the ER. Things have been OK here so far. All the staff and patients are really nice, and I have an ocean-view room, which is actually scenic enough to trick you into thinking you're vacationing in some resort. Ha-ha, yeah, but not quite. I've been trying to restrict but have also been *so* hungry, which has led me to consume quite a bit of boxed cereal. Ugh! I just want to be thin!

Oh man, I hate myself right now. I can't stop eating. I've had so much cereal, milk, and crackers that it's repulsive. I've had at least 4,000 calories for the day so far. It sucks here because the dining room area is always open and in it there is a large fridge crammed with juices, milk cartons, puddings, apples, and Jell-O. On a table next to the fridge sits an endless supply of boxed Cheerios, Raisin Bran, peanut butter tubs, saltine crackers, graham crackers, and tea. Ah! To make matters worse, everyone I express to about how fat I am, all reply with either, "You aren't *that* fat" or "It's only temporary and fixable." I just want to be the thin one again! I can't take this anymore. I'm jumping out of my skin!

June 9, 2012

It's frightening how depressed I am when I'm able to truly take off my smile-plastered mask. The psychiatrist increased my medications today, and I can only hope I start to notice a difference in my mood and certainly my binging behavior. What is it going to take to help me? Medications? Therapy? Lockdown? Time? A miracle? What am I trying to control? What am I trying to avoid? The unknown? Success? Failure? Feelings?

June 15, 2012

Things have *not* taken a turn for the better here. My binge eating has only climaxed past what I ever could have imagined, and my own body is making me claustrophobic. I literally spend my days sitting in the dining room eating bowl after bowl of cereal and dipping graham crackers in peanut butter and vanilla pudding. On top of this, I also eat my 3 meals a day, which I purposely order extremely restrictively. Hmm...connection?

I got put in restraints last night. Let's just say I did something so utterly stupid in a pathetic attempt to try to make myself throw up all the food I had just binged on, but obviously things didn't go as I had magically planned. I am just so distressingly fat and want to die! I just need some sort of escape, some relief, some sort of break from my own torturous mind.

June 16, 2012

You're not going to believe this. Or maybe you will. Last night I was absolutely at my limit and felt I was going to explode, both mentally and physically. Since there isn't much to do or places to go in a locked-down psychiatric unit, my options were limited as to how I would alleviate my stress. What I did find was a pencil. What I did do was impulsively jam it into my skin as hard as I could. It was one bloody, painful, and idiotic mess. I got assigned a 24-7 sitter. *Really?* How many times has this happened in my life? I can't even pee alone! Yep, the door must be wide-open with the nurse staring right at me. So not worth it. I don't even know what the point is anymore. I binged tonight as well. I just give up!

June 22, 2012

Letter from God:

Dear Brittany,

I see your struggles. These chaotic moments in your life are merely times of change and transformations used to guide you through trials of strength and character building. Failure and giving up are not a part of the plan, understand? Get back up on those 2 beautifully and talentedly made legs of yours and start molding into that mature, assertive Brittany we both know you are. I will take care of the aftercare planning for you as always because things happen for a reason. Every day is a new day despite the despair and ugliness that led to it. So, suit up, chin up, look up, speak up, stand up, and do the actions based upon your mind, not feelings.

XOXO

~God

July 18, 2012

Fuck! Yeah...not the best way to start a journal entry. I'm at Cottage Hospital right now in the psychiatric ward in Santa Barbara. Almost exactly 1 year later, too, which is weird. What the heck is wrong with me? After finally being discharged from the last psych ward, I decided not to go back to Sovereign or to my apartment near PFC and instead come home. Yep, home—back to trigger town and memories of madness. Given the fact that I put on over 20 pounds during my inpatient stay, I was in a very dark and isolated place when I arrived back in San Luis Obispo, which in turn led to my psychiatrist, Dr. Guimaraes, admitting me to Cottage Hospital.

I am so beside myself right now. I have so much to say, but what's the point anymore? Where's my energy? Where's my fire? My courage? My tenacity and perseverance that helped me survive the impossible? I'm fading fast. ED has trapped me for a long time, and I understand the meaning of that, but depression...oh wow, that is something else. The sadness and hopelessness I feel is impossible to explain. What's worse is the anger and the rage. The problem? It's hidden. It's hidden so deep and is so untouchable. It's at the core of the blanket of sadness. Anger toward my mom, myself, my classmates, the doctors who gave up on me, my eating disorder, losing Scandalous, losing my place at UC Davis, my parents not visiting much while I was dying at Torrance, and the list goes on! There is just so much built-up rage! I don't know how to get it out, so I implode and take it out on myself. Self-harm, restrict, overexercise, binge, swallow 30 laxatives...no big deal. *Seriously*, Brittany? Here I am 1 year later...still battling ED, battling worsening depression, living at home, isolating myself, fat, abusing laxatives, self-harming, no friends, hate myself, still haven't finished my college degree. I just keep strategically tiptoeing around my core problems. Unfortunately, they are buried so deep and are so traumatizing that I can't even fathom beginning to do the work of healing. Yet, this just means I'll be stuck seemingly forever!

Just fuck my life. I'm miserable! I can't do it. Nothing ever gets better. Things only continue to get worse, so I *give up*! I don't want to do this anymore. No wonder eating disorders have the highest mortality rate from suicides. After almost 11 years, I am so burnt out it's not even funny. I've tried *everything*!

July 19, 2012

Erg! I slept maybe 1 hour last night. My roommate was snoring out an orchestra, or was it an opera? She's an older lady who is I believe an alcoholic...very sweet, though. Anyway, between the elephant breathing, a new environment, flat pillows, a soft mattress, bright lights, and changing temperatures, it was a rough night. One thing is clear in my mind...I will not stop on my weight loss journey until I hit the 120s, and I make *no* guarantee I will stop then. I *do* think I will stop by 100 pounds, but it all just depends. Oh, and here I go fantasizing about bullshit again because I'm so far away from any of those things happening, which in turn will only work against me and I will probably binge...wait, no, I won't binge. I *won't*!

Shit! I just finished lunch, and I feel so bloated and am such a fat pig! By accident, some chowder type of soup got put on my tray, so what happened? My healthy brain and ED battled it out:

Healthy: "I'm cold, and I'm already barely eating. It's OK to have the soup."

ED: "Are you *kidding* me? You're already obese and are now thinking of detouring from an already lenient diet plan? Ha! You are pathetic!"

Healthy: "Well, they forgot my coffee, so I won't be having my 2 creamers, and my fruit cup is less than the 100 calories I counted it for."

ED: "Oh, you disgust me! Just have it and do better tomorrow!"

I met with my psychiatrist earlier today. He's very nice. I just don't know yet how I will be helped here. I'm getting off one medication and increasing another, but that's it for now. I suppose I'm not even really open to many medications given their side effects of possible weight gain. I just feel so hopeless and numb, which is really making me want to self-harm. Cottage Hospital has a zero-tolerance policy for that, though, so if I do hurt myself I will be transferred. How do I keep it a secret? I have no Band-Aids.

I prolonged to start eating my dinner, which caused some concern and reason for the staff to threaten to move me to a room closer to the nurses' station where they could observe me. Well, screw that! Yeah, I did eventually eat, but let me tell you, if that's the game you want to play, I won't eat! And, yes, I know I sound like a 4 year old. Hmm...to stop eating and drinking...now wouldn't that be the ultimate punishment? The ultimate pain and discomfort? The ultimate suicide? And the ultimate control? I can do it again. Maybe I do want to play that game again. Maybe the feelings and memories wouldn't be so haunting if I became them again. An overdose would be easy...too easy. Pathetic really. I'd rather make myself suffer. After my impossible weight gain right after almost losing my life to anorexia I've wanted nothing more than to get my identity back...of at least being skinny...at *least*! I've struggled with being overweight and obsessive now since late 2009. Enough is enough! By late 2012, I plan to be thin. So, why do I feel like such a hypocrite writing this? Because deep down I know...I know the truth. I'm smarter than this. To give in to ED is a familiar fashion to me, but I can't deny my secret wish of wanting to be free, happy, healthy, and alive.

July 20, 2012

I got moved to the isolation room last night just for my safety. Everyone was so nice about it, though, and I was happy enough to get a night away from the lawn mower that was my roommate. I actually slept really well, which was nice and somewhat of a relief. Today has been a repeat of yesterday. I don't even have the strength or am in tune anymore to fake a smile. The staff had me switch to another room, which is closer to the nurses' station. The bed is more comfortable and my new roommate is nice, but, unfortunately, I believe she snores as well.

I've been doing well with my restrictive meal plan. I do get hungry between meals, especially because it's so boring here, but too bad. I don't have interest or joy in anything anymore, and it scares me. I want to hurt myself. I want this all to be over—all to end. I've struggled for so long. I can't take this pain of sadness and numbness on top of it all. I see no glimpse of hope or future for myself. And to add the icing to the cake, the guy I've been madly in love with since middle school now has a new girlfriend and I can't stand to see his Facebook updates with her. That was supposed to be *me*! That is until ED decided I couldn't have any other relationships whatsoever. I am so over this! And I wish I could get over the loss of this guy, but I love him and I always will.

July 22, 2012

Please! This really *can't* be my life right now! I ended up binging last night alone on the snacks leftover in the dining room. I had 4 ½ peanut butter and jelly sandwiches, 1 ½ turkey sandwiches, 15 packets of crackers, 3 graham crackers, 7 Yoplait yogurts, honey, 2 oranges, 1 apple, 2 string cheeses, 3 Babel cheeses, 2 hot chocolate packets, and carrot sticks. That was at least 4,200 calories in that hour alone and about 5,000 for the whole day. *When* does this nightmare end?

Well, I most certainly did self-harm! I picked at an old scab until it bled, not giving a crap if there would be consequences or not. I went to bed after 1:00 a.m. This morning ED just finished breakfast with his fellow ED roommate named Krista, who is a lady in her 40's or so. She's quite timid and troubled and certainly didn't touch breakfast, but apparently she never does. Yeah...I didn't need that added trigger this morning. I'm already full of rage and ready to burst. I'm going to hurt myself. I could not care less what happens to me. I can't sit with these feelings of fatness and of betraying myself by getting so out of control and binging in the first place. I suck! I'm worthless! I'm a failure!

Oh, I am *so* franticly mad right now. Dad wanted to come to visit me, and I want him to visit, but I also wanted him to bring me some laxatives because of last night. He said no, which led to an awful conversation over the phone. I'm going *crazy*!

38

An Apocalypse of My Own

"There is such a freedom being able to sit still...
with yourself... with your questions... with your
thoughts, dreams, and doubts. In fact, I can't think
of anything more frightening, threatening, and liberating." ~Britt

July 25, 2012

Hello, there. It has been a few days now, which you know is never
a great sign. After the binges at Cottage Hospital I was overcome by
rage and impulsive self-hatred and behavior. I grabbed a pencil and
attacked myself again. I figured I already had a scar anyway, so who
cares if I make it worse? Anyway, it resulted in 1:1 monitoring, and
a 90-minute, late night ambulance ride to Valencia, California, to a
place called Henry Mayo Newhall Memorial Hospital at their behavioral health unit. The staff at Cottage Hospital was trying to get me a
bed at Vista Del Mar or somewhere closer, but thank goodness there
were no beds available. What a blessing it has been.

It's a pretty nice unit here in the sense that it's quite big, has a
large dining area, a TV room, large minimal bedrooms with floor-to-
ceiling windows, and a large outdoor patio with a basketball hoop.
The best part for me is that there is no available food. Breakfast,
lunch, dinner, and 3 snacks are put out at certain times and that's it!
No food is available in-between designated times. Yes, finally! This is
exactly what I've been needing, eating disorder-wise. Clearly I needed

a higher level of care than Sovereign could offer because I couldn't control myself with having unsupervised access to food.

The most devastating news was that I was told my weight...170 freaking pounds! Ah! And that was my admit weight at Cottage Hospital *before* my 3-day binge. Oh, I almost died right then and there! There is no way I will be stepping on any scales here at Henry Mayo! My first day here all my meals were ordered for me, so a bunch of high-calorie crap food was served on my tray. Of course, already being in a binge mode after what happened at Cottage meant that I chose to eat the shit I was served and only further my anger, disgust, and detachment from myself. I was definitely feeling my rage and impulsivity rise after lunch. It was as if I was in a trance now as I took hold of a pencil and went after myself again. Predictably, I got placed on a 1:1 status, but it's actually OK this time. I'm able to use the bathroom alone, which is the important part, so I just don't care anymore.

All the staff members here are absolute angels, though, *really*! Every one of them has all the time in the world to encourage me, get to know me, and hang out with me with such compassion and acceptance. When I cut myself, the only thing all the nurses said was how much they care about me and want to help. There was none of the critical condescending tone that I'm so conditioned to hearing. I finally called home and had a good talk with Dad. I cried for a while, but he was actually so supportive, encouraging, and understanding. He made me feel better about my weight, too. If I were just around my goal weight I feel that so many of my issues would resolve. I might still be weird with food to an extent, but at least I could wear my clothes, socialize, work, play tennis, and move on with my life. The loneliness and depression would be lifted. Right? I mean, once I get to where I want to be physically, everything should be fine, right? Why is it that this is never the case, though? If anything, I'm holding myself back in fear because I'm placing such high expectations on my life at a certain weight.

The other patients here are wonderful so far. Now on day 3 here, I do find myself even smiling a bit. Hey...I'm even journaling! I've been eating healthy meals, and I eat all 3 snacks as well, even if it means eating a gluten-containing granola bar or peanut butter.

I'm proud of myself. My hunger isn't getting too out of control either. In some ways I wish so badly that I could stay here for at least 1 month…wonderful staff, sleeping well, no chance of binging, good groups, structured schedule, and a time to learn to accept myself and climb up out of my black hole.

July 26, 2012

Today has actually been decent. My 1:1 sitter today is this really cool guy who is around my age. I've had a really nice time talking to him all day. The advice and words he spoke to me definitely left an impact for the better…I can't give up on myself. I've been up and out of bed almost the whole day as well as talking with a lot of people. The severe negativity and depression as well as impulsive urges seem to come in waves, but they are softer waves for now. The psychiatrist here wants so badly to help me. I just don't think it's possible, though.

July 27, 2012

Last night was awful. The staff brought out *3* trays of snacks, which is far more than they needed, and I struggled. My total calories for the whole day totaled around 2,050, but that's still at least 500 too many. With the chaos of certain patients screaming and others with eating disorders themselves engaging in food talk, I let my anger overcome me, resulting in me harming my fat, ugly body. My sitter eventually came into my room, and I was crying.

Anyway, that was last night, but today has been a bitch as well! I just overate at lunch. It's so hard eating with such discipline when everyone else orders all these yummy-looking desserts, bread rolls, sandwiches, and breakfast items. They don't even blink twice about eating them either, which is the most baffling part to me. Often, the patient won't even finish all the things he or she ordered, so the food is offered up for grabs, which only causes my OCD to surge more inside knowing that the food could go uneaten and therefore wasted. I *have* to calm down and not get frantic about the food. At least the calories I'm eating shouldn't cause me to gain weight.

July 28, 2012

I met with my psychiatrist's father today, who is also a psychiatrist. He was quite a special man, although it was only our first encounter. We didn't even discuss medications or anything of that sort. He spoke so compassionately, yet firmly. What he said to do was to go to the mirror and look and look and look and look and look and look and look and look and look... *without judgment!* He said there are 62 things our minds think, including judgment, jealousy, anger, etc., and none are good. He instructed, "When your mind starts to judge, say, 'Shut up,' and keep practicing until you believe it." He also explained that we are all energy, and energy is matter, and matter cannot be destroyed or created. Therefore, I, as a person, cannot be destroyed or created, so I might as well be successful or else continue forever to struggle against hating myself. Only *I* can change... only *I*.

September 28, 2012

Goodness, it has been a while since I've journaled. There are so many things to catch up on, but frankly I want to focus on the present, so I will only do a brief recap. I first want to mention that I had gone about 6 weeks completely binge-free and eating in somewhat of a healthy and normal manner. Wow! That is the longest period of abstinence I have had from ED in about 10 years. Things just began to click once I got home from Henry Mayo. Mom and I have kind of been doing the Maudsley approach, which is where the parent plates the child's food. She served and portioned all of my meals, and it was a very healing and liberating process to team up with her against ED. Needless to say, I started changing physically as well. In fact, the physical transformation I have made in the past 2 months is pretty amazing, come to think of it. I have started back playing some tennis with Paige, and I even started taking tennis lessons from my first real coach again. I haven't hit with him in almost 10 years, so it is quite a special and big deal for me. Now that I have a level enough head on the tennis court and a focused attitude, his coaching style is just what I need. The amount my game has risen in just a few lessons with him is head turning.

I also started working with my psychiatrist Dr. Guimaraes again, and he's been a very key person in my life lately. I see him for medication management, sure, but I've also been seeing him along with Erin for therapy. He and I have really uncovered some things that have never surfaced before. He is extremely book smart, but he is also highly in sync intuitively and alternatively, which sheds a light on my life that is often covered in shadows.

I'm hoping to transfer and get into California Polytechnic State University in San Luis Obispo next year. It's a bit of a long shot, but my grades have always been stellar and I have a unique situation. It's weird, but San Luis Obispo actually feels like home for the first time in my life. Anyway, this has been a nice little recap thus far, but the drama is just yet to begin. September 20th, the day I confirmed I would be coming back to work at Premier Fitness Camp, woo-hoo, right?

Ugh... no, not quite. All of a sudden, I realized that I was about to leave a lifestyle that I not only enjoyed to a degree but that was safe, healthy, and progressive. I would be an idiot to go back to living alone in Carlsbad, you might think. But what about my amazing apartment, my one-of-a-kind coworkers, my great personal trainer, my tennis buddies at the amazing La Costa Resort, my independence, and my commitment, for goodness' sakes? Should I stay or should I go? I explored the pros and cons of both choices, but ultimately it was going to have to be my decision. I ended up choosing to go to at least try it out again.

One week before I was supposed to start back at Premier, Dr. Guimaraes told me I could still change my mind about going. He told me I absolutely didn't even have to test it out at all and that I could choose to stay in San Luis Obispo. Umm, thanks, Dr. Guimaraes, but I think it's time you come back to reality here. I can't back out of a job they've so nicely and unusually been holding for me 6 days prior to starting! What I didn't realize was that it was I who wasn't living in reality.

Fast-forward a few days later, and it's now Tuesday. I'm up early at 7:00 a.m. for a hair appointment. My hairdresser asked me about my job, Carlsbad, and Premier Fitness Camp, and would you believe it, I was speechless! Completely tongue-tied. It was *such* an effort to talk about it—so much resistance. It caught me completely off guard and frankly startled me enough to listen to my heart and not my head. Here was a neutral person amidst my conflict with no judgment or interest either way, and my heart got the chance to speak. Uh-oh!

Well, first things first: gimme food! I arrived back home around 9:30 and started eating. Not flat-out binging, but eating and without pause. Fast-forward a few hours later and I'm now stuffed, panicked, and overwhelmed with the truth. I *can't* go back to Carlsbad. It would be congruent to jumping into a tank full of sharks…bad news! To make a long story shorter, after some hysterical talks with my parents and sister, I sent off a long, honest, and personal text to Mary with trembling hands. Oh boy. Well, Mary left me a voice mail saying it was OK and she understood, but she also said how sad she was. Oh, did I ever feel like an unprofessional failure. Then again, I made this decision because I value my health and well-being, which is a new and important step for me. Mary sent me the most compassionate text later that evening, which really helped me breathe a sigh of relief.

To finish the night off, I also took 18 laxatives—ugh! Factoring in that I hadn't taken laxatives in almost 2 months, I was in for a rough night—and that it was. Let's just say I've never had more pain and discomfort in my life! It was so bad I had to even call and wake up Mom to be with me sitting on the toilet because I was ready to allow her to call 911. Never had I thrown up so much as well. It was just a horrific night, but thank goodness I made it through. I stayed in bed all the next day completely out of it.

Slowly I got back on my feet and even started seeing Erin again, which has been so nice. Boy, does she threaten ED. Never have I known or worked with someone that causes ED to squirm so much knowing she will not back down and will call out *all* of the bullshit. Tennis continued getting better and better, but with the improvement came new opportunities. Pretty soon I had more people than I knew what to do with wanting to hit. On top of my lessons and joining a tennis doubles league, I was starting to get overwhelmed.

379

It was a big jump for me just to go from being a shut-in at my house to hitting on occasion with my dad to now having people wanting to schedule something every day. It caught me off guard and left me feeling vulnerable.

ED: "Whoa, Brittany! What the heck do you think you're doing? Don't you realize that you are filling up every day of the week with a commitment? Not only any commitment but also one that requires competition, effort, judgment, and pressure? Tennis is just one more way to judge if you are good enough. That's a lot at stake. Besides, if you think you're going to start getting out and socializing, think again! *Hello!* What about *me*? You know that I need at least 3 days in a row from you in order to pull off a binge and laxative session. And at the rate you are saying yes to people, I don't see that you and I will be together much. You are scared of success. You are scared of failure. You are scared to have friends. You are scared of change. You are scared of rejection. You are scared of the unknown and what you can't control. Once you get healthy, don't you know what that means? No more excuses, pressure, expectations, perfection, responsibility, choices, exposure, feelings, and growing up. You *need* me. I know how to keep you safe and sheltered from all of the chaos."

Me: "No, ED, I really want to play tennis with all these people. I feel good knowing so many people want me in their lives. I should be OK."

ED: "But look at you! You are so bloated today, and you just spent 30 minutes arguing with your dad about body image. Even he admitted you look bloated and 1 pound or so overweight in the tight shirt you're wearing. Not to mention you are already chewing gum out of control tonight."

Me: "Ah shit, I hate this!"

(Open fridge to see chicken from the market sitting there. The kind on the bone, which just so happens to be my favorite.)

I eat it. I'm hungry, but I'm also emotional and frantic.

ED: "Ah! There you go! Now don't you feel better? Come on, eat that celery and ranch dip, too! And guess what? I even saw 1 extra protein bar in the freezer earlier today. Hooray!"

I upsettingly, yet numbly, continued eating. I knew I was now in binge mode and there was no going to bed for me. I stayed up very late staring blankly at the computer, watching horses on YouTube with a mindless jealousy. Accompanying me were 2 pears, 2 extra-large almond packages, and 1 protein bar. Oh, yeah...and ED was there, too, of course. It looks as though I'm canceling my tennis for tomorrow and Saturday now. I suppose I will binge a bit tomorrow and then take the laxatives. Now I won't be able to sleep thinking about what I'm going to binge on next. Gee, thanks, ED; you really do always know how to keep me "safe."

October 14, 2012

I had done everything right. In fact, I was almost ready to let down my guard. It was my 24th birthday and the best birthday I think I have ever had. The "best birthday," however, was competing with my past. All my past birthdays have been nothing short of heartbreaking, exhausting, and tearful. It would only make sense that somehow my 24th would end up the same. So, I found myself in a weird state. I completed the day exactly as I had expected and wanted: lovely meeting with Dr. Guimaraes, gym, dinner at home with parents, dog walk, and frozen yogurt with my parents. It was 2,500 calories at most. And, come on—it was my birthday after all, so go away guilt! Anyway, I was about to head downstairs when ED piped up to wish me a happy birthday.

ED: "What are you doing! Don't go to bed yet! It's your birthday, your day to go all out and not care. You didn't even overindulge. *Come on*, at least open the fridge and take a look around. Once your birthday is over, it's over, and you have to go back to eating the same foods in appropriate portions. Have some fun while you still can! Yes, yes, that's it! Eat that whole chicken and pour some BBQ sauce on it. Heck, yes, you better eat that banana, too! Oh, so you're going downstairs now? Well, good luck sleeping."

Me: "Ugh, I feel so bloated, uncomfortable, and anxious. I know I had no more than 3,000 calories and that it was my birthday, but I still feel guilty. The only way I know to signal the end of a binge and turn off my anxiety is to take the laxatives. They are a symbolic thought stopper and a symbolic binge stopper. Since I can't seem to turn off my anxiety, I feel I will need to take laxatives. And if I'm going to take laxatives I might as well eat some dangerous foods to make it worthwhile."

ED: "Yes, yes, that's *right*! Come on, let's think about all the foods we can binge on Sunday. It's past 3:00 in the morning now, and it's not as if you are going to just go to sleep and forget about it. Give in. Besides, the next times you're going to binge will be Halloween, Thanksgiving, and Christmas. Only 3 more times in a few months. You can do that. You can still get away with weight loss as well. We could get more frozen yogurt, candy bars, coffee drinks, and even some protein shakes. It's going to be hot the next couple of days and the ladies' doubles is canceled this Monday, so you can easily cancel your private tennis lesson as well while you're recovering from the laxatives. *Come on*, Brittany, we are binging Sunday! You're lonely, you're sad, you're pathetic, and *I* control you."

Me: "*Shut up, ED!* I don't want to binge! I don't want to take laxatives! I actually had an amazing birthday even though I didn't have a bunch of friends over. I'm actually very proud of myself and how far I've come. I'm happy with my opportunities and the progress I am making. I am doing a fabulous job taking care of myself, and I'm allowed to treat myself every once in a while without it turning into a freaking disaster. I don't have to binge to relieve pressure or anxiety. In fact, I *want* to have my tennis lesson. I *want* to see my body make progress. I *want* to work with Dr. Guimaraes and help other people. I *want* to be an inspiration to others and show them that ED never had control to begin with. I *want* to feel proud. I *want* to find balance and peace. I *want* to know I am healthy and safe and not put my life at risk. I *want* recovery and I *want* to change. This is the new me, and there is no ED involved!"

Somehow I managed to fall asleep. When I awoke late Sunday morning I was still anxious, but I felt I had the ability to make decisions for myself. I ate my normal breakfast, and then Dad and I got in the car to go play doubles. I told Dad about eating the extra chicken and banana and how uncomfortable I was last night. I also told him how badly I wanted to binge. Bingo! ED squirmed and protested, but I didn't keep it a secret. I told on ED. I told another human being who was on Brittany's side what ED was up to. That immediately took away most of ED's power and the likelihood that I would binge. What a relief! You might think that I would always tell someone else when I feel the urge to binge if it decreases the chances of it happening so much, but that's just not so. The power my eating disorder has when it wants to binge or take hold is immensely overwhelming and practically blinding. Everything about ED is secretive; that's the fun in it all, anyway.

What can we get away with without being caught? Silly really, but ED is not a team player, so when there are others calling him, or *it*, out on destructive behaviors, ED vulnerably retracts.

39

Repeat Offender

"A laugh here, a smile there, a faint rainbow in the sky, and the sight of burning pink clouds. Life is full of treasures everywhere. It just depends on what you choose to see." ~Britt

November 19, 2012

I'm currently on a train to San Clemente...yep, you guessed it: I'm heading back to Sovereign Health. Third time's the charm, right? I was going to go back to Rosewood Ranch, but for a variety of reasons, I am going to try Sovereign first. I have to say I'm a little nervous. I'm going into it focused but with a restrictive mind-set, which is no good either. I'm just so sick of my body and weight. I've had a lot of binges, laxative overdoses, and hours spent crying in pain on the toilet. Enough is enough! To be fair, I've held myself together quite well considering all the events and recent triggers in my life. Surprisingly, most of my triggers have been positive ones, but that still creates a whole new dilemma for me.

Long live the binge, I suppose. I wish I could believe more than I do that this is the truth. Maybe it's not fair to ask myself that question yet...will I ever binge again? Well, everyone overindulges sometimes, so that's OK, but I do hope never to purposely set out to overeat for emotional reasons and most importantly never take laxatives again.

Overeating to me is tied with my fondest memories as a child: being on the East Coast for the summer beach trip. My grandma's gourmet cooking was pure heaven to me: pancakes, French toast, bread, pies, cookies, cereals, Chex mix, ice cream, muffins, pastries, fries, cakes, sandwiches, fruit salads, deviled eggs, potato skins, candy-coated pretzels, jelly beans, melons, taffy, yogurt, Wheat Thins, croissants, éclairs. Yeah, food was definitely correlated to my happiest memories growing up. Ironically, a lot of the above foods are my main go-to binge foods now. It's as though I want to relive those happy memories I had before my life turned into madness. I need to learn to make happy memories with things other than food...like real people and real friends. I also need to learn that those binge foods are not off limits. Would I punish, hate, or be angry with a little girl for wanting a cookie or sandwich once in a while? No way! I have to learn how to have a balanced relationship with food. And I'm not just re-learning; I'm truly starting from scratch in a way because I never did have a healthy relationship with food to begin with.

From ages 5 to 13: binge/overeater/food hoarder
From ages 13 to 20: anorexic and compulsive overexerciser
From ages 20 to 22: binge eater
From ages 22 to 24: bulimic

I decided to write a "goodbye binge" on paper to see if it would help ease my cravings:

Cereal with milk
Pancakes
Frozen yogurt with candy
Ice cream
Bagel with cream cheese Peanut butter
Pizza
Doughnuts
Cheez-It crackers Frappuccinos Protein shakes
White shell macaroni
Chex mix
Cookies
Subway

Cesar salad
Hamburger
Milkshake
Cheesecake

November 20, 2012

Today has been OK. I must say, it's so nice to have such a warm welcome from all of the staff here. Right now it's just me and 2 other girls in the ED program, which is kind of nice and a big change from all the drama during my last stay. I had an awesome therapy session today. My therapist is also the program director of the eating disorder track at Sovereign and she is really quite brilliant, firm, and straightforward, which I need. She told me I'm the "most professional eating disorder client" she personally, and Sovereign, has ever encountered. I have to understand that success is not equivalent to being number-one and to quit putting unrealistic expectations on myself because no one else puts them on me. They only serve to set me up for a guaranteed failure. Just live! I know how to fail but not succeed. I really couldn't have made a better decision to come back here.

It's exactly what I need even if it does mean I'm here for a couple of months... it will be worth it.

I had a really great session with my dietitian today as well. She said my ideal weight range would be closer to 130 to 140 pounds because I'm athletic and have a lot of muscle. She said that by looking at me she assumed I was already at or near that weight range, which was a really nice compliment, but I assured her I was probably in the upper 150s. I got weighed backward, so who knows. I've been doing so well with trying to abstain from aspartame. Since I'm a gum addict and all gum has aspartame, I've been chewing this natural organic gum, which literally lasts 5 seconds before it becomes inedible. It's also made with real sugar and it has more calories, so I do have to be careful with how much I chew.

We went to the gym tonight, and, boy, that was hard. The gym we went to had mirrors everywhere, including in front of the machines, so I got to stare at my body working out the whole time, ugh! Let's just say that I was *not* happy with what I saw. I know it's a process and that I will see changes if I'm patient, but I'm just so uncomfortable with myself right now. I've been ridiculously tired both yesterday and today, but this is emotionally draining stuff.

November 21, 2012

Cycle of addiction:

Restless, irritable, disconnected ~ Remember "good" feelings ~ Specific foods remembered ~ Start out with thoughts of "control" ~ Go out of control ~ Negative feelings afterward ~ Promise or vow to never again....

November 26, 2012

I miss the control.
I miss Remuda Ranch.
I miss being young.
I miss Stanford.
I miss being sick.
I miss UC Davis.
I miss my memories.
I miss Torrance.
I miss having to gain weight.
I miss UCLA.
I miss my bones showing.
I miss all the games I used to play.
I miss the drama.
I miss being the skinniest and sickest.
I miss the excuses.
I miss my childhood.
I miss the struggle.
I miss the secrets and the lies.
I miss the "easy" life.
I miss the double digits.
I miss the XS clothes.
I miss the gap between my thighs.

I miss the compulsive exercise.

I miss the fierce control I had over food.

I miss shocking doctors.

I miss not having to make any choices.

I miss the simple, isolated world.

I miss *anorexia*!

November 27, 2012

Help me! I'm so stuck! ED has completely taken me over. All I can think about is calories, food, weight, and my body. Why do I hold on to something intangible so tightly? Why am I so afraid to live? To be happy? To try? To love? I know I can always fall back on ED, so why not try something else? The truth is I never wanted to give up anorexia... I was cheated, bribed, forced out of it... or so I like to believe... it couldn't have really been *I* who lost control. Sure, when I was obese, when I'm binging, when I'm abusing laxatives, I wanted to give up ED and be done, but that didn't include anorexia. All my memories, identity, and hard work are tied to being an anorexic. I know anorexia. I'm experienced in it; I am an expert. It's comfortable, and I like to think I am or was one of the best. Then again, what am I saying? Is this even *me* talking at all? Is this *you*, ED? Why can't I get through my head that anorexia, binge eating disorder, and bulimia are all driven by the *same* eating disorder? The same core issues! Sure, they are different forms, which result in different behaviors, which therefore lead to different appearances, but I can't keep fooling myself into thinking anorexia was so different from what I'm going through right now. It's still the same damn eating disorder trying to kill me. So, why can't I let it go?

What about life? What about truly living, not merely existing? Well, it's new, it's unknown, it's more competitive, it's harder to be one of the best, and it's cruel... at least I grew up living in what I considered a cruel world. I'm scared. I have to start from square one and rebuild a shattered life. But deep down I want to. I have so much to offer. I perceive using my talents to be so difficult and such a huge commitment, but I know my thinking is distorted and blown out of proportion. All I have to do is the best I can in each given moment. So what if my boyfriend and I break up? So what if I get a C in a class? So what if I lose a tennis match? So what if not everyone likes me? *Big freaking deal!* I always have my family and I know there are people that truly care about me. And, yes, ED could be there, but just because something doesn't go perfectly, it doesn't mean I have to fall back on ED to justify the failure. *No!* I'm stronger than that! What's it going to take? I'm once again filling up on lettuce, avoiding carbs, grazing at night, and consumed constantly by ED's voice—so much so, that it's as if I'm in another world.

I had a really good and bad session with my dietician today. It was bad in that she really let me have it regarding my disordered behaviors, but it was good because that's what I need to hear:

- Stay present-focused. One meal at a time is *all* I need to think about. Not what I ate earlier or what I will eat later.
- Do something fun to take my mind off ED...read a light book or do artwork.
- Think of myself in 10 to 20 years. Do I want to keep doing this.
- Quit the grazing at night. Eat 2 things and be done!
- Quit filling up on lettuce. I am not a rabbit, and it is not normal.
- Chewing gum is 2 to 3 pieces per day to freshen breathe, not to curb hunger or give my mouth something to do.
- I'm too talented to keep this game up.
- Use anger to rise above ED; do not be a victim.
- I need to be courageous. I need courage to try something new.
- Listen to hunger cues and not my head.
- Eat in the moment and what sounds good, not what ED says is OK.
- Stop using food as a punishment! Stop emotional eating!
- Focus on successes and not the negatives.
- If it's uncomfortable, do it!

Here are some other notes that I felt had meaning I took from my treatment team today:

- Think how much animals have taught and given to me over the years. They aren't in my life anymore, but I will always remember them and smile. That rings true for people, too!
- If I do things without a struggle, they are meaningless. I don't have to reach my goals perfectly, especially because I learn more from my mistakes than getting things right or from things that come easily.
- I want the success but not the discomfort.
- When it comes to my body and portion sizes, I am psychotic.
- Goals must be something I can achieve.
- I don't always have to prove people wrong.
- I'm so stressed about giving up ED that I'm turning to ED to cope.
- What feels better? A hug from someone I love or 1 hour with ED?

November 28, 2012

I really liked process group today. It made me think about a lot of things I've never even considered. "I want to," "I will," and "I don't want to" are *much* different than "I can't" or "I have to." When we use the latter phrases, we don't own our decisions. It's up for bargaining. Own your choice, and be honest so people understand clearly. Using the words "can't" or "have to" is always *false* because we don't *have* to do anything—but if we don't there could be consequences. If you can say no, people will respect you and value your word. If you are always saying yes, people might question your authenticity or if you really mean it. Always saying yes stems from low self-esteem and wanting people to like and accept me. If I don't want to do something, say no, just like I can say no to my eating disorder.

Perfect is nonexistent. Doing the best of your ability on a given day is equivalent to "perfect." Perfect to *me* doesn't have to be perfect to others or meet unrealistic standards. Perfect is a matter of opinion.

For me, eating nonfat Greek yogurt is *not* a success because it's easy, safe, and provides no opportunities for growth or learning. In this instance, nonfat Greek yogurt is unhealthy. I keep reciting the alphabet of food…it's easy now, and I can do it unconsciously. I need to learn to recite the food alphabet backward so that I can grow mentally and emotionally.

Safe equals lonely, boring, sad, and deprived. Staying "safe" is a big punishment as if I don't deserve anything good, exciting, or different.

Food rules and rituals equal instant success and gratification. *But* I can break those same rules and be a success as well.

December 4, 2012

This is me countering ED thoughts:

ED: "You shouldn't have eaten all those grapes!"

Me: "I was hungry, and it's fine to eat grapes. They will always be there, so don't panic!"

ED: "Ah! You were supposed to fast all day! How could you have eaten all that chili and cornbread, especially after yesterday's binge?"

Me: "Just because I binged the previous day doesn't mean I have to starve myself to compensate. Besides, I was hungry and really wanted to try the chili, and cornbread is my favorite!"

ED: "You are so fat! You will never look or be skinny again!"

Me: "Shut up, ED! You are delusional! I do have the capability to be skinny again, but as long as my health comes first."

ED: "You must starve and restrict for over 1 week to undo the damage of your binges."

Me: "That will only slow down my metabolism and plunge me into a binge-restrict-binge cycle. I am going to eat normally as if nothing happened."

ED: "That girl is so much skinnier than you are! She's also been on that elliptical far longer than you were planning to do. Psh! To think you were once an anorexic-exercise queen. *Pathetic!*"

Me: "Excuse me! First of all, just because she is thinner doesn't make her superior or happier or someone who has a good life. For all I know, she could be mean and miserable, flunking college, and have just gotten fired from a job. Looks don't tell you anything about what really matters. And I don't have to compete with everyone I see or encounter. I can work out for the length of time that is best for *me*—end of story!"

December 6, 2012

I had a good session with my therapist today. Some key points to remember:

- I am not my voice. It is just a part of me.
- Rules take me out of my life.
- Rules give me no personal say or preference as to what I would like. Goals and guidelines are good and healthy measures and motivators. Rules don't help me reach my goals.
- Rules only equal consequences.
- Rules are black and white; good or bad; follow or break.
- Rules replace boundaries for me.
- Rules don't define whether I am good or bad.
- I make me so small when I let rules define me. "Hi, I'm Brittany, and I ate 2 percent fat yogurt for breakfast today versus nonfat, so I'm a failure." Not true!
- I let rules dictate my self-worth and weight. I do have a choice!
- My rules defeat me, which creates a predictable and familiar outcome.
- I feel I need external approval based on my appearance, but that is not me!
- I'm doing nothing to improve my self-esteem. I have to practice giving myself credit for the small things. I need to give myself credit for things that are not related or associated to weight whatsoever.

- Ask myself, "What would I like?" Not, "what am I supposed to have?"

December 10, 2012

Help! I can't stop eating! I'm so hungry, yet so nauseated. I'm so depressed and have no light, positivity, energy, or effort left in me, and it's freaking me out! My head hurts, my mind is blank, and I feel defeated. What am I supposed to do? I can't get my hands on more laxatives because that would be bad news at Sovereign, yet I just want to binge and would *have* to take laxatives then. I'm not really even craving anything in particular, but the urge is so automatic right now based on emotional stress. I'm overwhelmed by every ounce and aspect of my life and in turn I'm starting to binge again massively and *in treatment*, where I'm supposed to be safe. ED is too strong for here. Should I go to a higher level of care? I'm so, so lost.

December 18, 2012

Only I can control myself. I keep looking outward for things and people to control me so I can rebel. People can only influence me; they don't have any more power than that. I have all the choice and control within.

Oh no! Oh no! Oh no! The following list I am about to write is one I wish could be no more real than a dream...or nightmare: yogurt, almonds, blueberries, 3 apples, 1 cup granola, coffee with creamer, 4 Nutri-Grain bars, 1 roast beef sandwich, 1 cupcake, chicken salad, 1 pear, 4 tablespoons dressing, 50 pieces of salt water taffy, 1 Grande Frappuccino light, 1 extra-large oatmeal cookie, 1 Cold Stone strawberry ice cream, 1 protein bar, teriyaki chicken, rice, veggies, 1 banana, 2 extra-extra-large bowls of Honey Nut Cheerios with milk, and 20 laxatives.

This is my second time taking laxatives here this time around, and I fear this was my last chance. I know I will be too sick to get out of bed to be taken to clinic and groups tomorrow morning, so is this it? I just blew the warning I was given.

Conversation between my dad and the eating disorder program director at Sovereign:

"Mr. Burgunder, this is the program director at Sovereign. Brittany took laxatives and made herself sick again. She can no longer stay here. Most people think I am too optimistic and overly willing to give patients extra chances. I have done everything I can to help Brittany, but she has not changed. You have to pick her up by tomorrow."

"This is a really tough time for her to come home. Can she stay for a few extra days until Saturday?"

"No. Her behavior is too upsetting to other patients. I really have tried everything that can be done. There is nothing we can do for her here. Brittany is the most determinedly ill patient I have ever encountered. I am sorry."

40

Tell Me You'll Open Your Eyes

"Change your routine, take a risk, throw out the scales, and get rid of those who support having an eating disorder because really they are supporting your death." ~Britt

January 18, 2013

I've been back living with my parents in San Luis Obispo now for a few weeks. So far things have been just OK. I'm so caught in-between. Part of me wants to starve, become anorexic again, be forced into treatment centers where the fun of life becomes fooling the nurses and the only hardship is competing to be the sickest. I want that back. But to be honest I suppose it's not really anorexia I miss but the scenarios it creates. I miss being sick and having people worry. I miss being taken care of. I miss having an excuse and reason to be unhappy or unsuccessful.

There are problems with my thinking, though. The main problem is that choosing health and recovery can be, and is, so much more wonderful. I can play tennis, get back to riding horses, have a proud family, relationships, careers, go to college, have no regrets, and move forward with my life. It certainly is a 180-degree contrast from the life I'm used to living. It's scary, unfamiliar, and, in a way, a risk to my identity. Life has its ups and downs. I have to be responsible for my actions and choices. I have to grow up. I don't get to hide behind a mask.

Growing up is hard whether or not people have an eating disorder. I recognize the choice I have and that's hard. I always had a choice, but the right one is so clear to my heart yet so challenging to my mind. But there really is only one difference between those who move on with life and those you see endlessly struggling for decades in and out of treatment with eating disorders. That one difference that separates those who move on and those who don't is a tough *choice*. I don't want to be one of those older patients in treatment centers or psych wards continuing to waste my life, yet taking the leap of faith and giving recovery 100 percent is so frighteningly unknown. Sigh. This is just so tough, but I know I'm not alone with these feelings. But I am stronger than this, and I deserve to live and be free. It's time to leave the past behind. It's time to become me.

April 24, 2013

Please...
- I want to prove those who doubted me wrong.
- I want to be happy.
- I want to be loved.
- I want to love myself.
- I want to be proud of myself.
- I want to accept myself.
- I want a horse in my life.
- I want to be forgiven.
- I want to have a purpose.
- I want to make a difference in this life.
- I want to help people.
- I want to be healed.
- I want to be at peace.
- I want to change the world for the better.
- I want to speak to the world.
- I want to save people's lives.
- I want to visit my grandparents.
- I want to feel safe flying in airplanes again.
- I want to have close friends.

- I want to feel needed.
- I want to marry the man of my dreams.
- I want to stop pretending I'm always OK.
- I want to purge the anger I hold inside.
- I want to purge the sadness in my heart.
- I want my life to make sense.
- I want to be a symbol of hope.
- I want to learn to relax.
- I want to be able to eat freely.
- I want to be able to eat out and spontaneously.
- I want to have balance in my life.
- I want to have happy dreams.
- I want to make sense of my past.
- I want to stand up for myself.
- I want to have inner confidence.
- I want to treat myself kindly.
- I want to be healthy always.
- I want to live a long, happy life.
- I want to be able to eat dessert without binging or feeling guilty.
- I want to wear my nice things without feeling undeserving.
- I want to be successful and not be fearful of it.
- I want to be a role model for others.
- I want to be an inspiration.
- I want to be a life teacher.
- I want my family to be happy.
- I want to move forward from my past.
- I want to know I'm beautiful for who I am on the inside.
- I want to work through my trauma.
- I want to get close to people.
- I want to have experiences and adventures.
- I want to take leaps of faith.
- I want to be safe always.
- I want to believe in myself.
- I want to trust in my abilities.

- I want to know who I am.
- I want to have fun.
- I want to enjoy my talents and not see them as burdens.
- I want to know that I am possible.
- I want to be recovered from ED always and forever.
- I want to love my inner child.
- I want to be in the right place at the right time.
- I want to set good boundaries.
- I want to live without anxiety, fear, depression, and OCD.
- I want to understand that there was never anything wrong with me.
- I want to be defined by my heart.
- I want my weight to be insignificant.
- I want to be free.
- And I want to be *Brittany*! No strings attached.

May 30, 2013

I'm letting go...today was a great family therapy session with Erin in which I made an interesting connection. ED lost some of its personal relationship/identity this last week. I am opening my eyes to the fact that ED was merely a coping skill for my real issue, which is the anxiety, depression, and OCD. ED is *not* a friend, a parent, a savior, or *alive* by any means. ED is a part of me but *not* me at the same time. It is simply that my low self-esteem was so extreme it split me in 2 to the point that I had created 2 people.

Almost like the devil on one shoulder and the angel on the other. ED is now shifting from a personal relationship to merely a coping method that I used. ED no longer has feelings, emotions, human characteristics, or power.

I am recognizing that an eating disorder was *not* my fault, only a way to self-medicate to make my mind feel better. Another new thing for me is that I am *talking* about my anxiety, OCD, and distress versus just talking about being fat and diverting from the real issue and feelings. I'm not afraid to say over and over to Erin and my parents how anxious I feel and uncomfortable. I'm finally using my voice and not feeling weak or vulnerable because of it. I feel empowered. I feel brave. For once in my life, I'm letting it out not holding it all in.

I can feel now. It hurts, but that's OK. It's OK to have a chemical imbalance. It's OK to need medication for support, even if it's just for a little while. It doesn't mean you are weak, flawed, or incapable. It means you are strong, proactive, and willing to help yourself. It's OK that genetically I have flaws, and it's OK not to pretend to be perfect and ask for help. Surrender! It is in the surrender that you regain your power and control in the way you have been searching for all your life.

41

Letters of Love . . . or Not

Dear Kasey,

If only I knew then what I know now. All you ever wanted was your big sister to love you, to like you, to play with you, and to be there for you. And every time I pushed you away, I teased you, and I ended up in hospitals every year it was your birthday. I was never there for you. You grew up with a sister, but how could you even call me that? You didn't understand. You thought I was ruining the family on purpose. You thought I hated you. The truth is I loved you so much I couldn't get close. I spent every day filled with guilt, regret, and shame that I couldn't be what most big sisters were...a friend and a guide through life. I was never there for you to teach you about boys, dealing with drama, and getting through school. I was never there for you for anything. You lived with an empty soul. You lived with a monster. You watched our family fall to pieces. You watched our parents cry and fight over how best to save me. You watched your sister die. You said goodbye to me.

This is something I can't undo, but I can ask for forgiveness. I can tell you I didn't choose this. I can tell you that I love you more than life itself. You have become one of the most vital people in my recovery. It's you who is now teaching me about boys, dealing with drama, and dealing with school. You are my role model and my inspiration. Your strength to cope with a broken family without turning to unhealthy behaviors yourself is an act of rare courage and heroism. You provide a light and compassion all to your own. You are my best friend in the whole wide world and always will be. This was never about you. I used you as a target to deal with unresolved trauma. An eating disorder was the only way my brain figured out how to save myself and others around me from my wrath. So, I turned it inward.

It wasn't my choice. It wasn't my fault. I didn't do or say the things I said on purpose. In fact, it wasn't even me. You know this now, and your acceptance and encouragement toward my steps forward have been my saving grace. I would take a bullet for you, and forever and always you will be my hero, my inspiration, my role model, my best friend, and my little sister.

-Love,
Britt

Dear Mom,

Don't you know it wasn't your fault? Don't you know you didn't cause this? Don't you know there was nothing you could have changed in the past to make this not happen? Don't you know you were the best mom you knew how to be? Don't you know you've already done more than enough? Don't you know it's not your responsibility to fix me? You hold so much blame on yourself for my eating disorder and my unhappiness. You're my mom; of course you want your kid to be OK, and of course you want to be able to find a solution and answer. Unfortunately, an answer and solution could only come from me and me alone.

Your journey alongside me has been fierce. I've watched you cry, I've watched you scream, and I've watched you write e-mails to any and every person you thought might offer a new form of help. I watched people ridicule you, look down upon you, and label you. "Oh, she must be an awful mother! Just look at how sick her daughter is. She must be oblivious and ignorant!" If only they knew. You took the wrath and judgment of doctors, therapists, professionals, and treatment programs telling you that you have a hopeless daughter and one who can't be helped. You've tried giving me freedom; you've tried watching me at all times. You've tried everything within your will to make me well and make me see what the rest of the world saw.

I will never forget when you visited me at Torrance. The tears you held back baffled me. I thought I was just fine. If only I knew...if only I knew the doctors told you this was the end. If only I knew you were there to say goodbye. If only I knew you were planning my funeral in Yosemite. You told me that you sat in that ice-cold room filled with doctors and looked everyone in the eye and said, "You may not know it now, but my Brittany will gift you in ways you don't know yet." You and I share the same tenacity and fight that allowed us to never give in. Every doctor stood in that room with you telling you all the ways I was going to die, and you *demanded* to hear all the ways they were going to save me and keep me alive.

You are my fiercest protector, companion, and lover. You had the courage to look into every professional's face and tell them they were wrong. You, Mom, display an intuition and love so deep and profound it works its own miracles. We have butted heads over and over. You were wanting to help; I was wanting to do it for myself. Through our journey, we are learning to use our stubbornness and strong wills as one. I would be lost without you, and I mean that on so many levels. To know that you have gone to hell with me and back and will be there for me no matter what is a testimony to who you are as a human being, but in my mind you are an angel.

And it's not about fixing the problem anyway. It's not about placing the blame on something or someone. After all, maybe you did save me. When a person can stand by the side of another who is seemingly reckless, mentally disturbed, hopeless, and doomed and not leave...and continue to love unconditionally...and not judge...and continue to have hope...that is a form of healing in its own. Mom, you couldn't have fixed what happened, but because of you, here I am. Here I am proving them all wrong. Here I am living a life full of meaning, purpose, and gratitude. Here I am as Brittany, and that is good enough.

~Love,
Bootsie

Dear Dad,

My other half, my twin, my best friend, and the only one who knows my thoughts before I say them. I have always been Daddy's little girl and always will be. I share my fondest memories with you before ED ripped us apart. I can't even imagine how you held yourself together the way you did. Night after night I would hear you secretly cry above my room. How could I save you? How could I make it all go away? I couldn't. All I could do was lie and pretend I was trying as ED took hold stronger. To be faced with conserving your daughter who had so much potential and so much to offer is unthinkable.

All your little talks every day trying to motivate me, trying to make me see the bigger picture, trying to give me hope...well, they did...it just took quite a few years. You have always been honest with me and have been the one person I felt I could confide in, if even only a little bit. I still remember my first binge as though it were yesterday and how exhilarating it was to share that with you. In fact, I share all my greatest triumphs, memories, and struggles with you.

It's you who can hold me when I'm breaking down crying. It's you who can challenge the lies ED feeds me. It's you who can give me a glimmer of hope into who I really am. You are one heck of a man. Every day you work your hardest for our family and others. You are a role model, inspiration, teacher, friend, supporter, and dedicated to all, but to me you are even more.

You saved me. You stood by me and trusted me when no one else would; maybe even when you shouldn't have trusted me you did. Your faith in me despite what every single person told you is what turned a tragedy into a miracle. You have and will do anything for me. But all you want is for me to be happy and to see myself for who I really am.

That means more to me than you know. Your support in allowing me to take the road less traveled has given me confidence to find my true self and meaning in this world. Because of you I have opportunities, possibilities, and something to look forward to. Because of you I don't merely exist, I live.

~Love,
Brittany

Dear Brittany,

You sweet, precious thing. You didn't deserve *any* of this. This was *not* your fault. There was never anything wrong with you. You weren't bad. You weren't flawed. You weren't abandoned. Don't you know how loved you were? Don't you know how unfair it was to be bullied? Don't you know you did the best you could to cope? Every day you got up, put yourself together, painted on a smile, and did the best you could. Your courage and perseverance amaze me. Your compassion and willingness to hold on inspire me.

Don't fret that you took a different path. It will all come together. It is all coming together. You are so loved. You are so accepted. You are so perfect. I love you. I accept you, and ED will never be allowed to touch you again.

You don't deserve punishment. You aren't responsible for the world. You don't have to be something so remarkably great. You are great just for waking up each day. You get to be happy. You get to enjoy life. Your job is not to please others. Relax. Giggle. Heal your inner child. Don't be afraid to let your walls crumble because on the other side of those walls are hundreds of open arms waiting to take you in. Don't be afraid to feel love and know you are worthy of it. You have been through more than most can even fathom, but the fact that you are embracing it toward a greater good is something that only the select few can do.

You are here for such a greater purpose. Don't be afraid of your intuition. Don't be afraid to follow your heart. Don't be afraid to be in the spotlight. Don't be afraid to speak your mind and stand up for yourself. Don't be afraid to question the world. Life is not out to get you. Life has challenged you, tested you, and been cruel to you, sure; but it has also opened your eyes and made you realize *why* things happen that just aren't fair. Life has made you realize that *you* have the power to change your reality and how you react to life's difficulties. It has trained you into one of the finest warriors.

You are unique. You walk your own path. Let people walk with you, but keep yourself first. This is a journey so grand and so special that you have been chosen to walk it because *you* are not only strong enough to handle it and survive it, but use it for a greater purpose. I am so proud of you; I am *so* unconditionally in awe of you. If I could choose a best friend, it would be you. I love you, Brittany, and always will.

~Love,

Me

Dear eating disorder,

You are a liar, a thief, a bully, a manipulator, a killer, an illusion, and a prison. But I could never hate you. To hate you would be to hate myself. You were everything about me I couldn't deal with turned inward, which exploded outward in chaotic destruction.

There were times I called you my best friend, my *only* friend. There were times you were somebody else—an enemy and a stalker who would never leave. But you were always me. I was fighting me. I was destroying me. I was trying to cope with me. I label you ED, but what you were was the dark side of who I was. You became an escape and an imaginary thing to give a name to explain the things I did. I was silently crying out for help. But I didn't feel I deserved help. My dark side tried to help me survive. It tried to give me boundaries, rules, rituals, and feedback. ED, you were my way of self-medicating a much deeper problem.

I never took the time to look at the beginning of my life. It was too traumatic. I couldn't make sense of it. In the simplest of forms, you became my imaginary worst friend. But you were a friend nonetheless to help me cope with what I couldn't see, what I wasn't ready to face or look at, and what I couldn't make sense of. So, ED, I thank you. I thank you for stepping in and taking care of certain needs in my life that helped me cope, albeit negatively. Many times I used you as if

406

you had an identity, as if you were a tangible thing and almost human.

Many times I used you as an excuse, an escape, and an outlet to place blame. After all, it couldn't be *me* who lost that tennis match, who didn't have friends, who was ruining my family, who turned down social events, who made the gym my priority, who was slowly killing myself, and who was lying and manipulating. No, not *me*; it was because of *ED*. I never took responsibility.

But, ED, I accept that responsibility now, and you don't even deserve the name ED anymore because you are not a separate entity. You are a mental illness. You are an eating disorder, sure, but even that can be a stretch. With a troubling childhood, I found ways to cope with OCD, anxiety, trauma, depression, and fears. It played itself out with food, but that was merely a symptom of the problem. Now that I'm dealing with the problem, the symptoms diminish. I am no longer my own enemy, and I choose to water and feed the positives in my life. So, eating disorder, thank you for teaching me I'm stronger than I ever believed imaginable, thank you for making me realize how precious life is by placing me on my deathbed, thank you for showing me a perseverance so amazing I am in awe, and thank you for never, ever, *ever* having a place in my life again.

~Your worst enemy,

Brittany

42

A Weigh Through

"The only way to move forward is to focus on the good in your life and the good that you are doing for others and yourself. My past has shown me things in life, others and myself that I wouldn't wish upon anyone, but I can choose to pick up the pieces and build a beautiful life for myself and help others to do the same." ~Britt

IMAGINE CLIMBING A MOUNTAIN. When you first start it seems as if it will take forever to get to the top. In fact, you are already tired, wonder if the view at the top is worth it, and are starting to fear you might get lost or encounter a bear. But you slowly continue on. After all, you've been told by enough people that the climb is worth it. But what if you can't do it? What if you aren't in good enough shape?

You sit down on a rock to rest and notice a beautiful stream and the sound of singing birds. It's not so bad after all. You eventually gather your physical and mental strength to keep going. You are almost at the top now; you can actually see the peak. But this is the steepest part. You fall multiple times, slipping on the slick gravel. Your knees are banged up, and you debate whether to stop and call it close enough. How could this be worth falling down so many times? "Maybe I'm just a bad hiker and don't deserve to make it to the top."

But then you think of all those people who told you that you couldn't make it. You also think of all those people who whispered in your ear not to give up because anything is possible. You brush yourself off and start climbing again. This time you do so more slowly and cautiously. It seems to take you hours, but almost in shock you realize you made it. Goosebumps trickle up and down your arms and legs as you take in not only the view, but what you just accomplished. Looking down you see how far you've come. During the journey up, you lost sight of your progress because you were so focused on the end result. But you did have that nice moment sitting on the rock listening to the birds and the stream. The journey wasn't that bad. It took you a long time to get to the top of that mountain, longer than some people you know, but you still made it. The accomplishment and freedom you feel within is indescribable. You're proud of yourself; you feel strong, confident, and able to conquer anything. You did it. You didn't give up when it got hard or when you fell. This is recovery. This is working through hardships. This is life. This is your journey.

Recovery doesn't mean life gets easier. It just means it gets better and worth living. I think sometimes people are afraid of recovery (just as I was) because they believe that once they get there then they will have no excuse to have a bad day or make a mistake. The truth is life is full of ups and downs, tears and smiles, success and mistakes. This is living. This is feeling. I still have plenty of days where I don't want to get out of bed, where I'm tempted to binge, where I overdo the exercise and look in the mirror with disapproval. The difference is that I recognize these urges and, for the majority, don't act upon them. However, there are still days where I screw up, but I pick myself back up and keep going. This is what recovery is. This is how you move forward. If recovery were all smiles, sparkles, and success then I would question your judgment and believe you are in denial. Recovery is work. You don't reach recovery and then kick back and relax. I'm not perfect. I've been through a lot and have taken those experiences to create a great life, but I'm not here to preach to you or make you think recovery means you have to have it all together. I can't reiterate enough that recovery is possible and meant for each and every one of you no matter *what*—and I mean that from the heart. Keep your head up; keep moving forward and allow yourself the space, patience, and compassion to have ups and downs.

It's not when you've messed up, fallen backward, given in, made a mistake, done something harmful, or given into temptation that defines you as a failure or provides justification to continue screwing up. It's what you do with the aftermath. Do you pick yourself back up? Do you let the tears fall and then turn them into forgiveness? Do you get up the next day and take care of yourself properly? This is what separates those who fail from those who succeed. I hate the word *failure* in any form because it's been a word I've used to label myself all too often. But it's time to be blunt and honest about recovery and those who make it and those who don't. If you want to succeed, you have to want it bad enough that a stupid slipup is just that and nothing more because *you* are worth so much more.

It's a process of learning to let go, stop fighting, trust those who have earned the right to be trusted, be patient, practice self-forgiveness, and find your inner peace. You are courageous, and you are brave. Let yourself feel emotions; don't numb them away. Remember who loves you. Remember you have good intentions. It's OK to struggle. It's OK to be sad. It's OK to feel lonely. It's not OK to let that be acceptable as your truth. Keep pushing forward. You never know when the walls that cage you in are going to crumble.

Remember that this process has nothing to do with appearance. So, why do we give so much power to our reflections as if they define our whole beings? A mirror is simply a reflection of perception. We do not see ourselves as we are. We do not see ourselves as whole people. When we look in a mirror, we do not see our hearts, our souls, our personalities, and our dreams.

The mirror became an obsession for me. It became something I could rely on for instant feedback. But then I couldn't rely on how I processed that feedback. At my lowest weight, the mirror still told me I was not worthy of being called anorexic. Now when I look in the mirror I see a girl full of light, happiness, and strength. But I also see a survivor, a warrior, and a girl who has been through so much pain. The mirror no longer decides whether I get to have a good day or bad day, whether I'm beautiful or ugly, or whether I'm accepted or not. The mirror is not the enemy. Your relationship with yourself is.

When I took away the power I so freely gave to the mirror, I could start seeing myself through clear lenses.

So, go to a mirror and look yourself in the eyes. No, nothing else, just your eyes. There is nothing wrong with you. You are a uniquely crafted work of art that isn't copied by anyone. You have a good heart. You have good intentions. Those attributes define your beauty. What you see is not what others see. What you feel is not what matters or is necessarily real. Believe me when I say you are not alone; you matter, you are beautiful, you are good enough, you are not too broken, and there is the most beautiful hope and life awaiting you.

Things happen in life that sometimes can't be made sense of. You could say it's not fair. You could say it's your fault. You could say everyone else has it easier. Perhaps you're dealing with depression, an eating disorder, addiction, anxiety, abuse, self-harming, or a traumatic event. It consumes you and sometimes even becomes your identity. But I believe the challenges you are given in life are directly proportional to your ability to overcome them and the amount of strength you hold inside. If you have the ability to live with something so negatively haunting, then you sure as heck have the ability to use that power to turn it around and change it into something amazing. Look at your challenge as a gift. This obstacle is going to teach you a lot about life, yourself, others, and your goals. It's going to make you an interesting person, a person who has compassion for others and a humbling confidence. People who have life easy tend to get lost in the crowd.

Whatever you are dealing with, know that it is not your fault and that it is fair. If you choose to take that inner strength buried deep down inside and overcome your demons, you will have opportunities and a freedom that is far greater than most people have. Use your challenges to empower you. Know you are capable of greatness because you are.

Some of my most profound changes, progress, and insights have come at various rock-bottom stages in my life. It's certainly not pleasant to be in such a state, but it is also a place where we are more open to listening to our hearts, our intuitions, and our natural instincts to do what is truly right and healthy for us. It is an opportunity to reevaluate your life and what isn't working. You can't give up at this point, though. I can't tell you how many times I've had to pull myself kicking and screaming out of a dark hole, and it can get tiring and feel never-ending. But that is not the truth. The truth is that if you keep picking yourself back up one step at a time, your rock bottoms won't be so deep each time and your ability to change is at its highest. When it's that dark, you have no choice but to rely on your heart to illuminate your way.

You don't have to be OK. You don't have to be happy. You don't have to wear a mask, and you sure as heck don't have to be perfect. Anger, sadness, regret, and loneliness are all just as valid feelings as being happy and upbeat. Don't be afraid to be real because most people aren't. What you do have to do is wake up each day and try your personal best. To some that could be working a stressful job, to others that could be going to class, to some it could be following their meal plan, and to others it could simply be getting out of bed. Try not to compare with others. Try not to get caught up in the social media world either because it's only easier to create a false illusion and identity. If you have just one person you can trust and who loves you unconditionally, you are blessed. But know that you always have yourself and you are good enough just as you are in this moment. Stop trying to change yourself. Stop trying to numb out. The world is unknown and sometimes scary and cruel, but it is also full of joy, opportunity, growth, and meaning. If nothing else, go to a mirror, look yourself in the eyes, wrap your arms around yourself, and tell yourself you are deserving and accepted and that there is absolutely nothing wrong with *you*.

Comparing yourself with others is toxic—pure poison. There is nobody else like you, and that alone is phenomenal. Stop wishing you were this or that. Stop wishing you looked like this or that. Stop wishing you had this or that. Stop wishing at all! At least those types of wishes. Start smiling instead. Smile at your heart. Smile at your ability to function. Smile at your intentions. Smile at your existence. Smile at your struggles. You are human, and it's in our nature to compare and be jealous, but you are so much more than pointing out what you don't like about yourself. Start focusing on the good in you, and trust me, there is plenty. You are unique. You are irreplaceable. You are here for a reason.

It is very tempting in tough times, stressful times, triggering times, and dark times to feel the magnetic lure of your old ways. Perhaps they aren't even your old ways yet and are still a part of your daily means to cope. It would be so easy in a way to forget about the stress and go eat 1 dozen doughnuts. It would be so easy to avoid food and let yourself feel hunger. It would be so easy to purge everything you eat or overdose on laxatives. It would be so easy to get on a treadmill and run 'til you can't feel anymore. It would be so easy to take a razor to your wrist. It would be so easy to pick up the bottle of booze or pills. It would be so easy to hide under your covers and hibernate.

Yes, these are coping skills you've learned to believe fill a void in your life. But you have to realize they are only a Band-Aid and a way to numb yourself from your true feelings and difficulties. Living with destructive coping skills is absolute hell, don't get me wrong, but facing life and its ups and downs is much braver, harder, and rewarding. You're stronger than that. Why give into your negative thoughts? Why give away your power to familiarity and the illusion of safety?

I can think of my best day in relapse…I saw my lowest weight and then looked in the mirror and felt a sense of accomplishment for a brief period as if I had achieved being the best anorexic. Ha! What a prize. Shortly thereafter I was in the ICU, facing liver failure, relearning how to walk, and having my family plan my funeral.

I also remember my worst day in recovery. I felt that I had overeaten but promised myself I would not take laxatives and instead sat through the discomfort, self-hatred, and embarrassment. I wanted to scream, I wanted out of my body, and I wanted to undo the damage that most people would call normal eating. So, do you really think I have to tell you which day I would choose to repeat? Don't take the easy way out. You are here for such a greater purpose that does not include abusing yourself.

It's tough to change. It's hard to leave what you believed to be true. It's even harder to ask for help. But stop for a minute and think about the future. It's so easy to get caught up blindly and mindlessly in the moment and go through the motions of life like a robot. Do you really want to be doing and feeling the way you are in 1 year, 5, 10? So often it's easier to say, "I'll start tomorrow" or "I will be happy when..." But these are excuses that keep us miserably safe and excused from true greatness, purpose, and joy. All change begins with baby steps. No step is too little. No progress is too small. But if you never start, the years will pass you by in a trance. Reach out. You can't do this alone. You are deserving and important and have value. Don't let anyone or yourself tell you otherwise.

No matter what you are dealing with that is negatively affecting your life, know that you are not meant to fight your battles alone. I am an incredibly stubborn person and used to be a major control freak and perfectionist. I spent 10 years silently struggling. I saw treatment professionals and went to plenty of treatment centers, but I was never honest and I always put up a defense. I felt it was my fault for having an eating disorder, and so it was up to me and me alone to fix it. Asking for help and letting others in to support made me feel as if I was weak and incapable.

It's only now in hindsight that I realize how wrong and deadly that thinking was. Asking for help is not only courageous, it is the smart and strong thing to do. It doesn't make you weak; it makes you proactive and admirable. We are not meant to walk this path alone, especially when dealing with hardships. Don't feel ashamed of what you are going through. Don't feel you need to fool those around you into thinking everything is just fine. Don't live a lie and take off that mask. It is so liberating to speak your mind, receive help, and not worry so much what others think. The right people will always stand by your side.

How do you let go of addiction, self-harm, eating disorders, over-exercise, fear, or negative thoughts that keep you depressed, isolated, and socially afraid? Most people hold on to some sort of behavior that does not serve them positively, but for many others that behavior is literally killing them, whether it be slowly or quickly, mentally or physically. Yet, why does it also seem to destroy us to let such a thing go? Why is this behavior and way of life so important? We believe it's holding our life together. It's a delusional belief that we *can't* live without it, but the truth is we *can*. We become loyal to the chaos and the abuse because we know no other way. It's familiar and comfortable. We think it's keeping us safe. The only way to survive and truly live is to take a risk and make the choice to change. The behavior and way of life is killing us; letting it go…I promise, will not.

So, if you are out there debating whether to ask for help, or if you are struggling silently, please take it from someone who wishes she did a decade ago. I'm lucky to be where I am now, but my life could have easily ended tragically because I walked alone. And remember that you are deserving of help no matter what your height, weight, age, gender, diagnosis, or thoughts. You are all deserving of recovery no matter *what*. In fact, it will save your life.

I challenge you to look at the pain you've pushed aside. Look at the hurt you've masked under your smile, eating disorder, addiction, or other issues, be they good or bad. It's time to be real with yourself and authentic to others as well. Take off the Band-Aid and heal the wound. It will hurt at first, but the result is a scar that fades with time that will be sealed from infection and disease.

My work has only just begun in looking at things I've allowed my eating disorder and perfectionistic identity to cover up, but already it has freed me from some very large burdens and given me clarity as to what my goals are and the strength to pursue my passion fearlessly. Take off your masks; take off your Band-Aids. I promise you won't be laughed at or hurt again, and I promise you won't bleed forever.

My past hurts more than you know. My past hurts more than even I know or want to accept. But then how can you move forward if you don't? A smile, an upbeat attitude, and external successes won't cover it up anymore. I have come too far to pretend my life has been a fairytale. It's been anything and everything *but* that. But accepting that I can't change my past I can now feel all the pain I hid inside. I can now work through it. I can become even stronger. I can learn to live more fully than most because of it. I can use it as a gift of healing to others and also more importantly to myself. Because if you learn from your past and break the chains and false illusions that it somehow defines you and your future, you can begin to live in the present and cherish the journey and beauty in your growth. And that's the choice I am making one day at a time. And it is because of this that I can now create a fairytale ending.

43

Perfect in Every Weigh

"I don't believe in the word hopeless because the strength that lies within every person is enough to create many miracles." ~Britt

WHEN I FIRST BECAME overweight and then obese, I still had a Facebook, sure, but I let everyone believe I was still anorexic and that my life was still "just amazing." No one would have ever known otherwise since I isolated myself. I lived vicariously through others' photos and glorious status updates only to confirm I was a pathetic failure. I would spend hours every day comparing myself to others and secretly wishing they would post something bad about their lives or an ugly photo so I wouldn't feel so alone. Gee, talk about a great way to live life, right? At one point, I even made a separate eating disorder profile to try to motivate myself back into anorexia when bulimia was in full throttle. All this did was fuel my eating disorder more and not in any of the ways I would have liked. With social media sites like this, often people are looking for one of 2 things: either validation that they really are inadequate to justify their low self-esteem, or a confidence boost for themselves when they see or read something negative about someone else. Both ways are harmful, artificial, and self-defeating in the end.

In a way, eating disorders are much easier to have a relationship with than a boyfriend, girlfriend, or friend. They are, in a false sense, more reliable, consistent, predictable, and easier to commit to than a person where feelings are involved. But this becomes a hollow, meaningless, and miserable existence. Sure, the gym will always be there, the food (or lack thereof) will always be there, but at the end of the day, you will tuck yourself in at night and hold back the tears of another day full of regret and sheer loneliness. Relationships are hard and always contain good times and bad times. But if not for the bad, the good times have no value. People take work and require you to be vulnerable in a sense because not everyone will like you. That's OK because that has nothing to do with *you*! It will take time to find the right group of people, but with patience, persistence, and perseverance, you will find that group that accepts you unconditionally. Remember, you don't need a lot of friends to be happy—only those who make you feel good just as you are.

Eating disorders are *not* one size fits all. No matter what side of the scale you are on—whether you are underweight, overweight, or even at an ideal weight—eating disorders will kill, and it can happen to *you*. You are not invincible. It isn't a comparison: "Well, I'm not as bad off as him or her, so I'll be OK." It also isn't about how many times you've gone to treatment, how medically compromised you are, or whether you meet all of the diagnostic criteria.

Eating disorders don't offer second chances and don't target only those who look physically sick. Eating disorders of all forms are a disease. They are about what you can't see. They are about your mind.

They are a mental illness, which means that most people will believe they are *never* sick enough or acceptable enough for treatment or help. This is a distortion in your mind, and too many people won't get help because they die beforehand. You don't see yourself in the same light as others do. Having an eating disorder is walking around with a ticking time bomb that could explode with no warning. With anorexia, you don't reach XX pounds and then think, "OK, I can ask for help now" or "I've reached my goal weight, but now I'm scared I might die, so I'm going to go to treatment." Likewise, with binge eating disorder, you don't reach XXX pounds and then think, "OK, I'm now obese. I will ask for support" or "I can't stop binging, and I'm always short of breath, so I'm going to check myself into treatment." The same goes for bulimia. You don't wake up one day purging blood and think, "OK, now I need help" or "My laxative abuse is so debilitating that I can't leave my house; maybe I need treatment." If you believe receiving help for an eating disorder has the prerequisite of coming face-to-face with a crisis, then most of the time it will be too late.

Eating disorders will always make you believe you are indestructible and that it will never happen to you. Eating disorders will make you believe you can and have to fix it on your own because you'd be a weak failure if you asked for help for such a silly problem. Eating disorders tell you that you are *fat* at 56 pounds. Eating disorders will tell you that taking 30 laxatives is normal because you read someone once took 100. Eating disorders will tell you that you are not allowed out of your house until you aren't obese anymore. Eating disorders will tell you, "You can stop tomorrow. Just one more time." Eating disorders will tell you that it's OK to exercise 5 hours a day because athletes do it.

Eating disorders will tell you that it's OK to have chest pain: "It will go away like last time. Don't worry. Yeah, people die, but not you. You're fine." Eating disorders will also tell you that once you reach XX pounds, you will be happy and perfect. All your worries will vanish. Eating disorders turn you into a manipulative monster and an untrustworthy person. What's worse is that eating disorders will make you believe in the reasons for manipulation and the lies and destroy all trust in yourself.

Eating disorders are not a choice nor are they easy to defeat, *but* you are not completely powerless to their wrath or demonic spell. You *do* have certain choices and responsibilities in moving forward toward a better life. An eating disorder is *not* your fault, just as any other disease, such as cancer, is not your fault. However, recovery requires certain lifestyle changes, choices, and an attitude of willingness. Wanting recovery, choosing recovery, and achieving recovery takes daily reaffirming and recommitting, but we have to choose it for ourselves because no one else can. It's time to stand up wherever you are in your struggle and say, "I deserve better, and I'm going to make it happen."

Remember that the body can recover from a physical standpoint to baseline health in a matter of months, but our minds, habits, and ways of thinking, which have been imprinted into our brains on a daily basis, may take years to change. It takes a lot of time, patience, and kindness to work through rewiring your mind. Also, just because you look healthy on the outside doesn't mean you have to feel upbeat and happy all the time on the inside. One's physical health does not always equate with being content, successful, or without problems and confusions. All too often people who are insensitive or uneducated about eating disorders make the assumption that because you look well, you are well and things are now great. This couldn't be further from the truth. Yes, we may be out of immediate life-threatening danger, but that's all that may be different.

On the contrary, I've learned that sometimes when we look our healthiest, we may be closest to death. When we are struggling with bulimia, binge eating, or laxative abuse, it is easy to maintain a physical image of normalcy for a set period of time. All too many nights, I would sit in the bathroom frantically praying to get through the night alive. Over and over, I would swear in fear that this would be the last time. I would get up the next day, paint a fake smile on my face, and keep the doors locked tight around my personal life. So what if I didn't make it through one of those nights? What if the laxatives took their toll? What if my stomach did rupture after consuming close to 20,000 calories? To be honest, every single person besides my parents would be absolutely shocked and confused. "But she looked healthy. But she didn't look sick. But she said things were going great." Of course, that was all a deception.

It took tremendous courage for me even to seek out a therapist when my eating disorder transformed. I felt ashamed that I was unable to maintain the control I once had. I felt embarrassed that I was now almost obese. And I felt as though therapy was a waste of time because clearly I couldn't be sick if I was no longer skinny and in fact was now overweight. This is where our magical thinking becomes the biggest barrier to getting help and ultimately saving our lives. If you look up the word "sick" in the dictionary, it is defined as "mentally or emotionally unsound or disordered and affected with disease or ill health." Nowhere does it mention anything related to body weight.

This is where you have to look deep inside yourself and ask the question no one wants to ask: "Am I worth receiving help and recovery no matter what?" I will give you the answer. The answer is *always* yes—no matter how thin, fit, fat, tall, short, old, young, or what gender you are. Everyone's rock bottom is different. Some people's rock bottom is simply being unhappy or having a certain behavior that makes them feel guilty or interferes with their lives. No matter what the barrier is, everyone is equally deserving and qualified for help, for support, and for recovery. If anything, it would be my hope that people value themselves enough to seek help before they come anywhere near a rock-bottom state.

Life gets tough, and sometimes the easiest way out of life is to get yourself so sick, mentally or physically, that you can escape. But be wary of thinking a change of environment will help or that a new treatment center will be the answer. Don't get me wrong—sometimes it does take multiple treatment centers and programs before it clicks for people, but I believe mostly that this is not the answer. The answer lies in staying put in your discomfort and working through the underlying issues. Once you leave your environment, an element of progress is lost, and you will eventually have to return home and face it again.

But remember our eating disorder is in control, and we are not thinking rationally. We will do anything to look for the easy way out, the magical click, or that aha moment. We are looking for the escape to focus on what is familiar, comfortable, and safe for us. By now we know how eating disorder programs work. It's not scary, we know the system, all the rules, and know how to manipulate them. But this is the definition of a chronic relapse as you are merely masking and deferring the core issue. Recovery is *not* easy. You *must* do the work—period. A short-term escape or stabilization can temporarily be beneficial to regroup yourself, but residential treatment is often cut too short to instill a lasting change, thanks to insurance and cost issues.

Even when money isn't an issue, residential treatment can become too safe, luxurious, and sheltered so that transitioning back to reality can be a big shock and relapse trigger.

These eating disorders have shown me that I am a strong person who doesn't need a crutch to get through the daily ups and downs of life. This journey is something that I will never regret. The gifts of recovery are greater than I ever could have imagined.

I can smile now and truly mean it. I can learn new tennis techniques rather than having to relearn how to walk. I can have fun and socialize, even around food. I am trusted by others and trust my actions, my words, and myself. I can go to bed at night without worrying I will die in my sleep. I can exercise and enjoy it without it being a punishment or something that is harming me. I can go out to dinner without looking ahead at the calories or ordering everything plain and on the side. I can feel for the first time and am learning how amazing it is to be able feel sadness, joy, and anger and know it will pass. I have a future now and am forming meaningful relationships. I can think about what really matters for once and relax without constantly obsessing over food, weight, and calories. I can be spontaneous and travel again. I am confident in myself and can set boundaries. I feel alive and am not simply functioning on autopilot. I have a purpose and newfound passions. I am thinking about what makes me happy rather than how to stay out of treatment. I'm collecting new friends, not hospital wristbands. I can laugh, engage with people, and use my intelligence toward good things. I can carry on a conversation and pay attention to what the other person is saying without my mind wandering about what I ate, what I will eat, what I won't eat, how much I exercised, what foods I'm going to eat for my next binge, and how many appointments I need to cancel so I can take laxatives. I can look in the mirror and say, "Hey, I'm proud of you and like the person you are," and mean it. I can finally be me, which is all I ever needed to be.

To those who get fooled into believing the stigmas around eating disorders, please know that this is *not* about weight, food, or a 5-letter word called the scale. Eating disorders are mental illnesses no different from schizophrenia in the sense that what the sufferer is experiencing is real in their eyes. This is why comments such as "Just eat" or "Just eat less" or "You look fine" or "You are way too skinny" are not only insignificant to the receiver but also will be deemed a lie. Those with eating disorders are dealing with a misconception with their minds. They are living in a world where nonsense and chaos makes sense and the truth is twisted into manipulation. Because this is a mental illness, it also means food and weight will never lead to a resolution. At 56 pounds, I thought I was *fat.* I thought I looked normal. I thought I was OK to go back to college. I thought there was no way I could be considered anorexic. Do you think I enjoyed gaining 165 pounds in a little over 1 year? Do you think I chose to become 221 pounds and obese? You know the answer. *No way!* But again, this is a disease of the mind. There is no picking and choosing what happens to you physically—or mentally, for that matter—without help and support.

Eating disorders can take on different physical shapes, but that is merely a side effect of a much deeper matter—what is going on inside your brain. I was just as miserable at 56 pounds as I was at 221 pounds. It didn't matter. It changed nothing. I was still being ruled by the same voice in my head telling me I wasn't good enough and that I needed to act out in destructive ways to cope with underlying issues and fears. An eating disorder is *not* something you try on for a few weeks. It's not a fad diet. It's not about wanting to be a model or fit into certain clothes.

This is the only way you know how to get through each day. This is about having self-esteem that is not only nonexistent but also fiercely negative. This is living each day the same to the exact minute thanks to your OCD. This is about having a meltdown because you accidently ate 1 extra strawberry. This is about counting the calories in vitamins. This is about secrets, lies, manipulation, and turning against everyone who loves you. This is about breaking up with the man of your dreams because your relationship with the gym has become stronger. This is about being so afraid to truly live that you would rather slowly commit suicide. This is about having no boundaries or respect for yourself. This is about shame and feeling so utterly undeserving of *anything*. This is about fear and the fear of life itself. This is about control. This is the only way you know to keep yourself from exploding inside. This is about taking all your disappointments, failures, fears, imperfections, and brokenness out on yourself. This is about blaming yourself for *everything*. This is about focusing on anything but the things that hurt the most in life. This is about numbing away trauma, abuse, heartbreak, and dysfunction. This is about escaping reality by creating a reality you believe you deserve. This is about wanting to feel safe and protected. This is about being so utterly lonely you'd rather purposely isolate than be teased or labeled a loner.

This is about hating yourself so much you paint a fake smile on your face every day so no one would suspect the hell you hold inside. This is about trying to make yourself invisible to the world so you won't be taken advantage of again. This is about shielding yourself from rejection, hurt, emotions, and the unreliableness of people and events. This is about feeling guilt for wanting and needing more than you can bear or admit. This is about being so afraid to get close to someone that you won't even allow your mother or father to hug you. This is about self-medicating when you should probably be in therapy and/or on medication. This is about having no trust in anyone, including yourself. This is about creating an inner world of chaos that you soon become familiar with and seemingly takes care of your unmet needs. This is about creating boundaries through rules the eating disorder comes up with. This is about having so many emotions you don't know how to express that you turn them inward and go exercise for 5 hours until they dissipate. This is about having anxiety that is so suffocating that you create insane rituals to calm yourself down. This is about not knowing how to use your words. This is about not having a voice. This is about being so terrified of rejection that you reject yourself first. This is about survival. This is about being so afraid of success and failure that you use your eating disorder as an excuse for falling short of your ability. This is about wearing a mask so no one can see the real you. It's easier to say, "They didn't . . . I didn't . . . because I'm fat, anorexic, have an eating disorder" rather than have to think it's actually about *you*. But it's *never* about you anyway; it's always about them. This is about feeling different and flawed. This is about feeling as if it's you against the world. This is about creating such a controlled life that you soon become out of control. This is about surrendering your rights as a human being.

It isn't about food or weight. It really isn't even about an eating disorder. It is about having desperately horrific coping methods to deal with a false sense of self you've learned to believe is true. This is about fear of the unknown, the present, the past, and yourself. This is about needing something in your life you can rely on. This is about secrets and shame. This is about building walls around you so high that nobody can reach you or hurt you.

This is about a chemical imbalance and an addiction to escaping reality. This is about living your life in and out of treatment centers to the point where the IV pump becomes your lullaby. This is about tearing apart families, relationships, dreams, hopes, and friends. This is about having a mental illness that takes over every aspect of your life and control.

But this is also about having an inner strength so immense it scares you. This is also about having the ability deep down to make a different choice. This is also about choosing to say, "I need help." This is also about trusting in the unknown and breaking every rule and ritual that has seemingly kept you safe and alive. This is about being sick and tired of being sick and tired. This is also about holding on to hope and faith that life can be different. This is also about realizing people do care and want the best for you. This is also about realizing you cannot recover on your own despite creating the eating disorder on your own. This is about accepting help without feeling weak. This is about using your sensitivity and intelligence toward better coping skills. This is also about divorcing the one and only thing you feel is there for you or makes you special. This is about growing up and taking responsibility for yourself, your life, and your actions. This is also about talking and using your words to get your needs met. This is about choosing to live, not merely exist. This is about allowing yourself to start to feel again and begin to understand feelings don't last. This is also about finding your voice. This is about mourning your inner child and all that was stripped away from him or her. This is about believing you matter, have worth, and can rise above this. This is about embracing who you are even with imperfections. This is also about forgiving yourself. This is not about food or a desire to be skinny. This is the hardest battle you will ever fight and one that can be won if you choose to set yourself free.

Recovery is selfish, and that's a good thing. Don't let the ignorance of a person, a doctor, a friend, a coach, a parent, or yourself tell you otherwise. Also, don't believe yourself when you say it isn't that bad or that there are others worse off than you are. It's a trick your mind will play with you to your grave. It's those who continue thinking they aren't in that much trouble who end up dead. Recovery is a long and patient process, and often people go into what I like to call remission before they reach a point of true recovery—and that's OK. People suffer in different degrees, but the solution is equal among all and that is reaching a point of true recovery, peace, and happiness for oneself.

My journals, which make up this book, are a testimony to my existence. They were a way to prove I had a presence in this world. It was a way to witness myself. Much of what I realize at the end is what I have actually known or have been told from the beginning. It didn't matter if I was receiving the best treatment or the worst treatment during the course of my eating disorder. What it really comes down to is an internal choice that comes from within and one that can be made only when one is ready.

Looking back on my life, I wonder how I got so lucky. My eating disorder was an outward expression of how I felt about myself on the inside. It was never about weight. It was about walking a self-destructive path based on a false belief that I was never good enough, loveable, or acceptable. I believe there are things in life both tragic and miraculous that one can't understand through words but rather through the heart, and that is where the healing lies.

Epilogue

"May you walk with your head held high, your heart full of acceptance, and your mind at peace." ~Britt

July 23, 2013

    I just booked my ticket last night to go on the annual summer beach trip in Delaware with all of my dad's family. Thanks to my eating disorder, I haven't been in 7 years. I am really nervous in some ways, but mostly I am excited. I've been going on this trip every single year since I was in the womb—literally—and my happiest and maybe only happy childhood memories are of this trip.

I've been thinking about my life a lot lately, and I have had to make some big decisions. I was going to attend Cal Poly this fall, but I have decided to defer my enrollment a year. At first, all I could feel was anger toward myself and that I was nothing but a failure who backed out of something again but that was just me thinking what *others* would think of me, not my heart. In my heart, I know it was the right decision. Right now I'm working my way through recovery and healing myself. My health is my number-one priority, and I can't lose sight of that. In fact, it's been 8 months now since I've taken laxatives or used any harmful behaviors.

Tennis has been going really well and has been a great outlet and way to integrate myself back into life. I've made some true friends through it and have been learning to enjoy the sport while still having performance goals and playing competitively. I've also decided it's time I add horses back into my life. They have always been a passion of mine and offer a healing of their own. My relationship with my family and sister is pretty incredible. This journey has affected us all and changed us, sure. But we have grown in strength and closeness at an exponential rate as we continue to learn and love one day at a time.

August 8, 2013

I've been in Delaware now for 1 week. I can't even begin to describe to you how overwhelmed I am with love, happiness, and pride. In so many ways I thought I would never make it back to the beach. I figured my eating disorder would always be a barrier. I thought I would never see my grandparents again before they passed. I am so proud of myself for being here, but there is so much more than the fact that I've shown up. I've been on this trip with my eating disorder for quite a few years before I stopped coming altogether. Those beach trips were filled with tears, silent whispers, isolation, stress, and misery. This year, though, I feel free. I feel like the little 5 year old who couldn't get enough of my family, atmosphere, food, games, conversations, and joy. I am myself again. I have an identity now that I know is wonderful, loveable, and good enough—and that's me and only me.

I don't think my smile could stretch any bigger nor could my laugh be any louder. My grandparents joked with my dad that they think he made up that I was struggling so bad all these years because I'm as normal, healthy, and happy as can be. And you know what? It's real this time. It's me.

The only way to move forward is to focus on the good in your life and the good that you are doing for others and yourself. It's so weird being back with my favorite relatives in Delaware after a 7-year absence. In a way I feel whole again...as if all the traumatic events that happened in-between never were. As if I have a chance to redo my life. As if I could turn back time. As if I know who I am again. But that doesn't help me. Attitude is everything. I had my moment of sadness, sure, but it's just so incredible that I'm even here, healthy, happy, and whole in this moment. My past has shown me things in life, others, and myself that I wouldn't wish upon anyone, but I can choose to pick up the pieces and build a beautiful life for myself and help others to do the same. Family is so important and precious. Their support, acceptance, belief, unconditional love, and encouragement have turned me into an individual who will reach for the stars and let nothing stand in my way of grabbing them.

Sometimes I can't believe how far I've come. A little over 8 months ago, I was kicked out of a treatment center. I've made the choice, I've made the changes, but recovery isn't linear, and it sure as hell is not perfect. Life has its odd ways of showing you your opportunities when you stick with it, though, and sometimes my hardest days are my days of the most growth. In life, you start learning what's truly important. Sometimes I feel as if I've lived 20 lives. In some ways I have. Be kind to yourself.

Everyone is fighting his or her own battle, but the choice is always yours to say this is not how it's going to continue or end. No matter if you are dealing with an eating disorder, laxative abuse, self-harm, depression, anxiety, PTSD, OCD, exercise addiction, suicide, or anything else, just know you are not alone and there is hope.

I have survived and experienced all of the above and then some. I have gone from 56 pounds lying in a hospital bed and a sure funeral to 221 pounds at fat camps. I have created a life in ways far better than I could have imagined. That doesn't mean I don't still have goals or that I am always happy with my body image. It does mean I have other ways of coping and other things in my life that can take ED's place. I have taken back my rights as a human being. It doesn't happen overnight, but anything is possible. I'm possible. You're possible. We are *all* possible.

About the Author

BRITTANY BURGUNDER LIVES IN San Luis Obispo, California and has continued to strengthen her recovery and build a happy life. She transferred to Cal Poly as a psychology student and is passionate about helping others. Brittany continues to pursue her love for writing by blogging on her website and publishing articles. She also enjoys playing tennis and riding horses. She looks to inspire people to believe in and love themselves above all else.

Stay connected with Brittany by visiting **brittanyburgunder.com**.

Printed in Great Britain
by Amazon